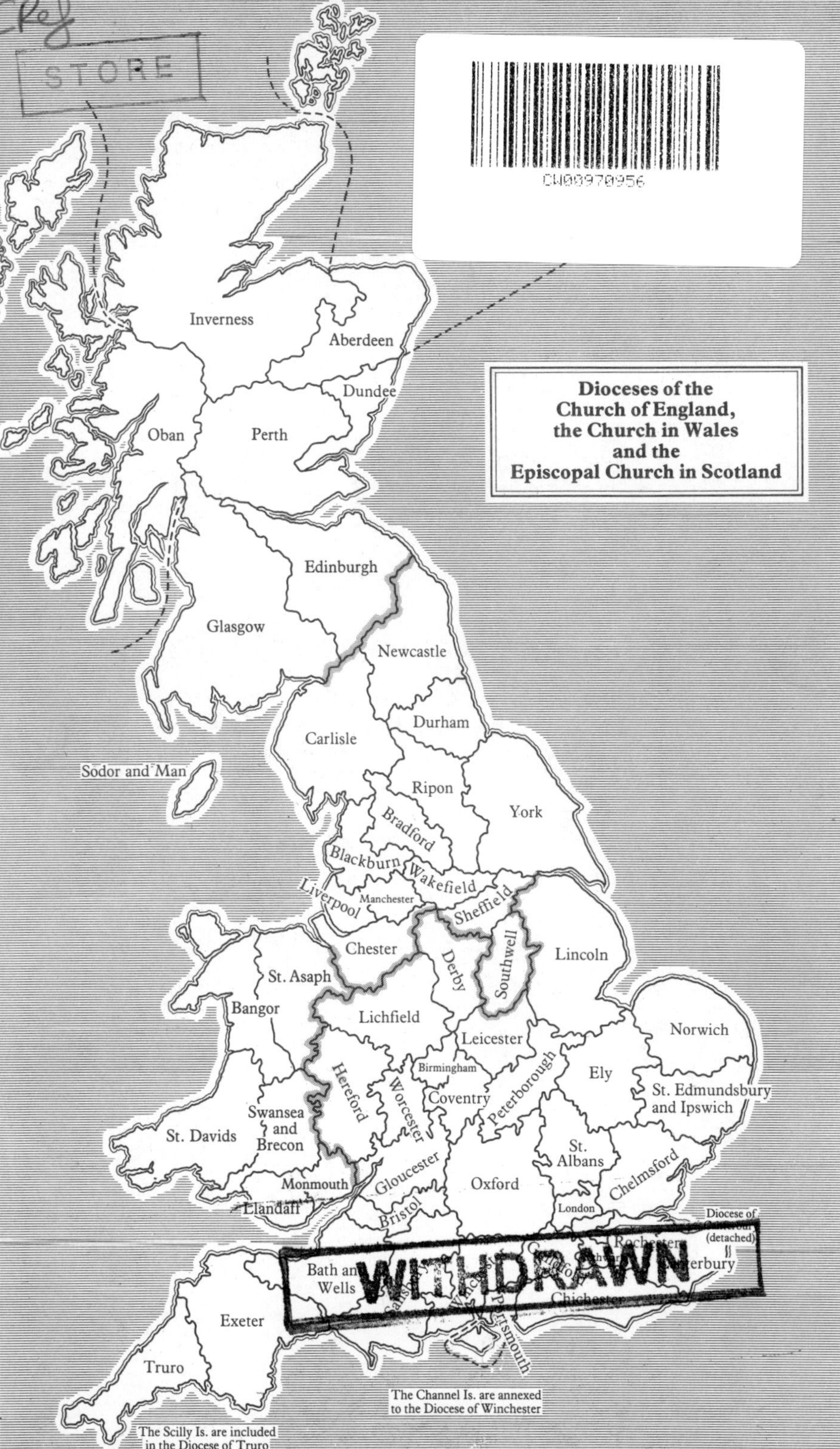

Dioceses of the
Church of England,
the Church in Wales
and the
Episcopal Church in Scotland
Inverness
Aberdeen
Dundee
Oban
Perth
Edinburgh
Glasgow
Newcastle
Durham
Carlisle
Sodor and Man
Ripon
York
Bradford
Blackburn
Wakefield
Liverpool
Manchester
Sheffield
Chester
Derby
Southwell
Lincoln
St. Asaph
Bangor
Lichfield
Leicester
Norwich
Birmingham
Hereford
Worcester
Coventry
Peterborough
Ely
St. Edmundsbury
and Ipswich
Swansea
and
Brecon
St. Davids
St.
Albans
Monmouth
Gloucester
Oxford
Chelmsford
Llandaff
Bristol
London
Diocese of
(detached)
Wells
Chichester
Portsmouth
Exeter
Truro
The Channel Is. are annexed
to the Diocese of Winchester
The Scilly Is. are included
in the Diocese of Truro

CHAPELS & CHURCHES: WHO CARES

Chapels & Churches: Who Cares

An Independent Report
by Marcus Binney and Peter Burman

Published by the British Tourist Authority
in association with *Country Life*

Printed in Great Britain by
Billing & Sons Ltd, Guildford, London and Worcester.

CONTENTS

FOREWORD

Leo Dryden, the music hall artiste, used to sing a popular number called the Miner's Dream of Home:

I listened with joy
As I did when a boy
To the sound of the old village bells
The log was burning brightly
Twas a night to banish all sin
For the bells were ringing the old year out
And the new year in.

Tears were in every eye as the audience joined in the chorus and the backdrop showed clumps of trees round the village green and above them that essential feature of the landscape of our islands—the church tower. This calm unsentimental report chronicles a disappearing feature of our landscape—the church, chapel, kirk or meeting house. The way we can save our remaining places of worship is by becoming fond of them. This is not possible when they are locked and with no indication of where the key may be found. We take churches so much for granted that it isn't till they are gone that we realize they are part of our lives because they are part of our landscape.

A place is recognizable by its places of worship. They mean more than the town hall or the council offices. They draw the houses together just as the mothering dome of St Paul's dominates the City of London and the spires of Lichfield cathedral symbolize the Midlands and the outline of St Giles's crowns Edinburgh.

The vaulted church interior of many vistas, gilded rood screens, twinkling candles and mitigated light through stained glass windows is one sort. The box-pewed meeting house with clear glass windows and a cushioned pulpit dominating all is another sort. Either sort used has an atmosphere of its own which no museum can give.

Every chain-store, office block, slab of flats and monster hotel makes a church or place of worship more desirable and more of an essential oasis. This factual report shows in readable prose and effective photographs the havoc that has been wrought by worship being given almost last place in our planning. But it also shows what superb churches and chapels, kirks and meeting houses there still are. We are told that apathy is our enemy. This report is a herald of better things.

JOHN BETJEMAN

ACKNOWLEDGEMENTS

In preparing this report we have visited a great number of churches and chapels and talked to numerous people concerned with the care and the future of churches, all of whom have given generously of their time and provided an enormous amount of useful information. Among those who took us to visit churches we are particularly grateful to Andrew Anderson, Neil Birdsall and Lady Harrod in Norfolk; Peter Cleverly in Suffolk; David Verey in Gloucestershire; Seiriol Evans in Cambridgeshire; Ken Powell in Leeds; Ted Hubbard in Liverpool; Donald Buttress in Manchester; Patrick Brown in Bristol; Hilary Aggett in Southwark; Oliver Baratt in Edinburgh and Robin Ward in Glasgow.

Dr Christopher Stell has given freely of his unique knowledge on nonconformist chapels. We also owe a special debt to the Rev Bessie Sellwood who has allowed us to draw much material from her marvellous thesis on early meeting houses, which deserves to be published as a book in its own right. Of the later nonconformist chapels we have learnt a great deal from David Barton, Clyde Binfield and Christopher Wakeling, all of whom are working on this subject. For much of the information on Scotland we are indebted to the tireless scholarship of David Walker and John Gifford. John Gerrard of the Scottish Civic Trust and Colin McWilliam have been unstinting in their help. Harry Graham, Secretary of the Historic Buildings Council for Scotland has taken great pains to ensure the Scottish information is accurate.

The encyclopaedic knowledge of Richard Haslam, who is now working on *The Buildings of Wales,* is the basis of much of what we have said on Wales and Welsh nonconformity. We have learnt much from the work of Professor I. G. Jones from whose learned articles we have taken the two tables on page 54. John Hilling, Peter Howell, Olwyn Jenkins and Professor Anthony Jones of Texas Christian University have all helped open our eyes to the qualities of Welsh chapels and churches.

We naturally owe a great debt to the officials of numerous church bodies. In particular we are indebted to Desmond Ward of the Church Commissioners who has constantly kept us up to date with information about redundant churches as well as to his colleagues J. E. Shelley, Martin Elengorn and E. J. Robinson. Margot Eates, the Secretary of the Advisory Board for Redundant Churches, and her staff have also been a constant source of ideas and information, so have Ivor Bulmer Thomas, the Chairman of the Redundant Churches Fund until the end of 1976 and John Bowles the Fund's Secretary and his assistant Jean Southern.

We have also corresponded with all the Diocesan Redundant Churches Uses Committees and many Diocesan Advisory Committees as well as Redundant Churches Furnishings Officers. Among other denominations we are particularly indebted to the Rev W. R. Jones of the Church in Wales, who has supplied us with the lists of listed Welsh churches. the Rev George Patterson of the Church of Scotland and the Rev Brian J. Meney of the Episcopal Church in Scotland. Edward Milligan, the Librarian of the Society of Friends, has been especially kind as has the Rev George Dolbey of the Methodist Division of Property. We are also indebted to the Rev D. L. Golland of the Unitarians and David Whale of the Baptists. Hugh Llewellyn Jones of the Historic Churches Preservation Trust has taken much trouble on our behalf and Christopher Mann of Wells and Co has greatly illuminated the problem of fund raising for us.

In our chapters on tourism we have received much information and advice from the British Tourist Authority and the Regional Tourist Boards. We also owe a special debt to Max Hanna of the English Tourist Board and the creator of the pioneering English Heritage Monitor, who has generously allowed us to use his tables of listed Anglican churches. In compiling the lists of demolitions we have been hugely aided by the unique knowledge of Basil Clarke and in addition to those we have already mentioned John Briggs, Andor Gomme, Rodney Hubbuck and David Lloyd have supplied us with many additions and corrections. For the information on wild life in churchyards we are indebted to Peter James of the Natural History Museum, George Barker and Ted Offord, the British Trust for Ornithology and the Royal Society for the Protection of Birds. Of the many people who have been valuable sources of ideas and information we are particularly indebted to Richard Morris, John Physick, Michael Archer, Michael Gillingham, David Watkin, John Cornforth, David Williams, Judith Scott, Dr White, Sophie Andreae, Donald Findlay, Alan Crawford and Matthew Saunders. We also are indebted to all the members of the editorial advisory committee who have steered this project on its way: from the Department of the Environment Lloyd Warburton, Simon Ridley H. O'Sullivan and Peter Arnold; Lionel Wadeson of the General Synod of the Church of England and Sandy Parnis of the Churches Main Committee. A very special word of thanks is due to the staff of the British Tourist Authority who have printed and published this report in record time: among them we are particularly indebted to Leonard Lickorish the Director General, Douglas Webb, Harold Booty, Edward Butler, Dick Gough, Dick Thomas, Cyril Palmer, John Warsany, Peter Baynes, Ray Hewett and the designer John Bailey. Geoffrey Lee of *Country Life* has kindly edited the manuscript.

Susan Cowdell and the staff of the Council for Places of Worship have typed numerous letters on our behalf. Caroline Ridler of *Country Life* is responsible for making sense of the huge list of demolitions and for obtaining many missing facts and the greatest debt of all is to Anne Hills who, as organizing secretary of the exhibition Change and Decay at the Victoria and Albert Museum has undertaken the enormous task of the correspondence, including letters to all the planning authorities in the country, and twice typing a long and immensely complicated manuscript in record time. Without her this book would not have been written.

The research and writing of this book have been financed by grants from the Department of the Environment, the General Synod of the Church of England, and, through the Churches Main Committee, the Church in Wales and the Roman Catholic Church. The initial impetus came from Dr Roy Strong under whose auspices the exhibition Change and Decay has been presented. The book nonetheless is an independent study representing personal views alone.

INTRODUCTION

This report is a survey of the churches and chapels of all denominations —Anglican, Baptist, Calvinistic, Congregational, Episcopalian, Methodist, Presbyterian, Quaker, Roman Catholic, Unitarian—including meeting houses, Jewish synagogues and churches of sects such as the Countess of Huntingdon's Connexion, the Catholic Apostolic Church and the Christian Scientists. There are today between 60,000 and 70,000 places of worship in England, Scotland and Wales but despite the rapid growth in population this figure is already far lower than in 1950, let alone 1900. As congregations decline, and grow proportionately older, and as the costs of maintenance and heating soar, churches are being closed, sold, demolished or simply abandoned in increasing numbers. How many—in both national or local terms—are worth trying to keep? The Church of England has some 8,500 wholly or substantially medieval churches but what of the other denominations?

The conclusions of our survey are alarming. In the past 15 years nearly 1,000 churches and chapels have been demolished: at least 200 of these have been buildings officially listed as of special architectural or historic interest; many others, had they survived today, would now be considered listable and many more by virtue of their towers or spires or their prominent position had townscape value. In Glasgow 33 "listed" churches have gone since 1956: in the Diocese of London 19 of the 38 churches declared redundant since 1970 have been demolished, and since new uses have been found for two of the remainder most of the others are only too likely to follow. In Birmingham, Liverpool and Manchester 19th-century churches have gone in dozens and with them not a few Georgian ones—Bristol, Hull, Newcastle and Sheffield follow not far behind. Since 1968 the Church of England has declared 639 churches redundant principally in the Dioceses of Salisbury (52), Lincoln (36), Oxford (35), Norwich (34) and Chelmsford (32). Between 1960 and 1970 3,000 Methodist churches were closed: currently some 220 of the 2,200 United Reformed churches are for sale. In Scotland the Episcopalian Church may soon be faced with a sudden spate of closures following the reduction of its clergy by one-fifth; the Church of Scotland which, due to the disruptions of the 19th century, has two churches in every small town and village, is now closing churches at a sharply increasing rate. The Church in Wales is this year embarking on a programme of closures of remote and often beautiful churches: Welsh chapels are being sold off in hundreds. In Clwyd the Conservation Officer estimates that "over 30% of the chapels in our county are either in total ruin and the target for vandalism of unspeakable irreverence or have Estate Agents signs affixed to the outside".

The problem is at its most acute with inner city churches whose congregations have been driven out through clearance and redevelopment, and with remote country churches, sometimes grand sometimes small, which have far too few people to sustain them. In cities like Leeds, Liverpool and Manchester once a church is closed or declared redundant it becomes an immediate target for vandals. In such cities numerous fine churches by notable architects have been wrecked or even burnt out within weeks of the congregations' departure. And even where protective measures have been effective these churches are left in such a pitiful, even disgusting, state that it is only too easy to see that no one is likely to wish to take them over. Broken glass is everywhere, the walls are sprayed with graffiti, every object of any religious significance is smashed or mutilated.

In Norfolk medieval churches lie abandoned in the fields. In every county there are churches where congregations have simply locked the door after the last service and left the church a prey to the elements and to vandals as they have gone off to worship in the next village: choir music is scattered on the floor, the pews covered in bird droppings, dead flowers remain on the altar. Quite a number of these churches have been isolated since the black death, yet a faithful few have tended them: now, though nothing has changed for several centuries, they are made redundant.

Nor does the problem end here: numerous churches with fine interiors, retaining fine fittings made by accomplished craftsmen, are being reordered to fit in with new concepts of worship: altars and screens, pulpits and reredoses, choir stalls and pews, sacramental objects and vestments are discarded and even destroyed. Ancient graveyards are stripped of tombstones recording the occupations, fortunes and relationships of villagers and townspeople over several generations for no better reason than to make grass-mowing easier.

Yet for every endangered church there is another, comparable in size and circumstance which has resoundingly overcome its problems. Numerous parishes have valiantly raised daunting sums to pay for repairs: for every church that languishes for lack of worshippers there is another that is a flourishing focal point of the community, in regular use for meetings and events throughout the week, with festivals, fêtes, concerts and recitals continuing throughout the year. This type of extended use—bringing to the church many of the activities that traditionally took place in the parish hall—is increasingly showing the way a church can play a vigorous and dynamic role in the life of a village or town. Equally there are many congregations, faced with a church which is intimidatingly large, that have subdivided it internally, adapting the aisle or the west end or the chancel for secular use. In cities a growing number of churches are converting their crypts into family clubs that are making them once again the centre of social life in the neighbourhood.

The number of conversions to new uses is also so great as to dispel any argument that churches are impractical or uneconomic to convert or adapt. Churches and chapels have become youth clubs, old age pensioner's day centres, children's nurseries and night shelters for the homeless. They have been transformed into museums, concert halls, theatres and libraries. Town churches serve as urban studies centres: country ones for field studies. Others have become sports halls, studios, craft workshops and offices—still others survive as stores and barns. Countless nonconformist chapels and a growing number of Anglican churches have been converted into houses. Best of all more and more churches are finding a new life in their original role, as churches for new sects or for groups of immigrants, ranging from Polish Catholics to Greek, Russian and Serbian Orthodox, Christadelphians, Pentecostalists and Seventh Day Adventists, mosques and temples.

There remain, nonetheless, a very great number of churches which, whether for their sheer quality or character, their history or completeness, it would be quite wrong to alter. These range from princely parish churches to humble meeting houses and missions. Quite apart from their priceless artistic and historical value they are a very real asset to our fastest growing industry—tourism. Churches are one of the few buildings to which the visitor can almost universally gain access: there is hardly a church anywhere which does not tell something of the history of the community in which it stands. This report sets out to ask a dual question; how can churches help tourism, and how in turn can tourism help churches? The growth of tourism is vital to Britain's balance of payments: visitors from abroad bring much needed foreign currency; every British person who takes a holiday in this country rather than going abroad is saving precious foreign exchange. Churches, we believe, could play a much greater role in this major industry. At national, regional and local levels there is an opportunity to forge a relationship between church and tourist authorities which can only be to the well-being of both.

PART ONE–LEGACY

CHAPTER ONE

The Importance of Historic Buildings to Tourism

Tourism is one of the UK's strongest and fastest growing industries. In the past 10 years, overseas visitors' spending in this country has risen at almost treble the rate of tourist spending in the world as a whole. From just over £190 million in 1965 spending reached the high figure of over £1,600 million in 1976 and is expected to reach over £2,000 million in 1977. Tourism earnings have risen against a background trend of a weakening balance of payments position to achieve a surplus on the tourism account of £629 million last year. This amount has grown fourfold in only two years and is now more than half of the manufacturing industry surplus. All the signs for 1977–78 point towards a tourism surplus of £1,000 million with an increasing share of total exports accounting for 15% at the moment.

Overseas visitor spending, together with expenditure of British tourists holidaying in their own country, which would more than double the amount, provide enormous wealth and economic strength for the regions of Britain, with very great potential to come.

Recent studies have shown that every £1 million of tourist spending generates an increase in total industrial output of over £3 million. This massive investment goes to create incomes and jobs in local communities, where it is becoming increasingly necessary to fill the place of major industries such as agriculture and manufacturing which are suffering from cutbacks in their labour forces.

Tourists also contribute heavily to central and local government revenue through taxes such as VAT and excise duties on petrol, alcohol and tobacco. This brings in an extra £300 million a year to the British economy.

Tourism is therefore a very tangible phenomenon with an extremely positive effect on the life of communities in Britain. One of its most crucial roles is that it protects and enhances the heritage of each region and gives many cultural attractions, such as the local museum, a viable economic life that would otherwise cease because of lack of funds.

	UK Balance of Payments	*Tourist Balance*
1965	£ −28 millions	−97
1966	+100	−78
1967	−301	−38
1968	−275	+11
1969	+462	+35
1970	+735	+50
1971	+1,048	+47
1972	+131	+19
1973	−842	−1
1974	−3,380	+154
1975	−1,635	+245
1976	−1,423	+620

Tourism thrives on maintaining Britain's heritage and its present and future success very much relies on the unique and attractive resources the country has to offer. Historic buildings are one of the main, if not the most important attraction, for the millions of people who visit Britain every year.

Surveys carried out by the British Tourist Authority show that visiting historic places tops the list of attractions for both English and non-English speaking visitors and takes precedence nearly every time over seeing friends, shopping, visiting museums and going to the theatre.

Historic buildings and places, therefore, count as this country's principal attraction to overseas visitors. Among them churches must rank high, but they have very rarely been considered as an individual group in the research that has been carried out. Whether as the most regularly accessible of all historic buildings or simply as major accents in the townscape and the countryside, they rate above any other type of historic building in number, distribution and quality. This is evident from the following table which shows the number of churches officially listed as of historic interest in relation to other historic buildings in each tourist region.

In every region it is evident that churches far outnumber the other historic buildings open to the public. While, it is true, there is an increasing problem of locked churches and the official lists of churches leave much to be desired (both topics discussed elsewhere) it is evident the Church of England's churches (quite apart from those of other denominations) are major potential attractions in every area. And though in number ancient monuments rival and exceed churches in certain

Region	*Listed Buildings Dec. 1976*	*Outstanding Conservation Areas Dec. 1976*	*Scheduled Ancient Monuments Dec. 1973*	*Buildings Open to the Public 1977*	*Listed Churches C of E Jan. 1977*	*Cathedrals C of E and RC*
Cumbria	4,830	9	363	80	188	1
Northumbria	5,640	15	612	53	283	4
North West	14,230	25	218	52	447	7
Yorkshire	16,120	14	1,091	108	860	6
Heart of England	28,860	47	1,282	143	1,481	8
E. Midlands	14,430	17	778	81	1,721	7
E. Anglia	26,020	51	698	122	1,908	5
Thames & Chilterns	18,790	25	510	118	954	2
South East	30,050	48	701	138	881	5
Southern	7,230	11	440	37	369	3
West Country	46,100	65	3,516	203	1,969	7
London	29,290	47	111	73	486	4
England	241,590	374	10,320	1,208	11,547	59

areas, there is often so little to be seen above ground level that they have little interest for most tourists. And, of course, among those that are really popular ruined abbeys such as Fountains, Rievaulx and Tintern figure very largely.

It is significant, too, that the highest numbers of historic churches are to be found both in the areas now most popular with tourists and in those which it is Government policy to direct tourism towards. Norfolk, for example, has 704 listed churches, Suffolk 483 and Devon 529. South Yorkshire, a region poor in historic buildings, nonetheless has 103 listed churches. Similarly Merseyside which only has three major buildings open to the public has 88 listed churches. A similar pattern emerges among churches listed Grade A, the top category, though here also considerable revisions in the listing are due.

In all there were 2,248 Grade A listed Church of England churches in January 1977. Fifty-nine per cent of these are located in the East Midlands, East Anglia and the West Country, regions which contain only 23% of the population of England.

Tourist Region	*Grade A Listed Churches, Church of England, January 1977*
Cumbria	4
Northumbria	26
North West	60
Yorkshire	173
Heart of England	169
East Midlands	581

Tourist Region	*Grade A Listed Churches, Church of England, January 1977*
East Anglia	428
Thames and Chilterns	239
South East	119
Southern	46
West Country	322
London	81
England	2,248

Grade A Listed Churches in Anglican Dioceses

Diocese	Churches	Diocese	Churches
Lincoln	275	Winchester	35
Oxford	174	Coventry	30
Peterborough	165	Sheffield	25
St Edmundsbury	150	Worcester	25
Norwich	126	Chichester	23
Salisbury	117	Bristol	20
Ely	105	Derby	18
York	88	Durham	16
Leicester	75	Rochester	16
Canterbury	73	Lichfield	15
London	71	Birmingham	13
Bath and Wells	70	Manchester	11
Exeter	70	Portsmouth	11
St Albans	65	Newcastle	10
Southwell	48	Southwark	10
Chelmsford	47	Liverpool	9
Ripon	46	Wakefield	9
Hereford	45	Guildford	7
Truro	45	Bradford	5
Gloucester	41	Carlisle	4
Chester	39	Blackburn	1

CHAPTER TWO

Church of England

The religious buildings of the world, more than the castles and palaces of temporal rulers, more even than the great wonders of nature, are dominant symbols and powerful magnets in the world's tourist trade. The temples of the Nile, the ziggurats of Central America, the holy places of Palestine, the mosques of Islam, the Hindu temples of India, the stupendous Buddhist shrines of Borobudur and Angkor Wat, the pagodas of China and the cult-gardens of Japan, are all places of pilgrimage to tourists as much as worshippers. The ability of their romantic allure to transcend national, political and denominational barriers is evident from the fame they retain even when, like the monasteries of Tibet, the holy places of Mecca and the temple-cities of Burma, they are virtually inaccessible. Groups of smaller temples, shrines and churches also form the principal tourist attractions of a whole country or region: the Byzantine churches of the Peloponnese, the romanesque churches of Auvergne and Apulia, the monasteries of Serbia, the half-timbered churches of Hesse, the rococo churches of Bavaria, the stave churches of Norway and the mission churches of California each form the basis of the most absorbing of holidays.

In a more general sense much of the scenic beauty of the world's towns and cities derives from well-placed religious buildings. What would the view of Istanbul across the Golden Horn be without the minarets of its great mosques? What would Moscow be without the golden domes of the Kremlin's churches? Would Isfahan or Samarkand be legendary without their mosques? What would the view of Rome from the Pincian hill be without its domes and façades or that of Prague from the Charles Bridge without its steeples?

Even against this background Britain has a legacy of churches with an appeal—whether architecturally, historically or scenically—that takes second place to none. In Stonehenge, Britain has the world's most majestic pre-historic monument, and if little of substance survives from nearly four centuries of Roman settlement, there are numerous sites to tell the story of the tenacity and devotion of the early Christians, notably in Northumbria and Wales. Though these are sometimes remembered in no more than unique dedications like the church at Atcham, Salop, dedicated to St Eata (d. 685) a companion of St Aida, there still remains a remarkable number of Anglo-Saxon churches, and some like Escomb in Durham, surviving almost unaltered. Many timber Saxon churches were replaced in the generations immediately following the Norman Conquest, and today we still have a prodigious number of stone churches dating from the 11th and 12th centuries, quite a few with stone vaulting. In Gloucestershire, the development of Norman architecture can be watched step by step, while in Salop square Norman towers are common throughout the country and virtually complete Norman churches survive at Heath and Linley.

English Gothic, though influenced by the Continent, developed in a variety of individual ways culminating in the unsurpassed virtuosity of the Perpendicular. Most surviving medieval parish churches grew over two or three centuries, and, according to the availability of natural materials and the degree of regional prosperity, almost every county in England can show distinctive types of construction and style. Obvious examples are the timber-framed belfries of Essex and the Welsh border counties, the churches of the limestone belt (the Cotswolds, the Leicestershire and Lincolnshire churches with their spires and gargoyles), brown sandstone churches in Herefordshire, granite in Cornwall and brick and flint in the Chilterns. Whereas the Norfolk and Suffolk churches show a virtuoso handling of stone and flint (often deploying flint "flushwork" in the form of decoration or inscriptions) Somerset, with its superb natural building stone, produced a series of stately towers which, collectively, are one of the architectural wonders of Western Europe.

Of this great legacy there survive today no less than 8,500 wholly or substantially pre-Reformation churches in the hands of the Church of England: some 1,100 of these are concentrated in just two counties, Norfolk and Suffolk, which, with Somerset, benefited from the prosperity of the late-medieval wool trade. After the Reformation there was a pause in church building, though significant changes in furnishing and decoration were, of course, taking place. In the 17th century relatively few churches were built, though some people, like Sir John Shirley of Staunton Harold in Leicestershire, "did the best things in the worst times and hoped them in the most calamitous". His remarkable church, built during the Commonwealth, belongs, exceptionally, to the National Trust: other examples are the estate church at Euston, in Suffolk (1676), St Katherine Cree in the City of London, St John (1632–33) in the centre of Leeds, now being taken into the care of the Redundant Churches Fund, Willen in Buckinghamshire by Robert

Hooke, rescued from redundancy by the establishment of the new town of Milton Keynes, Buckinghamshire, and the tiny abandoned chapel in the fields at Humby, near Grantham, Lincolnshire, which is the only 17th-century church in the county and surely deserves to be rescued.

The rebuilding of the City of London churches after the Great Fire by Sir Christopher Wren and his ablest assistants was a response to a unique opportunity. In spite of some lamentable losses there still remain some thirty-eight 17th- and 18th-century churches in the City and, whilst today they must vie with multi-storey office blocks, they nevertheless form one of the best reasons for visiting the City after St Paul's Cathedral. An enterprising programme of lunchtime services, concerts, pulpit dialogues and lectures draw visitors to the City and attract City workers.

In the 18th century, traditionally castigated as a time of torpor in the Church, there is abundant evidence of parishes faithfully repairing their churches, providing communion vessels, often of magnificent quality, and other furnishings such as organs of high architectonic quality, which have all too often been subsequently swept away or altered out of recognition. Where they survive they have a scarcity value and particular significance for the growing interest in performing and recording early music on contemporary instruments. There are two main strands of Anglican church building in the 18th century—first the desire of a private landlord to improve his own demesne, which at its best produced buildings like Robert Adam's Gunton in Norfolk and Capability Brown's Croome d'Abitot in Worcestershire; and second a growing mercantile class in prosperous towns which produced swagger new churches like St Philip, Birmingham, Whitchurch, Salop and Blandford Forum in Dorset. Both Warwickshire and Worcestershire are well-endowed with fine Georgian churches. In the capital the passing of the Fifty New Churches Act in 1711 produced a series of architectural masterpieces: St Martin-in-the-Fields (paid for by the parishioners, one of whom was the King) and St Mary-le-Strand both by Gibbs, whose *Book of Architecture* (1728) was a *vade mecum* for Georgian church builders on the far side of the Atlantic, and Hawksmoor's great Stepney churches, Christ Church, Spitalfields, St George-in-the-East and St Anne, Limehouse, which could provide a means of drawing some of the legion of visitors to the Tower of London into one of London's most depressed boroughs. The development of London to the north and west led to a spate of church repairing, church building and refurnishing, as outlying villages were absorbed, producing numerous proprietary chapels of which few have survived—St John's, Downshire Hill, Hampstead is one good example.

These two major strands were intensified in the 19th century and immeasurably enriched, architecturally, by a desire to make a statement about "correct" worship. Hence Brighton, Sussex, is not only attractive for its bracing sea air and handsome stucco terraces, but for the prodigious number and variety of its churches and chapels, ranging from the almost palpably aggressive low to no less aggressively high. Some of the finest 19th-century architects (Barry, Bodley, Burges, Pearson, Scott) worked here, so that in Brighton the 19th-century contribution to church architecture and townscape can be studied in microcosm.

No one has yet properly evaluated the relation to landscape of the great 19th-century estate churches, but just as "Athenian" Stuart at Nuneham Courtenay, Oxfordshire and Nicholas Revett at Ayot St Lawrence, Buckinghamshire, produced churches akin to garden temples, so at Studley Royal and Skelton-on-Ure in Yorkshire (both by William Burges), at Sherborne, Warwickshire, and Privett, Hampshire, one can readily identify churches of special quality and distinction which are no less carefully related to landscape in a quasi-feudal setting.

At the same time there was a strong feeling that even the poorest communities deserved the best buildings in which to find their relation with God. It was this feeling (not universal, admittedly, and hence parishes like Cromford, Derbyshire, where there was one church for "carriage folk" and another for the "poorer sort") which resulted in buildings like Pearson's St Augustine, Kilburn, London, with its soaring spire, St Columba, Haggerston, London, by James Brooks, and William Butterfield's St Alban the Martyr, Holborn, London, all built in poor and even squalid districts with a positive missionary purpose. Beauty had spiritual meaning: it spoke of holiness and therefore the source of the holy.

CHAPTER THREE

Liturgy and Music

For the casual visitor as well as to the regular worshipper one of the most immediately striking facts about churches and cathedrals is that they are still very much in use for the purpose for which they were designed. At one end of the scale is the church used once or twice a year, like Waterden, near Walsingham, in Norfolk; in the summer it is surrounded by the ripening corn, one day in the spring of this year wild aconites were in glass jars on the altar. It is the English epitome of what on the Continent it is usual to refer to as "pilgrimage churches", and the annual service is a very happy affair. At the other end of the scale are services like the Enthronement of the Archbishop of Canterbury or other diocesans, or the Christmas or Easter High Mass in Westminster Cathedral presided over by the Cardinal Archbishop of Westminster.

The special contribution made by the free churches to hymnody is widely recognized—for example some of the fine hymns of Charles Wesley are included in the *English Hymnal*, regarded as one of the bastions of High Anglicanism—and the Poet Laureate has caught the flavour of low church enthusiasm for hymn singing and for splendid tunes in *Undenominational*:

Undenominational
But still the church of God
He stood in his conventicle
And ruled it with a rod.
Undenominational
The walls around him rose,
The lamps within their brackets shook
To hear the hymns he chose
"Glory", "Gospel", "Russell Place"
"Wrestling Jacob" "Rock"
"Saffron Walden" "Safe at Home"
"Dorking" "Plymouth Dock"

I slipped about the chalky lane
That runs without the park,

I saw the lone conventicle
A beacon in the dark.

Revival ran along the hedge
And made my spirit whole
When steam was on the window pane
And glory in my soul.

(Reproduced by kind permission of SIR JOHN BETJEMAN and JOHN MURRAY from *Collected Poems*, 1970.)

The *English Hymnal* also includes excellent translations of a considerable number of the great medieval Latin hymns (e.g. *Pange lingua*, or "Sing my tongue, the glorious battle . . .") thereby preserving some of the most remarkable devotional verses of our civilization in regular use as part of a continuing tradition of music and worship. Although there are some very good modern hymns it is one of the merits of most collections that they cast their net wide over a vast spectrum of periods and traditions. So that for every one of us who reads the Latin lyrics of Peter Abelard tens of thousands of us regularly sing one of them, and for the few who read Augustan poetry a congregation vast beyond imagining regularly sings one of the poems of Joseph Addison.

The pride of place given to preaching and hymn-singing in Nonconformist worship is reflected in the galleried interiors and prominent pulpit, and the universality of the organ—often of quite an early date by comparison with Anglican churches. The post-Restoration use of an organ during Anglican parish worship only became widespread after the effects of the Oxford Movement and the recommendations of the Cambridge Ecclesiological Society began to be assimilated, from the 1840s onwards. It was in the mid-19th century that chancels were brought back into use, placing within them choir-stalls for a surpliced choir of men and boys and emulating the style of cathedral worship.

Now that the chief liturgical emphasis is upon the celebration of the Eucharist, a uniting act of fellowship in which all present endeavour to participate as fully as possible, surpliced choirs have in most places fallen out of fashion. In churches where Matins and Evensong is still a prominent pattern there are sometimes choirs in the late-Victorian style, like the very good choir at St George's, Stockport in Greater Manchester, a turn-of-the-century church of cathedral-like grandeur designed by Paley and Austin.

Whatever the liturgical and musical tradition there is a great deal of activity, and some of the best 20th-century British composers (Ralph Vaughan Williams, Benjamin Britten, Lennox Berkeley, William Walton, Michael Tippett) have written for the liturgy, either on a modest or a grand scale. The Royal School of Church Music has done much to raise standards throughout the country, by its system of affiliated choirs, its publications, and its extremely well-attended courses for organists and choristers. The School is located in Addington Palace, Croydon, in Surrey, formerly the country house of the Archbishop of Canterbury, and in this year celebrates its Golden Jubilee.

An intriguing possibility, if it could be accomplished without self-consciousness, would be the recreation of historic liturgies in appropriate settings. A good example was the superb Victorian Evensong in St Paul's, Knightsbridge, London, attended by members of the Victorian Society in 1969. At Edington, in Wiltshire, the great Priory Church refounded by the Black Prince is annually the setting for a week-long festival of cathedral music begun 20 years ago. The special features of this festival are the singing of the regular office, the *Opus Dei,* to superb music and sung to the highest professional standards: this provides a framework within which new services have been evolved, like the Procession of the Christian Year, and much new music introduced. To hear Byrd's *Five Part Mass,* sung liturgically, in this very special building which provides a unique transition on a large scale between the Decorated and Perpendicular styles is a very special experience—and worshippers come every day during the festival (and to other special events during the year) from a wide radius.

Experiment is the key to much which is worthwhile and happening in the field of liturgy and church music. Although this does not mean that we are unappreciative of traditional liturgical practice, which is in some places too thoughtlessly set aside, it is encouraging to encounter such an experience as the *Mass for the Sun Rising* celebrated in March 1977 at St Peter, Morden, in Surrey, with specially composed music performed very ably by young musicians from the Inner London Education Authority's specialist music school in Pimlico. The music was linked to a series of dances, culminating in the administration of the bread and wine to the whole congregation (which was large and enthusiastic).

In the chapter on cathedrals we have referred to the pattern of daily worship and the practice of professional choirs and organists which link the cathedral with education (where they were originally the pioneers) in a continuing tradition, and with some of the liveliest figures in contemporary music-making. Not only is worship offered daily in the cathedrals, but they provide especially suitable settings for great festivals in which worship or a specifically religious dimension plays an important part. The most famous of these must undoubtedly be the Three Choirs Festival, to be held in 1977 at Gloucester, where (as the Dean has told us) "... it will be the 250th of these Festivals, it will last two days longer than usual, and it looks as though it will be the finest ever held. The great new feature of the second and final Sunday will be a celebration of the Eucharist with the three choirs (Gloucester, Hereford, Worcester) sharing in it, as a great act of thanksgiving for this Festival and for the long tradition behind it."

It would be invidious not to mention in the same breath the justly celebrated choirs of certain of the Oxford (Christ Church, Magdalen, New) and Cambridge (St John's and King's) Colleges, and it is significant that one third of the current £3 million appeal for Canterbury Cathedral is for the musical establishment.

CHAPTER FOUR

Other Denominations

The history of English ecclesiastical architecture has in this century been so dominated by the buildings of the Established church that those of other denominations have been all but passed by. Yet numerically Anglican churches are in fact in an overall minority. For while the Church of England has some 17,500 churches and chapels of ease, the Methodists still have about 8,500 churches; the Roman Catholics have 2,588 parish churches and 1,213 other churches and chapels also accessible to the public; the United Reformed Church (formed in 1972 from the Congregationalists and the Presbyterian Church of England) had in January 1975 2,093 places of worship; and a further 1,729 churches belong to the Baptist Union. The Quakers have between 350 and 400 meeting houses still in use, and the Unitarians some 200 chapels. To these must be added churches of the Christian Scientists, the Pentecostalists, the Christadelphians and numerous smaller and newer sects. Then there are the churches of old and new immigrant groups, notably Jewish synagogues, Orthodox churches, and a growing number of mosques and Hindu and Buddhist temples. In all, statistics kept by the Registrar-General show there are no less than 675 different denominations, sects and faiths—and a total of over 30,000 non-Anglican buildings in England that are licensed for worship.

The tendency to overlook the buildings of the nonconformists is due not simply to taste and scholarship but to the sheer problems of access. With the exception of a few shrines of dissent—the Quaker Meeting House at Jordans, Buckinghamshire, where William Penn is buried, Wesley's New Room at Bristol, or the famous Octagon Chapel at Norwich—nonconformist buildings are unlikely to be found open except at times of services when they are again difficult to visit. Whereas Anglican and Roman Catholic churches are traditionally open all day for prayer and contemplation, to dissenters a church has no special significance except when the congregation is gathered.

Yet the growth of nonconformity is a central strand of English history, closely associated with the struggle for civil liberties and equal opportunities. In Kenneth Lindley's words: "these chapels are the expression of one of the greatest revolutionary movements which the world has seen and of a religious experience which was capable of so enlarging the lives of those caught up in it as to transform the humblest of labourers into the greatest of men". Dissenters have provided many of the vigorous empire builders and industrial and commercial entrepreneurs, as well as men like Joseph Priestley who made outstanding contributions to the development of science and medicine.

Dissenting congregations are recorded in the 1580s and the first homogeneous sect to appear were the Baptists, followed shortly by the Independents. Initially English nonconformity was led mainly by university graduates, but it flourished early in commercial centres such as Bristol, Gloucester, Ipswich and Norwich. With the temporary disestablishment of the Anglican Church during the Commonwealth, dissenters openly took over many parish churches, and even turned cathedrals into preaching-houses—hence the major refurnishings which took place after the Restoration. Nonconformity proper begins with the Act of Uniformity in 1662. As a result of this measure some 2,000 ordained clergy who were by conviction Baptists, Presbyterians and Independents refused to conform and were ejected. This was followed in 1664 by the Conventicle Act forbidding dissenters to meet for worship. However, certain towns like Mansfield, Nottinghamshire, which were not incorporated, were not forbidden to Puritans, so early conventicles flourished there. Some relaxation came with the Declaration of Indulgence but many of the finest nonconformist buildings date from the years immediately following the Toleration Act of 1689, and were built mainly for the Presbyterians and Independents. In the first half of the 18th century the pace of chapel building declined, but a new momentum came with the meteoric rise of Wesley and the exclusion of his followers from parish churches. Growth during the early 19th century was even more rapid, and in the census of 1851, to the anguish of the establishment, it emerged that attendance at nonconformist chapels was numerically higher than in the Church of England. The redoubled frenzy of church and chapel building in the 1860s and 1870s was partly a result of these findings, and soon after the turn of the century the nonconformists reached their apogee—only to enter a drastic decline which continues today.

Expansion must have been encouraged in part by lack of Anglican churches in the growing centres of the Industrial Revolution: Leeds in 1831 had a population of 70,000 and only one parish church and two chapels of ease. Nonconformity has always been strongest in the industrial north and there are towns like Leyburn, in Yorkshire, where there was no Anglican church until 1837 and Great Whittington in

Northumberland, a substantial stone-built upland village, where there is still no Anglican church. In villages where squire and parson held joint sway, there tended to be less chapel life, but where there was no dominant landlord, as say in the Fens, nonconformity grew faster.

The geographical pattern established in the early years of dissent has generally survived. Presbyterian/Unitarian chapels preponderated in Cheshire, south Lancashire, southern Yorkshire and Derbyshire, continuing in a line through the Midlands, to Somerset and North Devon. In Sussex and Kent a comparable belt of Baptist and Unitarian chapels survives. Independents, now mainly Congregationalists, were most numerous in Somerset, Wiltshire, Northamptonshire, Bedfordshire and East Anglia. The Quakers, who began in Westmorland, spread into Cumbria, Yorkshire, Lancashire, the North and West Midlands, Oxfordshire and Gloucestershire, Buckinghamshire and Hertfordshire. Methodism has always had a great stronghold in Lincolnshire, the county of Wesley's birth, and Primitive Methodist chapels abound in Cornwall.

The earliest chapels are usually simple but dignified buildings hardly distinguishable from the farmhouses and cottages of the surrounding countryside, whether of Cumbrian stone and slate, Devon cob and thatch, or East Anglian plaster and tile. From 1739, when Wesley began his travels, new buildings became larger and took on the character of preaching houses. A number of these buildings are interesting examples of central planning: the nonconformist chapel with its single focus on the centrally placed pulpit was much more adapted to this than the more complicated ritual of Anglican and Roman Catholic worship.

Forbidden until the 19th century to build steeples, chapels were readily adaptable to the temple form of the Greek Revival, epitomized by the handsome Hexastyle Doric portico of the chapel in Stamford Street, London, of which only the façade now remains. Many of these buildings have major townscape value; of Redruth, Cornwall, Pevsner says: "The main street, running downhill and up again, is the typical shopping street of any county, made interesting only by the Wesleyan church of 1826 at its north end." In the late 1840s steeples began to appear (one of the first was E. Walters' Congregational church, Cavendish Street, Manchester, built in 1847–48), and more and more congregations set out to rival and even eclipse the parish church. Telling examples are the prominently placed Unitarian chapel at Todmorden, Yorkshire (J. Gibson, 1869), and the Union Congregational chapel at Ashton-under-Lyne, Lancashire, which both have spires outshining the parish church. The chapels of the later 19th century so far from degenerating into uniform coarseness are, at their best, among the more notable buildings of the Arts and Crafts revival and *art nouveau,* as was recognized on the Continent (though nowhere else), as long ago as 1901 by Muthesius in his *Die neuere kirchliche Baukunst*. Even architecturally insignificant chapels often have decided townscape value, and many are the only enlivening accent in an otherwise monotonous area. Inside, where admission is possible out of service hours, chapels of this date can have a particular quality due to the homogeneity of architecture and fittings. Whereas in Anglican churches pews and galleries can appear ill-at-ease with pillars and columns, nonconformists consistently achieved a remarkable degree of internal harmony, often through the use of elaborately curved and raked pews.

Early Meeting Houses

The earliest dissenting meeting houses are fascinating buildings, and though little larger than cottages, are worth travelling a great distance to see. The first dissenting congregations usually met in existing buildings and where these survive they have almost all passed into other hands. The chapel at Kirkstead Abbey, Lincolnshire, which became Puritan in 1645, became Anglican again as long ago as 1791, but the ancient St Mary's Chapel at Broadstairs, Kent, avowedly Independent from 1691, survived in use until 1918 when it was acquired for use as a parish hall by the nearby Holy Trinity Church. At Tavistock, in Devon, the present Unitarian church is in the great hall of the former abbey granted in 1691 to the Presbyterians by the Duke of Bedford.

Next came what might be termed the *incunabula* of dissent, built for very "low church" or Puritan-minded congregations. The earliest and most memorable of these is at Bramhope, just north of Leeds, built in 1649 in the grounds of the manor house by a strongly Puritan squire, Robert Dynetey. Today a new motel stands guard in place of the house, but the chapel was beautifully restored a few years ago by the former Wharfedale Rural District Council. Like many early meeting houses it is a long, low single-storey building, dominated inside by an imposing three-decker pulpit half way along one wall opposite the entrance—though there is, nonetheless, a small communion table at the east end. Inside it is complete and untouched, with candle sconces on the pulpit, hat pegs on the walls and brass name plates on the box-pews. Other buildings in this group are the chapel at Great Houghton (1650), near Wakefield, Yorkshire, again built for a country house since demolished, and a chapel at Guyhirn (1650) near Wisbech, Cambridgeshire, which became Anglican and was falling into decay until rescued recently by the Redundant Churches Fund.

The oldest of all surviving dissenting chapels is the small stone meeting house at Toxteth, Liverpool, built in 1618, which stands in the corner of an extensive graveyard. The interior, however, though charming, is later. Two of the most intact and remarkable early dissenting chapels are at Walpole, near Heveningham, in Suffolk and Monks Lane near Corsham in Wiltshire. Walpole chapel was converted in 1649 from two cottages built half a century earlier; Monks Lane, though equally cottage-like in appearance, was built as a chapel about 1670 and has an extraordinary dormer window like the eye of a cyclops over which the tiles rise in a gentle serpentine curve. Both have miraculously untouched interiors complete with box pews and creaking galleries, all in plain unvarnished woodwork. Corsham has a stone-flagged floor, pews panelled inside and out and music stands for the singers. Other good early chapels are at Guestwick in Norfolk (1652, intriguingly altered in the 1840s), and Newport Pagnell, Buckinghamshire. By 1700 a basic pattern had emerged with box pews and galleries on three sides facing an imposing pulpit in the middle of one wall with a small communion table below. From about 1700 the denominations begin to develop a clearer identity, and though many chapels have changed hands it is better to describe them separately.

Dissenting meeting houses also have their own distinct layout and furnishing about which some generalizations can be made. They tend to be either square or oblong, dominated by a pulpit in the centre of one wall, usually with a sounding board of some elaboration. These vary from single to triple deckers and can be square, hexagonal or octagonal, bow-fronted or tulip shaped, approached by one or two flights. Where there are galleries the fronts tend to be panelled, while below walls are often also panelled up to head height. In quite a number of cases the ceiling is supported by one or two massive columns, sometimes former ship masts. Communion pews, which rarely survive, were placed beneath the pulpit; but few meeting houses had a font, though a brass or iron ring fixed to the side of the pulpit was often used to hold a pewter bowl brought in for the occasion. All denominations have a minister's chair, sometimes with special historical or personal associations. Congregational singing which became widespread by about 1700 was usually led by a clerk or precentor from the desk below the pulpit.

Another interesting item to be found in most early meeting houses are hat pegs. Hats were taken off for prayer and for the sermon and before long for the whole service—hence the characteristic long pegs to support tall puritan hats, originally only on one side as the sexes sat apart. Occasionally these are found on the gallery fronts so those upstairs could reach over to hang their hats. In the North these were sometimes painted in a black and white bull's eye pattern: hence the Yorkshire expression: "his eyes stood out like chapel hat pegs". Interior memorials were not tolerated until the late 18th century, though quite a few meeting houses have their own graveyards with historically interesting groups of headstones. Many nonconformist buildings also bear a date—though this can be that of foundation, not erection. Another feature of interest is the communion token—issued as a proof of fitness to take communion. At first these were printed cards but increasingly they became smaller tokens of lead, brass, pewter or tin. All Quaker and most Baptist meeting houses had a library, and in some places these and, more rarely, chained books remain.

The Baptists

The Baptists today are not a Church as such but a union of largely autonomous churches, a number of which though included in the *Baptist Union Directory* are not in fact in the Union. In January 1976 1,749 are listed in the Yearbook.

Associations	
Bedfordshire & South Huntingdonshire	39
Berkshire	38
Bristol	54
Buckinghamshire	31
Cambridgeshire	38
Devon & Cornwall	69
East Midland	167
Essex	74
Gloucestershire & Herefordshire	47
Hertfordshire	43
Home Counties	16
Kent	63
Lancashire & Cheshire	167
London	255
Norfolk	32
Northamptonshire	61
Northern	38
Oxfordshire & East Gloucestershire	41
Southern	82
Suffolk	28
Sussex	45
Western	29
West Midland	126
Wiltshire & East Somersetshire	23

Associations	
Worcestershire	23
Yorkshire	120
Total	1,749

Baptists have always laid great stress on the importance of freedom of conscience and religious liberty and held that baptism should be administered to believers only, and with this goes the practice of total immersion. Baptists in England begin with John Smith (d. 1612), an ordained clergyman who became a separatist about 1605. He was forced by persecution to emigrate to Holland, where in 1611 he formed the first English Baptist Church, which met in Newgate Street, London, the next year. This was the origin of the General Baptists, who repudiated the Calvinistic doctrine of predestination, to be distinguished from the Particular Baptists, founded in 1633 who led a completely separate existence until fusion of the two in 1891 into the present Union. Growth of the Baptists was particularly marked in the first half of the 19th century with the number of churches rising from 652 in 1801 to 2,789 in 1851.

Among the small number of 17th-century Baptist buildings to survive, the best are at Loughwood, Tewkesbury, Gloucestershire and Winslow, Buckinghamshire. The Tewkesbury chapel, dating from 1623, is one of the most remarkable of all early nonconformist buildings—and inside has a repose and domesticity reminding one of a de Hooch painting. Loughwood is a converted cottage dating from 1653 and remarkably complete. Winslow (1695) still has its original quarry tiled floor.

Notable Early Baptist Chapels	
Sutton-in-the-Elms, Leicestershire	1650
Downton, Wiltshire	1673
Winslow, Buckinghamshire	1695
Burford, Wiltshire	1700
Cote, Oxfordshire	*c.* 1704
Gamlingay, Cambridgeshire	1710
Tetbury, Gloucestershire	1721
Taunton, Somerset	1721
Stevington, Bedfordshire	1721
Exeter, Devon	1725
Roade, Northamptonshire	*c.* 1730
Tiverton, Devon	1730
Upton-on-Severn, Gloucestershire	1734
Bratton, Wiltshire	1734
Alcester, Worcestershire	1735
Tottlebank, Lancashire	1740
Blunham, Bedfordshire	1751
Bessels Green, Kent	1770
Walgrave, Northamptonshire	1788

Cote, Oxfordshire, retains its original family pews and communion pew set lengthways to the pulpit. Bratton, Wiltshire, is an exceptionally handsome redbrick chapel with a spectacular pulpit, wide enough to seat four people and approached by twin curving stairs. Here too the original rails enclosing the communion table survive. Few early Baptisteries however remain. Adult baptism was usually practised in rivers, though at Tottlebank, Lancashire, traces of an open-air pool remain.

Towards the middle of the 18th century many Baptist congregations dwindled and became extinct or Unitarian. With the revival in the early 19th century Baptist chapels followed the pattern of other nonconformists but, perhaps because they appealed more to the poorer sections of the community, they built some churches of cathedral-like proportions. Examples are the magnificent Baptist Church of the Redeemer in Birmingham (demolished in 1975) and the cathedral-like Coats Memorial Baptist Church at Paisley, Strathclyde by H. J. Blanc (1886–94). On only a slightly lesser scale is the massive Baptist church in Osborne Road, Jesmond, Northumberland (1889) in bold competition with its Anglican contemporary and neighbour St George's. Towards the end of the 19th century it is apparent from the Baptist Yearbook that there was a great spate of construction and many of the buildings which resulted, though notionally Gothic, are among the more interesting (and little studied) Arts and Crafts buildings of the period.

No overall figures on the number of listed Baptist churches are available, but it is likely that not only most of the buildings dating from before 1850 are worthy of inclusion but a substantial number of the later 19th-century buildings are as well.

United Reformed Church

The United Reformed Church was founded in October 1972 by Union of the Congregational Church in England and Wales and the Presbyterian Church of England. The Church is divided into 12 provinces which in January 1975 had a total of 2,092 places of worship. About nine-tenths of these were formerly Congregationalist—the Presbyterian churches were mainly in the North.

	Province	*Places of Worship*
1	Northern	145
2	North Western	189
3	Mersey	116
4	Yorkshire	170
5	East Midland	149

	Province	*Places of Worship*
6	West Midland	187
7	Eastern	188
8	South West	181
9	Wessex	189
10	Thames North	179
11	Southern	228
12	Wales	171

(Figures from 1976 Yearbook)

Congregationalism, with Episcopacy and Presbyterianism, is one of the principal types of ecclesiastical polity. Traditionally it regards each local church as an independent self-governing unit, though the merger of 1972 has brought a greater element of central co-ordination. The first Congregational gatherings can be traced to London in the late 1560s, and in 1580–81 Robert Browne formed the first known Congregational church in Norwich. Between 1631 and 1640 Congregational churches around London grew to about 80; but the earliest buildings to survive date from after the Restoration. Like the Unitarians, the Congregationalists later inherited some of the best buildings of the Presbyterians and the Independents, and, as at least initially they tended to be relatively prosperous, their early buildings are well-finished and handsomely fitted out. Among the best chapels dating from the century following 1660 are Newport Pagnell, Buckinghamshire (1662), Stainton, Yorkshire (1698) and Tisbury, Wiltshire (1726).

In the 19th century the Congregationalists were responsible for a great number of imposing chapels. Many of the best provincial architects were regularly employed—Mawson and Lockwood, the Pritchetts of York and Darlington, the Habershons of London and Newport; John Tarring (at his best with Early English spires) and Sulman. On occasion they employed leading figures: Waterhouse built a number of their chapels, Butterfield designed one in Bristol and S. M. Daukes was responsible for the grand Congregational church at Broughton Park, Salford, Greater Manchester (1874). This was built in best 14th-century Gothic with everything to order including furniture and silver, and the spire seen across Clowes Park recalls Salisbury Cathedral. In many northern towns they set out to rival and even eclipse the Anglican churches: at Halifax the great 210 foot spire of the square Congregational church, built by the Crossley family, dwarfs the marvellous late medieval parish church—though Scott was quickly called in by a rival Anglican family to build the great church of All Souls, Haley Hill, across the valley. The big Gothic Congregational church of 1874 at Tynemouth, Tyne and Wear, also stands high above the main street. The Presbyterian church at Embleton, Northumberland (1833) rises proudly in the village square. From the turn of the century dates the roaring redbrick Congregational church at New Brighton, Merseyside, in a suburbia of splendid Wirral gentility—again the spire seen across the Mersey on a stormy day is a memorable piece of Northern cityscape. A number of Congregational buildings of this date have a flair and liveliness anticipating *art nouveau*; many also have excellent fittings. Faulkner Armitage, for example, who carved the choir stalls at Chester Cathedral, also made the pulpit for Wycliffe Congregational Church in Warrington, Cheshire.

According to Chesterton's, who manage the property of the United Reformed Church, about 10% or some 200 of these churches are listed. This again appears a remarkably small number.

Unitarians

Today the Unitarians have at least 250 churches in Britain, including about two dozen in Wales and four in Scotland. Although this is small compared with the Methodists, the Baptists or the United Reformed Church, the Unitarians undoubtedly possess *relatively* the highest proportion of fine historic buildings. This is because the Unitarians inherited many of the best early buildings of the Independents, the Presbyterians and the General Baptists. The earliest English Unitarian tracts were the work of John Biddle, published in 1652, who established conventicles. The first formal Unitarian church was established at Essex Street in the Strand, London, in 1774, just at the time when the early dissenters were growing weak, and the Unitarians inherited a substantial number of ambitious late-17th-century and early-18th-century chapels built by rich merchants in important commercial centres such as Norwich. These were usually built of the finest materials and, if restrained without, often contain interior woodwork as fine, or almost as fine, as would be found in any contemporary college building at Oxford or Cambridge.

This sense of grandeur is well caught in Wesley's description of the Norwich octagon: "Today I was shown Dr Taylors meeting house perhaps the most elegant in Europe. It is eight sided, built of the finest brick and the interior is as clean as a nobleman's Saloon: the very latches of the pews are of polished brass. How can this be a fitting house for the poor coarse gospel." At Ipswich, Suffolk, the Unitarians have a no less remarkable (former Presbyterian) building which Defoe said was: "inside the best finished of any I have seen, London not exempted". In Cheshire the Unitarians have a group of three chapels at Knutsford, Wilmslow and Allostock all evidently built by the same architect at the time of the Act of Toleration. Further north is Rivington, Lancashire (1703), islanded among reservoirs, and almost completely preserved. Atherton, Greater Manchester, is another little altered chapel (1722) with all its box pews and galleries resting on giant Corinthian columns. Other important chapels are at St Saviourgate, in York, in the form of a Greek cross, and at Taunton, Somerset, which has an exceptionally handsome interior. Among later-18th-century chapels that at Lewins Mead, Bristol (1791), is large and ambitious with a good interior, and Bridport, Dorset (1794), which though modest is complete inside with galleries resting on Ionic columns.

The comparative wealth of the Unitarians continued in the 19th century, particularly around Manchester. As a result quite a number were well-endowed, which is one reason why many are carefully maintained today. Chapels were built in a remarkable variety of styles, ranging from a spiky filigree Gothic to a sturdy polychrome Romanesque. With a few exceptions congregations show a great love for their buildings and look after them with evident pride and care—and quite a few have been well repaired and restored in the last two decades. Unitarian chapels, it is also worth noting, often have delightful graveyards—one of the earliest is at Chesterfield, Derbyshire. These can contain headstones of considerable interest.

Unitarian Chapels	*17th Century*
Allostock, Cheshire	1690
Ashton-in-Makerfield, Greater Manchester	1697
Bridgwater, Somerset	1688
Frenchay, Bristol, Avon	1691
Chesterfield, Derbyshire	1694
Cirencester, Gloucestershire	1672
Dean Row, Wilmslow, Cheshire	1688
Knutsford, Cheshire	1689
Toxteth, Liverpool	1618
Macclesfield, Cheshire	1690
St Saviourgate, York	1693

Unitarian Chapels	*18th Century*
Atherton, Greater Manchester	1721
Belper, Derbyshire	1788
Billingshurst, Sussex	1754
Bridport, Dorset	1794
Lewins Mead, Bristol	1791
Chorley, Lancashire	1725
Crewkerne, Somerset	1733
Ditchling, Sussex	1740
Dudley, West Midlands	1717
Egerton, Walmsley, Lancashire	1713
Evesham, Hereford & Worcester	1737
Exeter, Devon	1760
Great Hucklow, Derbyshire	1795
Hale Barns, Greater Manchester	1723
Hepton, Norfolk	1741
Hinckley, Leicestershire	1722
Hindley, Greater Manchester	1700
Horsham, Sussex	1721
Ilminster, Somerset	1719

Unitarian Chapels	*18th Century*
Ipswich, Suffolk	1700
Kendal, Cumbria	1720
Great Meeting, Leicester	1708
Lewes, Sussex	1700
Gatacre, Liverpool	1700
Stoke Newington, London	1708
Maidstone, Kent	1690
Mansfield, Nottinghamshire	1701
Newcastle, Staffordshire	1717
New Mill, Lydgate, Yorkshire	1768
Newport, Isle of Wight	1774
Norwich, Norfolk	1756
Rivington, Lancashire	1703
Sevenoaks, Kent	1716
Fulwood, Sheffield	1728
Stannington, Sheffield	1742
Sidmouth, Devon	1710
Tamworth, Staffordshire	1724
Taunton, Somerset	1721
Tenterden, Kent	1746
Wakefield, Yorkshire	1752
Warwick	1780

(Note: dates are those of building as given in the Yearbook and do not take account of later remodelling or alteration)

Society of Friends

While the chapels of Baptists, Congregationalists and Methodists are to some extent interchangeable, the Quakers have a distinctive architecture of their own. There are today between 350 and 400 Quaker meeting houses still in use, and a remarkable number of these are 17th and 18th century. The founder of the Society of the Friends of the Truth, George Fox, began his first travels in the Midlands in 1648–49. Going to the North-west in 1651–52 he quickly gained followers, particularly among the groups of seekers in Westmorland. Contemporary estimates suggest that there were between 6–8,000 adult male Quakers by 1660 and some 10,000 by 1689. The Quakers did not benefit from the relaxations on dissenting worship following the Act of Toleration and large-scale emigration continued in the 18th century. This is a reason for the survival of so many early meeting houses. The early 19th century saw something of a revival, but in contrast to the other nonconformists there was little Quaker building between 1850 and 1914—a period when many early buildings belonging to the other denominations were rebuilt.

Externally most Quaker meeting houses are purely vernacular in character with little to distinguish them from the farmhouses of the surrounding landscape. They were built with cooperative labour, of local materials. Inside the same simplicity is to be found, wainscotting and seating are generally of unstained and unpolished deal, or, more rarely, of oak. Originally benches were backless but by the end of the 17th century the characteristic open back bench was becoming widespread. Though the benches are simple in the extreme the design and sometimes ornament of the benchends provides an opportunity for unexpected exuberance.

The characteristic feature of the Quaker meeting house was the elders' stand, running the length of one of the walls. This consisted of a block of seats facing the rest of the congregation. At its simplest it is a single bench, but more usually there are two tiers, and sometimes three, entered by short flights towards the ends or, more rarely, in the centre. The front of the stand was sometimes panelled, alternatively there was a handrail and shaped balusters. Men and women originally sat separately, and at the back there is usually to be found a women's gallery. The fronts of these usually have ingenious movable shutters which can be raised or sunk to make the gallery into a separate room for monthly meetings. Otherwise Quaker meetings houses are characterized by extreme simplicity—no internal memorial plaques were allowed: hassocks where they survive were intended to protect the feet from floor draughts and damp, and never used for kneeling.

Architecturally the character of meeting houses varies sharply from region to region. At Almeley Wooton in Gloucestershire is one of the few black-and-white meeting houses to survive. Ettington in Warwickshire has one of the smallest, measuring a mere 23 by 18 feet externally. The lowliness of the congregation is further evident in the use of second-hand materials: the window catches for example are all of different patterns and clearly re-used from elsewhere. In place of the wainscotting found elsewhere woven rush matting is pinned to the walls; hassocks and seat-cushions are of the same material.

The famous meeting house at Brigflatts in Yorkshire is a typical North Country farmhouse outside. Dating from 1673 it has white-washed stone walls, a York-flagged roof, a door studded with oak-nails, and a (now unique) dog-pen at the foot of the gallery stairs, for farmers' sheepdogs. Little changed since the 18th century, and now beautifully cared for, it is undoubtedly a place of Quaker pilgrimage. Other well-preserved meeting houses are to be found at Colthouse, Cumbria, Swarthmoor, Yorkshire, Settle, Yorkshire and Farfield, Cumbria—at Skipton, Yorkshire, the fine elders stand is carved with the initials of children who sat there in the early 18th century while the building was used as a school.

In the London area there is an interesting group of late-18th-century meeting houses—Uxbridge (1755), Wandsworth (1778), Brentford (1785) and Esher (1793). To these may be added Plaistow (1823) and Peckham (1847). In the second half of the century there was little Quaker building except in Leeds (1863) and Bradford (1877). Between 1900 and 1914 there was renewed activity and Fred Rowntree built two delightful meeting houses at Hampstead, London (1907) and Golders Green, London (1913), the latter modelled on Jordans, Buckinghamshire. Between the wars, Hubert Lidbetter, author of *The Friends Meeting House* (1961), built two distinguished medium-sized meeting houses at Birmingham (Bull Street) and Liverpool (Hunter Street) in the Georgian tradition.

Methodists

John and Charles Wesley held their first outdoor service for the Somerset colliers in 1739. Both were Anglican clergymen and at first set out to complement Anglican worship, usually holding services and meetings on weekdays. But as an increasing number of Anglican clergy refused to give communion to Methodists, because of John's ordination of pastors for the American mission, they soon had to establish their own places of worship. Many of the first Methodist chapels were in converted houses: the simplest procedure was to make a hole in the ceiling of a ground floor room, with men sitting below and women above—from the start the sexes were separated as in the primitive church. The first wholly Methodist building was the New Room in Horsefair, Bristol, begun in 1739. Here the central pulpit is dramatically approached by stairs which descend on either side from the gallery: some of the original backless forms survive as a reminder that Methodists originally had no pews, and benches were for rich and poor alike.

Wesley himself made a distinct contribution to Methodist architecture. He disapproved of the term meeting house and eschewed any resemblance to earlier dissenters. Architecturally, the form he favoured was the octagon—inspired by the chapel at Colegate, Norwich, which he called: "perhaps the most elegant in Europe". Between 1761 and 1776 he built, or was associated with, at least 14 octagon chapels. Only three of them survive, Yarm in Northumberland and Heptonstall in Yorkshire (both 1764), and Arbroath near Dundee (1772). Gone are Rotherham, S. Yorkshire (1761), Whitby, N. Yorkshire (1764), Snowsfield (1764), Aberdeen (1764), Edinburgh (1765), Chester (1765), Nottingham (1766), Thirsk, N. Yorkshire (1766), Bradford, W. Yorkshire (1766) and Gwennap, Cornwall or Carharrack, Cornwall (1779). Octagons, he felt, were best for the voice; he also considered, as he wrote to E. Bolton in 1769, that "A preaching house cant be too light and airy therefore your windows must be large And let them be sashes opening downwards; otherwise the air coming in would give the people cold".

By 1784 Wesley's followers had built more than 350 chapels which, according to William Miles's *History of the Methodists,* had risen to 1,540 by 1812. Of these only 131 remained in 1970. Expansion during the first half of the 19th century was even more rapid with membership rising from about 80,000 in 1791 to 338,861 in 1848. The term Wesleyan does not appear until the early 19th century when it was introduced to distinguish Wesley's own followers from other branches: the Methodist New Connexion (founded 1797), Primitive Methodists (founded 1805–10), the Bible Christians (1815) and the United Free Methodists who having failed to reform their church from within separated in 1857. The Free Methodists, New Connexion and the Bible Christians joined in 1907 to form the United Methodist Church, which was followed in 1932 by a full union with Wesleyans and Primitive Methodists to form the present Methodist Church.

This expansion is clearly reflected in church building. In 1851 the official total of Wesleyan preaching places had risen to 5,682; by 1873 it was 7,854. The Wesleyan Chapel Committee Reports show further that between 1860 and 1900 approval was given for 4,612 new chapels (including replacements). At the time of union in 1932 there were approximately 14,500 Methodist churches. The numbers had fallen to 11,500 in 1960 and 8,500 in 1970. So far the only attempt to assess this remarkable legacy is George Dolbey's pioneering *The Architectural Expression of Methodism: the first hundred years* (1964), and this general lack of awareness is reflected in the fact that (according to the Methodist Department of Property) only 300 to 400 Methodist churches are listed. Of these just five are Grade I: Central Hall, Westminster, the City Road Chapel, London, and the house next door, the Bristol New Room and the Nicolson Square Church, Edinburgh (Category A). Certainly any church before 1800 should be listed simply on grounds of rarity; so should the great majority of pre-1840 and perhaps pre-1860 buildings. After 1860 townscape value and interior completeness should make many more buildings good candidates for listing.

After Wesley's death, Methodist chapels fell into three main groups, the large 1,000-seater urban church, the smaller town chapel and the country chapel, to which must be added in the later 19th century the remarkable series of Central Halls in major cities. The larger chapels represent the emergence of Methodism from a simple domesticity to a formal dignity and even stateliness. Given the context in which they were built some were almost swagger buildings—Tiviot Dale, Stockport, Greater Manchester (1826), for example, cost the princely sum of £12,009. Other grand buildings of this type are Carver Street, Sheffield, S. Yorkshire (1804: 1,000 seats), Bishop Street, Leicester (1815: 717 seats), Brunswick, Newcastle upon Tyne (1820: 1,120 seats), Wesley, Redruth, Cornwall (1826: 1,382 seats) and Priory Place, Doncaster, S. Yorkshire (1832: 1,000 seats). Almost all have an impressive range of ancillary buildings, principally classrooms and Sunday schools, and a manse or house for a chapel keeper. Structurally these buildings are remarkable for very broad clear spans, usually unsupported by any internal columns. The great galleries which run round three or four sides are supported from below, usually on slender cast-iron columns, and thus from any part of the building there is an uninterrupted view of the pulpit. These galleries are often oval in shape, with pews curved and raked in unison.

In the 19th century increasing importance was placed on the administration of the sacrament, and the communion table, which in some chapels was kept in an apse, was brought out in front of the pulpit, and often communion rails were introduced. Towards the end of the century the original two- or three-decker pulpits were often replaced by a rostrum, a broad raised platform where communicants could stand and a pulpit with seating for several people. These rostrums are often of considerable grandeur in themselves: a good example is the handsome twin-staired Renaissance rostrum-pulpit introduced in 1900 at Priory Place, Doncaster, S. Yorkshire. Often the carving and joinery is of high quality and in addition there is excellent metalwork in the form of communion rails and light fittings. The other principal feature of the large urban chapel is the organ—reflecting the importance attached to music in worship, especially to hymn singing—that in the Brunswick Chapel, Leeds (now disused) is one of the best Georgian organs still in existence: at Bishop Street, Leicester, there is an organ reputed to be by Father Smith.

Secondly come the small-town churches, and it is here that Methodist architecture has suffered its greatest losses, partly through replacements but even more through redundancy resulting from amalgamations and declining congregations. These buildings generally seat between three and four hundred and tend also to be of the auditorium type, scaled down versions of the large urban chapels, often with the characteristic oval galleries. Both inside and out they portray the growing dignity of Methodist worship. Good examples are at St James Street, Monmouth, Gwent (1837) and Bridport, Dorset (1838).

The third group are the country chapels, small and simple but often of great charm and character. The early chapels tend to be purely vernacular in character, but in the later 19th century they developed a distinctive style of their own, an obvious example being the red and grey brick chapels to be found in villages all over Lincolnshire. Inside, pulpits are almost all single decker: from here the whole service was taken, and the sermon delivered. An attractive example is Withypool, Dorset (*c.* 1800) which has ogee-headed Gothick windows.

Methodist Chapels before 1800 still in use in 1970

Addingham Wesley Place, Chapel Street, West Yorkshire	1778
Arbroath St John's, Ponderlaw Street, Angus (Tayside)	1772
Berwick-on-Tweed Walkergate, Northumberland	1797
Bewdley Hereford and Worcester	1794
Braithwell South Yorkshire	1799
Bramley Main Street, South Yorkshire	1789
Braunston High Street, Northamptonshire	1797
Broadmead John Wesley's Chapel, New Room, Bristol, Avon	1748
Countersett (Rented property), North Yorkshire	1710
Crich Wesley Chapel, Chapel Lane, Derbyshire	1765
Deveral Cornwall	1794
Earlswood Valley Monmouthshire (Gwent)	1791
Farnley Hill Stonebridge Lane, West Yorkshire	1797
Fontmell Magna Dorset	1794
Fryup North Yorkshire	1799
Goadby Leicestershire	1795
Greetland West Yorkshire	1780
Harewood West Yorkshire	1790
Hawnby North Yorkshire	1770
Hayfield St John's, Derbyshire	1782
Heptonstall Northgate, West Yorkshire	1764
Hoghton Chapel Lane, Lancashire	1794
Ireshopeburn High House, Durham	1760
Little Walsingham New Walsingham, Norfolk	1794
Lofthouse West Yorkshire	1790
London Wesley's Chapel, City Road	1778
Lower Foxdale Isle of Man	1798
Newbiggin Durham	1750
Newhaven St Michael's, East Sussex	11th or 12th century
Raithby (Wesley's Chapel), Lincolnshire	1779
Rastrick St Matthew's (shared), West Yorkshire	1798
Ravensworth North Yorkshire	1784
Reeth North Yorkshire	1796

Methodist Chapels before 1800 still in use in 1970

Salem	Watleys End, Bristol, Avon	1790
Seend	Wiltshire	1775
Shelley	West Yorkshire	1785
Southfield	(Rented Property) Lancashire	1796
Trowbridge	Church Street, Wiltshire	1771
Stapleford	Wesley Place, Nottinghamshire	1782
Whittlebury	High Street, Northamptonshire	1783
Wilton	United Free Church, Crow Lane (shared)	1791
Winchelsea	East Sussex	1785
Yarm	Cleveland	1764

Some Smaller Denominations

The great majority of nonconformist buildings which are of outstanding architectural interest were built by the half dozen major religious groups. But of the innumerable smaller denominations, many have a remarkable architectural heritage.

The Moravians, who strongly influenced John Wesley, built many chapels in England. The most interesting of these, such as at Fulneck, Yorks (1742) and Fairfield, Manchester (1785), are found in groups of buildings in which the Moravian communities worked, lived and worshipped.

The Countess of Huntingdon's Connexion, established in the mid eighteenth century by the Countess, Selina, had a curious amalgam of Methodist and Congregational ideas. Its buildings were equally distinctive. That at Bath (1765) is a delightful example, admired by Walpole for its "true Gothic windows" and neat mahogany fittings; while the chapel at Worcester (1804–15) has a fine Victorianized interior.

The New—or New Jerusalem—Church was founded in 1788 by followers of Emanuel Swedenborg. Its buildings, which included octagonal and circular chapels, were invariably noteworthy, but sadly few remain. Accrington (1849 by James Green) and Melbourne, Derbyshire (1864 by B. Wilson) are interesting survivors.

The Salvation Army, which was created in 1872 by the former Methodist minister William Booth, needs little introduction. Initially its crusade was undertaken from adapted premises: redundant skating rinks and indoor circuses were conveniently plentiful at the time. But it soon began to build its characteristic castellated and turreted citadels, such as Aberdeen (1893–6 by James Souttar) and Sheffield (1894), which are such an important feature of many inner urban areas.

The Christian Scientists first began building in England at the beginning of this century, and were able to employ the very best architects. Their church in Curzon Street, London (1910 by Lanchester and Rickards) is a massive classical edifice. That at Victoria Park, Manchester (1903 by Edgar Wood) is perhaps the most original church of its date in England, in a dramatic proto-Expressionist style out of the Arts and Crafts tradition.

Roman Catholics

The history of post-Reformation Catholicism, as much as that of Dissent, is a story of valour and endurance. It is living proof, too, of the way religious beliefs can be upheld through long periods of great adversity by a determined and dedicated laity. Equally it is a romantic story, associated for the best part of two centuries with ancient country houses, notably in Lancashire and Oxfordshire, complete with hiding places and priest holes which are far from being mere legend.

There are in England some three places where mass has been said continuously since the Reformation: these are Stonor Park, Oxfordshire, Sizergh Castle, Cumbria and Brailes, Warwickshire. For a long time services were held in upstairs rooms or outbuildings, the real purpose of which could be easily disguised: at Brailes in Warwickshire a trap door in the ceiling enabled the altar to be lifted into the roof. The Stuart sequence of Catholic royal marriages meant there were chapels at Court, as well as a number of embassy chapels, where mass could be attended, but it was not until the reign of James II that there was a short respite which allowed the first public chapels to be built. In 1689, however, Catholics were cut off from the benefits of the Act of Toleration, and it was only the Catholic Relief Act of 1778 which freed bishops, priests and schoolmasters from the risk of arrest and persecution. Following the Catholic Relief Act in 1791 Catholics were no longer liable for prosecution for hearing mass or not attending Anglican churches, provided they took a suitably worded oath. They could also build churches, without bells or steeples, if these were certified by Justices of the Peace. It was not until the Catholic Emancipation Act of 1829 that they were legally allowed to found schools, academies or colleges and establish religious orders and convents.

Most of the early Catholic places of worship surviving are therefore country house chapels. Sometimes these are within the house; sometimes attached or adjoining: elsewhere as at Lulworth, Dorset or Brough, Cumbria, they are treated as ornamental features in the park or grounds. Among the most notable are Cobham Hall, Kent; Croxdale, Durham; Mapledurham, Oxfordshire; Spetchley, Hereford and Worcester and Wardour Castle, Wiltshire.

Among the first churches are St John's Bath (1685), St Mary's Bristol (1730), St Wilfrid's York (1760), and St Aloysius, Oxford (1785). Two of the best are in the Isle of Wight at Newport (1792) and West Cowes (1796). An interesting group of Regency Catholic churches is still to be found in Lancashire, the traditional stronghold of English Catholicism. The best reasons for visiting Wigan (if not on an Orwellian pilgrimage) are the two contemporary Catholic churches built within 200 yards of each other as a result of a controversy between the secular clergy and the Jesuits—St Mary, and St John the Baptist, opened in 1818 and 1819. Preston, another largely Catholic town, also boasts a number of fine Catholic churches of slightly later date—including the Perpendicular, St Ignatius (1833–36) and St Austin (1838–40). In London two Regency Catholic churches were built at Hampstead and Somers Town (demolished *c.* 1969). Catholic churches were also built in spas and seaside resorts at this date—at Bath, Avon, Cheltenham, Gloucestershire, Darlington, Durham, and North Shields, Tyne and Wear.

In the 1840s the vast influx of destitute Irish provided a further spur to Catholic building, and if many of the churches are architecturally of minor interest, the fact that they were built in times of great difficulty, with the pennies of the poor, gives them in Catholic eyes a special historical value. Among the best of the inner-city churches of this date is St Anthony, Scotland Road, Liverpool (1832–33), which miraculously survived heavy bombing all around it and remains much as it was when new. Catholic churches are almost equally divided between the classic—such as the handsome Willow Lane Chapel in Norwich (1827), by John Thomas Patience—and Gothic, a good, light-hearted example of which is the little vaulted church at Lyme Regis, Dorset. Many of the best churches of this date such as St Mary, Sunderland, Tyne and Wear (1835) and St Marie, Bury, Greater Manchester (1841–42) have gone, making it all the more vital to preserve those that remain. With Pugin, Catholic churches enter a new more serious Gothic phase even though lack of money usually prevented his schemes being realized as he wished. As a group Pugin's churches have the added interest that many were inspired by a single patron, Lord Shrewsbury, beginning with the church at Uttoxeter, Staffordshire (1838), and continuing with St Alban, Macclesfield, Cheshire (1839–41), the Hospital of St John the Baptist, the Earl's patron saint, at Alton, Staffordshire (1840). The latter, a community of retired priests, is one of a whole series of monasteries, convents, seminaries and colleges, which are of great architectural interest but outside the terms of this report. Only two of Pugin's churches were built without severe financial restrictions,

St Giles, Cheadle, Staffordshire, built at Lord Shrewsbury's sole expense, with a steeple rising up over the centre of the town, and the great church at Ramsgate, Kent, which is the first major sight to greet visitors arriving at the hoverport. The second half of the 19th century saw a growing series of remarkable Catholic churches by eminent architects—the fine churches at Taunton, Somerset, and Abergavenny, Gwent (both completed in 1860) by Benjamin Bucknall, Joseph Hansom's St Walburge, Preston, Lancashire (1850–54) with a stupendous hammerbeam roof, the impressive cruciform St Mary and St Michael, Commercial Road, in the East End of London (1856) by William Wilkinson Wardell, designer of Melbourne and Sydney Cathedrals, Edward Welby Pugin's austerely grand St Gregory at Longton in the Staffordshire Potteries (1869) and his highly original Franciscan church in Gorton in Manchester (1866–72). Many of the finest Victorian churches in fact provide good reasons for visiting what would normally be considered the dreariest of places. The latter part of the 19th century saw the Catholics, like the nonconformists, building a number of adventurous Arts and Crafts Gothic churches, beginning with such as J. F. Bentley's Corpus Christi, Brixton Hill, London (1886) and Holy Rood, Watford, London (1889–90), both of which have excellent fittings, and continuing with the work of Leonard Stokes and F. A. Walters. Among the best churches of these two men are Stokes' St Clare, Liverpool, and Walters' St Anne, Vauxhall, London (1903–7).

Historically, the growth of Catholicism is difficult to chart in the early years after the Reformation, but in 1781 statistics based on returns by Anglican clergy showed a total of 68,373 Catholics; of these over 27,000 were then in the Diocese of Chester, which at that time included Lancashire, the traditional Catholic stronghold. By 1840 the number of Catholics was estimated at about 452,000 and the *Catholic Directory* of that year announced the number of churches as 457; of these 88 were in Lancashire. Today the figure has grown to 2,588 Catholic parish churches, to which must be added a further 1,213 chapels.

Diocese	*Parish Churches*	*Other Churches and Chapels Open to the Public*	*Private Chapels*
Westminster	215	42	140
Arundel & Brighton	115	55	—
Birmingham	230	103	—
Brentwood	92	44	44
Cardiff	101	38	28
Clifton	97	59	74

Diocese	*Parish Churches*	*Other Churches and Chapels Open to the Public*	*Private Chapels*
East Anglia	(Figures not available)		
Hexham & Newcastle	179	68	46
Lancs	110	64	—
Leeds	185	84	29
Liverpool	228	18	100
Menevia	67	53	41
Middlesbrough	93	48	37
Northampton	58	58	74
Nottingham	130	132	59
Plymouth	87	44	32
Portsmouth	119	77	—
Salford	208	22	77
Shrewsbury	103	38	23
Southwark	171	166	—

(Figures from *Catholic Directory 1977*)

No figures are available as to the numbers of listed buildings included, but taking the Directory of the Diocese of Clifton there appear to be some 145 buildings of consequence, the majority of which are post-1945. The following 35 date from before 1900, and give an indication of the proportion of historic churches to be found in one diocese:

Bath, St John the Evangelist (1685; 1861, etc.)
Bath, St Mary (1832; 1881)
Bridgwater, Somerset, St Joseph (1849; 1882)
Bristol, St Mary on the Quay (1730; 1790; 1843)
Bristol, Holy Cross (1872; 1922)
Bristol, St Bonaventure (1890; 1907, etc.)
Bristol, St Nicholas of Tolentino (1848)
Cheltenham, Gloucestershire, St Gregory (1809; 1857)
Chippenham, Wiltshire, St Mary (1855; 1936)
Chipping Campden, Gloucestershire (1854; 1891)
Chipping Sodbury, Avon (1838)
Cirencester, Gloucestershire, St Peter (1862; 1896)
Clevedon, Avon (1882)
Devizes, Wiltshire (1861)
East Harptree, Avon (1806; 1833)
Fairford, Gloucestershire (1845; 1852)
Frome, Somerset (1851, etc.)
Gloucester (*c.* 1789)
Kemerton, Gloucestershire (1843)
Malmesbury, Wiltshire (1867; 1875)
Minehead, Somerset (1895; 1898)
Nympsfield, Gloucestershire (1847)
Portishead, Avon (1887)
Salisbury, St Edmund, Wiltshire (1790; 1848)
Stratton on the Fosse, Somerset (1856)

Stroud, Gloucestershire (1857)
Swindon, Wiltshire (1848, etc.)
Taunton, Somerset, St George (1790; 1860)
Tewkesbury, Gloucestershire (1870)
Tisbury, Wiltshire (1898)
Trowbridge, Wiltshire (1876)
Weston super Mare, Avon (1851, etc.)
Wincanton, Somerset (1881)
Woodchester, Gloucestershire (1846, etc.)
Yeovil, Somerset (1887)

Synagogues

There were probably individual Jews in England in Roman times but the first records begin with the Norman Conquest. Jewish immigrants arrived soon after 1066 and important settlements were established in London, Lincoln and other centres. In 1190 came the ugly massacres of Jews in many cities, followed exactly a century later by Edward I's expulsion. The present Anglo-Jewish community dates from the Commonwealth. In 1656 the Spanish and Portuguese congregation in London was organized and this was followed towards the end of the century by the establishment of an Ashkenazi community. This increased rapidly and spread to the principal provincial cities and seaports. The London community has however always dominated.

In the 19th century persecution brought a further influx first from Germany and then from Russia following the outbreak of persecution in 1881 and a succession of pogroms, and then again from Germany after 1933.

Today there are some 375 synagogues in Britain, though only a small proportion claim to be of historic and architectural significance. This is in considerable part due to heavy losses through bombing in the 1939–45 war—the East End of London and the seaports, both traditional Jewish strongholds, suffered intensely. To an equal extent it is due to rebuilding of historic synagogues both before and after the war, a process which makes it all the more important to protect the remainder.

The oldest extant synagogue in the country today is Bevis Marks in London dating from 1701. In Exeter the synagogue in Mary Arches Street was built in 1763 and the cemetery in Magdalen Road dates from 1757. This has a handsome Greek Doric entrance and well preserved fittings—though today it is only occasionally used. In Liverpool the Princes Road synagogue is one of the handsomest in the country. At Plymouth is the oldest surviving Ashkenazi synagogue in Britain dating from 1762.

CHAPTER FIVE

Scotland

"Scotland and Greece are the two most romantic small countries in the world for what they can give of scenery and history, and both countries can add to the attraction of their mainland enchanting islands galore. To clinch the comparison, the Rock of Edinburgh and the Acropolis of Athens offer the finest combination of city landscape and seascape in Europe."

COMPTON MACKENZIE

Scotland has long had a powerful allure to visitors both from England and from abroad, whether for its glorious scenery, its distinct way of life and colourful traditions or its unrivalled fishing, shooting and stalking. The last decades have also seen a rapidly growing interest in its old towns and vernacular buildings (particularly as a result of the National Trust for Scotland's Little Houses Scheme) as well as its royal palaces, castles and country houses and gardens. Its churches however have remained the subject of a sense of inferiority. "Scotland", according to the leaflets on Historic Scottish Kirks produced by the Church of Scotland, "has comparatively few great churches to set beside those of England and the Continent." Yet Scotland's churches are not only keys both to its history and its townscape, but in most cases buildings of merit and individuality, remarkably well preserved and capable of comparison with contemporary buildings in most northern European countries.

Though Scotland has only a fraction of the number of medieval churches that England possesses this very fact led much earlier to the development of a distinctive Reformation architecture. While there was virtually no church building south of the border in the reigns of Elizabeth I, James I and Charles I, and little—apart from the rebuildings of the City churches—in the second half of the 17th century, there survive in Scotland a remarkable and all-too-little known group of buildings from these years, among which are a number of examples of ingenious central planning at least as noteworthy as better-known churches in Germany or Holland. The 18th century was a period of widespread church building, with churches often forming the principal element in a planned layout. In Colen Campbell, James Gibbs and Robert Adam, Scotland lost some of its best architects to the south, but from the 18th century on there were increasing numbers of major architects, at least as able as any practising in England, who are only now receiving the recognition they deserve. Those who built the noblest churches include John Smith, James and William Henry Playfair James Gillespie Graham, William Burn, David Bryce, John Honeyman, Alexander "Greek" Thompson, Archibald Simpson, Frederick Pilkington, William Leiper, Marshall Mackenzie, James Sellars, J. J. Burnet, P. Macgregor Chalmers, Ninian Comper, Rowand Anderson and Robert Lorimer.

Spires and towers are the major accent in the profile of many towns, as well as dominant elements in the streetscape. Few, if any, towns in Europe boast so many well-placed spires as Edinburgh where every brow and defile seems to carry a judiciously placed church. In Glasgow there is a saying that "a church is to be found on every street corner where there isn't a pub", and despite devastating redevelopment this is still apparent in the city centre. Smaller towns like Cupar, Fife and Dalkeith, Lothian boast fine sequences of spires. Perhaps the most memorable is the view across the river at Montrose where three stately spires follow in quick succession. Kelso, Borders (Roxburghshire), justly famous for its Abbey, contains a fine octagonal church of 1773, an outstanding church by Pilkington, an engaging Episcopal church by Rowand Anderson and an intentionally eyecatching Baptist chapel in red sandstone.

History

Much of the architectural and historical interest of Scottish churches is due to lively and determined rivalry between the Church of Scotland and other denominations such as the Episcopalians, the Free Church of Scotland and the United Presbyterian Church—to name the three of the most important. To understand this some of the background to the story is needed.

The Scottish crown had a protracted struggle with the Papacy in the 15th century over the question of patronage and the export of money. Following the break with Rome in England in 1540 the Catholic Party in Scotland looked increasingly to France for support, which only increased feeling against the Regent. The barons, inspired by Knox, looked south for help, and by the Treaty of Edinburgh (1560) the Protestants were left in control. Under the leadership of Andrew Melville, who returned from Geneva in 1574, a Presbyterian form of church government was rapidly introduced, and in 1592 the Scottish Parliament formally established Presbyterianism. James VI however was determined to create a Scottish Episcopate and in 1610, seven years after ascending the English throne, three bishops were appointed. In 1637 an attempt to introduce a Scottish prayer book, known as "Laud's Liturgy", led the next year to the signing of the National Covenant. The church remained Presbyterian until the Restoration, when Episcopacy was re-established. The Covenanters were then severely persecuted, some 300 ministers leaving their manses.

When William III came to the throne in 1689 the Scottish bishops and nobility failed to give him support. An assurance of loyalty was readily forthcoming from the Presbyterians, and in April 1690 a Presbyterian Church of Scotland was re-established. The Jacobite loyalties of many of the Episcopalians in turn made them subject to persecution. Open support of the 1715 rebellion was punished by penal laws in 1719 forbidding any Espicopalian clergymen to officiate to more than nine persons unless he took an oath of allegiance to the House of Hanover. After the 1745 rebellion the Duke of Cumberland destroyed many Episcopalian chapels, and in Sir Walter Scott's phrase the Episcopal church was reduced to "the shadow of a shade" with only four bishops and 40 clergymen. A few notable churches nonetheless were built at this time for English clergy or for congregations willing to take the oath of loyalty.

In the established Presbyterian church disputes over patronage had already begun to create problems, causing secessions in 1733 and 1761, which eventually merged in 1840 as the United Presbyterian Church. Increasingly the moderates in the Church of Scotland were overtaken by the Evangelical party. This culminated in 1843 in the severing split in the Church of Scotland known as the Great Disruption, in which 451 out of 1,203 ministers left to form the Free Church of Scotland. Very soon there were rival congregations in almost every town, a fact clearly reflected in the 1851 census. This showed a total of 3,395 places of worship in Scotland, divided as follows:

Churches in 1851

Church of Scotland	1,183
Free Church	889
United Presbyterian Church	465
Congregationalists, Methodists and Baptists	421
Episcopalians	134
Roman Catholics	117
Various	109
Presbyterian Minorities	77
	3,395

In 1874, the main cause of the disruption was abolished by Act of Parliament, but it was not until 1929 that the Church of Scotland and the United Free Church (formed in 1900 by the Union of the United Presbyterian Church and the Free Church) were reunited. A minority of the United Free Church remained outside the union under the same name. They must also be distinguished from the Free Church of Scotland, affectionately known as the "Wee Free's", consisting of those congregations which declined to merge with the United Presbyterian Church in 1900—mostly of Highland stock.

Listed Churches

Today it is the Church of Scotland which has the great majority of listed churches, according to figures supplied by the Scottish Civic Trust.

Listed Churches (October 1975)

Church of Scotland	1,050
Episcopal Church in Scotland	110
Roman Catholics	75
Free Church of Scotland	15
Congregationalists	15
United Free Church of Scotland	8
Methodists	5
Others	15
	1,293

The total of 1,293 corresponds quite closely to the estimate of 1,164 A and B listed churches supplied by the Historic Buildings Council for Scotland. Churches, like all other buildings in Scotland, are listed A, B, C: Category A is roughly equivalent to the English Grade I or II*: Category B to Grade II; Category C to Grade III, neither C nor III having statutory protection.

Under the wise direction of the late Ian Lindsay, Victorian buildings were included in the Scottish lists at an earlier date and in a much more systematic manner than in England. As a result Scotland's remarkable legacy of Victorian churches is well represented in the lists. To give an idea not just of the sheer number of worthwhile churches but also of the diversity of style and architect we give in the appendix the listed churches in Edinburgh with brief details.

From this it emerges that the Church of Scotland have some 50 listed churches in use, the Episcopalians 13, the Roman Catholics 8, the Congregationalists 3, the Baptists and the Free Church 2 each, and the Catholic Apostolic Church, the Christian Scientists, the Methodists and the Unitarians one each.

The Church of Scotland

Much has been said in the past about the destruction of medieval churches at the time of the Reformation (Knox's words, according to one Presbyterian historian, "were as sledgehammers beating down abbeys, images and altars"), but though a few were destroyed by mob violence and many were abandoned and allowed to fall into ruin, this merely rounded off the effect of centuries of military destruction, the ruins of Kelso Borders (Roxburghshire), Dryburgh Borders (Berwickshire), Jedburgh (Roxburghshire) and Melrose Borders (Roxburghshire) being due to the English invasions of 1544 and 1547. Today the Church of Scotland has some 60 substantially medieval churches still in use, shown in the following table. Those which would rate as substantial by English standards are marked with an asterisk, while those which were restored or largely renewed in the 19th century, often with a great deal of conjectural masonry, are marked with an R.

Medieval Churches in Use by the Church of Scotland

Abbey St Bathans, Borders (Berwickshire) (E. wall only)
Abercorn, Lothian (much added to in the 17th and 18th centuries)
* Aberdeen St Machar (nave)
  St Nicholas (transepts and crypt)
* Aberdour St Fillans, Fife (re-roofed in recent years)
Aberlady, Lothian (tower, church much rebuilt in the 18th century)
* Arbuthnott, Grampian (Kincardineshire)
Auchterhouse, Tayside (Angus) (largely rebuilt in 1630)
* Biggar, Strathclyde (Lanarkshire) (lacks tracery)
Birnie, Grampian (Morayshire) (Georgianized 1734, part restoration 1891)
* Bothwell, Strathclyde (Lanarkshire) (choir)
R Brechin Cathedral, Tayside (Angus) (reconstituted from Georgianized church 1899–1901)
Cockburnspath, Borders (Berwickshire) (much altered and rewindowed)
* Coldingham, Borders (Berwickshire) (choir, south wall rebuilt to simpler detail)
* Corstophine, Lothian
* Covington (Lanarkshire) (small, restored 1903 but with good original tracery and fairly complete by Scottish standards)
* Crail, Fife (partly Georgianized)
* Crichton, Lothian
Cullen, Grampian (Banffshire) (mainly 17th- and 18th-century character as now existing)
* Culross Abbey, Fife
Cupar, Fife (tower and part of nave)
* Dalmeny, Lothian
Dornoch Cathedral, Highlands (Dumfriesshire) (rebuilt from ruins without nave aisles)
Duddingston, Lothian (partly Georgianized)
* Dunkeld Cathedral, Tayside (Perthshire) (choir)

- ★ Edinburgh St Giles (all of exterior (except tower) and nave piers 1829–33 and 1870–83)
- Fearn Abbey, Highland (Ross & Cromarty) (partly rebuilt and re-roofed after 1742: E end is burial vault)
- ★ Fowlis Easter, Tayside (Angus) (small, but exceptionally complete although re-roofed)
- ★ Haddington, Lothian (choir and transepts recently re-roofed)
- Inverkeithing, Fife (tower)
- ★ Iona Cathedral, Strathclyde (Argyll) (re-roofed, nave partly rebuilt)
- Kilrenny, Fife (tower)
- ★ Kirkliston, Lothian (nave and tower)
- ★ Ladykirk, Borders (Berwickshire) —or Orkney?
- Legerwood, Borders (Berwickshire) (choir)
- ★ Linlithgow, St Michael, Lothian
- Linton, Borders (Roxburghshire) (much rebuilt and rewindowed)
- Lismore, Strathclyde (Argyll) (choir)
- Lundie, Tayside (Angus) (largely Georgianized)
- Markinch, Fife (tower)
- ★ Mid Calder, Lothian
- ★ Monymusk, Grampian (Aberdeenshire) (partly Georgianized)
- Mortlach, Grampian (Banffshire) (much rebuilt 1826 and 1876)
- ★ Paisley Abbey, Strathclyde (choir and central tower 20th-century rebuilds)
- Pencaitland, Lothian (much rebuilt)
- ★ Perth St John, Tayside (exterior of nave recast R. S. Lorimer)
- Prestonkirk, Lothian (choir)
- Ratho, Lothian (much rebuilt)
- Restalrig, Lothian (rebuilt by Burn from ruins in 1836)
- R St Andrews Holy Trinity, Fife (reconstituted from Georgianized church by P. MacGregor Chalmers)
- ★ St Monans, Fife
- St Vigeans, Tayside (Angus) (reconstituted from Georgianized church by R. Rowand Anderson)
- ★ Smailholm, Borders (Roxburghshire) (much rebuilt)
- ★ Stirling Holy Rude, Central
- ★ Stobo, Borders (Peeblesshire)
- Straiton, Strathclyde (Ayrshire) (transept)
- ★ Uphall, Lothian
- ★ Whitekirk, Lothian (re-roofed after fire, by R. S. Lorimer, but otherwise complete)

Medieval Churches in Use Owned by Universities

- ★ Aberdeen King's College Chapel
- ★ St Andrews St Salvator's Chapel
- R St Andrews St Leonard's Chapel

Medieval Churches in Use by Church of Scotland—Owned by local authorities

- ★ Dundee St Mary's (tower only, church rebuilt)
- ★ Kirkwall, Orkney, St Magnus Cathedral

Medieval Churches in Use by Church of Scotland—Owned by the Crown

- ★ Dunblane Cathedral, Central (Perthshire)
- ★ Glasgow Cathedral

Excluding those owned by the Crown only Edinburgh St Giles,

Haddington St Mary, Paisley Abbey, Perth St John, St Andrews Holy Trinity and Kirkwall St Magnus are really large buildings, though Aberdeen St Machar, Brechin Cathedral, Linlithgow St Michael, Perth St John, St Vigeans, Whitekirk, Aberdeen King's College Chapel and Roslin Chapel are all sizeable buildings. Historically, however, they have a special interest as Gothic architecture in Scotland developed very differently from England, particularly in the planning of churches.

The Reformation brought an entirely new type of worship to Scotland and with it a new architecture, related more closely to Calvinistic building on the Continent, particularly in Holland, than to the Church of England. The emphasis from the start was on preaching, and churches could only be as large as the voice would carry: as a result a number of larger medieval town kirks were divided into two or three for different congregations—for example at Aberdeen, Edinburgh, Perth and Dundee. However, new churches were quickly beginning to appear, the most remarkable at Burntisland, Fife (1592). Externally it is still vernacular in character, with Gothic angle buttresses but inside it is as ingenious an example of central planning as many contemporary Renaissance chapels in Italy. And whereas Italian architects never really reconciled perfect symmetry on both axes with the need for directional emphasis towards the altar, the single focus on the pulpit in the Reformed Scottish church made it possible for the congregation to sit on all four sides. During the 17th century experiments with central planning continued in a number of cruciform churches—among those that survive Fenwick, Strathclyde (1643), Kirkintilloch, Strathclyde (1644) and Lauder, Borders (1673) are all on a Greek Cross plan.

A frequent type of layout was the T-plan which, while sacrificing some symmetry, obviated the need to seat some of the congregation behind the pulpit. An early example is the 1636 kirk at Anstruther Easter, Fife. In a number of places a tower was added on the fourth side, as at Yester (1710) making the church essentially cruciform in plan. One of the most delightful churches of this type is at Durisdeer, Dumfries and Galloway, where the "fourth arm" contains a sumptuous baroque monument by Van Nost to the 2nd Duke of Queensberry (d. 1711). Most of these earlier churches have plain harled exteriors and their principal appeal lies in their internal arrangement which has quite often remained untouched, with box pews and galleries above. The traditional long communion table in front of the pulpit is still sometimes to be found, though other churches have individual communion tables in many of the box pews. Another characteristic feature is the laird's loft, spectacular in design and handsomely fitted out. Striking examples are the Forbes loft at Pitsligo, Grampian (Aberdeenshire) (1634), the Hopetoun loft (*c.* 1700) by Sir William Bruce, at Abercorn, Lothian, the Crawford Lord at Kilbirnie, Strathclyde (Ayrshire) (*c.* 1705), the Sutherland loft at Golspie, Highland (Sutherland) (1739) and Stirling loft at Lecropt, Perthshire (1826) by William Stirling.

A number of churches still retain delightful early 17th-century painted ceilings, such as are rarely found in England: the best are at Pitcairn, St Mary, Tayside (Perthshire) (*c.* 1635), Largs, Strathclyde (Ayrshire), Skelmorlie aisle (1638), and Stobhall, Perthshire (*c.* 1633).

The principal late-16th- and 17th-century churches in Scotland have a very special place in the architecture of this country in view of the dearth of churches of this date in England and Wales. They include:

Ayr, Auld Kirk, Strathclyde	1654
Anstruther Easter, Fife	1634
Birsay, Orkney	1664
Careston, Angus	1636
Cumbernauld St Ninian, Strathclyde (Dunbartonshire)	1659
Dairsie, Fife	1621
Dirleton, Lothian	*c.* 1615
Durisdeer, Dumfries and Galloway	1699
Edinburgh, Canongate by James Smith	*c.* 1690
Edinburgh, Cramond	1656
Fenwick, Strathclyde (Ayrshire)	1643
Fordell, Fife	1650
Kirkmaiden, Dumfries and Galloway	1638
Kirkintilloch Old, Strathclyde (Dunbartonshire)	1644
Lauder, Borders (Berwickshire) by Sir William Bruce	1673
Lyne, Borders (Peeblesshire)	*c.* 1645
Nigg, Ross and Cromarty	1626
Pettinain, Strathclyde (Lanarkshire)	1696
Sorn, Strathclyde (Ayrshire)	1658
Stewarton, Strathclyde (Ayrshire)	1696
Tibbermore, Tayside (Perthshire)	1632
Weem, Tayside (Perthshire)	1609
Wemyss, Fife	17th century
Yarrow, Borders (Selkirkshire)	1640

The dates given are those of construction—in almost every case the church will have been extended, enlarged or repaired, though without destroying its value or appeal.

This type of building, plain and vernacular externally, well fitted out within, continued to be built throughout the 18th and early 19th century in remote areas: the old parish church at Cromarty is the finest example, self-evidently untouched for two centuries. It has grown marvellously mellow with age, and there can be few churches anywhere with more simple dignity and atmosphere.

As the 18th century progressed an increasing number of full-blown classical churches were built, complete with porticoes and steeples in diminishing stages. Among the best are Aberdeen, St Nicholas West (1755) by James Gibbs; Glasgow, St Andrews (1756) by Allan Dreghorn, and Edinburgh, St Andrews (1782–89) by Andrew Frazer, of special interest because of its oval plan. The early 19th century saw churches in the manner of Sir John Soane, such as the North Kirk at Aberdeen (1826) by John Smith, in best Greek Revival; Elgin, St Giles —Doric—(1828) by Archibald Simpson; Montrose, St John—Ionic—(1829) by William Smith and in Commissioners' Gothic at Gillespie Graham's churches at Liberton (1815) Lothian, Keith (1819), Grampian (Banffshire) and Alloa (1817) Central (Clackmannanshire). As the 19th century develops an increasing number of Scottish architects of stature appear, and competition was the livelier as a result of the determination of rival congregations to outbid each other. Whereas in England the best 19th-century churches are often to be found in contemporary residential quarters, new suburbs or growing industrial towns, in Scotland many Victorian churches were built in the best positions in town centres and are as proud and self evident as the town hall or the railway station. Architects like Frederick Pilkington developed highly personal versions of Gothic, and used highly elaborate tracery and ornament, including every form of crocket, gargoyle, finial and pinnacle. Another exciting and exclusively Scottish development was the continuation of central planning even when Gothic forms were adopted. Whereas in England the Ecclesiologists and Tractarians brought a wholesale rejection of the 18th-century preaching box, in Scotland worship continued to be centred on the pulpit. The result is a number of highly original clover leaf plans such as Pilkington's churches at Edinburgh, Irvine and Kelso.

Towards the end of the century English liturgical influence increasingly made itself felt, inspired particularly by the superb churches of Bodley at St Salvador's, Dundee, and Butterfield at Millport on Cumbrae. A fair number of Presbyterian churches commissioned good glass from Cottier Morris and Holliday. The outstanding names in Scottish glass-making are Douglas Strachan, Chilton and Kemp, William Wilson and Gordon Webster. Some very fine glass was produced in Glasgow at the turn of the century by Stephen Adam, Anning Bell and Alf Webster.

Given the rarity of medieval churches Scotland actually suffered less from restoration than England, but, nonetheless, in a regrettable number of cases good and wholly appropriate Georgian arrangements of medieval buildings were ruthlessly stripped out and a highly conjectural and sometimes heavy handed process of reconstitution undertaken.

The Episcopal Church in Scotland

According to the Presbyterian minister, Dr Carlyle, "more than two thirds of the people of the country were Episcopals" at the time of the Establishment of the Presbyterian Church in 1690. The persecution following the 1715 and 1745 rebellions savagely reduced their numbers, but in 1764 the Scottish bishops produced a fine Scottish service book based on eastern liturgies, and 20 years later, in 1784, the first bishop of the United States of America was consecrated by three Scottish bishops in Aberdeen. In 1792 penal laws were repealed and from then on the Episcopalian church grew steadily, encouraged by the increasing Anglicizing of landed families who sent many of their sons to English public schools. This led to the Episcopal Church in many Scottish towns being described as the "English Church", which in view of what the Episcopalians suffered from the English is understandably resented. Even more important, however, the doctrine and liturgy of the Episcopal Church had a special appeal to the educated classes, strongest in Edinburgh, who were rebelling against the bleak forms of Presbyterianism. This tendency was stirred by the Romantic Revival and epitomized by Sir Walter Scott's departure from Duddingston Kirk, where he was an elder, for the first Episcopal church to be built in the New Town.

Partly, no doubt, because money was more readily available Episcopal churches tend always to have some architectural interest, and many are very good buildings indeed. Remarkably few have disappeared, despite declining congregations and today about 300 remain in use. A list in the appendix gives the most important with details of date and architect.

From this it is evident that the Episcopalians (or "Piscies" as they are sometimes affectionately known) are strongest in the north-east of Scotland and in Edinburgh. The earliest Episcopal churches have unfortunately fared less well than their successors. The small but very striking church of St Andrew-by-the-Green (1751) in Glasgow is now derelict and vandalized; James Adam's delightful octagonal Gothick St George's, Edinburgh (built in 1794 just after repeal of the penal laws), has been a plumber's showroom since the 1930s. The Episcopalians turned to Gothic early in the 19th century when neo-Classicism was still the dominant force in many Scottish towns; one of the best examples is St John's, well-placed in the centure of Edinburgh by William Burn (1818), with virtuoso fan vaults and pendants.

In the Victorian period, as is evident from the above list, the Episcopalians consistently used leading Scottish architects, notably John Henderson, Rowand Anderson and Ninian Comper, though some of their best churches are by English architects, for example G. E. Street's churches at Ellon and New Pitsligo in Aberdeenshire and Bodley's St Salvador in Dundee, as well as a number of cathedrals. The more complex liturgy of the Episcopalian church also allowed much greater elaboration of fittings; particularly of chancels—which, of course, have no place in Presbyterian worship.

The Roman Catholics in Scotland

Until the end of the 18th century the Scottish Roman Catholics were a small and decreasing minority. Two traditional groups of native Roman Catholics remained in the Hebrides and in Aberdeen and Banffshire but Catholicism only came back to the lowlands with the industrial revolution. Large numbers of immigrants, mainly from Ireland, came to meet the demand for labour in the cotton mills of Lanarkshire, and with them they brought their religion and their priests. In 19th-century Scotland, therefore, the Roman Catholic church was principally the church of the poor, and its priests, receiving about £40 a year, were the only clergy to live at the standard of the working masses. The liturgy and the authoritarian character which made so many converts in England were lacking. Many 19th-century Roman Catholic churches are therefore buildings erected on "the pennies of the poor", but in Catholic eyes they have a special historical value for this reason and are jealously kept up as a result. This method of building continued well into this century—Rosewell, Lothian (Midlothian), built by miners during the Depression is a good example.

Although an Act for the relief of English Catholics was passed in 1778 a similar measure for Scottish Catholics had to wait until 1793. There are, however, two chapels built before 1793 the older of which is still in use: the chapel of St Ninian at Tynet, Morayshire, a long, low, harled building of 1753 which was designed to be mistaken for a sheepcote, and St Gregory, Preshome, Grampian (Banffshire), only about three miles away. Built in 1788 this is the first Roman Catholic church since the Reformation which visibly proclaimed itself by a swept-up pedimented gable surmounted by a cross and inscribed "Deo 1788". A charming, if somewhat skin-deep Gothic, characterizes the earliest Catholic churches. The prototype was Gillespie Graham's St Mary, Edinburgh (1814): among its more engaging progeny are St Margaret, Ayr, Strathclyde (Ayrshire) (1827), St Mary, Fochabers, Grampian (Morayshire) (1828), Portsoy, Grampian (Banffshire) (1829), Tombae (1829) (Banffshire), St Andrews, Dundee (1836) and St Mary, Inverness (1837). One of the most ambitious Gothic churches of the period was Gillespie Graham's St Andrew, Glasgow, begun in 1815, and long regarded as the largest Roman Catholic church in Britain. A classical church of this date is St Mary, Abercromby Street, Glasgow (1842).

Many Catholic churches of this date were designed by Catholic priests, and thus belong to that always interesting category of buildings by amateurs of taste. These include Father Walter Lovi, the designer of St Thomas, Keith, Grampian (Banffshire) (1831) and the chapels at Wick, Highland (Wick) (1837) and Braemar, Grampian (Aberdeenshire) (1839), Fr Richard Vaughan, architect of the Sacred Heart, Lauriston Place, Edinburgh (1860) and Bishop James Kyle, Vicar-Apostolic of the Northern District (1828–69). Among the latter's works are St Mary, Dufftown, Grampian (Banffshire) (1825), St Margaret, Huntly, Grampian (Aberdeenshire) (1834) and the imposing twin-spired "cathedral" of Buckie, Grampian (Banffshire) (1857).

Pugin and Pugin designed a notable series of Roman Catholic churches in the diocese of Glasgow, including St Francis, Glasgow (1882–96); St Margaret, Kinning Park, Glasgow (1883); St Bridget, Baílleston (1893); St John, Portugal Street, Glasgow (1897) and Holy Cross, Croshill, Glasgow (1911). Also of interest are Wardell's Our Lady and St Andrew at Kelso (1858–72); Goldie's St Mary at Greenock (1862); J. A. Hansom's St Mary at Lochee, Dundee, with its remarkable octagon-chancel (1865); Burges's St John at Old Cumnock (1881–82); St Sophia at Galston by Sir Rowand Anderson (1886, Byzantine); Our Lady of Perpetual Succour, Glenlivet, by Archibald Macpherson (1897–1908, individual late Gothic) and *art nouveau* Gothic of J. T. Walford at St John, Portobello (1904–6); the tall-spired St Mary, Lanark (1912) by Ashlin and Coleman of Dublin, incorporating bits of George Goldie's 1859 church and the remarkable series of churches built by the Belgian-born architect Charles J. Menart. The grandiose Roman churches of St Aloysius (1908–10) and the Sacred Heart at Glasgow (1910), and the Auvergne Romanesque Church of the Sacred Heart at Torry, Aberdeen (1911), Reginald Fairlie's Our Lady of the Assumption and St Meddan at Troon (1911) and Sir Robert Lorimer's splendid St Peter, Edinburgh (1906–8, 1928–29), built for the aesthetes Canon John Gray and Andre Raffalowich. Except in the archdiocese of Glasgow the average Victorian Catholic church tended to be the work of local men such as Ellis and Wilson in Aberdeen, Mathieson and Cappon in Dundee, Buchanan and Bennet in Edinburgh and Andrew Heiton in Perth, with elaborate fittings bought from specialist Catholic church furnishers.

CHAPTER SIX

Wales

"I climbed one Sunday morning, on to the heights which overhang the town of Swansea, consigned on that one day, to silence and rest. Two kinds of buildings only evinced any signs of life, the high chimney-shafts, towering over the iron founderies, gave vent to black serpents of smoke, curled round by the wind into spiral coils, chasing one another over the tiled roofs; and from the church steeples I heard the sound of bells inviting to worship. Labour and Prayer—these were the elements which seemed to float in the air over this town spread out as it is on the edge of the resounding sea . . . Religion and Industry.

ALPHONSE ESQUIROS *Religious Life in England* (1867)

Wales has long been, and still is today one of the most intensely religious countries of Western Europe. It contains nearly twice as many Anglican churches per head of population, and the proportion of non-conformist chapels is higher still. While England has some 17,500 Anglican churches for a population approaching 50 million the Anglican Church in Wales has 1,721 churches for 2½ million inhabitants. Overall figures for other denominations are harder to obtain, but the Calvinistic Methodists have 1,235 chapels, the Presbyterian Church of Wales have 1,235 (including churches outside Wales), the Baptists have 875 churches and the United Reformed Church 175.

Historically the real growth of Welsh nonconformity dates to the first half of the 19th century. This is demonstrated in the 1851 census. In 1800 there were 967 Anglican places of worship: 50 years later this number had increased to 1,110. In the same period nonconformist places of worship had grown from 402 to 2,695. The Anglican increase rate had been 11%; the nonconformists 510%.

The Church in Wales

The Church in Wales was disestablished in 1920. It has six dioceses: four of these—St Asaph, Bangor, St Davids and Llandaff—are ancient, while Monmouth and Swansea & Brecon were created on disestablishment. The Act removed all property from the church and vested it in the Commissioners of Church Temporalities in Wales, who under the authority of the Welsh Church Acts transferred it to the Representative Body of the Church in Wales, the County Councils and the University of Wales. The Representative Body holds and administers all parish churches.

Christianity was introduced into Wales at a very early date: there is a tradition of three martyrs associated with Roman Caerleon, the headquarters of the second legion. Many churches are dedicated to 6th-century founders (Llan implies a sacred enclosure) and a number of these are commemorated in a single church. With a continuous Christian history of up to 1,500 years "sanctity of site" therefore has a very special meaning in Wales.

The early Christian churches have three characteristic sites, the sea coast, the valley or river bottom and the remote hills. The factor all three have in common is their isolation—sometimes no house is to be seen for two or three miles, and the hill churches are to be found as high as 1,200 feet. The chapelry of Yspytty Cynftyn in Dyfed (Cardiganshire), with its ancient church set in a celtic stone circle, is 16 miles from the parish church. Nucleated communities have developed only in the last 150 years in Wales and then only rarely or incidentally around the ancient churches. Hence their survival undisturbed through so many centuries and their present vulnerability.

Structurally, virtually all are post 1100, though in a few cases the plan may be older. The date of construction is often difficult to determine owing to lack of dateable features but most churches evolved gradually during the medieval period with something of note from every century. In type they range from simple cellular buildings of Celtic origin with walls of immense thickness to former Cistercian Abbeys (Conwy) and garrison chapels (Caernarvon). Distinct regional types, such as the double-nave in Denbighshire, are also to be found. Though only a few churches, like Gresford in Clwyd (Denbighshire), can compare with the greater wool churches of East Anglia or Somerset a large number, particularly in the dioceses of St Asaph, Bangor and St Davids, are rightly ranked as outstanding, and listed Grade A, as is evident in the table given in the appendix.

To these must be added numerous smaller churches—often no larger than cottages—which nonetheless have a sense of authenticity and an atmosphere that makes them both memorable and moving to visit. Sturdy, styleless and spartan, they are rough and plain without, perhaps with a bellcote, but rarely a spire or tower. Inside many remain without electricity, and simple furnishings—backless benches and box-pews, sturdy communion rails and communion tables, wooden chandeliers and coffin biers—have escaped both restoration and reordering.

Welsh churches, much more than English ones, tend to retain their medieval screens, often marvellously carved and retaining original paintwork. Another characteristic is the celure, or coved canopy of honour, found over the altar.

Few churches were built in the 17th and 18th century: the only complete example to survive is Worthenbury, dating from 1725. The second half of the 19th century, however, was a great period of Anglican church building—often on an ambitious scale—and in many cases by English families owning Welsh estates. Most of the best Victorian architects worked in Wales, Bodley and Butterfield at Penarth, S. Glamorgan and Elerch, Dyfed; Pearson at Port Talbot, W. Glamorgan; Street at Towyn, Clwyd and Scott in numerous places. In addition there were a considerable number of notable Welsh or Welsh based architects, including R. G. Thomas, Pritchard, and Hartland and Son, of Cardiff. These churches tended to be in the growing towns and often made ancient parish churches redundant.

Victorian restoration in Wales was on the whole less destructive than in England, and in many cases churches were in such disrepair that drastic action was probably the only cure. "Many of the churches in Wales", the Incorporated Church Building Society reported in 1851, "are in a much more dilapidated condition than any in England, and yet, like those in the latter country, are susceptible of complete restoration." Though most of these churches were undeniably in a very bad way, it is possible that they were no worse and no better at the beginning of the 19th century than they had been at the beginning of the 18th, and that "unfit for divine service" so often noted at the time, implied, as at Llanilar, in Dyfed (Cardiganshire), "a general wish on the part of the congregation for open seats and a better arrangement of the whole internal fittings, especially of the chancel". The worst restorations were carried out by English architects, over-versed in cathedral detail, who inserted features wholly out of sympathy with plain vernacular buildings: at the other extreme are the wonderfully sensitive and often invisible restorations carried out early in the 20th century by W. D. Caroe.

Today the Church in Wales has 685 listed buildings out of a total of 1,721 churches. This proportion of just over a third—compared with over three-fifths in England—appears to be on the low side, and it is probable that many simple vernacular buildings as well as more ambitious Victorian churches were omitted on the original round of listing but will be included as the lists are revised.

Diocese	Grade					
	A	B	C	I	II*	II
St Asaph	26	68	22	1	1	3
Bangor	51	53	36	—	—	1
St Davids	26	104	32	2	—	9
Llandaff	6	66	13	—	—	2
Monmouth	8	67	18	—	—	—
Swansea & Brecon	12	48	8	—	—	2
	129	406	129	3	1	17

Welsh Nonconformity

It was through their religion that the Welsh people recovered their own souls in the 18th and 19th centuries. It was supremely through the life of their own dissenting chapels, built by their own hands, that they found a road to personal maturity and independence which owed little or nothing to the English establishment and which often aroused hostility. The chapels were their own . . . they were the shrines of their communal identity in the most intimately personal sense.

DANIEL JENKINS

Chapels are an emotional sign to Welshmen, difficult perhaps for outsiders to grasp, let alone convey. They symbolize the survival of Welsh community spirit, of the Welsh language and Calvinistic teaching through times of unemployment, hard mining and hard agriculture. Even more difficult to comprehend is the sheer number of chapels, though the 1851 census again gives a picture of the extraordinary frenzy—for this is the word—of chapel building in the first half of the 19th century. In these years chapels in Monmouthshire increased 13-fold, Montgomery 14-fold, Flint 16-fold, Denbigh 10-fold and Glamorgan and Caernarvon 6-fold. In Caernarvonshire there were 64 Anglican places of worship in 1800 and 67 in 1851—an increase of three. By comparison there were 30 nonconformist chapels in the county in 1800 and 221 in 1851—an increase of 191. As can be seen from the table below the Calvinistic Methodists were well in the lead, building no less than 84 chapels in this one rural county in 50 years.

Growth of Nonconformity in Caernarvonshire (1801–50)

Denomination	*Pre 1800*	*1801 1805*	*1806 1810*	*1811 1815*	*1816 1820*	*1821 1825*	*1826 1830*	*1831 1835*	*1836 1840*	*1841 1845*	*1846 1850*	*Total*
Independent	6	2	1	9	2	11	8	8	3	7	2	59
Baptist	5	1	1	3	2	4	1	3	1	2	1	24
Calv. Meth.	19	1	4	9	11	9	13	11	13	12	1	103
Wesl. Meth.	—	4	3	1	1	1	6	6	7	3	2	34
Indept. Meth.	—	—	—	—	—	—	—	—	1	—	—	1

A similar pattern of intense chapel building between 1800 and 1850 emerges in the industrial south for example in Swansea. Here, however, it was the older dissenters, namely the Independents (22 chapels) and the Baptists (17 chapels) who filled the need of the rapidly growing population.

Growth of Nonconformity in Swansea (1801–50)

Denomination	*Pre 1800*	*1801 1805*	*1806 1810*	*1811 1815*	*1816 1820*	*1821 1825*	*1826 1830*	*1831 1835*	*1836 1840*	*1841 1845*	*1846 1850*	*Total*
Independent	3	2	1	2	1	3	2	3	2	2	4	25
Baptist	1	—	1	1	1	3	2	1	1	3	4	18
Calv. Meth.	1	1	1	2	1	—	1	—	2	3	1	13
Wesleyan	1	—	1	3	1	1	—	3	—	2	—	12
Primitive	—	—	—	—	—	—	—	—	3	—	1	4
Unitarians	1	—	—	—	—	—	—	—	—	—	1	2
C of E	20	1	—	—	—	—	—	—	1	1	2	25
Roman Catholic	—	—	—	—	—	—	—	—	—	—	1	1
Mormons	—	—	—	—	—	—	—	—	1	—	—	1

From this table it is clear that the Church of England (as it then was) did not begin to make provision for places of worship until 1839 when the nonconformists had already built 45 chapels. For example, the church at Llandeilo Talybont had seating for 260—adequate in 1801 when the population was 595—but far too small by 1850 when the population had increased to 1,408.

The large numbers of chapels surviving today is evident in the lists of places of worship kept by the Registrar General.

Nonconformists were persecuted in Wales until the end of the 17th century (the Religious Census of 1669 estimated that in the Merthyr Tydfil, Mid Glamorgan, district alone 300–600 people were attending secret conventicles). From then on its history is one of schism, beginning in 1692 with the great debate on Baptism. Between 1735 and 1795 the Independents and Baptists dominated, after that the Methodists and the quite distinct Calvinistic Methodists took the lead. Most chapels have been frequently altered and rebuilt and the dates dutifully recorded on a plaque on the façade—a typical example would run as follows: founded 1826, rebuilt 1846, enlarged 1866, improved 1886. A small number of late-17th- and 18th-century chapels survive relatively little touched: among the best is the Maesyronnen Chapel near Glasbury, Powys (1697–98), a beautiful vernacular building complete with original furniture and memorial tablets. Another very moving early chapel is the Congregational Capel Newydd (1769) in Gwynedd (Caernarvonshire), where earthen floor, box pews, and hat pegs along the wall have survived untouched since it was built. This, like many early nonconformist chapels, is rectangular in shape with the pulpit in the middle of the long rather than the short wall.

Towards the end of the 18th century the temple-form became the predominant chapel type—set lengthways back from the street with a pedimented gable over the façade. The earliest buildings tend to be astylar and somewhat domestic in appearance, but from the 19th century onwards more and more Greek and Roman detail was introduced. As often as not, however, the charm of façades lies in solecisms (like the rose window in the pediment of the chapel at Tremadoc, Gwynedd) rather than in correct classical grammar or proportions. Many make a play on the theme of the Alberti temple front: another variation is based on Diocletians Palace at Split—where against all the rules arches rest directly on the capitals of columns. This recurring tendency to make free with the Orders cannot simply be attributed to ignorance or provincialism but must have often been intended as a deliberate gesture of defiance. From the middle of the 19th century onwards neo-Gothic designs are to be found, and towards 1900 (a period usually dismissed as decadent or merely eccentric) a sturdy celtic vernacular emerges, with an overwhelming proportion of wall to window. From about 1850 more and more chapels were designed by professional architects. William Bage, who worked in the Merthyr Tydfil area, Evan Griffiths in Aberdare, Mid Glamorgan, John Humphreys in Swansea, George Morgan in Carmarthen, David Jenkins in Llandeilo, Dyfed—as well as preachers such as the Rev William Jones of Capel Jerusalem, who reputedly designed 200 or more chapels in the late 19th century. In addition a small number of chapels like the English Presbyterian church at Windsor Place, Cardiff, by Frederick Pilkington (1866) are by architects of national reputation.

Architecturally, the main value of chapels lies in their contribution to the townscape. In most cases they are the largest buildings in a town, the only accents rising above the massed ranks of terrace housing, punctuating vistas along the principal streets, and particularly where two or three and sometimes even more can be seen in a single glance, they, more than anything else, give Welsh towns their distinctive national character. Internally, chapels are very similar to their contemporaries in England with galleries on three sides focusing on a central pulpit. Joinery and woodwork however are often of remarkable quality and complexity, far surpassing any to be found in any other public buildings.

Chapels are to be found in greatest numbers in the industrial towns of the south and the communities which grew up around the lead mines and the slate quarries. At Blaenau Ffestiniog, Gwynedd, for example, a slate-quarrying town (Merioneth), there are more than 20 chapels.

The 1976–77 handbook for the United Reformed Church lists 172 churches—North Wales 30, East Wales 58, South Wales 44 and West Wales 40. As an indication of the proportion which might be regarded as of historic interest we give below a selection (an asterisk indicates a listed building).

North		Greenfield, Clwyd	1814
		Llanidloes, Powys	1818
		Welshpool, Powys	1784
East	*	Abergavenny, Gwent	1690
		Brecon, Plough, Powys	1688
	*	Brecon, Brechfa, Powys	1791
		Brecon, Ebenezer, Powys	1797
		Builth Wells, Horeb, Powys	1808
		Tretower, Powys	1814
	*	Llandrindod Wells, Caebach, Powys	1710
	*	Llanover, Gwent	1644
		Monmouth, Glendower Street, Gwent	1815
		Mynyddislwyn, New Bethel, Gwent	1758
		Talgarth, Powys	1806
		Hay, Powys	1804
	*	Maesyronen	1640
South	*	Llantwit Major, Bethesda'r Fro, Glamorgan	1808
		Maesycwmmer	1829
West	*	Haverfordwest, Albany, Dyfed	19th century
		Lanteg, Dyfed	1814
		Pembroke, Dyfed	1822
		St Florence, Dyfed	1810
		Rosemarket, Dyfed	1801
		Tenby, Dyfed	1822
		Tiers Cross, Dyfed	1815
		Wolfsdale, Dyfed	1827
		Zion's Hill, Dyfed	1823

The Presbyterian Church of Wales had (according to the 1975 Yearbook) 1,228 churches, including those in the rest of the United Kingdom.

The Baptist Union of Wales has 666 churches in membership, of which 173 conduct worship in English. In addition there are 209 other Baptist Churches in Wales, which are members of the Baptist Union of Great Britain and Ireland. The great majority of these were built between 1800 and 1914—all, in terms of date, eligible for listing. Interesting Roman Catholic churches are to be found in the recusant valleys to the north of Monmouth. In addition the Roman Catholics built some excellent churches in the 1930s.

In the first round of lists of historic buildings made in the early 1950s virtually no nonconformist chapels were included—and almost no 19th-century Anglican churches. And as far as we can ascertain not one nonconformist chapel is listed in Grade I, even though on purely historic grounds they must include some of the most important buildings in Wales. In the city of Cardiff for instance, before the 1972–73 re-survey there were no statutorily listed Roman Catholic or nonconformist churches; now there are some 15. This list is an excellent indicator of the wealth of interesting churches to be found in the capital of the Principality in what, second only to Glasgow, ranks as the best Victorian city in Britain. (See appendix.)

PART TWO–CHURCHES IN USE

CHAPTER SEVEN

The Ecclesiastical System of Control

Since 1913 the principle of the "ecclesiastical exemption" has been one of the most frequently discussed and frequently misunderstood aspects relating to the care and protection of churches in use. In order to be able to discuss the present position adequately it is necessary to understand both the historical context of the exemption and the effect both of subsequent legislation (ecclesiastical and secular) and the wider dissemination of awareness of the value of historic buildings.

At the beginning of this century the Englishman's home was still very much the Englishman's castle, and governmental interference in his manner of decorating, furnishing and altering it would scarcely have been tolerated in any degree analogous to what is now understood by "listed building control". It is not, therefore, surprising that the same degree of independence was readily accepted for the ancient parish churches of the country, many of which in any case survived under squirearchical patronage, or under the eyes of the Corporations of historic towns, or under the protection of City Livery Companies or other ancient guilds; the Ancient Monuments (Consolidation and Amendment) Act of 1913 was concerned with taking certain important but still essentially simple steps relating to "ancient monuments", i.e. sites or structures of antiquarian interest (barrows, crosses, Stonehenge and the like) and buildings which were for the most part roofless and scarcely likely to be "in use" again (Rievaulx, Tintern and so forth). During the discussions and negotiations which led up to the Act, however, and in the debate in the House of Lords criticism was levelled against the Established Church, directed principally against over-ruthless restoration, against the sale of church treasures (the subject of a dignified and timely protest by the Society of Antiquaries), and against plain neglect. It cannot be seriously entertained that in the face of even such justifiable complaints the Government of the day (any more than the Goverment of today) contemplated taking into anything remotely resembling "guardianship" the 8,500 or so ancient churches of England

and Wales. Nevertheless, the effect of the debate, both public and in Parliament, was salutary, for Archbishop Randall Davidson, brought back into the gaze of a no doubt largely forgetful nation the existence of the *faculty jurisdiction*. The origin of the faculty jurisdiction is generally traced back to 1252, when the Papal Legate Odo forbade the demolition of churches (for instance by high-handed Lords of the Manor, who might thereby deprive villeins of a place in which to worship) except on the granting of a licence or faculty by the Bishop.

In course of time the diocesan Bishops, always formidably busy men, delegated all, or many, of their legal functions to their Chancellors. The Chancellor, previously a cleric but now usually a leading lay lawyer, is the Bishop's *alter ego* in legal affairs and presides over the Consistory Court of the diocese. His function in granting faculties has carried on over the Reformation Settlement until the present day, and although the practice of exercising control over churches and their contents seems to have ebbed and flowed through the centuries there are many examples to be found—for instance in Basil Clarke's book *The Buildings of the 18th Century Church* (SPCK, 1963)—of the jurisdiction being conscientiously used, and the erection of whole churches, or towers or family chapels, and inside the churches the erection of organs, galleries or screens and the repaving of chancels and the like being properly sanctioned. (Such faculties, of course, are also valuable historical records, sometimes giving the name of the designer and craftsmen and very frequently the cost.)

In the 19th century, in that remarkable period of religious revival and the wave of restoration of old churches and the building of new ones that followed in the wake of the Oxford Movement, the evangelical revival and the influence of the Cambridge Camden Society, one reads in the standard literature little about faculties; but, according to Canon Clarke, although some work was done without them in most dioceses there was a steady stream. This is perhaps a good opportunity to mention the commissioners appointed in the 18th century to visit churches in which major work was to be done; and the architectural societies which sprang up in the wake of the Gothic Revival and played a constructive role in the encouragement of high standards. The Committee of the Ecclesiological Society reported on designs shown to it by its architect members (i.e. most of the leading architects of the day), and the provincial societies also acted as Advisory Committees. The Architectural Society of the Archdeaconry of Northampton was very good in this way; and the Church Building Society of Worcester diocese insisted that all plans submitted to it for grants should be approved by the Worcester Diocesan Architectural Society.

Archbishop Randall Davidson's undertaking to the House of Lords in 1913 was to the effect that the faculty jurisdiction would be brought down off the shelf where it appears to have been gathering dust, that it would be thoroughly dusted down and refurbished and put back into vigorous action. A Commission under the Chairmanship of the Dean of Arches (who is the Judge of the Appellate Court of the Province of Canterbury), Sir Lewis Dibdin, was appointed and its report recommended *inter alia* the setting up in every diocese of specialist committees to advise the Chancellor on artistic, archaeological and historical matters relating to the faculty applications before him. The Diocesan Advisory Committees for the Care of Churches are the direct result of this recommendation, but before they could be set up the holocaust of World War I intervened. At the end of the War the appalling sense of loss produced an understandable desire to erect monuments in the parish churches to those who had died in the struggle, and the lamentable absence of taste which was frequently apparent in the designs submitted was an added impetus to the bishops to make progress in the setting up of DACs. By 1923 all the dioceses had such committees, and in that year the Central Council for Diocesan Advisory Committees (later the Central Council for the Care of Churches and now the Council for Places of Worship) came into existence to co-ordinate them. In the words of Martin Briggs, *Goths and Vandals* (1952) "Need for these organisations was obvious enough: whether in respect of artistic judgment, historical fitness, or technical efficiency, many of the guardians of our ancient churches were not competent to deal with questions of alterations or repair, or even to forsee the threat of decay caused by an unventilated floor or an unblocked gutter, leading to an outlay of thousands of pounds when a few shillings might have saved it in the beginning."

By the early 1920s the Established Church in England and Wales (for in Wales the same system applied, and survived dis-Establishment) had evolved a system of *protection* which not only anticipated listed buildings control by a quarter of a century but has continued to be more detailed and arguably more effective in relation to interior decoration and to fixtures and fittings.

A faculty from the Chancellor of the diocese is needed for all works of repair (as opposed to simple maintenance jobs like repainting a downpipe), including repointing walls, and relaying of roof coverings; any works of rebuilding or replacement such as the reconstruction of a bellcote, the remaking of window tracery, or re-glazing. Inside the church a faculty must be sought for the introduction of *any* new furnishings (from bells, pulpits and *prie-dieux* to candlesticks, chrismatories and cancelli), or the removal or alienation—whether temporary (e.g. loan to an exhibition or museum) or permanent—of any of them. Liturgical rearrangement, or the repositioning of furnishings to meet changing needs and fashions, is also subject to faculty. Sensibly, however, an experimental rearrangement for a trial period can sometimes be authorized by the Archdeacon. The *Archdeacon's Certificate*, introduced in the 1938 Faculty Jurisdiction Measure, enables the Archdeacon to authorize by licence minor works the consequence of which will be no change in appearance—e.g. straight replacement of gutters, or a redecoration scheme following exactly the existing scheme. There is a safeguard here in that applications for an Archdeacon's Certificate, while they do not reach the Chancellor, must be approved by a majority of the DAC. (Archdeacons, incidentally, are *ex officio* members of DACs. Sometimes they are also chairmen, and this is not so satisfactory in relation to the certificate procedure since there might be occasions in which they could exercise a casting vote swayed more by feelings of sympathy towards the parish than by "artistic, archaeological and historical" considerations.)

The Archdeacon is, in a sense, the enforcement officer of the church's legislation—though it is doubtful, and for understandable reasons, whether many Archdeacons would express it quite like that: since their role (in helping their Bishop to care for the clergy, supervising parsonage houses as well as churches, sitting on all the diocesan committees from the Bishop's Council downwards) is a many-sided one, where such successes as they may achieve are likely to be the result of friendly exhortation and encouragement rather than from appearing in the guise of an ecclesiastical policeman. Archdeacons tend to cultivate the "lighter touch". However, this is not incompatible with a proper firmness, and where Archdeacons back up the advice and policy of their DAC, both generally and in relation to specific matters, there is likely to be greater respect towards the faculty system and greater effectiveness than if the Archdeacon appears weak and vacillating, readily persuaded from the DAC's advice by a parish pleading "pastoral" justification for something which on other grounds—and in the longer perspective of history—may seem quite unjustifiable.

The Faculty Jurisdiction Measure of 1938 was succeeded by a new Measure in 1964, and Rules governing the latter were issued in 1967 and 1975. The effect of the successive codification of the jurisdiction has generally been to make it "tougher", but in the final analysis it is the quality of the advice tendered by the DACs (and, where so invited, by the CPW) and the alertness of the Chancellor which render the system effective or not. There have been suggestions from time to time that Chancellors are too ready to grant faculties against the advice of the DACs and the CPW, particularly where applications to sell "treasures" are concerned—historic communion plate and armour (associated, generally, with particular monuments) being the most common. In fact, perhaps as a result of such pressure, successful applications to sell treasures to meet some crisis in the affairs of the parish have declined markedly since 1971.

Churches or chapels in use are *not* exempt from planning control, but only from listed building control over alterations. Planning control, *per contra,* has been only intermittently in doubt and covers all such matters as may be caught by the broadly defined expression "development" in successive Town and Country Planning Acts. These include (for example) changes in roof covering, any significant changes in the external appearance of the building.

It is surely a weakness or an illogicality in the system as it stands at present that the concept of a *locus standi* is so narrowly interpreted by the ecclesiastical courts. It has long been a source of irritation to the national amenity societies (the Society for the Protection of Ancient Buildings, the Ancient Monuments Society, the Georgian Group, the Victorian Society and now also SAVE Britain's Heritage) that they are not able to give expert evidence in a Consistory Court, unless through the subterfuge of a parishioner (who, of course, has a *locus standi*) calling on them as expert witnesses: and yet a case might often be materially assisted by such expert evidence, either in writing or by personal appearance of a representative. The four long-established national amenity societies have a quasi-statutory role in regard to secular historic buildings legislation in that they have referred to them by the planning authorities all listed building applications for demolition and a good many for alterations. If the DACs are to retain their self-confidence it would seem invidious and indeed unnecessary to suggest as some have done that *all* faculty applications should be referred to the amenity societies; but, if an application is serious enough in its implications to merit a hearing in Court, then it seems reasonable that in appropriate cases the Chancellor should invite a representative of the appropriate amenity society to assist him in coming to a decision.

It is no less absurd in the last quarter of the 20th century to deny a *locus standi* to a planning authority. The evidence of the county or district planning officer, conservation officer, or other such well-qualified officials as the county archivist or the county archaeologist could well provide material assistance to the court. The corollary of financial help from the community at large (whether through the Historic Buildings Council, the local authority under the Local Authorities

(Historic Buildings) Act 1962, or private non-parishioners concerned about the building) is surely a sensible degree of participation by the community at large in decision taking. If it cannot make its view heard at all, then irritation and dissatisfaction with the present system—for all its merits—will inevitably grow. If our suggestion were to be adopted it can scarcely be argued that it would cause intolerable delays as the majority of faculty cases are uncontentious and are decided by the Judge in Chambers with no necessity for a hearing.

Generally speaking, it is the knowledge that there is objection or evidence of dissension which will decide the Chancellor to hold a Consistory Court. If the Petitioners insist—as is their right—on an opportunity to put their case in the face of strong contrary advice from the DAC or the CPW, the Chancellor will usually decide to hold a Consistory Court hearing; alternately, a parishioner (not necessarily a worshipper, but someone who lives in the parish) or a member of the Electoral Roll (who may, paradoxically, not live in the parish but worship reasonably regularly in the church) may legitimately object to what is proposed, and again the Chancellor will generally consider it advisable to hold a Court. Sometimes there is a substantial body of opinion against what is proposed, but no formal objections are made. This is a great pity, and may well lead to serious derelictions of justice (with the Petitioners claiming, apparently with reason, that there is "no opposition"): the reason is likely to be that in the Consistory Courts costs generally "follow the action", and if the Petitioners are still successful the opposition may well find that they are saddled with the costs. The 1955 Report of the *Commission on Fees and Faculties* defined the purpose of the faculty jurisdiction as being to "protect the interest of succeeding generations of parishioners in their parish church, and in its contents", and it is more than a matter for regret that parishioners or others with a legitimate interest in the church are excluded from taking their case to the Consistory Court through fear of costs being awarded against them, or because of an illogically defined doctrine about *locus standi*. There is obvious room for improvement here and for modification of the system.

It is admirable that Chancellors hold their Consistory Courts very often in the church to which the application relates; not only does this obviate the necessity to hire a special room (and churches are, after all, readily apt for such a use as this) but, just as parish records make more sense in the building to which they relate, so an application for a faculty may also be more comprehensible (and its strengths or weaknesses be more readily apparent) in the building to which it relates. But in spite of their position *vis-à-vis* the High Courts the Consistory Courts might well with advantage lean a little more in the direction of Public

Inquiries—which they more closely resemble in *purpose*. The appearance in church of a bewigged and gowned Chancellor, Registrar and Apparitor, and the rigid procedures and formality insisted upon by some Chancellors (whom all must address as "Worshipful Sir") is hardly likely to elicit from a shy farmer churchwarden or an elderly lady member of the PCC their true attitudes towards an application for a faculty, unless they be of exceptional courage; and just as at Public Inquiries it is customary for the Inspector to ask after the formal witnesses have given evidence if a member of the public wishes to give testimony—and such persons would scarcely bother to be present if they were not interested—so the same principle might with great advantage be applied at Consistory Courts.

In spite of the Majesty of the Law being frequently apparent at Consistory Courts flouting of the Court sometimes goes unchecked and unregarded. A number of DACs regularly arrange tours of churches in the diocese where their advice has recently been sought, or where faculty decisions have been made, to see what the result has been: such checks should surely be the rule rather than the exception—not as in any sense "snooping", but as a sensible duly recognized regular practice. Again, to take one category of decision as an example, faculties have (regrettably in the majority of cases) been all too often given for "churchyard clearance" schemes on condition that certain headstones are retained and the inscriptions on those removed fully and accurately recorded. The testimony of such bodies as the *Society of Genealogists* and the *Council for British Archaeology's Churches Committee* suggests to us that such conditions as these, and other similar ones for faculties relating to other matters, may on occasion be cavalierly regarded by the parish. A system of checking and confirmation needs to be devised.

The "standing" of DACs in the dioceses varies a good deal, as does consequently the amount of notice taken of it. In some dioceses the DAC is serviced by the staff in the Diocesan Office, in others it is run from the house of the Secretary—often a clergyman with a relatively "light" parish not too far from the diocesan centre, but sometimes a layman. In the majority of cases they appear to be run very efficiently, but in several instances the agenda seem suspiciously thin (which suggests that a good deal of work is carried out in the diocese without the DAC's approval), and in two dioceses at least the minutes of the committee meetings are not even typed and circulated but written out laboriously in longhand by the secretary in an old-fashioned minutes book.

It was once said that the Church of England looked remarkably like the Conservative Party at prayer, and the legacy of this inheritance for some DACs is an attitude which looks suspiciously at specialists or too readily identifiable an expertise. This philosophy regards the ideal DAC as being made up of talented amateurs—country squires and clergy with an antiquarian bent and a generally well informed good taste. Another growing view is that DACs should embrace within their membership every relevant kind of expertise: organs adviser, bells adviser, art or architectural historian, an artist, an archaeologist, an archivist, an expert on lighting and heating systems, an architect or two with special skills and experience in the conservation of historic buildings, and so on. On the whole we favour the systematic development of the second kind of balanced DAC. "Experts" should not, after all, be construed as necessarily being narrowly expert: and we would certainly agree that the experts invited to serve should be those with a broad knowledge of and sympathy for ecclesiology generally. In the face of increasing professionalism in the field of conservation the church ought not to lag behind, and it is the professionals—the county archaeologist, archivist and so forth—who will have time to make the visits because it falls legitimately within their professional terms of reference. Although there certainly were attractive aspects of the old-fashioned kind of DAC there is no longer a sufficient supply of laymen or clergy with broad sympathies and deep antiquarian learning coupled with the time available to attend regular meetings, site visits and so on. If there are such people with the time available then it is likely that they will be retired, and this inhibits a healthy balance of age range.

Of the new kind of DAC there is a major advantage, in the influx of the professionals, and that is the chance of improved relationships with the local authorities, the museums service, universities and so forth. Frequently, if there is a local museum, the Director or some other senior member of the staff will be invited to serve on the DAC (e.g. at Ripon, where the Director of Temple Newsam House is on the DAC, or at Ely where the Deputy Director of the Fitzwilliam Museum is on the DAC); this not only provides a channel to further specialist sources of advice—on historic Communion plate, let us say—but the resources of the Museum's Conservation Department and the advice of its technical staff are likely to be made available. Again the appointment of the County Archaeologist (who can probably provide, or help to arrange for, men and money for an investigation on a church site) or County Archivist can furnish a valuable link between the diocese and the secular arm. We feel very strongly that these links are important and should be developed and that, for instance, where there is a conservation officer for the county or the major historic towns of the diocese the Bishop should consider inviting him to serve. There is also a strong case for having an artist on a DAC to balance the somewhat differing vision of the architect. Art historians, liturgists and others may provide an equally valuable link with a university.

DACs too frequently contain members—architects, generally, but it could apply equally to a stained glass artist or a silversmith—who sit in judgement on their own proposals. In our view this simply should not arise, and if a scheme comes up for which a DAC member is responsible it should be the invariable practice for him to explain his proposals and then leave the meeting; it is probably less invidious if the decision of his committee is thereafter conveyed to him in writing.

What happens if parishes carry out work (a lighting and wiring scheme, or redecoration, for instance) not realizing that they should seek the authority of a faculty or Archdeacon's certificate and the advice of the DAC, or worse still deliberately flout authority (e.g. the fine Bodley church of St Aldhelm's, Branksome, Dorset, where the original light fittings have been removed and the furnishings rearranged without consultation or permission being given)? A good deal could be done, in our view, to promote better relationships and understanding between clergy and the DAC, for example:

1. By devoting some time to the subject in theological colleges (a church is a clergyman's stock in trade and it is surely not too much to expect that he should have some inkling of how to look after it).
2. By including instructions in Post Ordination Training.
3. By regular discussions on questions such as the inspection system, security and so on at Deanery Synods.
4. By following the "best practice" as established in a very few dioceses and sending a letter from the DAC Secretary to every new incumbent or priest in charge as he takes up office, explaining the purpose of the DAC and its willingness to function positively in the giving of advice.
5. By providing a brief training course for Archdeacons, who take up office without any special qualifications or instruction and have specific responsibilities relating to the churches and a back up function in relation to the DAC's role.

Finally what happens (or could happen) to enforce faculty approval which is ignored or observed only where convenient to the parish? The status of the Consistory Courts as part of the High Court system has been mentioned, and the decisions of the Consistory Court can in the last analysis be enforced in the civil courts. We have never heard of this happening, and only very exceptionally does a Chancellor insist on the restoration of some furnishing or fitting removed without proper authority. Yet unless a healthy respect for the system is engendered it will too readily be disregarded by all but the temperamentally law-abiding. Major losses do occur as a result of parishes insisting on their independence, or refusing to recognize the applicability of the system as, for instance, when new drainage channels are dug, or new heating systems are installed, without opportunity for archaeological investigation of the evidence which will be revealed and then destroyed for ever.

The DACs of the Church of England and the Church in Wales form in association with the faculty jurisdiction a remarkably coherent system, and there is nothing to be found to compare with it in the other denominations. This system is, in important respects, e.g. as regards movable treasures, more effective than comparable control over secular buildings and their contents. Many of the particular weaknesses in it, to which we have drawn attention, could, we believe, be remedied with comparative ease—as, indeed, will be seen from the suggestions which we have made. We welcome the recent announcement that, once State Aid is available, the Church of England will initiate a further review of the faculty jurisdiction system: *inter alia* this will provide an opportunity for the consideration of improvements which would require changes in the Church's law.

The Church of Scotland is the Established church north of the Border, Presbyterian in government and not Episcopalian, and there is some semblance of control in that fabric repairs and maintenance are the responsibility of a special committee of each presbytery (smaller and more numerous than the diocese of an episcopal church) and matters of taste, broadly speaking, are considered at national level by the Artistic Questions Committee, which meets bi-monthly in Edinburgh. This was appointed by the General Assembly in 1934 to advise Ministers, Kirk Sessions, and Presbyteries on the design of church buildings and furnishings.

One former member of the Advisory Committee on Artistic Questions considered that it concerns itself largely with trivialities and has no power to discuss or at least to decide upon larger issues of protection and preservation.

The other major denominations in England, Wales and Scotland can be considered very briefly since they have either made very modest beginnings in instituting a system of conrol and supervision (other than financial or property holding), or have no identifiable interest in the matter. In very recent years Roman Catholic dioceses have established Artistic sub-committees or sub-commissions to the liturgical commissions which are in existence in every diocese. To some extent these are modelled on Anglican DACs. There is also a proposal to set up a national body analogous to the Church of England's Council for Places of Worship. Although the link with liturgical thinking is a valuable one from the church's point of view, it would be too optimistic to suppose that the Artistic sub-committee will be able to exercise control.

The Methodist Church has a well-established Chapels Department which is located in Manchester and is able to provide advice and support to local trustees faced with repair problems, redevelopment proposals, or redundancy. Final responsibility rests, however, on the local trustees who actually own the building, and there is no ecclesiastical control to supplement listed building control which becomes operative only after a church ceases to be "in use".

The United Reformed Church has a central administration but, unlike the Methodists, no specific department concerned with the buildings.

The Society of Friends has a Home Service Committee which keeps a watchful eye on matters appertaining to Meeting Houses, but exercise no control over them.

CHAPTER EIGHT

Maintenance

That great architect-engineer Sir Christopher Wren was also a man of sound practicality and common sense when it came to building maintenance. Consulted in 1676 by the Dean and Canons of St George's Chapel, Windsor, he counselled them to have the leaks in the roof repaired immediately, ". . . for drips come sodeynly, and doe great mischief". This is the essence of regular maintenance, for not only does a "stitch in time save nine" but the financial expenditure of a modest sum on a regular basis for cleaning out of gutters and soakaways, and replacing slipped tiles or slates the moment they work loose, can save a parish many thousands of pounds. A small fault rapidly leads to a large one, and dry or wet rot can cause untold damage to a building and be both difficult to eradicate technically and exceedingly costly. The same rule naturally applies to all buildings, but churches are on the whole larger and certainly more complex than most houses and therefore require more painstaking efforts and vigilance.

The 1967 Canons of the Church of England are very specific about the maintenance of churches, and the allocation of responsibilities, and in this they follow in the footsteps of the earlier Canons of 1604. For example, the Archdeacon is "to hold yearly visitations . . . [and] survey in person or by deputy all churches, chancels and churchyards and give direction for the amendment of all defects in the walls, fabric, ornaments and furniture of the same; in particular shall exercise the powers conferred on him by the inspection of Churches Measure 1951 . . ." (Canon C. 22). Canon F. 13 entitled "Of the Care and Repair of Churches" provides that:

"1. The churches and chapels in every parish shall be decently kept and from time to time, as occasion may require, shall be well and sufficiently repaired and all things therein shall be maintained in such an orderly and decent fashion as best becomes the House of God.
2. The like care shall be taken that the Churchyards be duly fenced, and that the said fences be maintained at the charge of those to whom by law or custom the liability belongs, and that the churchyards be

kept in such an orderly and decent manner as becomes consecrated ground.

3. It shall be the duty of the Minister and churchwardens, if any alterations, additions removals or repairs are proposed to be made in fabric, ornaments, or furniture of the church, to obtain the faculty or licence of the Ordinary before proceeding to execute the same; save that in repairs to a church not involving any substantial alteration or in the redecoration of a church, a certificate issued with the approval of the Diocesan Advisory Committee for the Care of Churches by the Archdeacon of the Archdeaconry in which such church is situated should suffice.

4. In the case of every parochial church or chapel, a record of all alterations, additions, removals or repairs so executed shall be kept in a book to be provided for the purpose and the record shall indicate where specifications and plans may be inspected if not deposited with the book."

And Canon F. 18 entitled "Of the Survey of Churches" states that: "Every Archdeacon shall survey the church, ornaments, and churchyards within his jurisdiction at least once in three years, either in person or by the Rural Dean, and shall give direction for the amendment of all defects in the fabric, ornaments and furniture of the same. In particular he shall exercise the powers conferred upon him by the *Inspection of Churches Measure 1955*."

The Canons in large measure provide the historical background, viz.: the Archdeacon has always had a very specific responsibility to see that the churches, chapels and churchyards in his Archdeaconry and their furnishings were decently kept and in order. Archdeacons of the 17th, 18th and 19th centuries seem to have been remarkably faithful to their charge, trudging round their enormous territories on horseback (usually there are two or three Archdeaconries per diocese, and the dioceses were vast until the creation of new dioceses in the late 19th and early 20th centuries). Churchwardens' accounts contain frequent references to preparations for the Archdeacon's visitation and to work which had to be carried out as a result of his inspection.

Up until the First World War many churches, kirks and chapels in England, Wales and Scotland were maintained in large part, if not exclusively, by the laird or Lord of the Manor or by leading local families. Even relatively modest country houses would often have a maintenance staff, who could be detailed to go and see to regular tasks and repair on the church. A country churchwarden today, used to climbing up ladders to inspect his own barns and carry out most of the repairs himself, may still occasionally do the same for his church. And the CPW publication *How To Look After Your Church*, 1970, urges every parish to consider appointing a Fabric Committee of "three or four vigilant and active members, who will keep the parochial buildings and their fittings and furniture under constant observation". Another possibility would be for the PCC (or trustees in the case of a Free Church) to appoint a Fabric Officer, preferably someone with a special interest and enthusiasm for the work. Sometimes the incumbent or minister may actually welcome the responsibility himself, and one clergyman has told us how he makes a point of inspecting his church when it is raining, so that he can spot any defects.

The chancels of the Church of England and the Church in Wales were frequently in the care of a lay Rector or patron who was legally responsible for the maintenance of that part of the church. Many lay Rectors still are responsible for chancel repairs, not a very welcome responsibility for a private person taxed up to the hilt, but perhaps the majority are the responsibility of corporate bodies such as Deans and Chapters, Oxford and Cambridge Colleges, and other ancient foundations and the Church Commissioners, who are landowners and consequently lay rectors. The Church Commissioners have responsibility for approximately 800 chancels, and other "big spenders" in this regard are the Dean and Chapter of Canterbury, Christ Church, Oxford, Keble College, Oxford, King's College, Cambridge, Eton College, and Winchester College. In all, Deans and Chapters are responsible for some 200 chancels, and Colleges for about 235.

The role of the traditional landlord in participating handsomely in church maintenance has understandably declined since the end of World War One, with the imposition of penal taxation and the break-up of so many estates. The backlog of repairs built up during the First World War seems hardly to have been overtaken when the Second World War came, bringing with it a further period of restraint in building repair work, and a shortage of men and materials. At least building prices were relatively stable between the wars, and £200 or £300 could make a major difference between the rescue or dissolution of a building which had fallen on difficult times.

In 1952 the National Assembly (now succeeded by the General Synod) of the Church of England set up a Commission under the Chairmanship of one of its members, Mr Ivor Bulmer-Thomas, to enquire into the size and nature of the problems confronting the Church with regard to the care and maintenance of its buildings, and the recommendations of the Commission had two important consequences: the establishment of the Historic Churches Preservation

Trust, and the passing into statute law of the *Inspection of Churches Measure 1955*, referred to by the revised Canons already quoted.

The *Inspection of Churches Measure 1955* is in its essentials a simple but profoundly important enactment, providing for regular inspection (not less frequently than once every five years) by a suitably qualified architect. The suitability of the architect has to be confirmed by the DAC—the idea being that an architect who, let us say, has made an admirable job of building new bungalows is not given responsibility for St Mary's, Beverley, simply because he happens to be a friend of the Vicar.

The Measure enjoins little else, except the making of provision for payment of the fees, and the establishment of separate diocesan schemes to provide for the detailed running of the scheme. If a church totally fails to carry out its obligations the Archdeacon can order an inspection and provide for payment of the fee out of the Diocesan Church Inspection Fund.

At the time of its inception the Measure represented a major advance in thinking, for although there were no doubt owners of country houses who had regular inspections by suitable architects, or public buildings where the same procedure was for some reason followed, no other category of historic buildings had this requirement as a mandatory provision. The sense of it, however, has commended itself widely so that (for example) it is now the policy of the National Trust, the Scottish Episcopal Church and a growing number of Roman Catholic dioceses.

The best practice in the writing of inspection reports is for them to be given in such terms that they will encourage the parish concerned to carry out a sustained programme of repairs, taking any urgent and immediate tasks straight away, and phasing second and third priority repairs (to be carried out within two and five years respectively) as advised by the architect. According to a joint working party of the CPW and the RIBA (published in *Church Inspection and Repair 1971*) the report should consist of:

(a) A brief description of the building
(b) The limitations of the survey, i.e. parts not opened up unless specifically required
(c) The general condition of the fabric, under such headings as Walls and Masonry, Roofs and Gutters, Rainwater Disposal, Interior Decorations, Floors, Fittings, Glazing, etc.
(d) Recommended works of repair, categorized as immediate, first priority (within two years), second priority (within five years) and long term, i.e. beyond the quinquennium (which gives the parish a hint to prepare and to save up).

A number of architects, including several who look after a great many churches, help the parish further by offering to attend a PCC meeting and explain the recommendations of the report and what it will entail, and also by attaching to their report explanations of repair procedure, recommendations for routine maintenance and even a list of publications on the care of churches.

The objective, for every church or kirk or chapel, should be regular evaluation of the state of the fabric (a professional evaluation quinquennially, with frequent visual checks in between) tied in with a consistent and continuing programme of care and conservation. "Stave off decay by daily care", said William Morris, and this straightforward and characteristically blunt maxim can scarcely be improved upon for sense, sensitivity and economical maintenance.

During the past few years there has been much discussion, and a certain amount of action, on the training of those who wish to learn the special skills required for historic buildings conservation. Architectural training has tended until very recently to neglect this aspect, as though every architect wished to design office blocks and new town housing and would have few opportunities of doing anything else. Schools of architecture now, at long last, encourage their students—who are often only too keen to do so—to look at existing buildings and consider their care, conservation and (where desirable) adaptation. At the same time the training of building surveyors now includes appropriate instruction, and there seems little doubt in our minds that a building surveyor may, depending on personal aptitudes, interests and training, be equally capable of inspecting and supervising work on many churches. The guiding principle should be the right man for the right job. The *Inspection of Churches Measure 1955* specifically states "architect" so there can be no change in the Church of England context unless and until there is a change in the legislation.

A further factor worth drawing attention to is that more enlightened architects recognize their own limitations and do not hesitate to take into their deliberations architectural historians, archaeologists, archivists, experts in wall paintings, bells, organs, heating systems and so forth. The inspection report does wisely, we feel, if it states the necessity of approaching such independent sources of advice; and the architect can, and frequently does, point out the need for an overhaul of security and fire risks, the investigation of levels of insurance, the testing of electrical wiring and the checking of lightning conductors, to name but themost obvious.

The architect may be the "conductor of the band", so to speak, but there is a large number and variety of skills which need to be properly deployed in maintaining an historic church.

CHAPTER NINE

Furnishings

The Church has long been the greatest patron of craft and craftsmanship in the country but as the companion volume to the report, *Change and Decay: the Future of Our Churches*, which we have edited, contains chapters on church metalwork, woodwork, monuments, stained glass and ceramics the observations here are brief. What can never be sufficiently stressed is that English parish churches are this country's sculpture galleries. Until at least the late 18th century the study of English sculpture can only be undertaken in our churches. Before the 18th century there are very few statues and busts, equally there has been little religious statuary since the Reformation. One result has been that English sculpture has not grown in value and esteem through constant trading on the art market: only those who have sought it out in hundreds of often remote parish churches have ever become connoisseurs of it. Yet just as a single marvellous altarpiece can make a pilgrimage to an otherwise undistinguished village church in Italy worthwhile and rewarding, so there are churches all over Britain, but particularly in England, which are worth visiting just to see a single spectacular monument or tomb.

The extent to which English sculpture is to be found in churches is evident from the following table based on Rupert Gunnis's *Dictionary of British Sculptors* (1660–1851). Taking the work of a dozen leading sculptors in this period, including the remarkable firm of Coade, this demonstrates the high proportion of the *oeuvre* of leading sculptors that is to be found in monuments in churches:

Table showing the Predominance of Church Monuments in the oeuvre *of Leading Sculptors*

	Statues	*Busts*	*Monuments*
John Bacon (1740–99)	21	14	80
E. H. Baily (1788–1867)	25	51	70
Sir F. L. Chantrey (1781–1841)	54	98	109
Sir Henry Cheere (1703–81)	3	29	31
Coade (firm fl. 1769–1820)	23	—	50
John Flaxman (1755–1826)	9	10	171
Grinling Gibbons (1648–1721)	5	—	15

	Statues	*Busts*	*Monuments*
Joseph Nollekens (1723–1823)	15	88	78
L. F. Roubiliac (1705?–62)	7	30	28
J. M. Rysbrack (1694–1770)	17	50	80
Peter Scheemakers (1691–1781)	17	23	75
Sir Richard Westmacott (1775–1856)	33	13	216

This applies equally to the work of the most interesting and significant provincial sculptors and masons: examples are William Cox of Northampton (1717–93), whose delightfully detailed tablets are to be found in many churches in his native county; the Fishers (father and son) of York whose monuments are consistently of a very high standard of craftsmanship, and Thomas King and Sons of Bath, the most prolific and popular of all the West Country firms of statuaries, whose monuments and tablets are to be found all over England and in India and the West Indies.

No one has done more to diffuse knowledge and instil enthusiasm about English sculpture than Sir Nikolaus Pevsner in the volumes of *The Buildings of England,* putting to rights years of academic neglect and unfavourable comparison with work on the Continent. Whereas much of the best sculpture in Europe is to be found in museums and art galleries, in Britain, after Westminster Abbey, it is to be found in the parish church. At one end of the scale is the Bedford Chapel at Chenies, Buckinghamshire, the richest storehouse of funeral monuments of any parish church in England, beginning in 1555 and running in virtually unbroken succession to an appealing proto-*art nouveau* monument by Alfred Gilbert. Hardly less remarkable are the monuments of the Spencers at Great Brington in Northamptonshire, or the St John's at Lydiard Tregoze in Wiltshire—and indeed similar series of monuments are to be found for almost all the great landed families in England. Then there are numerous churches which are worth visiting for a single spectacular monument, like Chillingham, Northumberland, for the sumptuous monument of Sir Ralph Gray, where figures of saints and angels escaped the iconoclasts of the 16th and 17th centuries, or the great Queensberry tombs at Durisdeer near the road south to England from Glasgow.

From the point of view of conservation monuments pose many problems: they are often of enormous size and fragile and their ownership is uncertain. Broadly, though subject to faculty jurisdiction, they remain the property of the family which erected them. A few years ago there was a move to sell the very fine Nollekens monument in Holy Trinity, Wetheral, Cumberland. This, however, was prevented and it is to be hoped that no chancellor will ever agree to the sale of a monument either by a parish or by a legal owner, as this would open the way to a flood of monumental sculpture coming on the market.

The second great treasure of our churches is the extraordinary wealth of church plate they contain. Though it is the parish church, once again, which usually has the most ancient and elaborate plate, even the humblest nonconformist chapels can have fine silver or pewter communion vessels. In recent years much alarm has been expressed at the sale of plate from Anglican churches. The following table shows the number of faculties granted for sale:

Year	*Total Number of Cases*	*Cases involving the Sale of Historic Plate*	*Cases Withdrawn*	*Faculties Granted*	*Faculties Refused*
1973	11	6	3	3	—
1974	12	6	3	2	1
1975	9	5	3	1	—
1976	9	4	—	3	1

The cases where faculties were granted were as follows:

Oxted, St Mary, Surrey (Southwark)
Cup and Cover 1634, 2 flagons 1675
Almsdish, etc.

Northian, St Mary, E. Sussex (Chichester)
Paten 1634
Alms plate 1724
and later flagon, chalice, paten

York, All Saints Pavement
St Crux cup 1635 and
several other items of plate
(Faculty varied later)

Camberwell, St Giles, London (Southwark)
2 Flagone 1691 (no sale)

Middleton, St Andrew, W. Yorkshire (York)
Chalice 1493: (sold to Goldsmiths Company)

Heddington, St Andrew, Wiltshire (Salisbury)
Flagon-tankard 1602

Watford, St Mary, Herefordshire (St Albans)
Cup and cover, 1618 gift

Wybunbury, St Chad, Cheshire (Chester)
Lidded Tankard 1677

Tottenham, St Benet Fink, London
2 Flagons 1658
2 Chalices and patens 1638
Salver—paten 1695

On balance the likelihood is that a Chancellor will refuse a faculty for the sale of plate and this is very encouraging. Another consideration is that the Chairman of the Historic Churches Preservation Trust (the Archbishop of Canterbury) and his fellow trustees have indicated that they will no longer make grants to churches that sell important works of art belonging to them, and it is to be very much hoped that similar conditions will be attached to the forthcoming state aid. Not only are such sales often a breach of trust—as plate was usually given in perpetuity for sacramental use—but the sums realized, however large they may appear at the time, usually look small in retrospect.

The third category of church contents most at risk are the numerous records to be found in churches. These include not only parish registers but documents of all kinds, as for centuries churches were the only public building locally available where such papers could be stored. The sad fact is, however, that many church records are not only in a total state of neglect, but that no one locally understands what they are. The solution in almost every case must be to deposit the records in the diocesan record office (usually the county record office) where they will be stored in proper conditions, be available to the public, and eventually be repaired by the conservation staff. Though parish churches contained the official registers of baptisms and burials until the middle of the 19th century quite a number of nonconformist chapels kept their own registers; the Baptist Meeting House at Cole, near Witney, Oxfordshire has its own register of births and deaths running from 1643 till 1837. This is the oldest non-parochial register known, but many Quaker meeting houses have records going back almost as far. In Scotland most church records are held in the Scottish Record Office though a fair number of Kirk Session Records and sometimes even Heritors' Records are still held locally. In a few cases, with the dissolution of congregations, records have disappeared or passed into private ownership.

All Quaker and most Baptist meeting houses had a library. Before the days of popular education these were often the only source of books available and ministers and richer members of the congregation gave bequests for purchases. Many of these libraries have now disappeared making it all the more important to identify and preserve the remainder. In addition there is a small number of Anglican churches which have libraries: the most famous being the parish library at Langley Marish, Buckinghamshire, housed in the best 17th-century painted room in England.

The other main threat to internal fittings comes with the reordering of interiors to suit new concepts of worship. In Anglican churches the modern desire to celebrate the eucharist facing the congregation has provoked a great deal of internal rearrangement: often this involves introducing a nave altar, which effectively makes the chancel redundant and in quite a number of cases choir stalls, high altars and reredoses have been removed. The desire to worship in the round has led to the wholesale removal of pews, and sometimes to the introduction of new seating arrangements which sorely conflict with the architecture.

While obviously each incumbent will wish to lead worship in his own way, in certain cases fittings are of such paramount importance that they should not be touched. Many schemes for reordering, though both destructive and expensive, suffer from the enthusiasm and transience of fashion: the secretary of one Diocesan Advisory Committee who had lived through two generations of changes told us that "when I began there was never a post without an application from an incumbent saying he could not exist without an English altar and a children's corner, now it is nave altars, kitchens and lavatories". He also pointed out that nave altars, however excellent for communion, could make churches less flexible for other uses: they are placed just where a couple being married traditionally stood. In Edinburgh, St Mark's Unitarian Church has had its pulpit removed, though the sounding board has been left in situ.

Roman Catholic churches have been subject to an even greater degree of internal reorganization than Anglican ones: a *cause célèbre* is the removal of Pugin's screen from the Cathedral of St Chad in Birmingham. Many of these changes result from Second Vatican Council, but the following list of internal reorganizations in the Diocese of Leeds gives an idea of the extent of these changes:

St Bede, Rotherham (1842 by Weightman and Hadfield). Reorganized 1959, rood screen and Easter Sepulchre removed

St Marie, Sheffield (1847 by Weightman and Hadfield). Rood screen (Hayball 1850); founders memorial tomb (Thomas Earp and George Myers 1850); Chancel decoration (H. T. Bulmer 1850); encaustic tiling in chancel and Norfolk chantry (Minton), all removed

Our Lady and St Paulinus, Dewsbury (1871 E. W. Pugin). High altar (Hayball) removed

St Joseph, Bradford (1887 by Edward Simpson). Reorganized 1968

St Patrick, Leeds (1891 by Kelly and Birchall). Gas fittings (Hardman, Powell and Co), High altar (1905); Sacred Heart altar (1926) all removed. Complete internal reorganization including chancel 1969

St Anne, Leeds, Cathedral (1904 by J. H. Eastwood). Internal reorganization in 1960. Mural decorations (Chevalier Formalli) removed

St Mary Carlton, Goole (1842 by Weightman and Hadfield). Rood screen removed

St Patrick, Bradford (1853 Weightman, Hadfield and Goldie). Interior reorganized. Original gallery steps removed *c.* 1969

St Hubert, Dunsop Bridge (1865 by E. W. Pugin). Elaborate painted decoration of walls and roof timbers in nave removed

St Joseph, Wath-upon-Dearne (1870 M. E. Hadfield and Son). Gas standards (Hardman and Co) removed

By comparison, there has been relatively little reordering of nonconformist chapels in recent years—with the exception of the Friends. Traditionally the benches in a Quaker Meeting House were always lined up facing the Elder's stand: these stands are now being removed and the benches rearranged facing inwards on all sides around a central table usually with a bowl of flowers set on it. As the benches, particularly on the inside, are too long to conform with this arrangement they usually have to be cut down.

CHAPTER TEN

Churchyards

'O Passenger, pray list and catch
Our sighs and piteous groans,
Half stifled in this jumbled patch
Of wrenched memorial stones!

'Where we are huddled none can trace,
And if our names remain,
They pave some path or porch or place
Where we have never lain!

'From restorations of Thy fane,
From smoothings of Thy sward,
From zealous Churchmen's pick and plane
Deliver us O Lord! Amen!'

THOMAS HARDY—extract from: *The Levelled Churchyard*

The brooding beauty of English churchyards has long been a source of inspiration, and at times of anger, to writers and poets, reflected in the fact that one of the most famous poems in the English language is Gray's *Elegy in a Country Churchyard*. In character churchyards range from the overgrown and all but wild to the trim and tidy garden complete with shaven lawns and beds of roses. Equally, there are distinct regional differences depending very much on the character of the local stone. Naturally perhaps the most glorious churchyards—with the best tombstones—are to be found in the Cotswolds where the dexterity of local masons has never been surpassed. Hardly less rewarding are the granite headstones of Cornwall, the slate of the Midland counties, where the art of calligraphy is to be seen in all its virtuosity, or the Pennines where whole churchyards are paved with large tombstones laid flat on the ground. Sometimes the actual shape of a churchyard is of interest: in Southern Shropshire 40% of the churchyards are round; elsewhere the church is built against the north wall because in medieval times only suicides and heretics were buried on that side. And though it is the English parish churchyard which is famous in literature and legend, many nonconformist chapels, particularly the early ones, are set in delightful graveyards: good examples are the Great Meeting at Leicester where many headstones survive, and the Unitarian Chapel at Chesterfield, Derbyshire. Quaker Meeting Houses, for all the plainness of their headstones, also have a quiet dignity and charm of their own. In Scotland churchyards often convey much of the independent, rugged self-supporting spirit of villagers and townspeople, at Lauder, in Borders (Berwickshire), for example, massive tombstones proudly proclaim the achievements of weavers, farmers, magistrates, burgesses and builders. In Wales, where many parish churches are externally very plain, the setting of the churchyard is all the more important and the tall slate headstones, which again take lettering superbly, often relate family history through several generations.

Churchyards often have no less important a role as oases for wildlife, and those who manage them can make a significant contribution to nature conservation. In intensely farmed areas like East Anglia, or in cities and towns, churchyards are often the only ancient grassland that has remained undisturbed and untreated by fertilizers and herbicides. Over the years a complex and relatively stable community of plants and associated animals has been built up: at South Elmham in Suffolk the County Naturalists Trust identified more than 300 varieties of wild flower and flowering grass including a very rare orchid.

The trees found in many churchyards are often of interest and beauty in themselves—yews, which provided the wood for the longbow in the Middle Ages were grown in churchyards because they are deadly to cattle. In addition, trees provide a source of food and breeding sites for insects, birds and mammals. The exotic conifers often found in churchyards provide havens for species such as the goldcrest and the coal tit that the surrounding areas frequently do not. The diversity of the habitat in a churchyard will be reflected in the number of species found there. At St Mary's, North Mymms, Hertfordshire, a rural churchyard, the species observed over four years during the breeding season are shown on the following chart.

Species Observed during the Breeding Season 1972–76

Species	*1972*	*1973*	*1974*	*1975*	*1976*
Pheasant	P	P	P	—	P
Woodpigeon	P	P	P	P	P
Swift	P	P	P	P	P
Swallow	P	P	P	P	P
House Martin	—	—	—	P	P
Crow	P	—	P	P	P
Rook	P	P	P	P	P
Jackdaw	P	P	P	P	P

Species	*1972*	*1973*	*1974*	*1975*	*1976*
Magpie	P	P	—	—	—
Great Tit	P	P	P	P	P
Blue Tit	P	P	P	P	P
Coal Tit	P	—	—	—	—
Nuthatch	—	P	P	—	—
Tree Creeper	P	P	—	P	P
Wren	P	P	P	P	P
Mistle Thrush	P	P	P	—	—
Song Thrush	P	P	P	P	P
Blackbird	P	P	P	P	P
Robin	P	P	P	P	P
Blackcap	—	P	P	P	—
Goldcrest	—	P	—	—	—
Spotted Flycatcher	P	—	P	P	P
Dunnock	P	P	P	P	P
Pied Wagtail	—	P	P	—	P
Starling	P	P	P	P	P
Greenfinch	P	P	P	P	P
Goldfinch	—	—	—	P	—
Linnet	—	—	P	—	P
Chaffinch	P	P	P	P	P
House Sparrow	P	P	P	P	P
Tree Sparrow	—	—	P	—	—

P indicates the presence of a species.

An idea of the relative density of each species is apparent from the following chart showing the number of territories or nests occupied in the same years.

Species	*1972*	*1973*	*1974*	*1975*	*1976*
Woodpigeon	1	2	1	1	—
Swallow	1n	1n	—	—	—
Rook	95n	94n	107n	106n	90n
Jackdaw	1	1	1	1	1
Great Tit	1	2	2	1	2
Blue Tit	1	2	2	2	1
Wren	2	3	2	2	2
Song Thrush	3	3	2	3	3
Blackbird	3	4	4	3	4
Robin	5	4	6	7	2
Spotted Flycatcher	—	—	1	1	—
Dunnock	3	4	4	3	3
Starling	2n	2n	2n	5n	1n
Greenfinch	1	1	2	—	1
Chaffinch	3	4	3	4	3
House Sparrow	3n	4n	5n	5n	5n
Tree Sparrow	—	—	1n	—	—

n indicates the presence of a nest.

A similar study of All Saints Churchyard, Boreham Wood, Hertfordshire, shows how even an urban churchyard with a main road on one side, a shopping centre on another and council offices on a third, can support a considerable variety of wildlife. Here in the same five years blue tits, song thrushes, blackbirds, robins and greenfinches were recorded every year; wrens, starlings and house sparrows in three years; great tits in two and woodpigeon in one.

Churchyards also have a special value for the colonies of lichens which grow on tombstones. Lichens are one of the most primitive forms of life and can establish themselves on bare rock (they were the first colonizers of the newly-emerged volcanic island of Sertsey, off Iceland), and as they feed entirely on the atmosphere they are extremely sensitive to pollution, particularly to sulphur dioxide. In many parts of England tombstones are in fact the only exposed rock faces they can colonize, and it can be cheaper to examine the state of lichen colonies than to use more complicated chemical means of monitoring air pollution. In Shetland, for example, tombstones are being used to measure pollution from the Sullom Voe oil terminal, and simple tests were carried out very successfully in Anglesey to assess hydrogen fluoride pollution. Lichens are very long lived and the particular advantage of colonies growing on gravestones is that they can be precisely dated. In addition, churchyards are often good sites for mosses and fungi.

The table or chest tombs found in many parts of the country can provide refuges for foxes and wildcats (not always desired guests it is true). The church building itself is, of course, often a nesting site for birds including owls; also bats, and although bats often induce a shudder and can do damage to brass and marble monuments inside a church, they are one of the groups of British mammals most in need of strong protective measures. The usual species found is the pipostrelle, but less commonly serotine, natterers and long-eared bats colonize churches.

If a churchyard is to sustain a rich variety of wildlife it is essential a sympathetic policy of maintenance is adopted. Ideally, churchyards should be thought of as rural parkland rather than well-kept lawns, and grazing by sheep, tethered goats, and occasionally geese or ponies is often the method most beneficial to wildlife. Usually the grass is best left uncut during June and most of July to give flowering plants a chance to flower and seed. And if at other times of the year the grass can be kept about three inches long this provides a habitat for voles, which in turn feed owls, kestrels and weasels. Traditionally, of course, a sexton was employed to cut the grass, though few parishes can now afford one. Nonetheless, where more voluntary labour is available and there is an interest in reviving traditional country skills, scything is a craft that should be kept alive.

One of the principal stimuli towards the tidy garden look has somewhat unfortunately been that commendable institution the Best-Kept Village Competition. An examination of the judge's reports for several counties shows that "neat and tidy" are consistently words of praise, and that churches are rated according to the attention they have received. It is somewhat galling to read that in the North Humberside Area (1976) at Humbledon the judges "approved of the resiting of the gravestones in front of the church to enable the grass to be easily cut". In Norfolk, however, the reports show an obvious concern for the traditional beauty and character of the churchyard. At Gayton, which came second, the judges commented that "the removal of gravestones, however, has detracted a lot from its appearance. . . . It was distressing to see a pile of broken gravestones in the corner of the churchyard. If these had been smashed during removal for maintenance this is to be deplored." At Northwold (third prizewinner): "Like Gayton the gravestones have been removed." The fact that gravestones are being uprooted even in prizewinning churchyards is an indication of the seriousness of the problem.

In addition to the obvious artistic value of the best graveyards and the vernacular charm or interest of many others almost all are a vital source of evidence to local historians, demographers and genealogists. They contain information about family relationships, occupations and fortune that is a vital supplement to the cryptic entries in a parish register, and when whole or part of a register is missing they are the only means many people have for tracing back their origins beyond the introduction of central registration in 1837, a subject of study which perhaps ironically interests more, not less, people in an egalitarian age. A study of a sample of seven churchyards which had been subject to applications to remove headstones shows how vulnerable such basic sources of information remain.

Churchyard	*A*	*B*	*C*	*D*	*E*	*F*	*G*	*Total*
Total number of monuments	525	471	731	187	24	40	23	2001
Number of inscribed monuments	519	467	731	186	23	39	19	1984
Number read in faculty lists	380	390	505	110	22	3	2	1412
Number read in independent recordings	503	466	721	185	23	39	19	1936
Percentage loss through application for churchyard clearance	24%	16%	31%	40%	4%	92%	89%	28%

In each case it is evident that almost every monument in the churchyard was inscribed; that the total recorded in the faculty application was consistently lower than that produced by independent recording and that considerable loss would result through clearance. In churchyard A, near to a naval port, over half the monuments were 18th century or earlier, and the clearance proposals were put forward by a local authority wishing to turn the churchyard into "a Garden of Rest". Churchyard B was also handed to a local authority to become a public open space, and in this case 97% of the monuments were destroyed. In churchyard D, around a mid-Victorian church, it was found that between 1950 and 1970, 72 out of 185 gravestones had been removed. Churchyard F surrounded an ancient country church with gravestones dating from the early 18th century. In 1972 the incumbent applied for a faculty to remove and destroy 40 headstones (and 86 footstones) to be disposed in the paving of two paths. More than half were 18th century and 34 out of 40 headstones were declared illegible, though in fact it proved possible to copy all but one inscription.

A number of the most unfortunate gravestone clearances have been in Wales; at Gresford, Clwyd (Denbighshire), the clearance of almost all the upright stones was condemned in suitably august terms by the Cambrian Society, the senior antiquarian body of the Principality: an equally lamentable clearance has also taken place at Aberystwyth, Dyfed. At Grantham, Lincolnshire, considerable numbers of slate headstones have been uprooted, and some used to wall in an unsightly rubbish tip.

Most country churchyards are dominated by the use of a single local stone and for this reason the increasing use of polished marbles and granite is particularly to be deplored. Highly polished black granite (often accompanied by glaring gold lettering) weathers extremely slowly and will look sorely out of place for decades. Equally inappropriate to a traditional churchyard are kerbstones (a practice imported from cemeteries where the burial space is formally sold) and coloured granite chipping. The solution we believe lies in control of materials, and to a lesser extent, type and dimensions, leaving people considerable latitude over both design and also wording.

The latest edition of the *Churchyards Handbook* proposes a set of model rules which each parish can adopt (with suitable local refinements). Framed copies of these should be displayed in the church porch and sent to local monumental masons. Equally, no commission should be given to a stonemason until particulars of the design materials and dimensions have been submitted to the incumbent and his approval obtained in writing. Such rules are, in fact, often laid down by Diocesan

Advisory Committees and forbid, for example, black granite, polished granite of any colour, white marble, synthetic stone and plastic. Incumbents do not always heed these rules and this will undoubtedly continue unless they are enforced on occasion by the Consistory Court. For however important it is for the individual to express a sense of grief and loss in a personal way it must be remembered that a churchyard is a communal burial ground and a determination to be different devalues the uniquely restful beauty that a homogeneous graveyard has.

Outside the Church of England there is some uncertainty as to whether churchyards come within the sphere of listed building control. In Scotland many churchyards are listed. Saxon and medieval crosses can also be scheduled Ancient Monuments. Under the 1972 Local Government Act local authorities can be obliged to take over the maintenance of disused churchyards and may contribute towards the expense of maintaining those still in use. In Scotland most parish churchyards still in use as graveyards have been in the care of county councils since 1925, though this responsibility has now been transferred to district councils. Most of these churchyards have the appearance of being well cared for but too often gravestones have been flattened to facilitate grass cutting, though in many cases the stones are in fact still there just under the turf. Since local government reorganization this responsibility has been transferred to district councils and it remains to be seen whether they are able to achieve the same standard.

CHAPTER ELEVEN

Archaeology

Church archaeology has been out of fashion for the past half century and as a result the great advances made in other fields of archaeological study have passed churches by. But since the founding of the Council for British Archaeology's Churches Committee in 1973, church archaeology has developed in the most vigorous and enterprising way, showing how excavation and investigation can deepen and indeed radically change our understanding not only of a church but the whole settlement around it. For example, the total excavation of the nave crossing and transepts of Hadstock church in Essex during 1974 by Warwick Rodwell, together with detailed examinations of the upstanding fabric, revealed that this well-known Anglo-Saxon building was not a single-period structure as had long been assumed. Three periods of Anglo-Saxon work were revealed, the earliest of which probably belongs to the pre-Danish era: it comprised a large five-cell cruciform church which it is suggested may be part of the 7th-century monastery founded by St Botolph at Icanho. Rebuilding on a monumental scale took place in the early 11th century and there is a possibility that this was Canute's minster, dedicated in 1020. The church was extensively repaired in the 13th and 14th centuries, following the collapse of the central tower. Subsequently the decline in the size and importance of the village saved the church from further extensive alteration.

At Asheldham, also in Essex, another all too brief investigation showed evidence of several previous structures dating back to the Iron Age. The first ecclesiastical building on the site was a timber-framed church beside a Roman road, this was superseded by a stone Norman church built on the road, using the hard core as foundations—the present road still makes a loop to the south of the churchyard. John Hurst and Maurice Beresford were long aware in their classic study of the deserted medieval village at Wharram Percy, Yorkshire, that the different phases of the church building provided a microcosm of the village's history when everything around it had disappeared, but excavation of the graveyard has supplied demographic data, information on physical types, robustness, health and mortality rates which will give scientific base to what has hitherto been largely speculation.

Most of the archaeological investigation of churches, as in other fields, is rescue work, carried out to discover and record evidence before it is disturbed or destroyed. The first major threat is the digging of drains and gullies around the bases of the walls. This has happened at Brightlingsea in Essex, where a drainage trench up to one metre deep was cut all round the church, cutting the church out like a card and largely obliterating any traces of an earlier building on the site. Where such drains are dug archaeologists should be called in: the parish may even gain as the trench will be dug without charge. The relaying of internal floors, or digging of heating ducts can be equally destructive of evidence—indeed the excavation at Asheldham, just mentioned, was provoked by the laying of a concrete floor. A third threat comes from the repair or redecoration of wall surfaces; where plaster is stripped, concealed medieval wall paintings can be destroyed. Even rewiring, when it involves the chiselling of conduit channels into the wall plaster, can damage hidden mouldings or concealed decoration.

The problem today is that the whole process of caring for churches has become divorced from investigating and understanding them. The Victorians well realized how archaeology could supplement the visible evidence used by the antiquarian or the architectural historian—though this too often encouraged conjectural renewal and restoration. Today archaeologists are often only called in when the scaffolding is up or while the work is actually being carried out. If valuable evidence is not to be destroyed archaeologists must be consulted at every stage, and all parties must realize that archaeology is not confined to below ground investigation and recording, but to the entire standing structure. To this end the Council for British Archaeology has appointed archaeological consultants for every diocese, and it is obviously desirable that these should be invited to join Diocesan Advisory Committees.

At a time when few major new medieval literary sources are likely to be discovered archaeology can illuminate not only the history of the building, the site and the settlement around it, but important aspects of national history as well. There is, for example, much doubt as to whether there was a continuity from Roman Christianity to Celtic Christianity in this country: church archaeology may provide the answer. The foundation of a major church in a former Roman town may be an indication of continuity of settlement—large churches were likely to have been built where people were living. Church archaeology can also provide answers to the nature of worship in the early church, again a subject of much theological and liturgical concern today. Were nave altars invariable at an early period and if so when did they give way to east altars? When did side altars, fonts and rood screens first appear? These are questions to which archaeology can provide answers.

Archaeologists should be consulted during all works of repair or redecoration, and also during any form of liturgical reordering or internal adaptation (which involve alterations to the level of floors), and equally if a church is to be declared redundant. Even the plainest church may conceal within or beneath it important evidence: no church should be demolished without taking archaeological advice, as the process of demolition will itself destroy evidence even underground, while investigation can help determine whether a church is worth preserving. Conversion to a new use can be archaeologically destructive, and professional advice should again be sought.

There is a good case for allowing archaeological work during the statutory waiting period after a formal declaration of redundancy. This will prevent any subsequent delays in sale or demolition stemming from the need for rescue archaeology: and in some cases the presence of a dig will help dispel the feeling that the church has been abandoned and thus discourage vandalism. The fact that the building would be covered by insurance during the period of investigation could prove attractive. In most cases, moreover, archaeological work is not at the expense of the parish or the diocese but is paid for by the Department of the Environment, local units or archaeological trusts.

Though church archaeology is growing rapidly in England, in Scotland neither the staff of the Ancient Monuments Department nor the Historic Buildings investigators know of any significant recent investigation of a church, though the Council for British Archaeology has recently set up a Scottish Policy Committee.

CHAPTER TWELVE

Finance

Need

Up and down the country churches cry out for large sums for repair and restoration: what is in many cases remarkable is their success in raising them. Imagination, energy and leadership, the hard work, enthusiasm and generosity of local people, primed by help from charitable trusts, and sometimes from local authorities and regional or central church funds, have met daunting targets. Part of the magic of a parish church is that it can look appealing to all the people of a village—and not just its own congregation—and in most cases it has the added advantage of being much the oldest building. Increasingly, however, churches of 18th and 19th century date and churches in inner city areas are being forced to set about raising large sums for repairs. In Birmingham, for example, St Saviours church at Saltley (built in 1850) is appealing for £50,000; in Brentwood, Essex, £30,000 is urgently needed for a striking Victorian church built in 1883 by E. C. Lee.

The greatest problems naturally lie in counties like Suffolk, Norfolk and Lincolnshire, richly endowed with proud medieval wool churches with only tiny congregations to support them now. A list compiled for the Suffolk Historic Churches Trust, with the help of the four architects responsible for quinquennial inspections of Anglican churches in the county, shows that just 33 out of well over 400 churches of medieval foundation require an overall figure of £857,850 to put them in sound repair. These figures are computed at October 1976 prices and it is estimated that a notional figure of some £2·5 million would be needed to put the remaining 400 in good condition.

Major Suffolk Churches in Towns or Large Villages requiring Substantial Repair

		Nature of Repairs	*Sum Needed*
	Bildeston	Repair after tower collapse 1975	£35,000
*A	Boxford	North side of tower, porches, windows, etc.	£40,000
A	Bury St Edmunds, St Mary	General over next 15 years	£65,000

		Nature of Repairs	*Sum Needed*
A	Clare	Final stage of roof and stonework	£19,000
	Combs	General, multi phase	£20,000
*A	Debenham	Mostly (part Saxon) tower	£20,000
*	Eye	Roofs N. and S. aisles	£20,000
*A	Hadleigh	Clerestory windows, etc.	£10,000
	Haverhill	Tower, etc.	£14,000
	Ipswich, St Clement	Roofs and tower	£5,000
A	Kedington	Glazing and stonework	£8,000
A	Lavenham	Tower, etc., next 15 years	£50,000
A	Long Melford	N. aisle roof, etc.	£80,000
*	Mendlesham	Tower and general	£10,000
A	Sudbury, All Saints	Tower £50,000, rest £30,000	£80,000
A	Sudbury, St Gregory	Tower only (rest complete)	£30,000
	Stowmarket	Spire rebuild, etc.	£40,000
			£546,000

Suffolk Churches in Rural Parishes in Need of Urgent Repair

		Nature of Repair	*Sum Needed*
A	Badley	General	£3,000
A	Barnardiston	General	£6,500
	Blyford	Tower	£15,000
	Burgh	Tower	£5,000
A	Bramfield	Detached round tower	£10,000
	Capel St Mary	Tower and general	£4,000
	Carlton by Saxmundham	Tower	£10,000
	Cavenham	General	£15,000
	Great Cornard	Spire	£3,000
	Chediston	Tower	£2,000
A	Denston	General	£10,000
	Erwarton	Tower, etc.	£17,000
	Fakenham by Ixworth	General	£5,500
	Falkenham	Tower	£10,000
A	Gazeley	General	£20,000
*A	Gislingham	Windows, roof, tower	£16,000
*	Henstead	Rethatch	£4,000
A	Hinderclay	General	£9,000
	Honington	Tower	£6,000
A	Great Livermere	Rethatch and general	£8,000
*	Monks Eleigh	Tower, etc.	£4,000
	Moulton	General	£11,000
	Martlesham	Tower	£7,500
A	Polstead	Spire	£5,000
	Preston	Roofs	£2,000
A	Shotley	Roof	£3,000
	South Elmham, St Peter	Tower	£7,500
	Sproughton	Tower, Clerestory	£6,000

		Nature of Repair	*Sum Needed*
A	Stowlangtoft	General (urgent)	£24,850
	Stratford St Mary	Clerestory	£8,000
A	Thorington	Routh tower split	£10,000
A	Thornham Parva	Rethatch, etc.	£4,000
	Tunstall	Tower	£15,000
*	Westleton	E. wall/window	£2,500
A	Wissett	Round tower	£10,000
	Yoxford	Spire	£12,500
			£311,850

A = outstanding.
* = competitive estimates and faculties obtained.

The ability to raise sums of such magnitude depends first and foremost on the attitude of those faced with the task. At one end there are those like the chairman of the appeal committee for the marvellous Victorian church of St Agnes, Toxteth Park, Liverpool who can write "Although our congregation averages only some sixty people, we are utterly determined that this fine Pearson building will be restored to its early glory." Others are in a more equivocal situation. The vicar of St Mary, East Moseley faced with raising £11,000 or more for his 19th-century church found the question "had been asked at Diocesan level if it is right for a small and not wealthy parish to accept such a task", though "at local level the feeling is growing that the parish should be brave and accept the challenge". At the other extreme, of course, are those parishes which rush to seek demolition or redundancy as soon as the repair bill is presented. The success of at least some churches in raising large sums is evident in the following list.

Church	*Date of Appeal*	*Target*	*Amount Raised*
All Saints, Margaret St., London	1976	£300,000	Appeal just launched
All Saints, Martock, Somerset	1976	£80,000	£52,000
All Saints, Northampton	1975–77	£150,000	£115,000 (Jan. '77)
All Souls, Langham Place, London	1975–76	£800,000	£655,000
Aylesbury Parish Church, Buckinghamshire	1976	£225,000	£170,000 (March '77)
Bildeston Parish Church, Suffolk	1975	£30,000	—
Blandford Forum Parish Church, Dorset	1976–77	£60,000	£30,000 raised Jan. '77
Great Malvern Priory, Hereford and Worcester	1976–77	£100,000	£65,000 (Jan. '77)
Great Witley Church, Hereford and Worcester	1976	£30,000	—
Hexham Abbey, Northumberland	1976–77	£75,000	—

Church	*Date of Appeal*	*Target*	*Amount Raised*
Holy Trinity, Bingley, W. Yorkshire	1974	£40,000	—
Leeds Parish Church	1974	£75,000	—
Nantwich Parish Church, Cheshire	1977–78	£200,000+	Newly launched
Oldham Parish Church, Greater Manchester	1976	—	£50,000 raised
Romsey Abbey, Hampshire	1974	£250,000	—
Saffron Walden Parish Church, Essex	1974	£100,000	£48,000 (late 1974)
Selby Abbey, N. Yorkshire	1974–75–76	£200,000	Target reached 1976
St Augustine's, Kensington, London	1974	£50,000	£50,000
St John's Wood Church, London	1975	£150,000	—
St Jude-on-the-Hill, London	1976–77	£40,000	£10,000 (early 1976)
St Lawrence's, Alton, Hampshire	1976–77	£90,000	£30,000 (Jan. '77)
St Margaret's, Lothbury, London	1974	£100,000	—
St Mary's, Latton, Wiltshire	1976	£150,000	—
St Michael's, Cornhill, London	1975	£75,000	—
Tewkesbury Abbey, Gloucestershire	1973–74	£200,000	£208,000
Thaxted Church, Essex	1975	£75,000	—
Wesley's Chapel, City Road, London	1974	£450,000	£250,000 (by Dec. '76)
Wimborne Minster, Dorset	1976	£150,000	£76,000 (Dec. '76)
Worksop Priory, Nottinghamshire	1974–75	£145,000	Completed 1975

These are large appeals mounted either with professional help or impressive local leadership. Yet a church like Hadstock, in Essex, which has raised some £25,000 in 10 years with a population of only 250 is typical of many. On a smaller but more urgent scale the parish of Mortlake, South London, raised a total of £2,159 in a few weeks by delivering leaflets to every household. The only expense was £90 for printing, and over half of the money came from people who did not attend the church. At East Worlington, in Devon, where the spire was struck by lightning in the summer of 1976, parishioners had completely raised the money by the following March.

Perhaps the most inspiring story of fund raising is that of the Augustine Buchanan church in Glasgow's Gorbals, situated in what was considered to be one of the worst slums in Britain. During redevelopment the parish was almost completely raised to the ground and church membership declined from 800 to 300. Yet during this time, in one of the poorest parts of Britain, through imagination and enterprise the parish reached their target of £10,000 for repairing and modernizing the church and its two halls. Beginning with a fabric fund of some £700 the parish invited all residents to become penny-per-day partners in raising a renovation fund. The response was far beyond expectations and brought contributions from many Roman Catholics. For nearly three years parish members made monthly calls to collect half-crown contributions, until the scheme had to be abandoned due to the amount of demolition in the parish. Undaunted another fund-raising project was launched with the title: "colour in a window and help raise £10,000". This consisted of a drawing of the church with its 16 windows and two multi-storey flats, also with windows. The price for colouring in a window ranged from 6d. to 2s. 6d. Fully coloured in the card realized £4. After £5,000 had been raised the church approached an architect who produced four schemes costing £7,000, £11,000 and £18,000. Believing that Charitable Trusts would come to their aid the parish chose the most expensive scheme. Their faith was rewarded and they received almost £10,000 in grants. The parish itself reached its own target of £10,000. In the words of the Minister: "a magnificent achievement for a down town church whose membership had dwindled to almost 300, its parish completely raised to the ground, its parishioners scattered to the four corners of Glasgow. Those who remained increased their givings and kept the level of our Sunday offerings to what they were when we had 700 members."

Church Funds

Many denominations have funds available at central or regional level which can sometimes, though by no means always, be made available for the repairs of existing churches. Sometimes such funds can be exclusively intended tor building new churches, in a few cases they are just for repairs. More often they are potentially available for both though new churches take the lion's share. Almost every Anglican diocese has a building fund from which it may allocate say £2,000 a year in small grants of £100 for repairs to churches: and though the amount is small it is a useful form of pump-priming. The Exeter Diocesan Board of Finance gave £12,000 in 1973 to church repairs: in addition it administers a separate Rural Churches Repairs Fund, which in 1976 made the following grants out of income.

	£		£
Little Hempston	500	Sheepwash	500
Barnstaple Holy Trinity	250	Landcross	250
Clyst St Mary	500	Moreleigh	500
North Tawton	300	West Alvington	50
Coffinswell	200	Doddiscombsleigh	100
Woolsery West	500	Bradninch	250
Colebrooke	300	Cove	115
South Pool	1,000	Rewe	250
Collaton St Mary	500	Cullompton	300
Westleigh	200	Littleham	250
Berrynarbor	25	Chivelstone	500
Fremington	25	Kenton	100
Clovelly	25	Oakford	300
St Giles-in-the-Wood	175	Hennock	200
Bishopsnympton	25	Harberton	200
Cornworthy	500	Holbeton	1,000

In addition the Diocese has a Loan Fund of approximately £50,000 from which loans are made to assist parishes to repair churches and church halls. The rate of interest charged varies, but for fabric repairs it is normally 3% per annum. These loans are normally repaid over a period of five years, so there is approximately £10,000 coming into the Fund in repayments each year, which can then be reallocated. In making grants and loans the Board takes into account the recommendations of the Quinquennial Inspection Report, the urgency of the work, and the ability of the parish to raise money.

The Suffolk Churches Capital Fund, set up after a big appeal, paid out £5,439 in 1975 in grants, representing the interest on the capital sum. In St Albans and Rochester Dioceses there are saving schemes by which parishes can save up towards repairs in anticipation of the Quinquennial report and borrow the balance interest-free from the Diocese. In certain cases money from the Diocesan pastoral account has been spent on church repairs: the church of Stanwell in Middlesex received £45,000 for repairs on pastoral grounds from the Diocese of London in 1975. The Chelmsford Diocesan Board of Finance Ltd has a Church Building and Repair Committee which makes grants and loans not exceeding £600 towards repairs, and in the last two years help has been given to Little Saling and Little Maplestead.

The main funds available for building and repairs in the Methodist Church have been gathered since 1968 into Circuit Advance Funds. Some circuits have sold a large number of chapels in recent years (or had one advantageous sale of a prime site), and the money accumulated goes not only to new building but acts as an insurance fund for financing emergency repairs like settlement, reslating and dry rot. In recent years, however, the Methodist Conference has extended the uses on which Circuit Advance Funds may be employed, thereby reducing the amount available for buildings. Nonetheless 75–80% of the 800 Methodist Circuits have such a Fund potentially available for repair work. In addition, all building schemes, including repair work (but no redecoration), which have been approved at Circuit, District and Connexional level qualify for a grant from the General Property Fund of 10% of the new money raised locally.

The Baptist Union Corporation has a Loan Fund, which grew with legacies and bequests until it now has an income of some £200,000 a year to cover all building and repair projects (including building and buying of manses) and the extension of existing churches. It is administered in the form of a revolving fund and on occasion money can be made available for emergency repairs. The Quakers also have a Meeting Houses Fund, modest in size, established about 1962. This again is mainly for new building but can also on occasion be used for repairs. Usually the Fund contributes about 50% of the cost, half (25%) in the form of a grant, and half in the form of a loan. Increasing pressure on the Fund may mean that the proportion will be lower in future. Repayment of loans is very sensibly attached to covenanted giving.

The Church of Scotland has its own Permanent Loan Fund with a capital value of some £775,000. The interest is made available in the form of grants and loans and can be spent on maintenance and repairs: in 1974 £138,000 was paid out in loans and £22,000 in grants.

The Church in Wales has been in a serious position since the loss of much of its property and wealth at the time of Disestablishment in 1920. Non-income producing property (churches, cathedrals and houses of residence) were vested in Representative Body of the Church. (Most churchyards and burial grounds were also handed over.) Some five-eighths of the income producing property was alienated irrevocably, on the grounds that it represented endowments made prior to Establishment in 1662, and was vested in the University of Wales and the County Councils. Another quarter was found to be English money and remitted to Queen Anne's Bounty and the Ecclesiastical Commissioners, while one-eighth was restored to the Church in Wales. The Church therefore launched an appeal which by 1934 had raised £722,552. Nonetheless, the effect was to deprive many churches of the sources of funds for upkeep: for example the late-19th-century church of Barmouth, which lost some £10,000 given towards its upkeep only a few years before.

Charitable Trusts

The number of charitable trusts prepared to provide funds for repairing churches is considerable, although the shortfall between need and available funds appears to be steadily growing and makes the introduction of state aid imperative. Foremost among these charities is the Historic Churches Preservation Trust, founded in October 1952. By September 30, 1975, the HCPT had raised a total of £2,211,000 and allocated grants to the value of £1,624,000 to 2,894 cases, and in addition transmitted a further £247,828 in specific donations. In its first ten years the Trust received some £922,500 in donations and promises, and its steady, indeed impressive, growth since then is evident from the following table.

	Annual Income	*Annual Grants*	*Church of England*	*Others*	*Cumulative Total of Cases*	*Cumulative Total of Grants*
1966	78,672	74,305	160	2	2,008	£931,996
1967	101,297	67,410	122	1	2,130	£999,406
1968	126,566	94,450	163	4	2,250	£1,093,850
1969	121,000	79,750	146	6	2,290	£1,173,000
1970	100,000	58,211	107	2	2,397	£1,231,211
1971–72	219,208	149,010	225	5	2,628	£1,380,221
1973	141,683	94,090	163	6	2,771	£1,474,311
1974	131,000	84,140	143	6	2,802	£1,558,451
1975	146,000	65,643	115	3	2,894	£1,624,000
1976	208,751	122,050	175	2	3,037	£1,846,050

An analysis of the Trust's work in the last 25 years also provides useful background to the patterns of demand that may develop when state aid becomes available. The Trust will consider applications for grants from all Christian denominations but, in practice, the vast majority of grants go to Anglican parish churches. The following table shows how grants to Church of England Churches were distributed on a county basis in the seven years between 1968 and 1974 and should be compared to the lists of outstanding (Grade A) churches on page 5. In these years the largest numbers of grants went to East Anglian churches—Norfolk 124, Suffolk 77 and Essex 60. Lincolnshire, by contrast, which has the highest number of Grade A churches of any county received only 40 grants; and Yorkshire, the largest county, containing the dioceses of York, Ripon, Sheffield and Wakefield (containing a total of 168 Grade A churches) received only 22 grants in the period.

Historic Churches Preservation Trust grants to Church of England Churches

Year	*Bedfordshire*	*Berkshire*	*Buckinghamshire**	*Cambridgeshire*	*Cheshire**
1968	3	1	4	3	2
1969	—	—	1	3	3
1970	1	—	3	1	3
1971–72	4	1	1	5	5
1973	1	1	2	5	1
1974	2	3	1	5	1
	11	6	12	22	15

Year	*Cornwall**	*Cumberland*	*Derbyshire*	*Devon**	*Dorset**	*Durham*	*Essex*
1968	4	1	3	8	1	—	11
1969	—	—	3	3	3	2	11
1970	3	—	—	3	4	1	5
1971–72	5	—	3	2	7	2	15
1973	2	3	1	1	9	1	12
1974	2	—	1	5	2	3	6
	16	4	11	22	26	9	60

Year	*Gloucestershire*	*Hampshire*	*Herefordshire**	*Hertfordshire*	*Huntingdonshire*
1968	11	1	—	3	2
1969	10	—	4	1	—
1970	3	3	2	1	1
1971–72	25	3	4	1	2
1973	5	6	5	—	1
1974	6	2	1	1	—
	60	15	16	7	6

Year	*Kent**	*Lancashire*	*Leicestershire**	*Lincolnshire**	*London*	*Middlesex*
1968	8	—	1	6	—	—
1969	6	—	2	3	1	—
1970	4	—	4	5	—	1
1971–72	9	3	6	10	—	2
1973	4	2	4	9	4	—
1974	12	2	6	7	—	—
	43	7	23	40	5	3

Year	*Norfolk**	*Northamptonshire**	*Northumberland*	*Nottinghamshire*	*Oxfordshire**
1968	35	9	4	1	4
1969	19	10	1	2	3
1970	14	4	2	5	4
1971–72	17	14	2	1	2
1973	20	5	3	4	3
1974	19	5	—	—	2
	124	47	12	13	18

Year	Rutland	Salop	Somerset	Stafford-shire*	Suffolk*	Surrey
1968	1	1	3	3	11	—
1969	2	—	8	3	14	—
1970	2	1	4	4	5	1
1971–72	2	3	6	5	17	1
1973	1	3	4	2	14	2
1974	—	2	5	3	16	—
	8	10	30	20	77	4

Year	Sussex	Warwick-shire	Wiltshire*	Worcester-shire	Yorkshire
1968	4	3	4	5	5
1969	4	7	3	—	5
1970	4	4	1	1	1
1971–72	10	7	4	4	—
1973	2	6	3	3	7
1974	2	5	3	3	4
	26	32	18	16	22

** = a County Trust in existence.*

The geographical distribution of HCPT grants obviously represents the general pattern of demand. Some counties have evidently been slow in coming forward—while Norfolk and Suffolk, where passions for churches run high, have lost no opportunity. There also appears to be some correlation with the existence of a county churches trust (indicated on the chart by an asterisk). Some of the counties without trusts come low in the table of grants, for example Berkshire with 6, Cumberland 4, Durham 8, Hertfordshire 7, Lancashire 7, London (extraordinarily) 5, Shropshire 10 and Surrey 4. Where there are enthusiastic people at county level, churches appear more likely to be conscious of what money is available.

By September 1975 the HCPT had awarded grants to some 2,894 churches, but of these less than a hundred had belonged to non-Anglican denominations. This imbalance again is evidently due to a lack of applications from Roman Catholics and nonconformists. This is probably largely due to ignorance on the part of individual congregations, but there appears also to be a feeling (quite wrongly) that the HCPT is really intended for the Church of England. The reference in *Listed Church Buildings* (1976), produced by the Methodist Division of Property, runs: "In one or two cases Methodist churches have received a modest grant from the Historic Churches Preservation Trust, but its headquarters are at Fulham Palace and most of its grants have gone to Anglican churches and cathedrals." This is hardly very encouraging, and since the HCPT does not give grants to cathedrals it suggests a lack of information and liaison at an important level. Between 1967 and

1975 the following grants were given by the HCPT to Roman Catholic and nonconformist churches:

		£
1967	Frenchay Unitarian Chapel, Gloucestershire	250
1968	Everingham Roman Catholic Church, Humberside	1,000
	Shepton Mallet Methodist Chapel, Somerset	200
	Northampton St John, Roman Catholic Church	750
1969	Warwick Quaker Chapel	500
	Bath, Prior Park Roman Catholic Chapel, Somerset	750
1970	Wilmslow Unitarian Chapel, Cheshire	200
	Loughwood Baptist Chapel, Devon	400
1971–72	Ashburton Methodist Church, Devon	100
	Lyme Regis Congregational Church, Dorset	250
	Uppingham Congregational Church, Leicestershire	250
	Midsomer Norton Catholic Church, Somerset	400
	Wardour Castle Roman Catholic Chapel, Wiltshire	450
1973	Liverpool Toxteth Chapel	150
1974	Roseworthy Methodist Church, Cornwall	100
	Manningtree Methodist Church, Essex	300
	Broadmead Wesleyan Chapel, Somerset (New Road, Bristol)	1,000
	Bewdley Roman Catholic Church, Warwickshire	550
	Salisbury St Osmond Roman Catholic Church, Wiltshire	750
	York St Saviourgate Unitarian Chapel	500
1975	Chipping Camden Baptist Church, Gloucestershire	250
	Needham Market Congregational Church, Suffolk	100

This list includes some of the most important dissenting meeting houses and chapels—the Unitarian chapels at Frenchay, Toxteth, Wilmslow and York, the Baptist chapels at Chipping Camden and Loughwood, and Wesley's New Room at Bristol. Some of the Roman Catholic chapels like Wardour, by James Paine and Sir John Soane, are also outstanding. Some of the grants are very small and none above £1,000: this may be explained by the fact that most are small simple buildings, but there are many larger nonconformist buildings, the best of which deserve more considerable sums. However, it is equally the case the HCPT grants to Anglican churches tend to be of the pump-priming type. Only a few receive grants of more than £1,000 in any year, and between 1966 and 1975 only 12 churches have received more than £2,000. They are:

		£
1966	Ingestre, Staffordshire	2,100
1967	West Walton, Norfolk	2,000
	Stanford-on-Avon, Northamptonshire	2,250
1968	Euston, Suffolk	2,000
1970	Bristol, St Stephen, Somerset	2,000

		£
1971–	Norwich, St John, Norfolk	2,000
72	Milton Abbey, Dorset	2,500
	Euston, Suffolk	2,000
	Great Witley, Worcestershire	3,000
1973	Deptford St Paul, London	2,000
	Great Witley, Worcestershire	2,000
1975	Hartlepool St Hilda, Durham	2,000

The Trust's report in 1962 stated it was "ready to consider the needs of any church or chapel built before the middle of the 19th century and having architectural features or historic associations worthy of preservation". Adding that its main task had been "the preservation of the countless small and little-known but lovely village churches". Over the years the Trust has broadened its scope to include quite major town churches, although so far few Victorian churches have had grants. This is another area where state aid is needed.

The HCPT has always emphasized that it would only consider grants when there was convincing evidence that "the amount needed for essential fabric repairs is beyond local effort". In too many cases grants are being sought by parishes which appear to have done little or nothing to help themselves (Annual Report, 1970). The Trust has also firmly discouraged the sale of church plate or other church treasures to pay for fabric repairs, and one of the conditions its attaches to its grants is that these should not subsequently be sold.

From an early stage the Trust excluded disused churches from the scope of its grants. The position of potentially redundant churches is more flexible. A few churches which have received grants have subsequently been declared redundant. Equally, there may be cases where the offer of a grant may prevent a declaration of redundancy. The problem is likely to be at its most acute where a diocese (or an incumbent) is seeking to declare a church redundant against the wishes of some of the parishioners or local people. "Purely pastoral considerations", the Archbishop of Canterbury wrote in his introduction to the 1962 Report, "cannot, however, be allowed to influence the attitude of the Trust whose purpose is to preserve for posterity buildings of architectural value." Many people would undoubtedly like to give money precisely to those churches which are most threatened, but in some cases churches with weak congregations have been excluded from grants. It was for this very reason that the Friends of Friendless Churches was set up.

The HCPT receives financial support from many sources and is now one of the small number of charities (like the National Trusts and the National Art Collections Fund) entitled to receive bequests of any amount free of capital transfer tax. Its work has also been greatly aided by the Pilgrim Trust, which produced no less than £175,000 in the first 10 years. Today the Pilgrim Trust makes a block grant annually to the HCPT, rather than making individual grants to churches. The HCPT's scope, however, is restricted to England, though there is now some hope that a sister body may be established in Scotland. In Wales no comparable body exists though the Pilgrim Trust, through the Representative Body, has helped a very considerable number of Welsh churches on an individual basis. Methodist churches have, on occasion, been helped by the Joseph Rank Benevolent Trust, though assistance has been concentrated largely on new churches. There appears to be a failure among some of the nonconformist denominations to make the best of their opportunities. In 1974 the Methodist Division of Property set aside £50,000 in the form of special European Architectural Heritage Year Grants. Yet according to *Listed Church Buildings*: "so much remained in the Fund by the end of the year that the Property Board decided to give (on conditions) £25,000 of the balance to the restoration of Wesley's Chapel, City Road, London, and this still leaves a substantial balance to be used".

In addition the Council for Places of Worship makes grants to the repair of furnishings in Anglican churches—a total of £53,000 being available in 1977. The CPW's grants are due to the generosity of a number of trusts, in particular the Pilgrim Trust (which has made a quite exceptional contribution to the conservation of churches and their artistically valuable contents), the Hayward Foundation, and the Radcliffe Trust. This is principally allocated as follows:

Bells	£1,500
Clocks	£1,500
Metalwork	£2,000
Monuments	£10,500
Organs	£5,500
Painted Woodwork	£7,000
Stained Glass	£6,000
Wall Paintings	£5,500
Wooden Furniture	£4,500
Textiles Decorative Plasterwork Books	£2,000

These sums are made available in substantial grants as well as smaller ones.

		£
1976	Southacre, Norfolk (monuments)	1,000
	Ashby-de-la-Zouche, Leicestershire (monuments)	2,000
	Colyton, Devon (monuments)	1,000

		£
	Amptney St Mary, Gloucestershire (wall paintings)	1,000
	Inglesham, Wiltshire (wall paintings)	1,500
	Little Witchingham, Norfolk (wall paintings)	1,900
1977	Barton Thurs, Norfolk (painted woodwork)	1,000
	Worstead, Norfolk (painted woodwork)	1,400
	Cambridge St Botolph (painted woodwork)	1,500
	Hortham St Faith, Sussex (painted woodwork)	1,500
	Acaster Malbis, North Yorkshire (stained glass)	2,242
	Birkin, North Yorkshire (stained glass)	2,500
	Wiggenhall St Mary, Norfolk (stained glass)	1,230
	North Elmham, Norfolk (stained glass)	1,000

County Trusts

In Staffordshire nearly 100 churches have received grants from the Friends of Ancient Staffordshire churches over the last 23 years: one grant has been made to a Roman Catholic church—the Regency church of St Peter and St Paul, Wolverhampton—and an application is being considered from a Methodist church in Stoke on Trent. In 1975 five grants were given of sums ranging from £75 to £150.

The Dorset Historic Churches Trust have given one grant to a non-Anglican church—the Roman Catholic church at Lulworth: this interdenominational support reflected the fact that Sir Joseph Weld, a Roman Catholic and now Lord Lieutenant, generously supported the Anglican church at Lulworth.

The Friends of Essex Churches which in 1975–76 gave £6,700 to 23 churches in sums ranging from £50 to £600 is an interesting example of how such a trust can win regular support from other local bodies—the County Council, the Augustine Courtauld Trust, the Charles S. French Charitable Trust and the Leather Sellers Company.

Buckinghamshire Historic Churches Trust, according to its 1975 Newsletter, has dispersed £62,240 since its foundation, to a total of 135 churches. One of the first to receive help was a Roman Catholic church and in the past five years the Trustees have approved grants to several Baptist Churches and a Quaker meeting house. Rutland Historic Churches Preservation Trust have helped two Congregational Churches, a Methodist Church and a Baptist Church.

The Devon Historic Churches Trust has also been notable in giving grants to nonconformist chapels—including £400 to the Methodist Church at Fore Street Brixham, £100 to the Baptist Church Budleigh Salterton, £250 to the United Reformed Church at Ottery St Mary, and £300 to the Methodist Chapel at Dartmouth: the Wiltshire Historic Churches Trust has helped the Moravian church at East Tytherton.

The Sussex Historic Churches Trust has given very substantial grants to Arundel Roman Catholic Cathedral and to the Roman Catholic Fitzalan Chapel at Arundel. It also makes interest-free loans towards repairs, and sponsors church guides, the profits from which go to individual churches. Since it was established in 1956 it has raised and largely spent £100,000, but is inclined to feel that the enormous amount of money required for Chichester Cathedral has had an adverse effect on its fund-raising.

The present secretary of the Herefordshire Historic Churches Trusts has concentrated on making the Trust better known by means of lectures, and has tried to make incumbents more aware of their responsibilities in the way of looking after their churches. The Northamptonshire Historic Churches Trust has helped 105 churches including three non-Anglican ones—the initiative for two of these in fact came from the Trustees. This imbalance, according to the secretary, is because the Trust has "no formal relation with the Roman Catholic or Nonconformist churches and have no knowledge of their needs in respect of buildings". By contrast the Trust is kept regularly informed of the needs of Anglican churches by the Peterborough Diocesan Advisory Committee which—in common with other DACs—is sent copies of all the quinquennial inspection reports.

Perhaps the most enterprising of all the County Trusts is the Norfolk Churches Trust. Faced with a threat of some 200 "redundant" churches in the Diocese, some dozen or so of which are already closed or abandoned, the Trust has concentrated its energies on first-aid repairs to churches—sometimes structural, but often simply cutting away accumulations of undergrowth and debris—and providing visitors with leaflets and a secure wall-safe in which to deposit contributions for the upkeep of the church. In the last three years small working parties have rescued a number of enchanting medieval churches which had been allowed to descend into a pitiful, indeed disgusting, state—the most notable is Little Witchingham, which has the additional attraction of an extensive series of 13th-century frescoes hitherto unknown. The rescue of this church from the jaws of dissolution won a European Architectural Heritage Year Award in 1975.

Recently the Lincolnshire Old Churches Trust has adopted a similarly dynamic policy towards redundancy and held a remarkably successful sale at Grimsthorpe Castle. Lord Ancaster put up a number of substantial items, and owners were allowed up to 90% of sale proceeds (less auctioneer's commission)—the Trust getting a minimum of 10%. The net proceeds to the Trust were over £4,000.

If the sums raised and disbursed by County Trusts are relatively modest they nonetheless have a recognizable catalystic effect and in some cases attract money that might not go to individual churches. Most Trusts are very anxious to be seen to be ecumenical, and clearly a much greater number of nonconformist places of worship could benefit by their work.

We recommend that local authorities should be encouraged to support their county historic churches trusts generously: an annual subvention of £2,000 or £3,000 per annum would not only increase the grant-giving ability of these trusts but, still more important, serve as a tremendous boost to their morale and enable them to be more confident of winning further grants and subscriptions.

Local Authority Grants

Local authorities were empowered to give grants and loans towards the repair of historic buildings including churches under the 1962 Local Authorities (Historic Buildings) Act. Similar provisions were enacted for Scotland in 1967. It is entirely at the discretion of the local authority to decide whether or not to give a grant, and it is important to emphasize that the grants are not limited to listed buildings. The Act was simply an enabling one, and while some local authorities have been enterprising and considerate others have given no grant aid at all. Over the last 17 years the total amount given in grants and loans has grown as follows:

Financial Year	*Grants*	*Loans*
67/68	123,339	20,571
68/69	194,219	17,141
69/70	129,302	94,768
70/71	191,146	85,598
71/72	290,765	45,268
72/73	318,933	64,420
73/74	315,944	68,457
74/75	439,350	33,552

The extent to which churches have benefited from these grants obviously varies from one local authority to another. Some local authorities, however, including the County Councils of Berkshire, Cheshire, Lincolnshire, Surrey and Wiltshire do not give grants to churches as a matter of policy. In Cheshire the reasons given are that "there are certain other funds devoted specifically to this purpose", and secondly that "alterations to ecclesiastical building in ecclesiastical use" are excluded from control under the planning acts. Certain exemptions have been made to this rule, as they have in Surrey where assistance has occasionally been given to small rural congregations. In Berkshire it is considered that there are other means available for the raising of funds for church repairs, while Wiltshire County Council is of the opinion that the restoration of churches should be a central Government responsibility.

Sometimes the grants have been very small, like the £69.50 given in 1971 by Cheltenham Borough Council for repairs to North Place Congregational Church (built in 1816 for the Countess of Huntingdon's Connexion and listed Grade II*), but more often they have been in the £200–£1,000 range. Since local government reorganization in 1974, for example, Leicester City Council have approved the following grants:

St Martin's Cathedral	(£500: November 1974)
St Margaret's Church	(£200: March 1975)
Trinity Hospital Almshouses and Chapel	(£900: October 1975 & April 1976)
Bishop Street Methodist Church	(£300: December 1976)
Charles Street Baptist Church	(£500: under consideration)

In this case—and others—it is very encouraging to find the local authority continuing to make grants despite current economic difficulties.

In view of the predominance of Anglican churches among grants given by the Historic Churches Preservation Trust and its associated county trusts, it is interesting to see how local authorities have spread the money between different denominations. Greater Manchester Council has given grants to 23 churches since April 1, 1974, including Congregational, Methodist, Moravian, Roman Catholic and Unitarian churches. The City of Sheffield, for example, has given £1,157 towards the cleaning of Holy Trinity, Nursery Street (Grade C, though now in nonconformist use) and £3,000 for treating dry rot in Upper Chapel, Norfolk Street (Grade II). The City of Manchester has given £3,384 to the First Church of Christ Scientist, Daisy Bank Road (Grade II*). Bath City Council recently gave £1,000 towards the cleaning and repair of Walcot Methodist Church. Dorset County Council has made the following grants:

Shaftesbury St Peter	(£250 in 1972, matched by the former Borough Council)
Lyme Regis United Reformed Church	(£250 in 1974)
Bridport Baptist Church	(£274 grant aid £274 loan—since repaid in 1973)
Morecombelake United Reformed Church	(£75 in 1974)
Longham Hampreston United Reformed Church	(£150 offered in 1976)
Blandford Forum Parish Church	(£500 in 1976 with matching sum from North Dorset District Council)

Wimborne Minster Church (£500 each from Wimborne District and Wimborne Town Council)

In Wales, Gwent County Council has given a number of grants to chapels, including £570 to Capel Babell, Cwmfelinfach, between 1972 and 1976, and £400 to Pen-y-barn Baptist Church, Pontypool. In Scotland, Strathclyde Regional Council and Glasgow District Council have given £5,000 each to Queen's Cross Church, Maryhill, Glasgow, now held by the Charles Rennie Mackintosh Society. The City of Edinburgh gave £8,000 in 1974 to the repairs at Barclay Church (Church of Scotland) and offered £3,900 to St James, Leith. Grants have been most successful when they have been given jointly by county and district councils, rather in the manner of the Historic Buildings Council's Town Schemes. The following table shows the considerable amount given in Staffordshire in this fashion.

Local authority grants to churches in Staffordshire

Church	*Grade*	*County Council Contribution*	*District Council Contribution*
1974–75			
St Nicholas, Abbots Bromley	B	£250	£75
St James, Longdon	B	£300	£300
St Edward, Cheddleton	B	£450	£500
Christ Church, Hilderstone	—	£250	£500
St Margaret, Draycott-le-Moors	B	£150	£500
St Michael, Horton	B	£250	£250
St Mary, Swynnerton	B	£150	—
1975–76			
St John the Baptist, Colton	B	£100	£150
St Lawrence, Rushton Spencer	B	£100	£200
St Giles, Whittington	B	£350	£200
St Peter, Elford	B	£250	£200
St Paul, Quarnford	—	—	£100
St Lawrence, Gnosall	A	£300	—
St Michael & All Angels, Colwich	B	£250	—
1976–77			
St Wilfrid's Roman Catholic Church, Cotton	II	£300	£200
St Giles, Cheadle	B	£450	£300
All Saints, Kings Bromley	B	£500	£320
St Michael-on-Greenhill, Lichfield	B	£400	£200
Holy Trinity, Edingale	—	£100	£100
Bethesda Methodist Church, Hanley, Stoke-on-Trent	II	£450	£250

In the north of England a great number of churches were stone cleaned with the help of "Operation Eyesore", as the Special Environmental Assistance Schemes were called in 1972–73. Grants of 75% were available in this period for cleaning (but not for repointing which was considered normal maintenance). Thus in Rochdale overall costs were divided approximately 65% from the Department of the Environment, 22% from Rochdale Borough Council, Greater Manchester, and 14% from the parochial church council—though obviously there were individual variations. The buildings cleaned, with the cost of work, were as follows:

St Clements, Spotland	£2,295
St Martins, Castleton	£3,785
Christ Church, Healey	£2,785
Trinity Presbyterian Church, Manchester Road	£4,963
St Aidans, Sudden	£3,624
The Good Shepherd, Entwisle Road	£1,250
St Mary, Balderstone	£3,415
St Peter, Newbold	£2,437
St Edmund, Falinge	£7,400
Zion Baptist, Milkstone Road	£550
Bagslate Moor Methodist	£650
Salvation Army Citadel, Lord Street	£6,300

Since 1974 Rochdale Metropolitan Borough Council has undertaken further stone cleaning financed from its own environmental improvement funds. The cleaning of Wardle Methodist Church (cost £3,150), which is in a conservation area, was financed on a 50/50 basis by Rochdale Borough and Greater Manchester Council. All Saints, Hamer (cost £3,750), St Barnabas, Littleborough (cost £4,000) and St Michael, Tonge Middleton (cost £5,200) were all financed by Rochdale Council with a 5% contribution from the parochial church council. The cleaning of St James, Wardleworth, a redundant Anglican church taken over by a Ukranian Orthodox congregation, was financed from the Greater Manchester Council's historic buildings fund. The impressive number of churches cleaned in Newcastle under Special Environmental Assistance Schemes is shown in the following list ("Townscape" indicates the church has townscape value though not listed).

City of Newcastle upon Tyne: Churches Cleaned under Operation Eyesore

Baptist Church, Westgate Road	Townscape
Baptist Church, Heaton Road	Townscape
St Anne, C of E, City Road	A
St Silas, C of E, Clifford Street	C
St Michael, C of E, Headlam Street	C
St Gabriel C of E, Heaton Road	C
Jesmond Parish Church, C of E	C
St Nicholas Cathedral, C of E	A
St James, C of E, Benwell	Townscape

St Augustine, C of E, Brighton Grove	Townscape
Walker Parish Church, C of E	Townscape
St Paul, C of E, Elswick	Townscape
St Stephen, C of E, Westgate Road	Townscape
Methodist Memorial Church, Bond Street	Townscape
Methodist Church, Dilston Road	Townscape
Cuthbert Bainbridge Methodist Memorial Church, Heaton	Townscape
St Andrew, Roman Catholic, Worswick Street	Townscape
St Lawrence, Roman Catholic, Fetton Street, Byker	Townscape
United Reformed Church, Gordon Road, Byker	Townscape
St James, United Reformed, Northumberland Road	Townscape
St Andrew, Church of Scotland, Sandyford Road	Townscape
Elim Pentecostal, Heaton Road	Townscape

During the same period a considerable number of churches were cleaned in North Tyneside, South Tyneside and Sunderland.

The Greater London Council has also done much for London's churches, giving grants ranging from £100 to assist the repair of a weathervane to £50,000 towards the restoration of St Paul's. Since 1970 the following grants have been given.

Grants given by the Greater London Council

Church	*Grade*	*Grant*
1970		
Bevis Marks Synagogue (1700–1)	I	£450
St Mary Magdalene, Paddington (1867–78 by G. E. Street)	A	£750
St Lawrence, Whitchurch (1714–20 by John James)	A	£750*
St Mary Magdalene, Islington (1812–14 by W. Wickings)	B	£500
1971		
St Raphael, Roman Catholic, Kingston (1847–48 by Charles Parker)	—	£500
St Paul's Cathedral (1666–1711 by Sir Christopher Wren)	A	£50,000*
St Mary the Virgin, Lewisham (1775–77 by G. Gibson)	B	£1,000
All Saints, Kingston (Medieval tower: 1708)	B	£2,000*
St Mary the Virgin, Bromley (Medieval)	B	£1,000
St Peter, Kensington Park Road (1855–57 by Thomas Allom)	—	£225
1972		
St Mary, Beddington (Medieval origin)	B	£1,234*
St John's Wood Parish Church (1813–14 by Thomas Hardwick)	B	£500
St Lawrence, Whitchurch (1714–20 by John James)	A	£1,000*
St John the Baptist, Old Malden (Medieval 17th & 19th centuries)	B	£500
St Peter & St Paul, Harlington (Norman & Medieval)	B	£1,000

Church	Grade	Grant
1974		
St Benet, Paul's Wharf (1677–85 by Sir Christopher Wren)	A	£1,000
St George, Bloomsbury (1720–31 by Nicholas Hawksmoor)	A	£1,000
1973		
Holy Trinity Church, Marylebone Road (1826–27 Sir John Soane)	B	£900
St James, Norland (1844–45 by Lewis Vulliamy)	—	£355
Church of Our Lady, Lisson Grove (RC) (1836 by J. J. Scoles)	III	£500
St Mary, Hendon (Medieval and 1914–15 Temple Moore)	—	£500
St Mary, Hayes (Medieval)	B	£500
St Margaret, Edgware (15th-century tower, church 1845)	—	£500
St George's German Lutheran Church, Alie Street (1762)	II	£500
St Mary, Bryanston Square (1821–23 Robert Smirke)	B	£1,500
1974		
St Pancras New Church, Euston Road (1819–22 W. & H. W. Inwood)	A	£750
All Saints, Kingston (Medieval tower: 1708)	B	£1,000*
All Saints, Margaret Street (1849–59 William Butterfield)	A	£750
St Augustine, Queen's Gate (1865–76 William Butterfield)	B	£1,250
St Paul, Deptford (1712–30 Thomas Archer)	A	£25,000
Church of the Sacred Heart, Trott Street (RC) (1872 F. A. Walters)	II	£100
Church of Our Lady Star of the Sea (RC) Greenwich (1851 W. W. Wardell)	II	£400
St Mary, Beddington (Medieval origin)	B	£1,000*
Holy Trinity, Southwark (1823–24 Francis Bedford)	B	£1,500
St Bartholomew the Great, Smithfield (early 12th century, etc.)	A	£1,500
Church of Our Lady Queen of Heaven (RC) (1868 for the United Methodist Free Church)	—	£250
St Peter, Eaton Square (1824–27 H. Hakewill)	B	£1,000
St Mary-le-Strand (1714 James Gibbs)	A	£3,000
1975		
All Saints, Carshalton (Medieval & 18th century)	B	£1,000
St Peter & St Paul's, Harlington (Norman & Medieval)	B	£250
St John the Baptist, Erith (largely 12th century)	B	£250
St Mary's Old and New, Stoke Newington (Old 1563. New Sir George Gilbert Scott)	B	£1,000
Holy Trinity, Upper Tooting (Anthony Salvin & Benjamin Ferrey)	—	£500
St Margaret, Hillingdon (Medieval)	B	£400
St Lawrence, Whitchurch (1740–20 John James)	A	£450

Church	*Grade*	*Grant*
1975		
St John's Wood Parish Church (1813–14 Thomas Hardwick)	B	£450
St Martin-in-the-Fields (1721–26 James Gibbs)	A	£1,000
All Saints, West Ham (Medieval)	—	£1,000
St Peter, Hammersmith (1827 by Edward Lapidge)	B	£450
St Barnabas, Pimlico (1847–50 Thomas Cundy II)	B	£1,500
1976		
St Lawrence, Whitchurch (1714–20 John James)	A	£1,000
All Saints, Carshalton (Medieval & 18th-century alterations)	B	£750
St Jude-on-the-Hill, Barnet (1911 Sir Edwin Lutyens)	A	£1,500
St James, Bermondsey (1827–29 James Savage)	B	£1,000
Wesley's Chapel, City Road (1777)	I	£1,000
St Paul, Deptford (1712–30 Thomas Archer)	A	£5,000
St Peter, Croydon (1849–51 Sir George Gilbert Scott)	II	£250
St Augustine, Kilburn (1871–77 J. L. Pearson)	A	£950
St Lawrence, Whitchurch (1714–20 John James)	A	£750
All Saints, Wandsworth (1906 Temple Moore)	—	£600
St Peter, Vauxhall (1863–65 J. L. Pearson)	Supp. List	£100
St Pancras, Camden (1819–22 W. H. & W. Inwood)	A	£1,000
St Mark, Kennington (1822 D. R. Roper)	B	£500
St Mary, Bryanston Square (1821–23 Robert Smirke)	B	£200
Southwark Cathedral (Medieval & 19th century)	A	£2,500
All Saints, Footscray, Bexley (Medieval & 19th century)	B	£1,000

* = *one of two or more grants.*

Certain London boroughs have also given notable grants to churches. Harrow, London, has matched the GLC's generosity to St Lawrence, Whitchurch, by grants of £750 in 1970 and £1,000 in 1972. Kingston-upon-Thames has given two grants of £5,000 to All Saints, Kingston. Barnet gave £2,202 to St Mary, Hendon in 1973, and Lambeth has given a series of grants including a probable interest-free loan of £10,000 to St Michael, Stockwell Park Road. The City of London, by contrast, considers the 1962 Act to be a matter for the GLC.

In conclusion it appears that though some local authorities are reluctant to give grants to churches or even refuse outright, others have rarely or never been approached. North Devon District Council for example reported "the only application received in respect of a church under the 1962 Act resulted in a grant of £300 towards the cost of repairs to Pilton Parish Church, a Grade A building". Payment was made in 1976. Other churches take note.

Local authorities can also play a useful part in initiating emergency measures to protect endangered churches. In 1976, for example, Rushcliffe Borough Council, Nottinghamshire, voted £500 for vandal proof fencing around the church of St Mary, Colston Bassett.

CHAPTER THIRTEEN

Secular Uses

The idea of putting a church to a variety of secular uses—commonplace in the Middle Ages—is now enjoying a revival. Such uses not only bring community activities into the church at a time when it is normally empty but make a substantial contribution towards its keep. Essentially they fall into two groups: first those which can take place in the church without any internal modification and second those which involve a measure of subdivision, alteration or extension. Many of these activities such as flower festivals, concerts, drama and recitals also have considerable relevance to tourism.

Much fascinating information about such activities is contained in J. G. Davies's *The Secular Use of Church Buildings* (1968). In the Middle Ages churches were almost invariably the largest building in a village or town and the nave served effectively as the village hall for most communal purposes. Churches were regularly used for eating and drinking notably at weddings, baptisms and funerals, and on the anniversary of benefactors' deaths. Secondly churches were used for dancing, sometimes associated with festivals or events in the Church calendar, sometimes of secular origin. Many a medieval fair owed its establishment to the observance of saints' days and pedlars and stall holders were charged for the right to sell produce inside or outside the church, providing a useful source of income for the upkeep of the building. In addition churches were used for many different kinds of meetings, notably councils, elections, debates and discussions, audits and the awarding of degrees, while many were in regular use for teaching. And though the fathers of the Early Church had been bitterly opposed to the theatre, in the Middle Ages churches played a leading role in the development of drama.

With the Reformation systematic attempts were made to prevent such non-liturgical activities, and between 1550 and 1640 some 200 separate articles and injunctions, both royal and ecclesiastical, were produced to this end. In many places churches continued, however, to be used for teaching and for meetings, and there were new developments, such as the Methodist love feast. The first of these was held at

Fetter Lane, London, on December 31, 1738, and from then on it became a standard feature of Methodism, celebrated in chapels throughout England, consisting of bread, biscuits or semi-sweet buns with water or tea.

In the last two decades however secular activities in churches have begun to flourish as never before. The most common of course is the flower festival, and in many cases these produce very substantial sums from visitors in the course of a few days.

The rapid increase in publicly-sponsored provision for the arts, principally through the Regional Arts Associations, is introducing a new dimension of activity in many churches. "Due to a great shortage of theatres and concert halls in the area", Lincolnshire and Humberside Arts told us "many churches are used for performances of all types, particularly music." South West Arts reported "Church buildings are terribly important to us in this part of the country as they are often the only available and appropriate spaces of concerts." "We have presented", wrote the Mid-Pennine Association for the Arts, "concerts by brass bands, choirs, ensembles and jazz groups in St Leonard's Padiham; Burnley Parish Church; Blackburn Cathedral; St John's Gannow; St John's Worsthorne: quite simply these are large capacity buildings and this area is short of halls." Similarly the South East Wales Arts Association wrote: "because we have a shortage of purpose-built art centres we need to use other buildings including miners institutes, schools, colleges, leisure centres and churches. Some of our local choirs of course use chapels the most notable one being Gymanfer Gany by Pendyrus Choirt in Tylorstown in 1974." The Yorkshire Arts Association organize an annual programme of 50 summer concerts in Yorkshire churches, which in 1977 is to be accompanied by touring craft exhibitions in churches. Similarly, the Windsor Festival includes events in St George's Chapel, Eton College Chapel, Windsor Parish Church and Cookham, Bray and South Ascot churches.

South West Arts also grant aids many events in churches and cathedrals—notably the Gloucester Cathedral Recital Fund and the Three Choirs Festival, which is to hold its 250th Anniversary in 1977 in Gloucester Cathedral. The Bournemouth Symphony Orchestra performs regularly in Truro Cathedral, which provides one of the largest spaces available in Cornwall, but there are also a number of small country churches in Cornwall on which festivals are based, such as the St Mylos Festival, St Columb Major, St Endellion and the East Cornwall Bach Festival at St German's church.

In Gloucestershire the Guiting Festival holds events in St Michaels church and the Stroud Festival in Dursley parish church. In 1975, the

Orchard Theatre, a small travelling theatre company based in North Devon, mounted a one-man show based on the life of Parson Hawker, of Morwenstowne, to mark the centenary of his death. With the help of the Devon Historic Churches Trust this was presented throughout North Devon. East Midland Arts have grant-aided the Derby Baroque Festival in Derby Cathedral as well as exhibitions and individual concerts; music at the parish churches of Higham Ferrers and Rothwell in Northamptonshire and concerts in St Matthew's Church, Northampton, have included the recent commissioning of a new work by John McCabe for the Northampton Philharmonic Choir. A recent month-long "Opera for You" tour included St Mary's Church Clifton and Brimington Church near Chesterfield. In 1976 East Midland Arts sponsored a major exhibition of sculpture at Worksop Priory (both inside and out). The Mid-Pennine Association for the Arts also report "a development of local arts and crafts exhibitions in churches or parish rooms".

Many of the churches in the City of London hold lunchtime organ recitals: the organists are often young musicians eligible for grant-aid from the Greater London Arts Association. Indeed there is a rich musical life in the City, with regular series of baroque music recitals in the 18th-century All Hallows on the Wall, music while you eat in St Olave's, Hart Street, and so on. The North Wales Arts Association directly sponsors an annual music festival at St Asaph's Cathedral—now one of the foremost national festivals in Britain. In 1976 Bi-Centennial Year, American music provided the theme with 15 works by 9 American composers. At Bangor Cathedral the Association sponsors a series of summer concerts; Theatre Roundabout also often performs in the two north Wales cathedrals. At Llanfullin church in mid-Wales there is a biannual music festival; similar festivals are held in south-east Wales at Lower Machen, Llantilio Crossenny and Abergavenny.

For the promoter churches can sometimes have a marked advantage over other buildings that may be available. The Courtyard Arts Trust said for example: "We are seeking to present events in a very aesthetic way. Some churches have a marvellous atmosphere—with subtle lighting you can get much better effects than on stage, more cheaply."

Churches are also often an ideal venue for "celebrity events"—readings of poetry and prose and short talks by well-known figures, and these are sometimes organized on a touring basis, with the help of industrial sponsorship. Churches also have great potential for children's events: in 1977 the Courtyard Arts Trust are organizing some 36 of these (though not all in churches); some churches organize their own arts programmes. The Baptist church at Sutton has regular drama and dance, including the Reigate Liturgical Dance Group, which recently performed a liturgical eucharist. St John's Church, Kingston-on-Thames, is used during term time by Kingston Polytechnic for lectures, exams and concerts as well as for flower festivals and Christmas sales: each year the local community puts on a play which runs for a week, as well as a local festival that provides a week of jamboree with the Salvation Army Band and popular films.

The following list gives an example of arts use of churches in Scotland.

Scotland: Cathedrals, Churches, Kirks used for Arts Events

Aberdeen	St Machar's Cathedral Melville-Carden Place Church
Crieff	St Michael's Church
Culross, Fife	Culross Abbey
Dumfries	St Andrew's Church
Dunbar	Dunbar Parish Church
Dunblane	Dunblane Cathedral
Dunfermline	Dunfermline Abbey
Edinburgh	St Giles' Cathedral (Church of Scotland) St Mary's Cathedral (Episcopal) St Cuthbert's Church Old St Paul's Church St Serf's Church (Goldenacre) University Chaplaincy Centre St John's Church St Andrew's Church, Leith St Mark's Unitarian Church Greyfriars Kirk St Margaret's Episcopal Church, Easter Road St George's West St Martin's St Andrew's and St George's Parish Church St Bernard's Church, Stockbridge Craigmillar, Richmond Church Roslin Chapel (Lothian)
Falkirk	Old Parish Church
Glasgow	Glasgow Cathedral University Chapel Wellington Church
Gourock	Old Gourock Church
Haddington	St Mary's Church
Helensburgh	Old St Andrew's Parish Church
Invergordon	Invergordon Church of Scotland
Kirkcaldy	Old Parish Kirk (St Andrew's Parish Church)
Lerwick	St Columba's Church
Oban	St John's Cathedral
Peebles	Old Parish Church
Perth	St John's Kirk
St Andrews	St Salvador's Chapel
St Monans	St Monan's Kirk
West Kilbride	Barony Church

Churches and chapels are also natural places for community meetings of different kinds, including consultations or briefings by local authorities and planning discussions. With the increasing desire to overcome the remoteness of local government and the establishment of town and parish councils and neighbourhood groups the church often provides a ready made meeting place. There are, however, a number of psychological barriers both on the part of the congregations and those who might use a church in this way. These were well illustrated in *Church Property and People* (1973) by Anne Holmes. One view put was that a "majority of the population are embarrassed by the idea of a church building and feel inhibited by being in a church. . . . There are others who feel that if the Establishment gets them in a church they'll be got at." Equally there was a certain resistance among the congregations "unspoken anxiety amongst the elderly" and "uneasy because it is unusual". The signs are, however, that these barriers are gradually being broken down.

Many congregations have made more permanent provision for multiple use by internal subdivision of the church by closing off the chancel, the west end of the nave, or the aisles and galleries. Almost always such adaptations mean sacrifices in architectural terms; the only consistently successful form of multiple use we have found is the conversion of crypts. In the 18th century many crypts were already used for storage; that at St Paul's, Deptford, London, was filled with barrels of rum; the crypts of many 18th-century proprietary chapels in London were let to wine merchants. Nonconformist chapels from an early date were often built over a basement or ground floor containing a series of rooms. At the turn of the century a Congregational church in a typical London suburb had a range of ancillary activities which anticipated many of the educational and social facilities and some of the recreational ones now provided by local authorities.

In more recent years crypts of a number of London churches have been brought into active use: at Christ Church, Spitalfields, the crypt is used to rehabilitate alcoholics; that at St Giles, Camberwell, is a centre for drop-outs. In October 1976 the work of deepening and extending the crypt of Nash's All Souls, Langham Place, to serve as a bustling and visually exciting parish centre for many activities was completed at a cost of £600,000.

The last few years have also seen more elaborate conversions of crypts intended to make the church a focus of community life—these have often been carried out with financial support from the local authority. At St Paul's, Deptford, the crypt is used daily by an old people's lunch club, and can be hired for the sort of activities a local hall would be available for—wedding receptions, and all night rock sessions.

An equally successful crypt conversion has been carried out at

St Peter Walworth, London. This is now a club with a licensed bar, and playspace for children. As a result it is one of the few places in the parish where a whole family can spend an evening. This is of great importance as it is situated in an area of high density council housing and many families and single people, who had never gone out in the evening before, now use the club.

Another highly successful club has been opened in the crypt of St Mary Magdalene, Munster Square, Marylebone, London. This again has a bar, a buffet and a youth club, and employs 5 full time and 10 part time staff. The club has a membership of 3,000, consisting both of local residents and many business people working in the office blocks along Marylebone Road. "It's best thing that's ever happened round here", we were told, by a local resident, while a 78-year-old widow was reported in the *Evening Standard* as saying "I never went out at all till this opened up".

Success has brought a clear profit of £1,000 per month, though the club has some way to go to recover the £55,000 that conversion has cost. The Rector began with a £5,000 loan from Whitbread's Brewery, and soon after secured a grant of £10,000 from Camden Borough Council. This grant was matched by the Diocese which generously also lent a further £10,000.

Another popular form of internal subdivision is to divide off an aisle as a hall inside the church. Where the aisle is wide enough this can provide an alternative and flexible space as at Holy Trinity, Upper Tooting, London, where a stage is being inserted so that the aisle can be used for a whole range of events. This solution also has the attraction of being easily reversible. Closing off the aisles or galleries in a classical church is a far less satisfactory solution: classical proportions do not take well to subdivision, and become distinctly gloomy if there is a marked reduction in light. Conversions of this kind are often carried out in the hope of providing lettable office space, but nothing is so intrusive as a typewriter clicking away in a gallery. Even where such a conversion is relatively sensitive in architectural terms, the noise of people at work destroys the sense of peace and repose that was formerly one of the church's main attractions.

Yet another way of providing a "social area" is to cut off the space under the organ gallery. This has been done at Blackheath and Clapham, London, but in both cases the outlay of more than £10,000 seems excessive in relation to the space gained. A more radical solution is to cut off two or three bays at the west end of the church: where a church has an unusually long nave, as at St Peter's, Spring Hill, Birmingham, this can be done with little detriment to the interior.

Extensions to the exterior of churches form an even more thorny problem than subdivision of the interior. Under the present law any new building in a churchyard must be attached to the church, and this means there will almost inevitably be a conflict between the old and new, whether in style, scale, materials, mass or silhouette. Most churches standing in churchyards derive a special quality from the fact that they were built to be seen and experienced in the round: any extension attached to the exterior is likely to affect the integrity of the design. More controversial are extensions to the sides of churches, for example the new Chapter House at Yatton, Avon, an award-winning scheme that has also attracted considerable criticism.

Another type of multiple use has been pioneered at Holme Cultram Abbey in Cumbria, which has been partially adapted into a tourist information centre with a shop and exhibition hall. This work has been aided by a development area grant from the English Tourist Board. In Chapter fourteen we argue the need for greater liaison between the Churches and the Regional Tourist Boards; one useful form of partnership would be the provision of tourist information centres in certain churches: in return for providing the premises the church would have someone permanently on duty while the church was open.

CHAPTER FOURTEEN

Churches and Tourism

The rapid growth in tourist literature and promotion following the Development of Tourism Act 1969 has, alas, done much too little for churches. All the new regional tourist boards produce excellent literature on places to visit, but in most cases churches come a poor fifth behind ancient monuments, historic houses and gardens, museums and art galleries, wildlife parks and bird sanctuaries. The explanation appears to be that while these other groups have central bodies with a direct interest in increasing the number of visitors the churches do not. The Department of the Environment promotes ancient monuments; the National Trust, the Historic Houses Association and individual owners promote houses, gardens and parks; local authorities and other bodies promote museums, but in most cases there is no one to ensure the inclusion of churches in tourist promotion at regional and national levels.

This omission is evident for example in the *West Country Tourism Regional Fact Sheets* (1975) produced by the English Tourist Board. Among the tourist facilities listed are:

Tourist Information Centres	52
National Trust properties open to the public	47
Department of the Environment properties open to the public	63
Historic Houses, Castles and Gardens (total)	176
Museums, Art Galleries, etc.	133
Zoological and other wildlife attractions	27

Included among designated natural resources are "444 conservation areas" (of which 30 had been designated outstanding). Nowhere are churches mentioned though the counties for which the West of England Tourist Board is responsible—Avon, Cornwall, Devon, Dorset, Isles of Scilly, Somerset, Wiltshire—contain, after East Anglia, the highest concentration of outstanding historic churches in Britain—and indeed the whole of Europe. The well-produced colour booklets on individual counties published by the West Country Tourist Board all contain

30 or 40 "places to visit"—but churches are omitted, though they are sometimes mentioned in passing in the gazetteer of towns and villages.

The Yorkshire and Humberside Holiday Guide 1977 (published by the Tourist Board of the same name) is filled with beguiling colour photographs of historic buildings and streets but churches appear rarely and then incidentally in general views. A list of over 80 places to visit, excellent on country houses, castles and former abbeys, mentions no churches at all. Yet the region not only contains numerous fine medieval, Georgian and Victorian parish churches, but has always been one of the great strongholds of English nonconformity—and contains some of the best and earliest dissenting chapels in Britain.

Norfolk and Suffolk together contain more than 1,100 medieval churches, but the handy and well-designed map and gazetteer produced by the East Anglian Tourist Board includes only the following:

Norfolk: Cley; Glandford; St Margaret's, King's Lynn; St Peter Mancroft, Norwich; Sall; Sandringham; Terrington St Clement; Walpole St Peter; Walsoken; The Wiggenhalls; Wymondham.

Suffolk: Blythburgh; St Mary's, Bury St Edmunds; Dennington; St Margaret's, Ipswich; Icklingham; Lakenheath; Lavenham; Long Melford; Mildenhall; Southwold; Stoke by Nayland.

Any brief selection must be somewhat arbitrary, and the compilers understandably wished to strike a balance between churches, ancient monuments, historic houses and museums and galleries. Yet the fact is that outstanding churches far outnumber any other type of historic building in East Anglia and deserve to be promoted as such.

The best example of imaginative and sympathetic promotion of churches as a tourist attraction is in Northumbria. "The Story of Northumbria as the cradle of Christianity is one of our major promotional assets", we were told by the Northumbria Tourist Board. The Board distributes a Christian Heritage leaflet and booklet free to all potential visitors, giving brief details of the growth of Christianity—the Celtic Church, Lindisfarne, St Cuthbert, the Council of Whitby—and churches to visit. In January 1977 the Board launched the first of a series of Achievement Holidays that will give visitors to the region the task of visiting 15 or so attractions with a common theme, answering a simple question at each and submitting their answers to the Board. Their "reward" will be an illuminated certificate and scroll. The first year's theme is the story of Christianity, and a list of 14 churches has been prepared for visitors. The Bishop of Durham is to sign each scroll awarded.

The Cumbria Tourist Board also told us that "we certainly regard the churches of Cumbria as being of major tourist interest". As part of the Bishop of Carlisle's working party dealing with mission and ministry to holidaymakers, the Board hoped to produce a church trail on the theme of: "in the steps of St Kentigern". Because of a shortage of money the text had to be incorporated in more general tourist board literature, but none-the-less it was a model of its type.

The Heart of England Tourist Board distribute free a very useful and comprehensive booklet on opening times and admission charges, but again this includes no churches at all. The Board, however, does produce an excellent booklet on brass rubbing giving details on brasses in a great many churches and conditions and charges for rubbing. In view of the rapid growth of brass rubbing as a pastime this could well be emulated elsewhere. The booklet published by the Board on the *Cotswolds* (30p), however, strikes a good balance between churches and other attractions, as do the Board's Fact Sheets on individual towns and scenic routes.

Much more could, indeed should, be done to signpost churches of historic interest. For many years the *Caisse Nationale des Monuments Historiques* has been erecting its characteristic blue-bordered signs to virtually every medieval church in France. Often these notices are to be found on most approach roads within two or three miles—always giving basic information such as "église romane—XII siècle". Similarly there is hardly a town or village in France that does not proudly announce its attractions to the visitor arriving by road on a series of signs: "son château, son église, sa musée, ses restaurants". In Britain though signs saying "welcome to this historic borough" are now common, it is rare to find any details of specific sights. Similarly Ancient Monuments have long been signposted, but with few exceptions these are prehistoric sites or ruins. More recently signs have been erected to historic houses (with a distinctive cryptogram); a similar programme should be instituted for churches.

Though regional tourist boards and local authorities could do much more for historic churches in their area, the church authorities themselves should take the initiative in calling meetings between clergy and ministers and the tourist boards to see what can be done. Many churches which are in need of funds for maintenance and repairs could raise much more from visitors. At Bradford-on-Avon, for example, Wiltshire, the sales of the guidebook to the perfect Saxon church pay for the costs of production, a caretaker and still leave hundreds of pounds a year over. One church on a Norfolk holiday route, according to Dominick Harrod in *Lincolnshire Churches*, has received £200 in the single month of August. A small, remote, almost private parish church in the park of a great house still earns enough, through a small charge for brass rubbing, to pay for church heating and lighting. The need here is for churches to invite gifts from visitors in a more positive way—to have a notice clearly stating what it costs to maintain and a special box marked "for repairs and maintenance". For while a Catholic or Hebrew visitor is unlikely to contribute to a box marked "church expenses" he may well want to support the church as a historic building.

One of the great assets of churches to tourism is that they are usually open all day and all the year round—unlike, say, country houses which are often open only on certain days even in the season, and then only in the afternoon. Ironically the very lack of admission charges and specific opening times is undoubtedly one reason why they are omitted from much tourist literature on places to visit. However, there is no reason why such literature should not say (as in the brass rubbing booklet mentioned above): "if locked, the key to be found at . . ." and "charge: left to the visitors generosity" or "donations to be placed in box marked fabric fund".

As tourism increases there is, alas, a growing problem of locked churches, particularly near industrial areas and motorways. In Wales many churches are now locked on Diocesan instructions against vandalism and arson. Elesewhere locked churches are sometimes a sign of indifference on the part of the incumbent or the congregation: certainly the number of locked churches has increased since the requirement to say matins daily, established in 1537, was waived in 1976—though in many cases the practice had lapsed long before. Whereas parish churches in England and Wales (both Anglican and Roman Catholic) have a long tradition of being regularly open, churches and chapels belonging to the free churches do not. Virtually the only time one can be sure of getting inside a nonconformist chapel is on a Sunday, and then often only just before or after a service. Indeed this is one main reason why nonconformist architecture is so undervalued, even unknown. A programme, therefore, needs to be set in motion to ensure that notices are placed in all churches or chapels of potential tourist interest saying where the key is available (preferably giving two options).

The accessibility of churches is the more important as more people (both British and foreign) take touring holidays, in preference to basing themselves on a single centre. A visit to two or three churches between each stop would take people off the principal roads and introduce them to delightful countryside they might not otherwise see, as well as bringing them into some of the most moving, fascinating and best preserved of all buildings to be found in Britain.

Greater promotion of churches could also play a vital part in encouraging foreign tourists to make repeat trips. For example, during their first stay in London most visitors will see the top 20 sights—including all those featured in BTA promotion abroad, and the promotion of a series of "lesser-known/little visited" landmarks could encourage them to come back. The promotion of lesser-known churches could also play a useful role in tourist management, particularly in London, helping to disperse people from the centre and to relieve congestion at places such as Westminster Abbey. The British Tourist Authority has already been pursuing such a policy.

Here there are opportunities to direct people to less visited but often fascinating parts of London, and to encourage half and whole day trips to places within a 100 miles radius. The London Borough of Tower Hamlets not only contains the Tower of London, one of London's top attractions, but a series of magnificent early-18th-century churches by Hawksmoor, as well as some spectacular Victorian churches. Co-operation between the local authority and the tourist board in making these attractions better known could attract tourist spending east of the city and help employment problems in a hard pressed borough. Similarly, church trails could be produced for parts of London where large numbers of hotels are situated: one obvious example is Kensington, which contains a series of sumptuous High Victorian churches; another is Heathrow Airport, where there is an extraordinary but little known group of small untouched medieval churches such as one would expect to find in a remote part of Sussex.

A number of Tourist Boards in 1976 and 1977 organized a fair for tour operators at which historic properties took stands. In 1976, 73 of these were taken by country houses, museums, local authorities, preservation societies (notably railway ones) but not a single church. Obviously it would be difficult in most cases to promote a church individually, but they could be promoted in groups, preferably in conjunction with other attractions in order to provide a day of mixed sightseeing. Recently the London Tourist Board took 50 coach operators on a trial visit to Richmond to see Ham House, Marble Hill and Orleans House—the latter being unknown to most of them. The visit was a great success, and as a result many are planning half-day excursions there. This idea could well be repeated in other parts of outer London with churches included prominently.

The attraction of churches to many tourists is not so much their architectural or historic interest but their celebrity value—who is buried there or has special associations with the church. For example, many Americans go to Battersea Parish Church because Benedict Arnold, the General who changed sides in the War of American Independence, is buried there. In the same way Chelsea Old Church is popular because Dickens was married there.

There is also a considerable potential for "pilgrimage holidays" on the model of those in Northumbria. Every year a great many people come to the north-west from north America (and other parts of Britain as well) on "pilgrimages" to look at early Quaker meeting houses there. These include not only Quakers, but many people claiming Quaker ancestry. This is inspired by the evident love the Friends have for their buildings, but it should be equally possible for the Methodists, for example, to organize pilgrimages "in the steps of John Wesley".

Tourist and church authorities, we believe, could to their mutual benefit develop a special programme of promoting tourism to churches, perhaps making it the theme of the very successful *années des châteaux* and *hôtels de ville* organized in Belgium. Such a programme should try to spread interest from parish churches to churches and chapels of all denominations and to direct people to Georgian and Victorian churches as well as to medieval ones. Such a programme could be a larger version of the joint British Tourist Authority/Heart of England Tourist Board marketing scheme for "the Undiscovered Marches". For this, 30,000 colour folders were produced in three languages and are distributed in target markets overseas.

In Scotland and Wales, chapels, churches and kirks have an important role to play in revealing a different and distinctive way of life and in offering an opportunity to depart from traditional routes and resorts.

The report *Tourism in Wales: a plan for the future* (1976) stresses the need to identify "buildings and places which may be suitable for tourism use"—Wales's ancient parish churches are an obvious candidate.

The same report also draws attention to two important sub-markets in the coach-tour sector which have general potential for historic places—and thus for churches. The first is the overseas coach tour ("Expenditure by these tourists is far higher than that associated with the traditional coach tour market"), and secondly the domestic senior-citizen coach tour, which "though generally lower-spending is far more amenable to seasonal dispersal".

Throughout Britain the promotion of churches we believe, has the particular attraction of providing a draw for the more educated higher-spending tourist and in helping to diffuse the impact of tourism both geographically and seasonally.

CHAPTER FIFTEEN

Churches and their Visitors

Figures of the number of visitors to churches are very rarely available. Very few churches charge admission fees, and seldom is anyone in attendance sufficiently regularly to keep a count. Most churches have a visitors' book, but there is still no means of measuring the proportion of people who sign it, and no attempt has been made to analyse the record on a comparative basis. This could be a worthwhile exercise as it would at least provide useful information of the numbers of overseas visitors to churches and the proportion of British residents who were clearly some distance from home. As a sample investigation we have written to the incumbents of a number of churches situated next to country houses open to the public, to assess the impact of visitors to the house on the church.

Almost all the churches experienced a considerable increase in the number of visitors when the house was open, but this did not necessarily mean an increase in takings in the collection box. Lanhydrock House, in Cornwall, had 52,000 visitors in 1976 and it is estimated that about one third of these also visited the church. Before the house was open the number of visitors to the church was probably not more than 1,000: last year the takings from the collection box were £734. More detailed figures were available from Gawsworth Hall, Cheshire (see table). These show a steady, though by no means dramatic increase.

Gawsworth Church: Income from Visitors

Year	*£*	*Names in Visitors Book*	*Number of Visitors to Hall*
1967	422	*c.* 4,480	Not Open
1968	446	*c.* 5,440	Hall open—no figures
1969	623	*c.* 10,000	" " " "
1970	616	*c.* 11,000	" " " "
1971	781	*c.* 9,200	46,079
1972	816	*c.* 11,200	57,211
1973	704	*c.* 7,400	50,084
1974	850	*c.* 7,000	54,226
1975	878	*c.* 8,900	50,220
1976	1,155	*c.* 9,000	53,980

Visitors to churches near country houses open to the public

House	*Admission*	*House Visitors*	*Increase when House Open*	*Box Takings £*	*Guide & PC*	*Church Open*	*Guiding*
Lanhydrock, Cornwall	70p	52,000	About one third	734	None	As house	
Hoar Cross Hall, Staffordshire	35p		Some	90	800–1,000	365 days a year	Yes
Sudeley, Gloucestershire		130,000		250		As house	
Lamport, Northants	35p		Great	25		Daily	
Sledmere, Humberside			Enormous	100	None	Daily	
Gawsworth, Cheshire	35p	50,100	Some	1,155	Notes free	Daily	Supervised
Hatfield, Hertfordshire	70p	131,600	Very significant	Some 100s		Daily	Vol. Guide
Kedleston, Derbyshire	40p		Yes	45% of annual income	None	As house	
Mapledurham, Oxfordshire	50p			325	Sold out	As house	
Dunster, Somerset	60p	85,600	Overcrowded already	1,000	20,000	Daily	
Berkeley, Gloucestershire	50p	99,000	Considerable	650		Daily	Yes
Sudbury, Derbyshire	70p	23,400	Yes	80	None	Daily	
Croft, Hereford and Worcester	50p		Yes	100	None	Daily	Yes
Skipton, N. Yorkshire	25p			400	3,000	Daily	Stewards
Rockingham, Northamptonshire	50p	34,200	Much	200 summer	None	As house	
Castle Ashby, Northamptonshire	50p	9,200	Yes	50		Daily	

Other churches, however, have found that visitors assumed that the church is "part of the show"—included on the ticket to the house. One incumbent actually found his takings down from £210 to £140: "the visit to the church" he said, "usually comes last on the tourists itinerary, their spending has been done at the house on entry tickets, guide books, refreshments, souvenirs, etc." The second table sets out some of our findings, and it is evident that even when takings are considerable they are still modest in the extreme in relation to the number of visitors.

There are a number of ways, however, in which churches could increase their revenue from visitors, without becoming overtly commercial or going so far as charging admission fees. First there should be a clearly marked "fabric box", quite distinct from general church expenses or missionary work, and also separate from sales of guidebooks or postcards. This should be accompanied by a crisp and well-presented statement of need. Many people—particularly those of other denominations or faiths—want to give to the church building, and it seems quite wrong that their contributions should increase the diocesan quota and be partially raked back into the Church's general expenses.

The availability of guidebooks varied considerably. Some, like Sandford Orcas, Dorset, produce a guidebook but do not envisage making a profit: at Lanhydrock, Cornwall, it was thought that any profit from producing a guidebook would be offset by a drop in takings in the collecting box. Dunster, Somerset, which sells about 20,000 illustrated leaflets of different kinds, does not reckon on any notable profit. At the other extreme Sandringham, Norfolk, sold 10,000 guide books a year, bringing in a profit of £1,000. At Skipton Church, Yorkshire, which is next to the castle, some 3,000 guidebooks a year are sold, bringing in between £100–£120. At Berkeley church, Gloucestershire, again next to the castle, profit from guidebooks and cards is about £200–£250 a year. Most country houses expect to make a profit of about 100% on the sale of guidebooks, and in some (though not all) churches there is decided profit potential in selling guidebooks. Finding the necessary capital can obviously be a problem, but where a church guide can also act as a village guide or local history there should be a possibility of obtaining help in the preparation, writing or production from a local authority, or indeed one of the new parish councils (as opposed to parochial church councils) which have some funds at their disposal for special projects.

Where churches are unattended some guidebooks or postcards are almost invariably taken without payment, which is obviously discouraging, but an increasing number of churches have someone present when there are visitors. During all bank holidays and festival periods the former incumbent at Berkeley "always spent most of the day in the church giving a brief talk on the main features of the building and its associations every 20–30 minutes". At Gawsworth, Cheshire, voluntary "church watchers" are on duty during the summer holiday, while at Hatfield, Hertfordshire, the church has a voluntary guide on duty every afternoon during the season, except Mondays when the house is closed. Visitors to Hoar Cross, Staffordshire, "are very appreciative of short guided tours . . . not too formal or stiff".

Guidebooks, leaflets and postcards have long been sold at churches, but now some parishes are considering how income can be increased through sales of gifts and souvenirs. Although this market has traditionally been considered beyond the pale, the success of the National Trust shops in producing goods of high quality, excellent design and in keeping with the place in which they are sold, opens a new line of thought. The average turnover in National Trust shops is now 40p per head, and half of this is probably profit. Churches could be developed crafts—the most engaging example of this is Worstead, Norfolk, where the village weavers are to found at work in the north aisle. Secondly, the church or the diocese could instigate its own buying organization, on the model of the National Trust shops, buying and commissioning goods in bulk. Churches, even more than the National Trust, have the ability to call on volunteers, making the potential profit margin all the greater. Certain major town churches, such as Tewkesbury Abbey, have produced their own highly successful souvenirs ranging from badges to a gold-plated replica of the city sword at £450—all of which have sold out.

Another promising source of revenue is the rapidly increasing popularity of brass rubbing. With fees ranging from 50p to £2 this can represent a significant source of revenue. Following the runaway success of the brass rubbing centre in the crypt of St James, Piccadilly, brass rubbing centres have opened in Gloucester Cathedral and Marlborough St Peter. In these centres the rubbings are made from replicas, and what emerges is the demand to rub not just local brasses but the best brasses from all over the country. The subject is as important as the design, rubbers are interested in historical figures: indeed one of the most popular brasses at St James, Piccadilly, is a memorial brass of William Shakespeare, which is not a replica but a new production.

CHAPTER SIXTEEN

Cathedrals

Control

The Cathedrals of England, Scotland and Wales are not an easy group of buildings to define. In England it is relatively simple: there are 42 mainland dioceses, all of which have a cathedral for the "cathedra" or throne of the Bishop and of these buildings nine are ancient cathedrals of the Old Foundation, that is from before the Reformation; eight are ancient cathedrals of the New Foundation, monastic in origin and refounded in the reign of Henry VIII; a handful (e.g. Ripon, Southwell) are major churches which became cathedrals of new dioceses in the 19th and 20th centuries; a further group (e.g. Wakefield, Newcastle) are "parish church cathedrals" of new dioceses which took a substantial and central parish church as the cathedral; and there is the small group of new buildings (e.g. Liverpool, Guildford and Coventry) and Bury St Edmunds where the late medieval nave by John Wastell has had added to it a new crossing, transepts and choir designed by Stephen Dykes Bower.

In addition to these there are the Roman Catholic cathedrals in England, the majority of them 19th-century buildings of a quality which cannot be said to place them in the highest rank—the exceptions being, undoubtedly, Arundel (by J. A. Hansom, 1868–69) and, pre-eminently, J. F. Bentley's Westminster Cathedral. The new Roman Catholic cathedrals of Liverpool and Clifton (Bristol) have attracted a good deal of attention and many visitors, and in both cases the furnishing and decoration of the building has been made the occasion for commissioning major works of art from artists of the calibre of Elizabeth Frink, Patrick Reyntiens, Simon Verity and Bryant Fedden. This is a trend, and a very welcome one, which may be said to have begun at Sir Basil Spence's Coventry Cathedral.

In Wales there are four ancient cathedrals (Llandaff, St David's, St Asaph's and Bangor): St David's is without question the most significant of these by comparison with the medieval English cathedrals, and a recent report on the cathedral and its precincts by Elisabeth Beazley and Martin Caroe has spotlighted the need to devise coherent and sensitive conservation policies—drawing in a wide variety of statutory and voluntary agencies—if the cathedral and its close are not to be swamped by the sheer press of visitors, and if visitors are to derive the maximum pleasure and value from their visit. Llandaff is a cathedral which received some of its distinctive character from the work of 19th-century architects, in particular J. P. Pritchard and J. P. Seddon, and in addition to a Rossetti altarpiece, it possesses one of the most striking 20th-century contributions to cathedral art and architecture in the form of Epstein's *Majestas*, incorporated into a brilliant design solution for the organ, and its tribune devised as part of the post-war reconstruction by the architect, George Pace.

It is in Scotland that the situation is most complex. There are ancient cathedrals of the splendour of Elgin which are now in ruins since abandonment at the time of the Scottish Reformation; there are cathedrals which have survived as great buildings (Edinburgh's High Kirk of St Giles, Glasgow, Aberdeen) but belonging to or in use by the Presbyterian Church of Scotland and no longer strictly speaking cathedrals: Glasgow, is crown property, maintained by the Council and St Magnus cathedral, Orkney, belongs to Orkney Island Council. The Episcopal Church in Scotland built cathedrals in the 19th century, and these include buildings of very considerable value such as William Butterfield's Cathedral of the Isles, Cumbrae and Sir George Gilbert Scott's Cathedrals in Edinburgh, Glasgow and Dundee.

Although the Bishop may have his "cathedra" in the cathedral, in England and Wales the governing body is the Dean and Chapter (or, for the parish church cathedrals, the Provost and Chapter or Cathedral Council). In Wales the cathedral buildings belong to the Representative Body of the Church in Wales, but in England the Dean and Chapter is a Corporation aggregate governed by Statutes, and their property is vested in them as a continuing corporate body.

Deans and Chapters have enjoyed such a long tradition of independence—independence of the Bishop and diocese, independence also from secular control—that it is neither surprising nor unreasonable to find that they prize it still. It is our view that cathedrals are to a large extent very responsibly cared for and administered—moreover, exhibiting signs of a vitality and wide appeal not easily found elsewhere—and this independence can be vigorously defended, up to a certain point. Not only have cathedrals enjoyed the same freedom from Ancient Monuments and Historic Buildings legislation that the parish churches enjoy, but they are also outside the control of the Faculty Jurisdiction, the Church's own system, as part of their inheritance of independence from the government of the diocese.

It would be untrue to suppose that cathedrals operate in a vacuum from which all else is excluded, so far as outside control over buildings is concerned. The Dean and Chapter's properties in and about the precincts of their cathedrals are subject to normal planning and (where appropriate) listed building consent. These include houses for the Dean and Canons, and frequently a cathedral school and other properties adding up in a number of instances—Norwich, Salisbury, Lichfield, Durham, Gloucester, Winchester, Canterbury, to name but the most obvious and substantial—to an ensemble of the greatest possible visual, historic and architectural value so that it is scarcely surprising that they are generally designated Outstanding Conservation Areas, with the additional control and possibilities of grant-aid which such designation brings. Ancient close walls, as at Peterborough and Chichester, may be scheduled as ancient monuments and, indeed, large areas of several cathedral closes are so scheduled. At St Albans where this is so, a public inquiry took place in early 1977 into the Dean and Chapter's proposal to build a Pilgrims' Centre on the site of the long-vanished Norman chapter house. All this is to make the point that in dealing with their properties Deans and Chapters are well acquainted with questions of architectural control over buildings or groups of major architectural and historic importance, and in places, e.g. Gloucester and Salisbury, close collaboration and partnership with the Historic Buildings Council has resulted in the up-grading and repair of many Dean and Chapter properties with help from outside sources. The current 1976–77 work in the Vicars' Close at Wells is being financed jointly by the Church Commissioners as landlords, the Dean and Chapter who own the Vicars' Hall and Chapel, the County Council and the Department of the Environment: an admirable example of fruitful collaboration between the secular and the ecclesiastical arms in the context of cathedral precincts. Another example of such collaboration is the repair of the oriel windows and the cleaning and conservation of the superb early-16th-century ceiling in the Prior's day room in the pele tower of the Deanery at Carlisle. The DoE and the English Tourist Board contributed approximately half the cost, and generous grants were made by the Pilgrim Trust and from other charitable sources, the remainder being found from Chapter funds. The room is open to the public and used for a variety of meetings.

With regard to the cathedral church itself, however, Deans and Chapters are quite unfettered except by their own resources of common sense, innate conservatism and also usually lack of funds. This has led to instances—albeit rare—where informed public opinion and authoritative advice has been set aside—the ruthless removal of almost all the

19th-century furnishings (reredos, screen, paving) from the choir at Salisbury, the removal of the spectacular Scott-Skidmore screen from Hereford (but not, as at Salisbury, its destruction), and the repainting of bosses in the western bays of the vault of the nave at Exeter are examples of such independence which have resulted in controversy and criticism from amongst informed and normally sympathetic observers.

There are three ways in which it might be said that control is exercised. In the first place a Dean and Chapter cannot easily afford to forfeit public support by pursuing policies which produce protests in the local or national press and could certainly stem the flow of money to an appeal. In the second place cathedral appeals (whether in the raising of huge occasional sums, or regular sums, as at Norwich, York, Lincoln and Chichester, and on a lesser scale almost everywhere by Cathedral Friends) depend for their success to a considerable degree on the energetic involvement of local prominent lay people. The tendency is for such key people to insist on the appeal money being paid into a special trust fund, whose terms inhibit the spending of the money so raised on "housekeeping" or other aspects of cathedral repair, however praiseworthy. For instance, at Wells, the current appeal is for the west front and the high vaults *only* and the money raised thereby cannot be used for other purposes. This, in our view, is eminently sensible as it protects the Dean and Chapter from suspicion and wonderfully concentrates the minds both of those responsible for raising the money on the one hand and for spending it on the other.

The third element of control is exercised, albeit with a light touch, by the Cathedrals Advisory Committee which exists under the umbrella of the Council for Places of Worship of the General Synod and is to that extent an "official" Church body, sharing its Secretariat with the CPW. The CAC was set up in the late 1940s, at the request of the Deans and Provosts, and reference to it—in spite of efforts to make it mandatory—is voluntary. There is some evident confusion as to what should or should not be considered necessary to refer to the CAC, and here perhaps the Committee itself could help by issuing guidelines on the lines of a Department of the Environment circular. We recommend, indeed, that this should be done, and that the CAC should take energetic steps to persuade Deans and Chapters that the present informal system is only a partial reassurance to the community at large. Everything, in our view, that would otherwise be subject to listed building control or faculty jurisdiction should be notified to the CAC who could then, like the Royal Fine Art Commission, decide what to call in.

The present CAC, under the Chairmanship of Sir Peter Scarlett, has a distinguished and widely representative active membership which includes the Presidents of the Society of Antiquaries and of the Royal Academy, art historians (including the Directors of the Victoria and Albert Museum and the Courtauld Institute), an architectural historian, a church archaeologist, a senior practising architect and a well-known practising artist. In order to function effectively the Committee needs to be kept up to strength; so many proposals affecting cathedrals demand a site visit, and a visiting delegation, and the recent appointment of a wider spectrum of members is to be warmly welcomed in consequence. The appointment of regional sub-committees has also been suggested.

The CAC is consulted by Welsh cathedrals from time to time but these otherwise look chiefly to their relationship with the Representative Body. Three of the cathedrals in Wales have the same cathedral architect, from a London-based firm with a unique experience of caring for cathedrals and a large number of parish churches through three generations. *Continuity of care* is important, in cathedrals as in parish churches.

In Scotland the situation varies according to the ownership (Crown Church of Scotland, Episcopal Church in Scotland), and it is of interest to note in the 1971–72 Report of the HBC for Scotland that a grant of £15,000 was made for urgent repairs to St Magnus Cathedral, Orkney, the HBC explaining itself thus:

> "It has been the policy of successive Governments since 1953, when HBCs were first set up, that repair grants should not be made for churches in use *for such buildings were not subject to planning control.* St. Magnus Cathedral is, however, owned by Kirkwall Town Council and the Secretary of State was satisfied that, in this case, the building was under public control."

There is only space for two brief comments about this: first of all cathedrals *are* subject to planning control, but are only *not* subject to listed building control. Secondly, it must be doubted whether ownership by a town council—indeed any form of public or private ownership—by itself protects a building from insensitive repair, without creatively deployed outside involvement and advice from appropriate sources.

Here we must introduce, however briefly, the topic of the cathedral architect: in the Church of England such a professional appointment is provided for in the Statutes, and taken as a whole the cathedral architects of England may be said to constitute a remarkable cadre of skills in the conservation of historic buildings. The late George Pace (who was good-humouredly dubbed the "Gilbert Scott of the 20th century" on account of the extent of his cathedral practice) wrote that ". . . one of the prime functions of a cathedral architect is to act as the conductor of an orchestra: to assess and advise, all against an unrivalled knowledge of his cathedral and an all-embracing knowledge of the art of architecture, the art and aesthetic of restoration, ecclesiology, archaeology and the like. The cathedral architect bears in mind all that is due to the cathedral:

as the House of God
as part of the *Opus Dei*
as having a very special high-level Aesthetic
as being beyond monetary value and part of a great heritage
as not being the sole responsibility of this generation: the time-scale for certain repairs will spread over four generations
as being a living building to be altered and adapted as may be necessary, but always at the appropriate high aesthetic level"

A possible danger, in our view, is that too high a view of his role—and it is a noble one, as expressed by George Pace—on the part of the cathedral architect might lead to a reluctance on occasion to consider seriously the import of other and equally well qualified judgements. In this connection we cannot commend too warmly the example of the Wells West Front Committee which, set up by the CAC and the Dean and Chapter as a council of "all the talents" available in England on stone decay problems and 13th-century sculpture, spent more than two years producing a satisfactory basis for the Appeal which would satisfy conflicting philosophies of repair and different technical approaches to the problems. The really difficult repair problems which confront a Dean and Chapter and their architects are immensely complex and we have not in this country devised a satisfactory method for dealing with them: listed building control, or any other form of "control", is not *per se* going to be satisfactory. The Wells experiment (in which the Dean, the Master of the Fabric, the architects, the master mason, the art historian, the sculpture restorer, the scientists and so forth, all sat down together and over a long period) looks like providing a useful model for the future and we would like to see it used elsewhere for dealing with special problems.

Tourism

It is not easy to obtain reliable information on the number of visitors to cathedrals, except for Salisbury where the sale of tickets in the six summer months provides a fairly precise check: in 1975 there were 550,000 visitors to Salisbury cathedral, and in 1976 600,000. Westminster Abbey, St Paul's and Canterbury Cathedral all give figures in the region of 3 million visitors annually, and it is evident on a a most superficial glance that these three buildings are sometimes overcrowded: the nave of Canterbury on many days during the summer resembles nothing so much as Wembley on Cup Final day, and many of the visitors are clearly from abroad. York estimates that it has approximately two million visitors annually, but so vast is the Minster that the feeling of being overcrowded is apparently rare. There are two issues therefore to be examined in this chapter. Why, in the first place, is it worthwhile singling out a cathedral, or a group of cathedrals, as is quite a popular combination for a visit; and how can the cathedrals draw upon their staggering visitor potential in such a way that the cathedral itself benefits, and in such a way that the cathedral is not swamped by the sheer pressure of numbers and the visitors are able to enjoy themselves and derive the maximum benefit—spiritual and aesthetic included—from their visit?

As a further introduction to this it may be worth recalling that, unlike country houses, cathedrals are open every day of the year as part of their primary purpose. This may be held to account in part for the higher number of visitors they have when compared to country houses (John Cornforth's *Country Houses in Britain—can they survive?* BTA, £1.50) distinguished between essentially family houses visited by a small number of people, houses attracting 40,000 to 50,000 a year; houses, primarily "show places", attracting 70,000 visitors a year or more; and a handful of houses, including Beaulieu, Longleat, Warwick and Woburn, where "a combination of a fortunate location and fully commercial management have put them in a sub-group of their own").

In cathedral visitor terms, Wells, with its appeal, perhaps, to the more discerning visitor and its poor communications—the nearest main line railway station being in Castle Cary, 14 miles away—is one of the weakest brethren among the great ancient cathedrals, with an estimated 75,000 to 100,000 visitors per annum. This immediately puts it in the "big league" by comparison with country houses and the comparison is instructive.

Possible reasons for the large number of visitors to cathedrals include:

1. The sheer quality of the buildings—simply to mention Salisbury, Durham, York, Canterbury—is sufficient to remind us of the level of medieval achievement in building them, and in creating the wealth of medieval or later stained glass, woodwork, sculpture and metalwork which adorn them.

2. They are, on the whole, situated in natural centres—Canterbury, Exeter, Bristol, Norwich, York.

3. They continue to have a significant role as a focus for the diocese

and county, and this must in itself account for many local visits. Moreover, as reported from Durham, the cathedral is visited again and again by people living in the locality.

4. It is an admitted phenomenon that visitors to stately homes prefer houses which are lived in to those that are not; so it is with cathedrals—the more visitors they receive the more they seem ready to respond, and to be "alive", and the more alive they are the more visitors they attract. The splendidly maintained choral services are often very well attended, and a tangible reminder that worship lies at the centre of a cathedral's *raison d'être*.

5. Some cathedrals—Truro, Exeter, St Davids, Salisbury, Winchester, Norwich, Carlisle, Chichester, Canterbury—are so situated that they form ready made "wet day" activities for the tourists who throng through the cathedral city, and these cathedrals report a marked increase in visitors on days where families are obviously being denied a visit to the seaside, the New Forest, or whatever it may be.

6. The recognition element. Most of us have grown up knowing all our lives about York, Salisbury, St Paul's and Canterbury. To visit them when opportunities occur is therefore a natural, almost inevitable, consequence in a way which is not true of country houses.

7. Cathedrals are not only centres of artistic excellence but of spiritual power: the man who would feel embarrassed and lost if it ever occurred to him to visit his parish church frequently finds the great scale of the cathedral all-welcoming and something touches him and moves him about the values which the cathedral has stood and represented for so long.

8. The procession of choir and clergy to sing Evensong may take some visitors by surprise, but it is remarkable what a large concourse of people sits in the Quire for the service and takes evident pleasure in the beauty of the music and the spoken liturgy, married to superb architecture.

9. Not only is there generally no entry fee to cathedrals (except at Salisbury where it is, however, voluntary), leaving financial support to individual awareness and response, but there is no sense of pressure, no hard-sell and no time limit. You have to leave when the cathedral closes for the night, but otherwise the place is your own.

Reasons such as these, some tangible some less so, may help to account for the enormous popularity of cathedrals.

In addition to the "unorganized" visitor and activity there are special attractions—festivals, musical or dramatic; exhibitions; services; flower festivals—and organized visits with a special purpose. Here again, location may be significant and at St Albans, for example, the

600 or so annual school visits, some of them admittedly from quite a considerable distance, the accessibility from London and the populous character of the two counties of Hertfordshire and Bedfordshire are significant. But, in addition, the cathedral staff has developed over the years a particular ministry towards visiting children, culminating in the annual Youth Festival, when the whole vast floor space is taken over by groups of children and young people. Whether for old or young, a cathedral has a special attraction as a "momentary monastery"—not quite a withdrawal from the world but an opportunity to relax, step aside from ordinary distractions, if only for a few minutes. To quote the Dean of Norwich again: "There is a new spirit, more courageous than 25 years ago. Cathedrals now take risks and arouse opposition; the Roman Catholic Bishop of Derry has been shouted down in the High Kirk of St Giles in Edinburgh, the Home Secretary has been booed in Chichester Cathedral. . . . Buildings can be shrines and places of inspiration, and the Close an 'Open' where everyone is welcome."

The cathedral has also an educational role, in the broadest sense, and we have been interested to see ways in which this responsibility is being tackled. From the earliest times the cathedrals have been centres of learning, and many of them still have fine—in some cases quite outstandingly fine—libraries. The library at Lincoln was designed by Sir Christopher Wren; that at Winchester has occupied the same room since the 12th century. The same sense of continuity is felt at Exeter, with its collection of Anglo-Saxon manuscripts, at Canterbury, at York, at Durham, at Salisbury (which has one of the three copies of Magna Carta, two of them indeed belonging to cathedrals, the other being at Lincoln). With treasures like these these cathedrals can scarcely fail to attract visitors, and yet we feel that in some places cathedrals have been slow to make their treasures accessible to the scholar on the one hand, and to the general public on the other. Problems understandably exist, security and finance among them, but a more determined will to succeed and financial assistance from some regional tourist boards would help resolve a number of them. Durham and Exeter have arrangements with their respective universities for the supervision of their libraries, so that professional staff are available on a full time basis at no cost to the Dean and Chapter; Winchester displays its treasures at regular hours; at Gloucester the student can arrange to work on precious manuscripts and incunabula, and they will be placed in the city library, with whom the Dean and Chapter have an excellent relationship, so that they will not be read unsupervised; at Canterbury the Dean and Chapter library is magnificently appointed with its own full time staff. At the other end of the scale are the cathedrals which have sold all or parts of their collections, or where a Canon Librarian—not necessarily appointed for his sympathy with learning or his knowledge of books—is only able to allow access to the library after prior permission by letter or telephone.

A positive approach is needed so that treasures become not only accessible at reasonable hours but also, if possible, revenue-producing in their own right through the sale of postcards, publication of facsimile editions, and so forth. It is extremely encouraging that the Dean and Chapter of Ripon, having come almost to the brink of selling their last remaining Caxton, have decided instead to form a display area for the greatest treasures of their library and to retain the Caxton *Boethius* as a centre piece.

We have already mentioned the formation of a treasury at Ripon, in the Saxon Crypt of St Wilfrid. The excellently lit display of ancient silver adds a valuable dimension to this remarkable series of chambers, which—for all their antiquity and significance—were less likely to have been appreciated by the generality of visitors before. The other treasuries, established with generous financial help from the Goldsmiths' Company, have also been mentioned; and the crypt exhibitions at York and Canterbury add immeasurably to any visitor's appreciation of the history and significance of the cathedral.

However, Norwich is so far the only cathedral to have established a Visitors' Centre as such, imaginatively sited in the upper west walk of the cloisters (previously inaccessible to visitors), incorporating an exhibition which covers:

(a) "The Building of the Cathedral."
(b) "The Vision Removed", dealing with the changes in religion, the Bible in English enabling everyone to try to be his own priest and minister, the abolition of the monastery and the conversion of the cathedral (largely for an enclosed religious community) into a building for the city and county.
(c) "The difficulties about any vision of God today, the challenge of the Third World, violence, and so forth".

The Norwich Visitors' Centre also includes an audio-visual room, devoted to a skilful presentation of the cathedral in slides and tapes, and a room for coffee and relaxation.

Cathedrals contain many treasures which could be shown to advantage in a museum-like setting, either in the cathedral itself or one of the ancillary buildings. Examples include the remarkable Romanesque carvings in Canterbury and Chichester, the sculptures in the north-west tower room at Lichfield, the archaeological finds at Winchester and many more. We feel that there is ample material in a number of cathedrals for museums related to the cathedral such as the *Museo del' Opera del Duomo* frequently encountered in Italy. However, it should not be thought that Continental practice is necessarily better than ours; at Rouen in 1975 when a party of three from the Wells West Front Committee asked to see the spectacular reliquaries and textiles in the treasury they were told they were the first to do so for eight years—but that only proves the point that if the public are not allowed to know of the existence of such treasures, except in remote journals, there is not likely to be much pressure to see them.

There may occasionally be opportunities for cathedrals to offer hospitality to outside collections in terms of space, and we draw attention to the establishment of a Stained Glass Museum at Ely. This ought to be an additional attraction to visitors, particularly as it provides access to a part of the cathedral previously inaccessible.

Hospitality, like learning, is something cathedrals have inherited from their partly monastic origins, and *The Times* on September 20, 1975, advised its readers that day-time visitors to Durham "should make tracks for the cathedral, where more than spiritual sustenance is now provided. Discreetly tucked away in a 13th-century crypt under the cloisters is an attractively converted self-service restaurant, recently opened under the combined auspices of the Dean and Chapter and a local catering firm." We can only hope that more cathedrals may follow Durham's example, for which there are good medieval precedents. At the same time we recognize that it is lack of capital rather than lack of will which holds back a number of cathedrals; and, large as these buildings are, it is surprisingly difficult to find the kind of space which was so happily available at Durham. Sometimes a house in the Close may be the answer, as with Centre 71 in Norwich, and at Canterbury the Plumbery is being converted into a Pilgrims' Centre for organized parties.

Cathedrals have equally a long tradition as centres for festivals. The medieval festivities around Christmas which produced the topsy-turvy situation of the Boy Bishop and the choristers taking over the cathedral, and the splendour of medieval music and liturgy, may be seen as the progenitors of this. The Three Choirs Festival, which began in 1767 and continued to rotate between Gloucester, Hereford and Worcester cathedrals, is the oldest established music festival in the world. Not only liturgical music, and not only classics of the cathedral repertoire, but the commissioning and performance of new works which have sometimes been of outstanding quality, have been features of the festival since the early days. The foundation of this festival is the professional cathedral choir, whose survival is of the highest importance as an integral, and deservedly popular, part of our English cultural heritage. To Pope Paul VI, the English cathedrals represent something very special in the achievement of the nation, and their choirs, he remarked, "sing like angels".

It would surely be otiose to enumerate more than a sample of the musical festivals that take place, or partly take place, in cathedrals. Winchester, Salisbury and Chichester have fairly recently taken a leaf out of the Three Choirs Festival in the West Midlands with their Southern Cathedrals Festival. In addition to the Southern Cathedrals Festival, Chichester now has its own Festival based primarily on the cathedral and as successful and ambitious as those at Bath or Cambridge. Wells Cathedral gives hospitality once a year to a concert which is part of the Bath Festival, Ely to the Cambridge Festival, York Minster to the triennial York Festival, and so on. There can scarcely be a cathedral which does not have a regular series of organ recitals. Birmingham cathedral, an elegant 18th-century building by Thomas Archer in the centre of the city, provides a home for the Birmingham Bach Society Choir; the Episcopal Cathedral of St Mary in Edinburgh is used during the Edinburgh International Festival. St Albans Abbey, under its enterprising organist Peter Hurford, has a biennial organ festival lasting a fortnight which attracts organists—competitors and listeners alike—from all over the world. Examples could be multiplied almost indefinitely.

The cathedral precincts of Salisbury, Winchester and Chichester have all served as the setting for major outdoor exhibition of the sculpture of Henry Moore; Dame Barbara Hepworth's *Crucifixion* stands south-west of the cathedral at Salisbury on that matchless sea of green lawn; the retiring Dean of Chichester, Walter Hussey, has made a notable contribution to the field of contemporary art by his commissions for the cathedral—the John Piper tapestries forming a reredos, a Graham Sutherland altarpiece in a side chapel, a lectern, pulpit, altar rails and door handles by Geoffrey Clarke and vestments designed by Ceri Richards.

On a more popular level cathedrals have staged some of the most spectacular flower festivals ever held—which not only have the advantage of involving many people in the making of them—but draw enormous numbers of visitors.

Finance

Up until the time of the reforming movement of the 1830s and 1840s which led to the establishment of the Ecclesiastical Commissioners to hold and administer the ancient endowments of the Church (except for glebe property, which has only recently been centralized by the *Endowment and Glebe Measure* approved by Parliament in 1976) the Deans and Chapters and the small army of Prebendaries enjoyed for the most part fairly substantial (and indeed in some cases enormous) revenues. In addition they were generally wealthy men in their own right, and it is not unusual to read of Deans and Canons after the Restoration or during the 18th and early 19th centuries paying for major restorations, or major new furnishings, out of their own pocket.

The whole point of centralizing the Church's ancient endowments was to redivide them more equally than the accidents of history had done, and the Ecclesiastical Commissioners (now united with Queen Anne's Bounty to become the Church Commissioners for England) were highly successful and scrupulously fair-minded in achieving this. In taking over capitular revenues the Commissioners undertook in perpetuity to meet the needs of certain "living agents"—that is to say the Deans and two of the residentiary Canons look to the Commissioners for their own stipends and the provision of a house. The total number of residentiary Canons varies from place to place. So the Church Commissioners continue to this day a generous, indeed sometimes lavish, expenditure on Deaneries and residentiaries' houses when they need repair or reconstruction, but make no provision for the cathedral church.

There are, naturally enough in so diverse an organization as the Church of England, exceptional situations. Durham, for instance, has an enviable financial independence through having retained considerable wealth from lands (including coal mines) and investments in Dean and Chapter hands. Southwell, which became a cathedral only in 1884, has been maintained for the Chapter until recently by the Church Commissioners; the agreement has now come to an end, and the 1975–76 Report of the Friends records that ". . . the programme of restoration of the exterior stonework carried out by the Church Commissioners was nearly finished, although the need for restoration work would continue, as a glance at the North Porch would show. The Provost said that the Cathedral Council had decided that a major appeal would be necessary and that preparations had already begun. He drew attention to the fact that the Minster had very little capital indeed and almost nothing compared to some of the old cathedrals; whereas the Friends of other Cathedrals are a great help, in Southwell they are an essential means of providing what could otherwise not have been carried out."

Something of the desperation which can be detected in some cathedral quarters may be gauged from the same Report, which points out that the effect of inflation includes the steep increase in ". . . the heating bill which had been £2,052 for the first quarter of 1976, which sum was £200 more than all the general collection for the previous year". The Dean and Chapter of Wells have been obliged by their financial circumstances to institute in 1976 payment for entry to the eastern parts of the cathedral. It needs to be stated emphatically that such developments are not the result of inactivity or mismanagement on the part of the cathedral, but derive essentially from the fact that, with resources no greater than those of a thriving parish church, the Chapter have to provide for the care of one of the largest and most elaborate buildings (in, say, the top 25) in England. The cathedral appeal at Wells, as we have mentioned, is for the west front and the high vaults—mostly for the west front—but even if it is wholly successful (and the appeal is already, at current prices, for £300,000 less than is known to be needed following the well-founded advice of the fund-raisers) the appeal is bound to be a disincentive to raising income for other aspects of cathedral maintenance. Roof coverings, lead-glazing and masonry need continuous unremitting patient attention on all such old buildings if the extremes of neglect and over-restoration are to be avoided.

In the discussions between church and state on state aid for historic churches in use it has been argued for the government that cathedrals do not self-evidently require financial help since cathedral appeals have continued to be exceptionally successful (York Minster raised £2 million, admittedly for an unprecedented crisis in the foundations of the central tower; St Paul's £3 million; and Canterbury is well on the way towards its own £3 million). It could well be equally argued that, with the addition of Westminster Abbey (a Royal Peculiar, in a like category with St George's Chapel, Windsor), these three cathedrals are perhaps the only ones capable of raising such huge sums. Moreover, the "Stop-Go" repair policies produced by dependence upon periodic large appeals are notoriously ill-advised not only for the buildings themselves but for the specialist craftsmen involved. In the case of the cathedrals themselves the temptation is always to do work—e.g. more stone replacement, than is strictly necessary—on the grounds that you never know how long it may be before it is possible to scaffold the cathedral again, and it is cheaper to do it now while you have the money. So, not slowly but too rapidly, the all important authenticity of the building may be eroded. At the same time, the Dean and Chapter will probably find it increasingly difficult to pay for the size of workforce established at the height of the appeal: after two or three years, St Paul's had to lay off a substantial number of masons and carvers, dissipating valuable and hard-won skills, because there was no longer—on account of inflation—the money to pay for them.

Black Chapel, North End, Essex. A rare, entirely timber-framed, medieval chapel, with priest's house attached (Christopher Dalton)

West Walton, Norfolk. One of the most sumptuous Early English parish churches anywhere in England—almost everything that remains dates from 1240. The completely detached bell-tower is an unusual feature (*Christopher Dalton*)

Tatenhill, Staffordshire. Medieval church and early Georgian rectory (Christopher Dalton)

Martock, Somerset. The great roofs of the West Country and of East Anglia are among the supreme splendours of our parish churches. Martock, sumptuously panelled and decorated, has recently been repaired (George H. Hall)

Baptist Chapel, Tewkesbury, Gloucestershire. Dating from 1618 and one of the earliest dissenting chapels in the country, it is now being restored by the local authority (National Monuments Record)

Congregational Church, Saltaire, West Yorkshire. Built in 1858–59 by Lockwood and Mawson, it has a stately interior which recalls the council chambers of contemporary town halls and is distinctive from the increasingly serious Gothic of Anglican churches in the 1850s (National Monuments Record)

Buckingham Baptist Chapel, Clifton, Avon. Built in 1842 by R. S. Pope in a forceful style influenced by French Gothic and on a college chapel plan. Initially an intrusion into the stucco street of elegant houses, it is now a significant element in the townscape on its own terms (National Monuments Record)

Jireh Chapel, Lewes, East Sussex. A representative example of late 18th or early 19th century chapel building using domestic elements—a coloured porch, glazing bars, and Adamesque circular motif (Christopher Dalton)

Methodist Church, Redruth, Cornwall (1864). *A giant order gives it the grandeur of a baroque church in Rome* (National Monuments Record)

Former Baptist Chapel, Belvoir Lane, Leicester. "Pork Pie" chapel designed by J. Harison now an Adult Educational Centre (National Monuments Record)

Bramhope chapel, near Leeds, West Yorkshire. A remarkable untouched puritan chapel dating from 1649 with the pulpit on the middle of the long side—a characteristic of early dissenting meeting houses. After years of disuse, the chapel was beautifully restored by Wharfedale Rural District Council (National Monuments Record)

Capel Salem, Senghennydd Mid Glamorgan (1899). Rugged Celtic vernacular (John Hilling)

The Chapel at Stonor Park, Oxfordshire. Stonor is one of the three places in England where Mass has been said according to the Roman Catholic rite without interruption through the centuries (Country Life)

St Mark's Unitarian Church, Castle Street, Edinburgh. Spectacular pulpit and reading desk on a dais in a church of 1834–35 by David Bryce (Royal Commission on Ancient Monuments, Scotland)

Rosskeen Church, Highland (Ross and Cromarty). 18th-century pulpit approached by twin flights of curving stairs (Royal Commission on Ancient Monuments, Scotland)

The Chapel at Burghley House, Northamptonshire. Most major country houses have, or had, chapels with handsome furniture for the daily worship of the household, a practice which often continued well into this century (Country Life)

Congregational Chapel, Roxton, Bedfordshire (1808). A most unusual and delightful design, thatched with a tree trunk verandah; interior with open-backed benches, west gallery, and family pew (Christopher Dalton)

All Saints, Isleworth, Greater London. Memorial to Sir Orlando Gee, d. 1705, a baroque monument of spectacular quality with a vigorous portrait bust and a fulsome epitaph (Duncan McNeil)

Cromarty Parish Church, Highland (Ross and Cromarty). Pews and galleries remain untouched since the late 18th century in this T-plan church (Royal Commission on Ancient Monuments, Scotland)

Burford, Oxfordshire. Monument to Christopher Kempster, one of the team of outstanding craftsmen deployed by Wren in the City of London (Country Life)

Catholic Chapel at Brough Hall, North Yorkshire. The estate continued in Roman Catholic hands and in the 19th century a substanting chapel was built in the grounds, to which was brought this sturdy and probably 12th-century font ornamented with carved ropework (Country Life)

Staplehurst, Kent. 12th-century door furniture is often under-appreciated and is nowhere more curious and striking than here with its representation of a shoal of fishes, a cross in a circle, a boat, and what appears to be a species of flying fish (Jane Geddes)

St James, Tong, West Yorkshire. Many Pennine churchyards are paved with large, boldly carved memorial slabs. The quality of the carving and the variety of lettering are among the special joys of churches and churchyards (National Monuments Record)

All Saints, Lewes, East Sussex. A romantic town churchyard. The church is now redundant and an alternative use is hoped for (*National Monuments Record*)

St Ann, St Peter's Square, Manchester. A town churchyard which is a peaceful oasis for Manchester's citizens and the only place in the centre of the city where wild life can survive. The church itself is an enterprising early 18th-century essay in provincial baroque (*Duncan McNeil*)

St Mary, Walton, Liverpool. The churchyard during clearance of the gravestones. Removals such as these destroy unique historical evidence in the form of inscriptions and sacrifice centuries of continuity in craftsmanship (*H. Ainscough*)

St Matthew, Upper Clapton, London. The reredos. The handsome church by Francis Dollman was gutted by fire caused by arson in 1976 and has subsequently been demolished: some of the furnishings were rescued for re-use elsewhere but much fine carving was destroyed (*National Monuments Record*)

John Street Church, Glasgow. This handsome classical building by J. T. Rochead (1859) is now disused and in poor repair. The basement is used for social work but the future of the church is a matter of serious concern on account of the quality of its plasterwork and furnishings (*Royal Commission on Ancient Monuments, Scotland*)

Cunninghame Free Church, Glasgow. This highly individual Gothic church, built in 1897–98 by H. and D. Barclay, was used for a time as a cash and carry store but is now disused and heavily vandalized (Royal Commission on Ancient Monuments, Scotland)

Renfield Free Church, Glasgow, by James Brown (1849). Though shops were incorporated from the start, the church stood on a valuable corner site and was demolished for redevelopment in the 1960s (*National Monuments Record, Scotland*)

Coade stone monument to Sir William Hillman (date 1800) from St James, Hampstead Road, London, lent to the Victoria and Albert Museum after demolition of the church in the 1960s

St Ruan Major, Cornwall. Abandoned and now ruinous (Christopher Dalton)

Babingley Church, Norfolk. A survey carried out for the Council for British Archaeology and the diocese, by the Norfolk Archaeology Unit suggests that one church in every eight is in some stage of ruin (Christopher Dalton)

Corpusty, Norfolk. Several attempts have been made to rescue and repair this fine medieval church, but the problem so far remains intractable (Christopher Dalton)

St Clement Sheepscar, Leeds, West Yorkshire. This had a wealth of rich carving, and good glass. Gutted by arson soon after it was declared redundant and demolished in 1976. Many urban churches suffer brutal attacks during the "waiting period" which follows the declaration of redundancy under the Pastoral Measure *(National Monuments Record)*

Countess of Huntingdon's Chapel at Evington, Leicestershire (1837). The Chapel, in a delightful early Gothic Revival vein, shows the impoverishment which has resulted from the demolition of the manse, the building of a mean low brick wall, loss of mature trees, etc. (National Monuments Record)

Stoer Church, Highlands (Sutherland), by Thomas Telford 1829. Characteristic long communion tables in a now abandoned church (Royal Commission on Ancient Monuments, Scotland)

Former Methodist Chapel at Eckington, Derbyshire. Demolished in 1977, though alternative uses had been suggested (Naticnal Monuments Record)

Former Unitarian Chapel, Devonport, Plymouth, Devon. Now a public house, with the visual appeal of the building intelligently exploited (National Monuments Record)

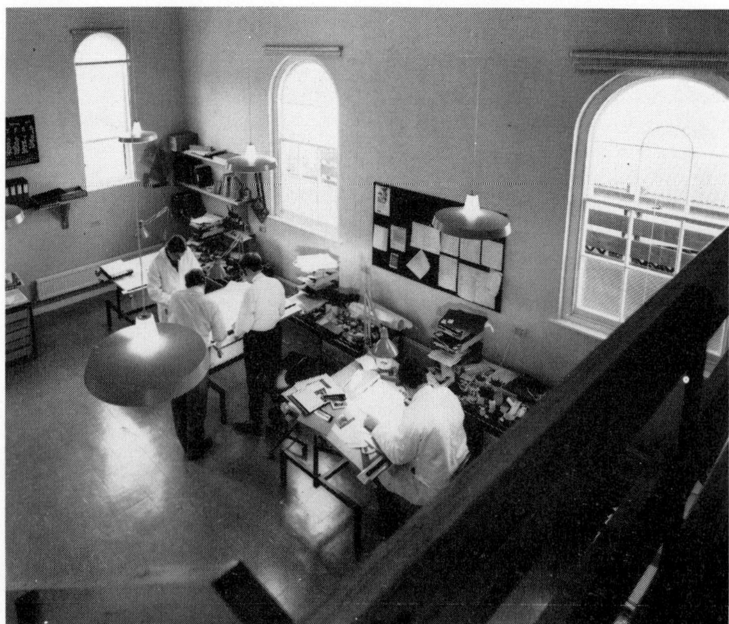

Former Nonconformist Chapel in Yorkshire. Now the office of Method Designs, it was converted with the help of the Council for Small Industries in Rural Areas (COSIRA)

Holy Trinity, Colchester, Essex. Refitted as a museum of country life and crafts in 1975, after a long period in which the church had stood derelict and abandoned. Structural changes have been kept to a minimum and the "teaching" aspects of the display have been well thought out (Colchester Museums)

that voluntary giving in the offertory boxes more than compensated. Today, however, public attitudes are different and the secularized family who cheerfully pay 75p a head to visit a "stately home" imagine, very often, that if a cathedral charges nothing for admission it must be because "they" or the state can perfectly well look after it for themselves. Nevertheless, even if the Salisbury scheme is voluntary and the number of actual complaints is small, it is our impression that charging for admission to the whole cathedral is sometimes resented—especially by Christians, who regard the cathedral primarily as a place of worship—and derogates from the successful impact of the building on the visitor. A cathedral *is* something more than a stately home, or a spectacle: it is the "House of God", and (as it continues to be for many) the "Gate of Heaven". Many uncommitted people feel moved when they enter a cathedral, people who would never enter their parish church: it is not simply the architecture which moves them but also the sense of continuity, the apprehension (however faint) of the never-ceasing *Opus Dei*, and the stance which a cathedral takes up against materialism, impermanence, superficiality, smallness. This is something infinitely worth safeguarding, and in countries where a palpably "Ministry of Works" attitude prevails in the care of great religious buildings it is evident that something is lost, however difficult it may be to define.

2. *Charging for admission to selected parts of cathedrals.* This, we feel, is a much more acceptable option and as we have said there is a long tradition in many cathedrals for charging admission to go up towers or descend into crypts. Charges could often be higher than they are (it costs 50p to go up the west tower at Ely, but 20p is quite common still) and well-organized tours promoted. At Salisbury a very well conducted tour up to the base of the spire costs £1 per head; and at York Minster, where the Dean and Chapter employ a Tourist Officer, the Superintendent of the Cathedral Works has a notice entitled *Conducted Visits to Parts of York Minster not normally shown to members of the public* which shows that such a demand exists. One of the difficulties encountered in meeting such a demand is the high cost to the cathedral of staff salaries. We feel, nevertheless, that cathedrals could be more imaginative in promoting tours with good guides of their own, especially to normally inaccessible parts of the cathedral, and also that they could reasonably take steps to deter "private" tour organizers who exploit a cathedral visit and make no contribution to its maintenance.

3. *Charging for admission to treasuries, museums and special exhibitions.* This seems to us entirely reasonable, indeed highly desirable. Treasuries have been established with the help of the Worshipful Company of Goldsmiths at Lincoln, Winchester, Norwich, Oxford (Christ Church),

Gloucester and Chichester and (on their own account) by the Dean and Chapter of Ripon. The Undercroft Museum at York received in April–September 1976 162,079 visitors, producing revenue of £41,168 for the Dean and Chapter. The exhibition in the crypt on the making and significance of the cathedral at Canterbury, a no less enterprising venture, received 99,973 visitors in the 1976 summer season. On a smaller scale is the exhibition in the crypt at Worcester, which had 35,000 visitors in 1976.

Treasuries, on the whole, attract a more specialist kind of visitor and produce income on a scale which can do little more than offset expenditure on their insurance and administration—which is not to say that they are not infinitely worthwhile both in themselves and in the contribution they make to solving the problem of custodianship for a country parish which finds itself the owner of an exceedingly valuable and rare, and probably fragile, piece of historic communion plate.

We feel that the success of the crypt exhibitions at York and Canterbury demonstrates the need for permanent interpretation exhibitions and also their very considerable revenue raising potential. We recommend generous help to other cathedrals from the English, Scottish and Welsh Tourist Boards to enable similar exhibitions to be established, since most cathedrals lack the capital to undertake such projects unaided.

4. *Cathedral shops* have enormous potential for disseminating the "message" of a cathedral, for enhancing its educational role, and for increasing its revenues. Several cathedrals, e.g. Norwich and Ely, have found recently that to replace a "stall in the aisle" with a properly designed and well-located shop produces a dramatic and gratifying leap in both turnover and net profit. However, profit margins are sometimes needlessly narrow and our hearts have more than once quailed at the low quality of goods offered for sale in certain cathedral shops. The National Trust has shown what can be done through establishing a policy for high standards in design, with reasonably priced goods, and by establishing a central buying agency.

5. *The "Ministry of Welcome"*. Here is another promising option, which is being put into practice at (among other places no doubt) Norwich, Exeter, Winchester, St Albans and Ely. The system involves good notices, explaining the welcome and the need for a contribution: "The Dean and Chapter Welcome You and Thank You For Your Gift. Without it, the Cathedral cannot be Maintained." At Chichester, Exeter and Winchester the visitor is welcomed near the entrance door and personally greeted by a robed attendant, man or woman. At Exeter the visitor is handed a small and attractively designed card to

complement the notices. The card indicates briefly that the visitor is "... making a pilgrimage to a place where Christians have worshipped God for 1,300 years, and you have before you one of England's most beautiful buildings. Most of what you see dates from the 14th century"; it then gives the times of the services, a few sentences relating to the physical nature of the building and to the life which goes on in it, and on the back cover of the card are two well-chosen prayers.

The Ministry of Welcome has two distinguishing elements:

I making the visitor feel welcomed and recognized, unobtrusively and gracefully;

II making it clear to the visitor that cathedrals are costly to maintain, depend on him as much as on anyone to survive, and indicating the *minimum* level of giving (usually 20p).

Before cathedral finance is relinquished a word further needs to be said about cathedral workshops and cathedral closes.

Cathedral Workshops

At Strasbourg the cathedral work force, called L'Oeuvre de Notre Dame, had existed continuously since the Middle Ages, and in the course of years acquired property and income devoted to the upkeep of the cathedral. There is nothing in England which can quite equal this, but a number of cathedral workshops have a marvellous sense of continuity (e.g. at Durham, and at Salisbury where lead is again being cast in the medieval "Plumbery") and may well have had an unbroken, or near-unbroken, existence. In a sense the great cathedrals have never been complete, and never will be, since their organisms are so vast and so complex that their building was necessarily succeeded by a process of gentle repair which will, if wise policies prevail, continue to the end of our civilization. At the present time 16 cathedrals have a Works Organization, manned in whole or in part by their own employees, and in most cases with a Clerk of Works in charge. Eleven of these are currently offering training to apprentices (Canterbury, Chichester, Durham, Exeter, Gloucester, Lincoln, St Paul's, Ripon, Salisbury, Wells and York). A minority of the workshops is able to take on outside work for parish churches or country houses in the vicinity or region. We feel that this is a promising line of development, which would merit substantial government aid, since it enables the works organization to continue—even to grow—at periods when cathedral finances may be low, and preserves rare skills at a time when the traditional small building firm with masonry and other skills is rapidly ceasing to exist.

In addition there are the traditional links between cathedrals as centres of excellence and high standards of craftsmanship which deserve to be maintained. To quote the Dean of Norwich again: "Creative craftsmanship . . . gives a feeling of confidence to those who come to the cathedral. The craftsmanship, so obvious in the building, and the concern to maintain and use the building are not purely historical—something which belongs to England's past. There is a sense of delight that our generation has done it. This is particularly important in Norwich Cathedral where the builders themselves did not hesitate to make major changes of style; for instance in the nave pillars which always intrigue visitors who, I think, subconsciously wonder whether we would have the daring and the courage to do this kind of thing today."

On the subject of cathedral closes it is relevant here to mention that their possession does not provide Deans and Chapters with enormous wealth. Indeed the escalating cost of repairs and maintenance to their beautiful, ancient (and therefore tender) fabrics usually more than offsets the rents received for those which are available for letting. Chapters may not even own what they appear to own, as at Wells, where a former noble inheritance has dwindled to little more than the present Dean's Lodging (a pleasant 17th-century house but a modest substitute for the historic Deanery sold in 1958 to the Diocesan Board of Finance for £6,000) and four modern Canon's houses tucked away in what used to be the former Deanery garden. The College of Vicars was inhibited from owning property or funds following the Cathedrals Measure 1936, and their property was taken over by the Church Commissioners, so that the Dean and Chapter (whose statutes require them to provide free accommodation for the Vicars Choral) have to rent those they need to fulfil their obligations.

The range of financial problems facing cathedrals is wide and varied, and includes the sheer scale of the responsibilities; the high cost of salaries, particularly when so many specialist skills are involved; the imposition of VAT on repairs, which tells particularly heavily when the money required has to be raised by voluntary effort. The smaller or less well-known cathedrals, it has been suggested to us, are especially vulnerable to financial difficulties, and "in a number of cases even routine maintenance is not possible on a comprehensive scale" we were told by John Phillips, architect to Truro cathedral.

Faced by those difficulties, what can cathedral authorities do? Clearly one possibility is to make a charge for entry, at least to some parts of the cathedral. Another traditional response has been the staging of major appeals, which have generally been successful. But, as one architect has told us: "Too much reliance on appeals results in alternating waves of feverish activity and sleepy pauses, and this can have fatal results on the continuity of craftsmanship." A more promising line seems to be the system of a High Steward's Committee, pioneered at Norwich and now employed also at York, pledged to raise a substantial annual sum and supported by influential local people who have the best interests of the cathedral very closely to heart.

PART THREE—REDUNDANT CHURCHES

CHAPTER SEVENTEEN

Redundancy

Almost every Christian denomination in Britain, with the possible exception of the Roman Catholics and certain small but growing sects, is faced with the problem of redundant churches. Only the Church of England keeps a readily accessible record of redundant churches, but the information we have received from many planning authorities gives a clear indication of the serious number of churches of architectural interest or townscape value which are disused or likely to become so in the near future.

In 1960 the Bridges Report estimated that some 790 Church of England churches would become redundant in the next 15–20 years. This figure was based on returns from diocesan bishops which indicated that about 370 churches were then redundant and that a further 420 odd were likely to become so in the following 15 to 20 years. According to the lists of listed buildings, supplemented where necessary by works of reference, it was calculated that 440 of these had considerable historic or architectural interest, and a further 86 had such interest to a lesser degree. The figures corresponded quite closely to those produced by the Bishop of Norwich's Committee on Disused Churches in 1948 which suggested there were (apart from ruins) about 400 churches which were seldom or never used. Of these 300 were thought to possess historic or architectural interest.

Following the recommendations of the Bridges Report a statutory procedure for dealing with redundant churches was set up in the Pastoral Measure of 1968. By March 31, 1977, 639 churches had been declared redundant and of the 539 cases subject to a final scheme 176 had been or were to be demolished, 224 appropriated to new uses and 108 vested in the Redundant Churches Fund.

The accuracy of the Bridges forecasts have been a matter of some contention. In *Problem Churches* (1971) Dr Gilbert Cope produced an estimate that some 6,000 churches will have disappeared, become preserved ruins, or been converted to secular use by the end of the century. The Redundant Churches Fund in its annual reports has always rejected such predictions of an avalanche of redundancies and upheld the Bridges estimates as broadly accurate. The Advisory Board for Redundant Churches, however, in its reports has consistently suggested that the Bridges figures will prove too low and in 1975 forecast that "by 1980 over 1,000 churches will probably have been declared redundant and that thereafter the redundancy rate will either be maintained or increased as the result of inflation and the redeployment of clergy". A fourth check exists in the number of cases of potentially redundant churches which go annually to the Council for Places of Worship for preliminary advice. In the last few years this has settled at an average of 90 a year, of which about 90% are subsequently declared redundant. If maintained this suggests that by the end of 1980 between 900 and 1,000 churches will have been declared redundant.

The Bridges Report divided Anglican dioceses into three groups: 8 Rural, 13 Urban, and 21 Mixed. The following table shows how the predictions for these three groups compare with the actual declarations of redundancy made by December 31, 1976:

	Redundancy in 1960	*Predicted Redundancy in 1960*	*Combined 1960 Total*	*Total Redundancies by End of 1976*
Rural (A)	121	157	278	167
Mixed (B)	164	182	346	284
Urban (C)	82	82	164	184
	367	421	788	635

Note: the division into Urban, Mixed and Rural follows those in the Bridges Report which were based on population statistics of ecclesiastical parishes and towns.

These figures show that while the total of redundancies is much lower than predicted in rural dioceses and considerably lower in the mixed dioceses, in the mainly urban group it has already exceeded the Bridges' estimate. The following table gives a breakdown of redundancies by dioceses, divided into mainly rural, mixed and mainly urban, following the Bridges categories:

Diocese *Group A*	*Redundant*	*Demolition Scheme*	*Redundant Churches Fund**	*Alternative Use*	*Unresolved*
Bath and Wells	15	2	4	6	3
Ely	22	1	13	2	6
Gloucester	8	2	4	1	1
Hereford	16	—	7	8	1
Norwich	34	2	3	18	11
St Edmundsbury	18	—	9	1	8
Salisbury	54	3	20	19	12
Truro	—	—	—	—	—
	167	10	60	55	42

Diocese	*Redundant*	*Demolition Scheme*	*Redundant Churches Fund**	*Alternative Use*	*Unresolved*
Group B					
Blackburn	2	—	—	2	—
Bristol	6	4	1	—	1
Canterbury	18	3	3	8	4
Carlisle	6	—	1	2	3
Chester	18	10	1	6	1
Chichester	9	3	2	3	1
Derby	5	1	—	2	2
Exeter	12	1	4	5	2
Guildford	7	3	1	—	3
Leicester	5	1	—	3	1
Lichfield	19	10	—	1	8
Lincoln	37	7	10	2	18
Oxford	35	3	9	16	7
Peterborough	12	2	4	3	3
Portsmouth	1	—	—	—	1
Rochester	15	4	3	4	4
St Albans	20	1	6	6	7
Wakefield	15	10	1	2	2
Winchester	19	2	6	8	3
Worcester	10	2	2	4	2
York	22	9	1	7	5
	293	76	55	84	78
Group C					
Birmingham	5	4	—	1	—
Bradford	4	2	—	2	—
Chelmsford	32	10	5	11	4
Coventry	8	1	1	3	3
Durham	9	4	—	2	3
Liverpool	15	9	1	3	2
London	37	18	1	6	12
Manchester	16	7	1	4	4
Newcastle	9	1	2	5	1
Ripon	14	5	2	1	6
Sheffield	14	8	2	2	2
Southwark	16	8	—	5	3
Southwell	4	1	1	—	2
	183	78	16	45	42

* *This column includes churches transferred to the Department of the Environment, or other bodies or owners to be cared for as monuments.*

From this it emerges that redundant churches in the urban group have the least chance of survival; a much smaller number are vested in the Redundant Churches Fund or find alternative uses while a far higher proportion are demolished. Among the rural dioceses some, such as Salisbury (54), Norwich (34) and Ely (22) have been very active in declaring churches redundant, though Truro has not yet declared a single church redundant. (The slight difference in the totals of redundancies for Groups B and C in the two preceeding tables is explained by the fact that the second table includes a small number of pre-Pastoral Measure cases).

From the relatively sparse figures available nonconformist churches appear to be closing at a considerably faster rate than those of the Church of England. Statistics kept by the Registrar-General show that of 74,089 places registered for worship since 1852 no less than 43,946 have closed. In recent years these closures have been running at a rate of 300–350 annually. The *Statistical Returns for the Methodist Church in England and Wales* (1970) show that a staggering 26% of Methodist churches became redundant between 1960 and 1970, the total falling from 11,500 to 8,500. In 1932 when the various groups of Methodist churches united there were 14,500 chapels in existence. This figure had been reduced to 13,524 by 1940. Following the Union of the Congregationalists and the Presbyterian Church of England in 1972 into the United Reformed Church over 200 out of a combined total of about 2,200 churches are on the market. Of nine United Reformed churches declared redundant between 1964 and 1974 (mainly 1972–74) in the Newcastle district, three, including one listed church built in 1750, have been demolished, six still survive and two are up for sale.

In Scotland, redundancy was a problem for the United Free Church of Scotland from 1900. In rural areas the early Secession churches of the United Presbyterian churches were widely abandoned as their congregations were progressively merged with those of the Free Church, the buildings of the latter being preferred as they were less than sixty years old whereas those of the Secession were anything from seventy to a hundred and sixty years old and often too small to hold the combined congregation. Many of these buildings which are usually of great simplicity and charm, survive as church halls, agricultural sheds, poultry houses, joiners' shops, furniture stores, and such like, often in depressingly bad condition. The further union with the Church of Scotland in 1929 merely aggravated an existing problem. In Easter Ross the established church was usually the casualty, but elsewhere, unless the Free Church was a later replacement of some quality, it was usually the established parish church which was eventually retained. Most of the early rural Free churches have suffered a similar fate to that of the early Secession churches.

The rivalry of the United Presbyterian Church and the Free Church with the Established Church thus ensured that every settlement of any size has had or had at least two Presbyterian churches. Under the Unions and Readjustments Commission 1,023 unions of congregations have taken place since 1929, and in each case one building has usually become redundant and been converted to a new use, demolished or simply abandoned. In the first few decades after reunion, we were told by the Secretary of the Church of Scotland Property Board, many congregations preferred to remain separate, but today, with a generation of churchgoers brought up after reunion, the number of unions—and thus redundancies is increasing sharply. The Episcopal Church in Scotland is faced with redundancies as a result of the need to reduce its stipendiary clergy (235 in February 1975) by a fifth.

In Wales, where according to our calculations there are more than double the number of Anglican places of worship in relation to head of population, we have heard predictions, still unofficial, that 100 out of 1,721 Church in Wales churches—mainly on isolated hillsides—will become redundant. Chapels, despite fiercely loyal congregations, are facing the same problem. In Cardiff for example 8 United Reformed congregations are to unite in 3 buildings.

To give an idea of the extent of the problem of disused and redundant churches we give below lists of churches causing concern to individual planning authorities. The Greater London Council gave us the following list of 31 churches:

Churches of interest or merit causing particular concern to the Greater London Council by reason of disuse, dereliction, possible redundancy or structural defects.

St George, Wells Way, Southwark
St Mary, Lambeth
St Alban, Teddington, Richmond
St Peter and St Paul, Teddington, Richmond
St Paulinus, St Paul's Cray, Bromley
St Andrew and St Michael, Tunnel Avenue, Greenwich
Christ Church, Jamaica Road, Bermondsey, Southwark
Christ Church, Cosway Street, Westminster (empty and nearly derelict)
Christ Church, Lancaster Gate, Westminster (serious structural problems in roof)
Paddington Congregational Church, Old Marylebone Road, Westminster (disused)
St Andrew, Willesden, Brent (in regular use, but has structural problems)
St Mary the Virgin, Perivale, Ealing (disused)
Christ Church, Willesden Lane, Brent (disused and vandalized)
St Michael at Bowes, Enfield
St Mark, Silvertown, Newham
Islington Chapel, Upper Street, Islington
United Reformed Church, Lower Clapton Road, Hackney
United Reformed Church, Muswell Hill Broadway, Haringey
St Stephen, Westbourne Park Road, Kensington and Chelsea

Christ Church, Spitalfields, Tower Hamlets
St Luke, Old Street, Islington (shell and tower only)
St James, Chillingworth Road, Islington (now a community hall)
Holy Trinity, Sydenham, Lewisham
St Mark, North Audley Street, Westminster
St Andrew (old church), Kingsbury, Brent (used infrequently for burials, etc.)
St Stephen, Rosslyn Hill, Camden
St Peter, Mile End, Tower Hamlets
St Bartholomew, Bethnal Green, Tower Hamlets
St Andrew, Plaistow, Newham
St Matthias, Poplar, Tower Hamlets

The majority of these are Anglican churches and though positive proposals have been put forward for some of them (for example the Tradescant Society hopes to take over St Mary at Lambeth) the future of the remainder is very problematic.

In Bristol a great many churches of the inner city area were damaged by the blitz in the Second World War but the subsequent reduction of the population in the city has had the result that many churches are now underused or out of use completely. The building of most concern is the splendid Lewin's Mead Unitarian Chapel, opened in 1791 and designed by William Blackburne. Of the 17 major 18th-century public buildings which Bristol possessed until 1940 only this chapel and Wesley's New Room in the Horsefair survive in anything like their original condition. An application to demolish this building was withdrawn shortly before a public inquiry but its future use remains a problem. A similar question mark also hangs over the Brunswick Methodist Chapel, part of a major group of buildings in a conservation area, until recently used as a warehouse. St John on the Wall, which incorporates the only remaining medieval gateway to the city, may also soon be redundant though its possible use as a museum is being discussed. Among churches with dwindling congregations which the city planning department fears may soon be faced with redundancy are the largely medieval All Saints—restored and cleaned as recently as 1973; St Thomas Redcliffe, built in 1791–93 and designed by James Allen and St Paul's Portland Square, built in 1789–94 by Daniel Hayne. There has nonetheless been considerable success in finding uses for some redundant churches: planning approval has been given for Hope Chapel, Clifton, built in 1786 by Lady Henrietta Hope to be used as a community centre; Holy Trinity, St Philip, which has been empty for some months may become a West Indian Community Centre, and St Mary Tyndal's Park is being considered by the BBC for use as a scenery store.

An example of the problem of disused nonconformist churches in the

Industrial Midlands was provided from Derbyshire by Bolsover District Council:

Disused churches in Bolsover District

Clowne, *Wesleyan Methodist* Church, Church St. (derelict and vandalized)

Creswell *Baptist* Church, Elmton Road (disused and vandalized after short period as shop)

South Normanton Mount Tabor *Methodist* Church, Market St. (disused and for sale)

Shirebrook *Methodist* Church Main Street (derelict and vandalized after short period as cafe)

Shirebrook *Congregational* Church, Church Drive (disused and vandalized)

Carr Vale, Bolsover *Methodist* Church, Charlesworth (disused: consent given for printing works in 1976)

A comparable list was supplied by Bedfordshire County Council of chapels currently disused—though some may receive planning permission for new uses in the near future:

Clophill Primitive *Methodist* Chapel, Old Silsoe Road

Lidlington Wesleyan *Methodist* Chapel, High Street

Marston Moretaine Primitive *Methodist* Chapel (1849)

Millbrook Wesleyan *Methodist* Chapel

Ridgmont Old Church of All Saints, Eversholt Road, Segenhoe (Grade I)

Shefford *Baptist* Church, Stanford Road

Steppingley Wesleyan *Methodist* Chapel

Wrestlingworth Ebenezer Chapel (Independent)

Bedford Howard *Congregational* Chapel, Mill Street

Riseley *Methodist* Chapel, High Street

Riseley *Moravian* Chapel, High Street

Sharnbrook *Baptist* Church, High Street (1865)

Billington Wesleyan *Methodist* Chapel, Gaddesden Turn (1838)

Caddington *Methodist* Chapel, Church Road

Stanbridge Wesleyan *Methodist* Chapel, Mill Road

Streatley Primitive *Methodist* Chapel, Barton Road, Sharpenhoe

Streatley *Baptist* Church, Sharpenhoe Road

An alarming number of interesting churches are currently disused in the New Town of Telford, Salop:

St Paul, Aqueduct (1851: condition reasonable)

St James, Stirchley (condition reasonable)

St Luke, Doseley (1845: very impressive, fair condition)

Methodist Chapel, Horton (1858: poor condition, vandalized: owned by TDC)

Bethesda Methodist Chapel, Old Park (1857: boarded up: owned by TDC)

Methodist Church, Park Lane, Mossey Green (very bad condition: owned by TDC)

Hill Top Methodist Chapel, Old Park (1853: poorish condition, some vandalism, owned by TDC)

Methodist Free Church, New Street, St Georges (1855: poorish condition, broken windows)

Methodist Church, Chapel Street, St Georges (very bad condition, much vandalized, surrounded by derelict land)

St Chad Mission Church, Lodge Road, Donnington Wood (isolated, very bad condition)

Note: TDC = Telford Development Corporation.

Not surprisingly perhaps the most disturbing forecast of likely redundancies came from Glasgow District Council:

Listing	*Glasgow: Likely Redundancies of Listed Buildings*
A	St Andrew, St Andrew's Square (1739–56 by Allan Dreghorn; major repairs needed, dwindling congregation)
A	St Andrew-by-the-Green, 33 Turnbull Street (1750–51 by Andrew Hunter; closed and deteriorating)
A/cda	Barony Church, Castle Street (1886–90 by Burnet and Campbell
A/cda	St George-in-the-Fields, 485 St George's Road (1886 by Hugh and David Barclay; in development area, low attendance)
A/ca	Belmont and Hillhead Church (1875–76 by James Sellars; repairs needed, congregation rapidly dwindling)
A/ca	Belhaven-Westbourne Church, 52 Westbourne Gardens (1880 by John Honeyman; congregation fallen drastically)
A/ca	Kelvingrove Parish Church, 4a Derby Street (1879 by James Sellars; congregation declining)
B/cda	Tollcross Central Church, 1088 Tollcross Road (1806 by John Brash; in Development Area)
B/ca	Dowanhill Parish Church, 93 Hyndland Street (1865 by William Leiper; poor repair)
B	St Margaret Polmadie, 110 Polmadie Road (1902 by McGregor Chalmers; extensive repairs, congregation rapidly declining)
B	Strathbungo Parish Church, 601–605 Pollokshaws Road (1886 by W. G. Rowan; congregation declining)
B/ca	Stevenson Memorial Church, 99 Garriochmill Road (1899–1902 by J. J. Stevenson; congregation may move out)
B	Trinity Parish Church, 176 Duke Street (1857 by Peddie and and Kinnear; in run down area, may merge)
B/ca	Crosshill-Victoria Church, 38 Dixon Avenue (1893 by J. B. Wilson; redundant, congregation gone)
A/ca	Ramshorn St Paul and St David (1824 by Rickman; congregation declining)
A	Barony North (1880 by John Honeyman; redundancy imminent)

Note: cda = church is in Comprehensive Development Area.
ca = church is in a conservation area.

Almost all these churches are by notable architects, and most are either in conservation areas or have been (or are to be) retained within Comprehensive Development Areas on grounds of architectural merit. Eight, in addition, have the top Grade A listing, and St Andrew and St Andrew-by-the-Green are two of the best and most important churches in Scotland. Of these churches listed by Glasgow District Council no fewer than eleven, St Cuthbert's and Queen's Cross; St Andrew; St Andrew-by-the-Green; Barony; St George-in-the-Fields; Belmont and Hillhead; Belhaven-Westbourne; Kelvingrove; Dowanhill; Stevenson Memorial and Trinity are of a standard suitable for consideration for Historic Buildings Council aid if the Secretary of State had funds with which to start the intended scheme.

The following notable Stuart or Georgian churches were disused in 1956 or abandoned:

Kinmuck, Aberdeenshire, Friends Meeting House (late 17th century: abandoned)
Oyne, Aberdeenshire (1808: disused)
Pitsligo, Aberdeenshire (1634: abandoned)
Ulva, Argyll (1827: Telford Parliamentary Kirk, disused)
Enzie, Banffshire (1785: disused)
Papa Westray, Orkney (1720: disused)
Edderton, Ross and Cromarty (1842: disused)
Rosskeen, Ross and Cromarty (1832)
Tarbat, Ross and Cromarty (1756)
Ui, Ross and Cromarty (*c.* 1825: Telford Parliamentary Kirk)
Ullapool, Ross and Cromarty (1829: Telford Parliamentary Kirk)
Falkirk, Stirlingshire (1806: Antiburger Church)
Kiltearn, Ross and Cromarty (1791)
Alness, Ross and Cromarty (1672)
Cromarty Gaelic Chapel (1783)
Lasswade, Lothian (1793)
Alves, Moray (1769)
Kirk o' The Muir, Perthshire (1744)

This list represents probably only one-quarter of the number of Stuart and Georgian churches of interest redundant, derelict or secularized by 1956. Since then, of those on the list above, at least Pitsligo, Kiltearn, and Alness have been unroofed, while Enzie and the very important church at Lasswade have disappeared altogether. Edderton is back in full use, Ulva when last heard of was in occasional use, Papa and Alves are wrecks, Oyne is a barn. Notable closures amongst Stuart and Georgian churches since 1956 where the churches as yet survive include Dairsie, Fife (1621); Glenbuchat, Aberdeenshire (1629); Dunning, Perthshire (1808 reconstruction of Romanesque kirk of which tower survives); Wemyss, Fife (1693); Newburn, Fife (1815); Temple, Midlothian (1832); Maryton, Angus (1791); Craig, Angus (1799) and Erskine Marykirk (1826) at Stirling.

The problem in Wales was well expressed to us by the County Planning Officer for Clwyd: "It is the chapel as opposed to the church which gives greatest cause for concern, and even here, the larger town chapels, although in reduced circumstances, are just about able to cope with rising maintenance costs in the face of dwindling congregations. It is the small, vernacular chapel which is suffering; chapels important enough at one time to warrant their erection and enlargement, even in tiny Welsh hamlets. A high percentage of these are lying empty and derelict—in many cases they are too small to be considered for residential purposes, and the problem of utilizing graveyards is enormous. Even when chapels are empty, there is little unanimity among the surviving trustees regarding the future of the building—the heart tending to rule the head in such matters. . . . These buildings, plain, small and uncomfortable, became the focal point for a completely new way of life. I believe that this social significance of the early vernacular meeting house is presently undervalued and hence the building type is in serious danger." A survey of 88 chapels in the county, carried out by the planning department, has shown that 25 of these are no longer used for their original purpose, and that of these only 4 have found an alternative use.

Examples of Anglican churches that are likely to become redundant in Wales are hard to identify but St Mary, Tintern, Gwent, a prominent landmark, listed in 1970, is now redundant and suffering from vandalism. Other disused churches are Llanfaenor, and Llangattock Vibon Avel, both in Gwent and St Illtyd, Llanhilleth, Gwent, believed to date from the 11th century, which has been closed for some years and is now deteriorating rapidly due to mining subsidence. In England redundancies of country churches are most likely to happen in East Anglia and Lincolnshire where there are many large medieval wool churches in tiny villages and hamlets. An alarming prediction of redundancies was made in *The Churches of Suffolk* published by the Suffolk Preservation Society. The author, the Rev John Fitch, says that of the 490 churches in the diocese of St Edmundsbury and Ipswich 218 serve under 250 parishioners; and of those 138 have under 200; and 45–50 under 100. According to Canon Fitch's grading system, of the 188 churches which he considers to be of exceptional quality, 78 are threatened, of the 235 quite good churches 109 are at risk and of the 49 "expendable" churches 31 may go.

Procedure

The Church of England's Pastoral Measure of 1968 is in the course of review—though the working party in its report on the proposed revision could not reach a consensus on a number of major points. Without entering into the more complicated points of procedure and ecclesiastical law, we consider that there are a number of aspects of the Measure as it now stands which give serious cause for concern.

In the process of redundancy there are normally three stages:

(i) a "declaration of redundancy"
(ii) a "waiting period" of up to one year and sometimes up to three

years in which an alternative use is sought for the redundant church

(iii) a "redundancy scheme" in which the Church Commissioners take the decision whether the redundant church (in whole or part) shall be appropriated for another use, shall be preserved as a monument, or shall be demolished.

Before a church is declared redundant preliminary advice is sought on its architectural and historic merit from the Council for Places of Worship; if redundancy goes ahead the Advisory Board for Redundant Churches will make recommendations as to its future in the light of its importance as a building, and the Redundant Churches Fund must be consulted as to whether it has the money to repair and maintain the church. The final decision in every case however is taken by the Church Commissioners, advised by their Redundant Churches Committee.

The first matter of concern is the waiting period. The Bridges Report attached great importance to this provision and it is certainly desirable that every opportunity should be allowed for consultation, discussion and exploration of possible new uses. However, once a church is declared redundant it enters a kind of limbo; the parish is no longer responsible for looking after it: this duty is transferred to the Diocesan Board of Finance. Yet as soon as any building is obviously closed and disused it immediately becomes a target for vandalism. In the country (where the Bridges Report forecast that most redundancies would occur) this may not be so serious, though the waste involved in replacing broken panes of glass—particularly leaded lights—is at the least unfortunate. In many big cities however the Pastoral Measure has proved to be nothing less than a vandal's charter. As soon as congregations move out churches are assaulted in the most vicious and savage manner: vandals break in and smash every object of furniture, defile every surface with graffiti, and systematically wreck the churches beyond repair. As a result numerous once proud and dignified churches are reduced to a state of degradation and defilement far surpassing the iconoclasm of the Reformation or the Commonwealth. In such cities a redundant church is not just a target for vandalism, but an invitation, and more often than not it is temptation to arson as well. Quite a number of churches have been gutted by fire within weeks of closure and as a result demolition has become inevitable even though an alternative use had been proposed: examples are the fine churches of St Clement Sheepscar, Leeds and St Philip Hulme, Manchester.

This is a harsh judgement, but the report of the Advisory Board for

1975 draws, in suitably measured terms, a very similar picture of its visit to Leeds "the former co-operation between the City Council and the diocese had been lost, diocesan committees and officials were struggling to cope with the effects of vast devastation upon churches left isolated in a wilderness of wasteland and the consecrated buildings stood closed, forlorn and abandoned to the attacks of vandals. Little has been done to remove the more important and vulnerable items of contents prior to the closure of the churches because the church wardens and parochial church councils had lost heart, and the resultant situation appeared to those of us who visited the City to be wholly deplorable." The effects of planning policies and comprehensive clearance on churches are discussed in Chapter 19, but what is equally clear is that as long as churches remain in use they are usually subject only to minor vandalism if any at all, even when they are situated in derelict run down areas or on the edge of vast tracts of waste land. Two good examples of this are St Matthew and St Edward, both in Holbeck, Leeds, and both admirably cared for by their congregations.

Would it not be far better if no church was to be declared redundant and forsaken by its congregation until a new use had been found and a new owner was prepared to take it on? What house owner for example would increase his prospects of selling his house by moving out, leaving it empty or abandoned and boarding up the windows? Equally, where a church is obviously of such quality and completeness that it should go to the Redundant Churches Fund it should be vested immediately and not subject to a minimum waiting period of a year: once again this invites vandalism and can only increase the eventual cost. The nave roof of St Mary, Islington, Norfolk, collapsed during the waiting period.

The second principal objection to the Pastoral Measure as it stands lies in two clauses allowing churches to be demolished forthwith. Under sections 42 (3) and 49 (1): "If the Advisory Board certifies that the redundant building is of such small historical or architectural interest that the demolition thereof would not in their opinion be objectionable on that ground" the Church Commissioners may demolish it immediately. Similar provisions exist under section 46 (1) (*c*), where a new church is to be provided to take the place of a church or churches in the same area. In this case the Church Commissioners may also authorize immediate demolition if the Board certifies that "all or any of the redundant buildings are of such small historic or architectural interest that the demolition thereof would not in their opinion be objectionable on that ground", or certifies that "features of historic or architectural interest in the redundant buildings are proposed to be incorporated in the new church" and the Board is satisfied with the proposal.

The problem here is that though most buildings given demolition certificates in this way may be of little intrinsic merit, they may be of townscape value and they may be in sound condition and readily convertible to a new use. The second clause is particularly dangerous as it can be used to demolish a series of churches in return for a single replacement. An example is the new church of Ardwick, Greater Manchester, which replaced no less than five nearby churches. The Pastoral Measure should therefore be amended to ensure that buildings which are in sound condition or give character to their surroundings are not demolished peremptorily. A further amendment should be introduced so that demolition did not become inevitable after three years. In certain cases it may take longer to find a new use (particularly in times of economic recession), and many churches could be mothballed at little cost beyond this period. In some important cases, like St Mary Lambeth, London, declared redundant in 1972 and still awaiting a solution, the Church Commissioners have exercised the discretion provided for in section 50 (1) of the Pastoral Measure and extended the three year period, but this should happen more frequently.

In 1976 the Church in Wales adopted its own procedure for dealing with redundant churches. This may be summarized as follows:

(i) When a church is closed for public worship the parish continues to be responsible for maintaining and insuring it.

(ii) The Diocesan Churches Committee, in considering whether it should be declared redundant, consults the Diocesan Advisory Committee on
  (a) "the architectural and historical merit of the building and its feature as part of the landscape"
  (b) the disposal of the contents.

(iii) The Diocesan Churches Committee after consultation with the Parochial Church Council, submits its proposals for the future of the building to the Bishop, with an estimate of the cost, including advice on the disposal of the contents.

(iv) As and when the Bishop is satisfied with the proposals he declares the church redundant and the Diocesan Churches Committee becomes responsible for maintaining and insuring it. This committee is also responsible for initiating action on the proposals.

The advantage of this procedure is that the parish remains responsible for looking after the building until a new use is found. There is, it is true, no equivalent of the Redundant Churches Fund, but there is a good chance that the more exceptional redundant churches will be taken into guardianship and since the majority are both small and sturdy they need not be a great burden on public funds. In contrast to the Pastoral Measure no specific provisions are made concerning demolition, but where the church was a listed building or in a conservation area this would require consent from the local authority in the normal way.

In the Church of Scotland redundancies usually result from mergers of congregations: the task of deciding which church is closed and disposed of lies with a board of assessors, composed of lawyers, architects and surveyors. With other denominations the responsibility for the decision to close varies according to the degree of centralization though the initiative almost invariably comes from the local congregation.

Attitudes

When is a church redundant? A leaflet on *The Redundancy of Churches* produced by the Diocese of Oxford begins "The Bishop of Oxford has stated that no Bishop or Committee ever makes a church redundant; they only declare to be what is in fact the case. It is the people who make a church redundant. The Bishop's tests for redundancy are:

Do the people wish to keep the church?
Do the people put the church to full use?
Can the people afford to keep the church when they have properly assessed their resources and their priorities."

The use of the word "properly" begs a lot of questions, for who decides what proper is? Not a few congregations have found their churches closed against their will and parishioners of Christ Church, Brixton Road, fought the proposal to declare their church redundant all the way to the Privy Council and won their battle. Similarly, the concept of "full use" is open to wide interpretation. Many small country churches are used only once a week or once a month, but are still lovingly cared for, even though the congregation may be in single figures, and they give great pleasure to visitors. As a Catholic priest in one of the rougher suburbs of Edinburgh put it to us: "You can't put a value on a church which stands as a monument to God's presence in the world." The researches of the Grubb Institute of Behavioural Studies have shown that a community which is deprived of its church feels that it has been devalued, and community life is itself weakened. In a letter to *The Times* the Institute's project director wrote that when people hear "of clergy recommending that churches should be closed or demolished or allowed to fall into disrepair they feel the clergy have now lost faith in the Christian faith". The community value of churches can be equally great in densely populated urban areas. The Minister of the Augustine-Buchanan church in Glasgow's Gorbals wrote that he had spent "the whole of my 25 years ministry trying to get people out of overcrowded slum dwellings into the church for worship and into the church hall for all types of recreation".

Of course, there are instances, like the church in Bethnal Green, London, where the new incumbent rang the bell three Sundays in succession and no one came. But there are equally cases where it is simply the attitude of the local clergy or the policy of the diocese which leads to closure. A church at Itchen Stoke, Hampshire (population 200), for example, was declared redundant even though a member of the team ministry lived next door. The Norfolk Churches Trust, which was carrying out rescue work on the church at Dunton was told by the incumbent and the rural dean that it was fine for them to be spending money on it "so long as they realize it is never going to be used". Yet near by another young incumbent has cheerfully taken on five churches, restored two of them, and is now raising money for the others. The same problem was echoed by the Herefordshire Old Churches Trust "the churches that are in most trouble are those where the clergy are not prepared to do any work of fund raising on their behalf".

CHAPTER EIGHTEEN

Demolition

In attempting to assess the numbers of lost churches we have concentrated on the post-war period, and principally on the years since 1970, and, as far as Church of England churches are concerned, mainly on events subsequent to the Pastoral Measure of 1968. For Anglican churches information has come largely from the Church Commissioners, for the other denominations, chiefly from planning authorities. In addition we have received invaluable help from a number of historians (see the acknowledgements).

Though the lists are far from complete they show that losses of churches have been taking place on a far greater scale than had hitherto been realized (see the appendix). And unlike the losses of country houses (some 1,500 notable country houses have gone since 1920) which reached their climax in the mid 1950s and have since fallen sharply, the number of chapels and churches demolished seems to be increasing every year. Indications are that the graph will continue to rise, though the number of demolition schemes for Anglican churches has *fallen* from 39 in the year to March 31, 1976, to 20 in the year to March 31, 1977, and the number of appropriations to new uses has risen slightly. Whereas controls over the demolition of secular buildings have been growing more effective in recent years, and the number of permissions to demolish held roughly steady, a different trend emerges from the lists of lost churches in the appendix.

Numbers of Listed Buildings in England for which Permission was Granted to Demolish

	Grade I	*Grade II*	*Total*
1971	1	200	201
1972	1	222	223
1973	1	444	445
1974	0	262	262
1975	0	350	350

These figures are the more disturbing in view of the very uneven listing of churches and chapels. In the first round of listing begun in 1945 most 19th-century churches and most nonconformist chapels were omitted, and since only about half the original lists have yet been revised there are many eligible churches that are still unlisted. For this reason we have included listed and unlisted losses, including, where obtainable, an indication of townscape value. It is true that some, particularly the lesser nonconformist chapels, would still be considered of marginal interest, but since this was the reason given for the demolition of many churches the loss of which is now regretted we have included them. In the words of the Director of the Greater London Council Historic Buildings Division: "The least exciting church usually has some townscape value, or at least it forms an interesting incident in an otherwise unrelieved area. Even among the unlisted churches which have gone there were probably only one or two so unremarkable that their absence would pass almost unnoticed."

The lists include a few medieval churches: quite a number of Georgian churches; dozens of churches by major Victorian architects, while those of notable provincial practitioners can be numbered in hundreds. Churches by Butterfield, Christian, Gillespie Graham, Godwin, Lorimer, Scott, Tapper, "Greek" Thomson and Woodyer have gone; as well as many more by figures such as Chancellor of Chelmsford, Foster of Liverpool, Foulston of Plymouth, Hayward of Exeter, Hill of Leeds and Raffles Brown of Liverpool. The majority of losses sadly have been in places which could least afford to lose good or prominent buildings. Manchester has lost some 40 Anglican churches: Liverpool 50, if churches of all denominations are included; in Birmingham 36 have gone; in Leeds 18; and in Sunderland 15. St Helens has lost 7 churches, Hastings 5, in Glasgow some 30 listed churches have gone since 1966; and in Sheffield 6 have gone since 1970. In London 8 listed churches have been demolished since 1972 and in the Borough of Lambeth alone 16 have gone since 1960.

Two of the most frequent causes of demolition in cities have been comprehensive development and roadbuilding. Almost every church demolished for housing clearance is a tombstone to a shattered and dismembered community. As for the churches demolished for roadworks—whether building, widening, straightening or improving—these are so numerous that it can only be that highway authorities, at both national and county level, have often considered churches entirely dispensable.

CHAPTER NINETEEN

Planning

Post-war planning policies of housing clearance and comprehensive redevelopment have been a major cause of redundancy and demolition of churches. The effects have been at their most acute in the city centres of major industrial towns, and the principal cause of losses of churches in cities like Manchester, Liverpool and Leeds, and London boroughs such as Southwark and Lambeth. In Glasgow's Gorbals, for example, the population was reduced in the 1960s through redevelopment from 36,000 to 10,000 with the result that though eight existing churches were retained only three were able to continue in use. The scale of these major shifts of population (and thus congregations) is evident in the following table:

Glasgow: Percentage Change of Population in City Wards

	% Change 1951–61	*% Change 1961–71*
Provan	+210·7	+9·0
Knightswood	+203·9	−6·0
Cathcart	+192·1	−1·6
Pollokshaws	+22·2	+4·8
Exchange	−37·9	−44·4
Hutchestown	−36·9	−43·9
Gorbals	−36·1	−68·2
Cowcaddens	−32·5	−42·4
Yoker	−14·0	+20·4
Maryhill	−4·8	+8·5
Kingston	−27·5	−63·1
Anderston	−32·3	−56·8
Towhead	−24·3	−53·9

In Birmingham clearance has been equally radical. The original five redevelopment areas in the city covered an area of some 1,380 acres of land, and of this total about 981 acres were included in a single compulsory purchase order confirmed in 1947. This contained some 30,000 houses in addition to shops, factories, warehouses and schools. Some 28 religious buildings, principally Anglican, have been demolished in the five areas; some had been blitzed but most went because of the enormous reduction in the number of parishioners. As the effects of such comprehensive redevelopment, not only on local communities but on jobs and small businesses as well, have become clear doubts have crept in, and the announcement of a subvention of £100 million in the budget of 1977, aimed at relieving the problems in inner cities, indicates policies are being put into reverse. These policies should have a major impact on stemming the decline of inner cities, and churches have an opportunity to play a leading part in this programme of revival. Gradually the churches themselves have begun to have doubts about the wisdom of displacing people in such huge numbers: one Roman Catholic priest in Roehampton expressed the feeling to us that "it has been one of the great mistakes to destroy well rooted communities in inner cities and create heartless housing estates which have little chance of becoming real communities". The continuing number of closures and demolitions in inner-city areas, however, suggests that the Churches have yet to respond to the change of direction in planning policies and the increasing emphasis on recycling rather than replacing existing buildings.

A further factor encouraging the demolition of churches has been the method of compensation used where churches have been affected by comprehensive redevelopment. Under the Land Compensation Act 1961, because normal methods of property valuation were thought unfair, churches are entitled to equivalent reinstatement in the event of compulsory acquisition. This means that local authorities will pay the estimated cost of buying a suitable site elsewhere and erecting a new church. This has created a huge bias in favour of demolition. One of the best examples of the needless duplication sometimes involved in this procedure is provided by Chesterfield, Derbyshire, where the Trinity Methodist Church was acquired subject to the payment of full replacement value, and the new chapel built just 100 yards away. Had even a fraction of the huge sums expended on this procedure been available for conservation many lost churches could have been repaired and adapted to provide the kind of facilities that are often included in new churches. In quite a number of cases the sites of lost churches have not even been re-used. In the Diocese of Blackburn we were told by the Diocesan Secretary: "the bulk of the 'down town' parish churches have been the subject of compulsory purchase orders or dangerous structures notices served by the local authority and these have been developed and the land conveyed to the local authority or held as an open space pending purchase when the financial climate eases (if ever)".

Fortunately there is increasing evidence to show that a growing number of local authorities are becoming concerned about the future of churches of individual merit or townscape value. Though churches have considerable exemptions from normal planning controls the majority of the local authorities we have corresponded with, particularly those in urban areas, keep a very close watch on the problems of churches. In Essex it is now the General Planning Policy of the County Council "to conserve and retain redundant church buildings as intrinsic historic features of the Essex scene".

It is to be hoped that similar policies will be adopted by other county councils in their structure plans. In almost all parts of the country some population expansion is envisaged and often this can give a new lease of life to churches with declining congregations. The rapid economic growth of Northampton for example has brought new residents to many of the surrounding villages. Holcot church, almost unused for 25 years, now has a congregation due to the proximity of a spur of the M1. One of the main encouragements to the Norfolk Churches Trust in its attempts to prevent churches becoming redundant has been the steady increase in population in many villages—overall of 10% between 1961 and 1971. The establishment of Milton Keynes, Buckinghamshire, has also rescued a considerable number of interesting churches from redundancy, including the rare late-17th-century church at Willen by Robert Hooke. In the earlier new towns new communities were rarely grouped round old churches with the result that they had to be duplicated at needless expense. Yet by centring a new development or suburb on an existing church of some interest, a planning authority will be giving it a focal point which could not otherwise be afforded. The Director of the International Council of Monuments and Sites made the suggestion that some isolated or remote country churches could become the sites of new villages. Most of these churches have once had settlements around them and though such development might conflict with green belt or agricultural zoning it should be explored in certain cases.

History goes to show the necessity of taking a long view where congregations are reduced to a handful. Nothing could be more tragic than the unroofing of the delightful 18th-century church at Alness, Ross and Cromarty, only two years before new housing sprung up all round it as a result of the oil boom. At Broad Camden, in Gloucestershire, a very fine early meeting house closed in 1874 was derelict in 1960 and in danger of demolition, but following a revival of Friends in the area it has been beautifully restored and reopened. The famous Blue Idol Friends Meeting House Thakeham, Sussex, was a factory between 1793 and 1869 while that at Marazion, in Cornwall, built in 1688, was disused from 1842 till 1910.

Church spires and towers are an important element in almost any townscape, and local authorities could do much more to protect them. In the last two decades planning permissions have all too often been freely given for high-rise development very close to major churches, and even cathedrals, marring both the distant silhouette of the town and many of the best views within it. One of the worst examples is the office block next to Peterborough Cathedral, but in towns and suburbs up and down the country the contribution made by spires has been eroded by ill-advised development. Where the new buildings are office blocks there is probably little chance that they will ever be replaced by buildings of less bulk, unless they prove impossible to let and uneconomic to maintain because built on assumptions that energy would remain cheap. There is, for example, at least a question mark over many high rise office blocks in cities like Birmingham and Portsmouth where there are huge areas of unlet floor space.

By contrast the post-war experiment of high-rising housing is now acknowledged in most cases to have been a failure, and very few council tower blocks are likely to be built in the future. In view of the antagonism most residents have to living in such blocks and the extraordinary costs of maintaining and repairing them it is doubtful whether many of them have a life span of more than 60 or 80 years. The average well built Victorian suburban church, by contrast, probably has a life of at least 200 or 300 years if properly maintained, so many churches, which are now overshadowed by tower blocks, could by the end of the century or shortly after dominate the skyline again. Most high-rise housing is surrounded by considerable areas of open space (usually largely wasted), and the same population density could be accommodated in standard terrace housing.

This summer a bill on the Protection of the Skyline was introduced into the House of Commons by Patrick Cormack, MP. This would give county planning authorities a duty to designate skyline views when preparing or revising structure plans and to formulate policies to protect these views. In making such designations the planning authority would be obliged to consult district councils: equally any district council could request inclusion of a specific view. To allow for the reluctant or philistine local authority the Secretary of State for the Environment would have reserve powers.

CHAPTER TWENTY

Ruins

The problem of ruined churches is much more extensive than is generally realized. In addition to the considerable number of roofless abbeys, priories and other substantial medieval churches now looked after as ancient monuments and regularly open to the public, there are large numbers of ruined churches, some forsaken as long ago as the Black Death, and some abandoned quite recently, for which no one takes responsibility. In Norfolk the Council for British Archaeology has estimated that there are some 249 churches in some state of ruination, ranging from abandoned buildings, which still retain a roof, to sites where most of the evidence is below ground. In addition there are, according to the CBA, at least 20 ruined churches in Yorkshire and some 15 in Nottinghamshire. The latter include the remarkable Norman church at Elston, the 14th-century tower of Bramcote, and the once stately church of Colston Bassett, Nottinghamshire, now saddening rather than pleasing, unroofed in 1892 when the local squire built a new church. In Herefordshire some 10 ruined churches are listed in the *Buildings of England* volume, in Bedfordshire there are ruins at Clophill and Segenhoe and in Cornwall at Merther, near Truro.

In Scotland it is not uncommon to find the shell of a small medieval or early post-Reformation church in the churchyard next to the parish church. This is due less to Reformation destruction (in general only major churches were destroyed) than to later replacement. In the Highlands there are also many ruins, notably in Ross and Cromarty, arising from poor popular support for the Established Church after 1843 and a subsequent preference for the Free Churches after the reunion of 1929. Among notable post Reformation churches in Scotland the following are now roofless.

Cushnie, Grampian (Aberdeenshire) (1637)
Tarland, Grampian (Aberdeenshire)
Appin, Strathclyde (Argyll) (1749)
Alloway, Strathclyde (Ayrshire) (1653)
Thurso, Highland (Caithness) *Old* Church (17th century)
Dalton, Dumfries and Galoway (Dumfriesshire) (1764)
Gladsmuir, Lothian (1695)
Balcarres, Fife (1635 mortuary chapel)

- Polmont, Central (Stirlingshire) (1731)
- Durness, Highland (Sutherland) (1619)
- Carriden, Central Lothian (1766)
- Glasserton, Dumfries and Galloway (Wigtownshire) (1732)
- Inch, Grampian (Wigtownshire) (1770)
- Sorbie, Dumfries and Galloway (Wigtownshire) (*c.* 1750)
- Delting, Shetland (1714)
- Metulick, Grampian (Aberdeenshire) (1780)
- Longside, Grampian (Aberdeenshire) (1620)
- Rosneath, Strathclyde (Dunbartonshire) (1780)
- Tulliallan, Fife (1675)
- Sauchieburn Berean Chapel (Kincardineshire) (1773)
- Quothquhan Strathclyde (Lanarkshire) (17th century)
- Lochcarron, Highland (Ross and Cromarty) (1751)
- St Boswell, Borders (Roxburghshire) (1652)
- Killearn, Central (Stirlingshire) (1734)
- Portpatrick (Wigtownshire) (1629)
- North Uist, Highland (Inverness-shire) (1764)
- Sleat, Highland (Inverness-shire) (1687)
- Glencorse, Lothian (1665 and 1669)
- Burray, (Orkney) (1621)
- Aberfoyle, Central (Perthshire) (1744)
- Balquhidder, Central (Perthshire) (1631)
- Blackford, Tayside (Perthshire) (1738)
- Alness, Highland (Ross and Cromarty) (1672)
- Kintail, Highland (Ross and Cromarty) (1719)
- Knockbain, Highland (Ross and Cromarty) (1764)

These ruins originated mainly as a result of the building of larger new churches between 1820 and 1900 and not of redundancies. Since then many churches at first used on a linked charge basis, perhaps encompassing as many as three churches, have been closed and unroofed, the congregations preferring to face the cost of travel rather than that of repair.

In Wales quite a number of parish churches were abandoned when newer churches were built in the late 19th century in the growing towns and villages, but it is often only in the last 10 or 15 years that they have become really derelict.

Repeated attempts have been made to persuade successive Governments to take ruined churches into guardianship, following the early precedent in Ireland where in 1869 over 100 ruins that had been church property were transferred to the Irish Office of Works for preservation. These efforts, however, have met with no success, and both the Bridges Report and the Pastoral Measure ignored the problem of ruins. In the sense that most ruins have been *de facto* redundant for decades if not centuries in a pastoral sense, this is understandable; however, the Redundant Churches Act 1969, though it continued exemption of Anglican places of worship from Listed Building Control did not exempt them, if they are scheduled, from the provisions of Ancient Monuments legislation.

Technically a ruin is in most cases the responsibility of a parish, which is legally responsible for third party liability, and the desire to pass on the burden has led some parishes or dioceses to seek to declare ruins redundant. A number of ruins and fragments have been vested in the Redundant Churches Fund, notably the shell of the remarkable rococo church at Hartwell, Buckinghamshire (where considerable repairs have been carried out). Two church towers, Lightcliffe Old Church, near Halifax, West Yorkshire and Saltfleetby, Lincolnshire, have been leased to the Friends of Friendless Churches. A number of other ruined churches have been vested in local landowners—technically as an "alternative use"—this may be the solution to the substantial ruin of the old church at Annesley in Nottinghamshire. Failing these two alternatives the ruin will have to be demolished. Since most such ruins have, left alone, survived for several centuries, it seems quite wrong that they should have to be eliminated simply because there is no suitable bureaucratic pigeon-hole in which to place them. Clearly, however, some provision should be made for the inspection and perhaps registration of ruins, and perhaps also for including them in a group third-party liability insurance covering the whole country.

Quite a number of ruined churches, and features such as towers, have been taken over by local authorities, principally those which are important elements in the townscape. Newton Abbot District Council, Devon, acquired and restored the medieval tower of St Leonard in 1972–73 at a cost of £11,000 aided by a grant of £2,000 and public subscriptions of £4,000. The tower of St-John-at-Wapping, Tower Hamlets, London, has been leased and restored by the Greater London Council. In Suffolk Beccles Borough Council purchased and restored the free standing tower of St Michael, and in Yorkshire, Calderdale Metropolitan Borough has acquired and plan to restore the magnificent spire of the Square Congregational Chapel at Halifax. The shells of a number of churches bombed in the Second World War are admirably preserved and maintained by local authorities: examples are Holy Rood, Southampton, St Agatha, Portsmouth, and the splendid Regency Gothic church of St Luke, in Liverpool, all of which are now pleasant and attractive gardens. In Bristol the ruins of three churches are maintained in this way: St Peter which has been repaired by the City Council as a central feature of Castle Park; Temple Church with its well-known leaning tower, maintained by the Department of the Environment, and the tower of St Mary-le-Port. In Scotland where local authorities look after many churchyards, they also look after any ruins within them with varying degrees of sympathy.

Other ruins have had new churches built within the walls; one of the most successful is Hawksmoor's St George in the East, London, where a modern church (and rectory) built within the shell are wholly invisible outside. This is a solution which is always worth investigating whenever, as from time to time will inevitably happen, a notable church is burnt. Very often, though, the roof and most of the internal fittings will have been damaged beyond repair, the walls and, equally important, the tower or spire will usually remain. In 1976, for example, the admirably well detailed church of St Matthew, Upper Clapton, in North London, by Francis Dollman, was gutted by arson. The walls, however remained, so did the fine tower which dominated the whole neighbourhood. As the incumbent wished to demolish the shell and dispose of part of the site to a housing association, a group of architects prepared a scheme providing an equivalent amount of housing and a small new church—which was all that was required—within the preserved shell. Unfortunately this scheme did not meet with the approval of the incumbent: indeed redundancy and possible demolition had been proposed even before the fire. Perhaps the most famous case of the re-use of a gutted church is the re-use of the bombed shell of St John's Smith Square as a concert hall.

Looking abroad, we have found other countries considerably in advance of the United Kingdom in the responsibility they take for ruins. In Denmark the state looks after all ruined churches. In Brittany the Caisse Nationale des Monuments Historiques began in 1963 a *Campagne de Sauvegarde* to restore numerous small, very ancient, chapels most of which are only used on the feast day of the saint to whom they are dedicated. This campaign is carried out with funds from the state (50%) the Department (25%) and the Commune (25%), with special funds from the Ministry of Agriculture for *renovation rurale*. So far emergency repairs have been carried out at over 60 chapels in Brittany (all *classé* or *inscrit*). The aim is consolidation through the use of the simplest methods—industrial tiles for roofing and simple carpentry.

A case is sometimes made for the deliberate ruination of certain redundant churches—the removal of the roof, perishable furnishings and stained glass: Canon Ian Dunlop argued that once a church was disused it was much better that it should become a ruin—with all the romance and association this can imply—rather than be kept a frozen mausoleum. Others, like Patrick Cormack, MP, fear that if ruination became a statutory possibility under the Pastoral Measure, or was encouraged in any way by law, all too many parishes and incumbents would gladly take the opportunity of shedding their responsibilities. Architects also take the view that it is often as expensive if not more so to maintain a building without a roof as to retain it complete.

In Wales quite a number of disused parish churches have been turned into "decent ruins"—recent examples are Llandeilo Abercowin and Eglwysfair-a-Churig, both in the Diocese of St Davids. "Ruination" in Wales, however, has too often resulted in the walls of a church being reduced to a level of only a few feet above the ground. This preserves the plan of the church it is true, but it utterly destroys any scenic quality it has; equally, decent and tidy ruins are hardly likely to have picturesque appeal.

The romance of ruins has long had a great appeal to travellers, and today ruined abbeys are among the most visited of all major buildings open to the public, comparing well with major country houses.

Visitors to Abbeys		*Visitors to Country Houses (1975)*	
Fountains Abbey, N. Yorkshire	270,000	Osborne House, Isle of Wight	260,200
Tintern Abbey, Gwent	163,900		
Rievaulx Abbey, N. Yorkshire	134,600	Hatfield House, Hertfordshire	131,600
Whitby Abbey, N. Yorkshire	130,000		
Melrose Abbey, Borders	66,700	Crathes Castle, Grampian	60,100
Dryburgh Abbey, Borders	46,200	Thoresby Hall, Nottinghamshire	46,400
Jedburgh Abbey, Borders	34,900	Sherborne Castle, Dorset	35,000
Furness Abbey, Cumbria	22,600	Blithfield Hall, Staffordshire	22,900
Cleve Abbey, Somerset	22,200		
Roche Abbey, Cornwall	20,900	Knightshayes Court, Devon	22,100
Torre Abbey, Torquay, Devon	20,000	Dyrham Park, Avon	20,100
Sweetheart Abbey, Dumfries	16,900	Trerice, Cornwall	20,000
Easby Abbey, N. Yorkshire	16,600	Littlecote House, Wiltshire	16,200
Byland Abbey, N. Yorkshire	15,800		
Thornton Abbey, Lincolnshire	14,700	Uppark, W. Sussex	14,700
Inchcolm Abbey, Firth of Forth, Fife	12,000	Nunwell House, Isle of Wight	11,000
Netley Abbey, Hampshire	12,000		
Arbroath Abbey, Tayside	10,500	Loseley Park, Surrey	10,700
Dundrennan Abbey, Dumfries and Galloway	10,300	Brympton D'Evercy, Somerset	10,000

Most of these abbeys are open every day throughout the year—an expense which few country houses could justify; on the other hand the signs are that visitors to country houses are growing faster than those to ruined abbeys. Nonetheless, the figures show the great importance of ruined monasteries to tourism, and suggest that the problem of the most substantial ruined churches is one that tourism could help solve. The best of the abandoned churches are as interesting to visit as the small abbeys, particularly where they are associated with a deserted village—which has an added history and allure of its own. Equally the potential of ruins for archaeological exploration also adds an extra dimension to their interest.

CHAPTER TWENTY-ONE

Churches as Monuments

Some churches are of such obviously outstanding quality that even when they are no longer required for worship it is imperative to preserve them intact. Here there are four solutions. Firstly, they can be taken into guardianship by the Department of the Environment (like other ancient monuments), or by the Scottish Department or the Welsh Office. Secondly, they can be vested in the Redundant Churches Fund—which is, however, restricted to Church of England churches; thirdly, they may be acquired and looked after by local authorities, and fourthly they can be entrusted to a suitable private owner or group of friends.

The Department of the Environment now looks after a number of churches (as well as many roofless ruins): these are mostly former private chapels rather than parish churches. They are:

Dover, St Mary in Castro, Kent
Tower of London, St Peter-ad-Vincula
Rotherwas Chapel, Herefordshire
Langley Chapel, Salop
Rycote Chapel, Oxfordshire
Duxford Chapel, Cambridgeshire
Lindsey Chapel, Suffolk
Abbotsbury, St Catherine, Dorset
Odda's Chapel, Deerhurst, Gloucestershire
Appledore, Horne's Place Chapel, Kent
Brinkburn Priory, Northumberland
Portsmouth Garrison Church, Hampshire
Chester, St Mary de Castro, Cheshire
Wharram Percy, North Yorkshire

Since 1968 the Department has also taken into guardianship two redundant Anglican churches, namely Studley Royal, West Yorkshire, and Canons Ashby, Northamptonshire. This is a very small number in relation to the total of 639 Anglican redundancies by March 31, 1977, but two further redundant churches, Barton on Humber, St Peter, Humberside and Kempley, St Mary, Gloucestershire, may soon follow.

In addition the Department now looks after two noncomformist chapels—Goodshaw Baptist Chapel, Lancashire and Unitarian Chapel,

Bury St Edmunds, Suffolk. To these can be added the Royal Chapels at Marlborough House, St James' Palace, Hampton Court, Chelsea Hospital and Greenwich.

The Ancient Monuments Branch in Wales has the chapel at Holywell, Clwyd, with an exceptionally fine timber roof dating from *c.* 1500 (the Roman Catholic shrine below is in separate ownership). Also in its care are Gwydir Uchaf Chapel, near Llanrwst, Gwynedd, dating from 1670 with an original painted roof and contemporary fittings and the parish church of Llangar which went out of use in the 19th century. This is now being repaired. Last year the Department also took into care the remarkable family chapel of Lord Newborough, at Rhug, Clwyd, which retains all its 16th-century painted woodwork untouched. In Scotland the Secretary of State has taken Dunning Old Church into guardianship for its Romanesque tower.

The total number of churches in the guardianship of the state is, nonetheless, very small and for this reason the achievement of the Redundant Churches Fund in a few years is all the more remarkable. The Fund was established in 1969 following a recommendation of the Bridges Report and now has 108 churches in its care. Already there is an impressive geographical spread, and the fact that there are more Fund churches in the Province of Canterbury than that of York largely reflects the greater concentration of churches in the south (13,337 parish churches in Canterbury and 4,559 in York in 1963). Among these are many remote churches in beautiful countryside: Shotley in Northumberland, approachable only on foot across the fields; Upton Cressett in a quiet and lonely Herefordshire valley; St George, Reforne, isolated in an enormous sailors' graveyard on Portland Bill, Dorset; Stocklinch Ottersey in Somerset, in a sylvan setting of trees and meadows; Friarmere, Yorkshire, on a windswept Pennine hill-top; Skidbrooke, islanded in a clump of trees in an empty expanse of the Lincolnshire marshes, and St Peter the Poor Fisherman, Revelstoke, Devonshire, with a breathtaking view over Stoke Bay.

Most of the Fund's churches are medieval, though it has a fine group of 18th-century churches, including Allerton Mauleverer, North Yorkshire, an interesting essay in primitive neo-Norman, and the delightful Croome d'Abitot, in Worcestershire, by Capability Brown and Robert Adam. The Fund also has some notable 19th-century churches including J. L. Pearson's St Mary, Chute Forest (1875) and G. G. Scott's South Tidworth, Hampshire, with an untouched interior of 1879–80.

Some of these churches came to the Fund in good repair, others were almost derelict and in view of this the Fund's average expenditure of some £15,000 on each church is a remarkable record. However, it has

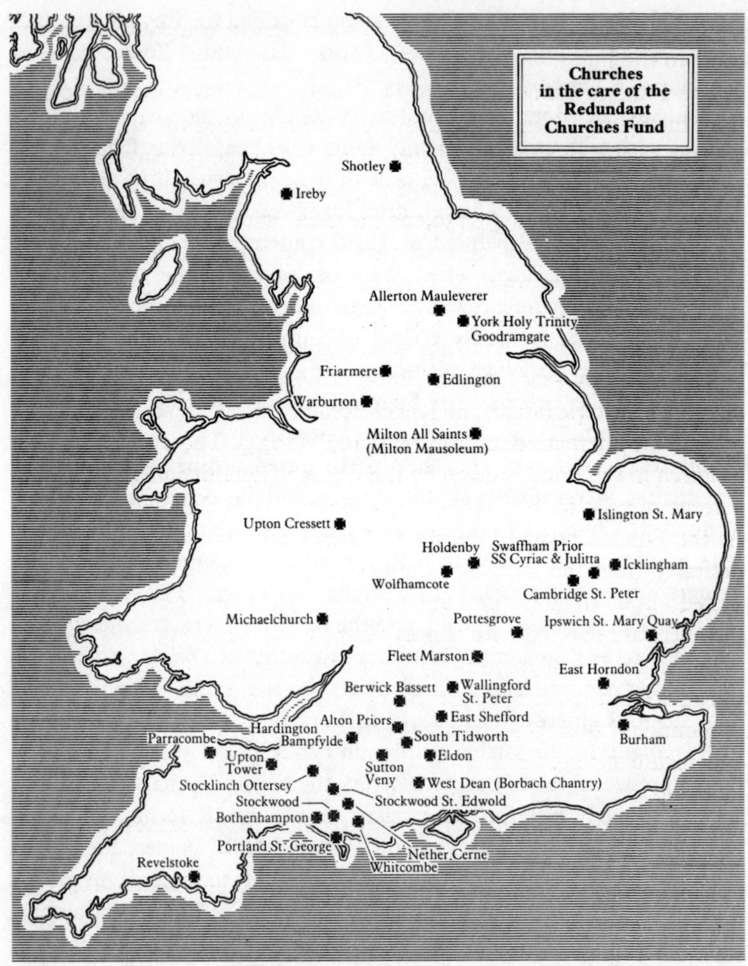

This map is based on a map in the Fund's Annual Report in 1974 and does not include churches vested since that date.

to be said that the Fund has not yet had to tackle a really large medieval wool church or a major Victorian urban church. Yet these two types of buildings, in financial terms, present the greatest problems of all.

While remote country churches are obvious candidates for the Fund, alternative uses have usually been sought for town churches which have become redundant: nonetheless the Fund now has St Nicholas, Gloucester (after several attempts at finding an alternative use failed), the 15th-century St Mary Quay, Ipswich, Suffolk, St Peter, Wallingford,

Oxfordshire and St Peter, Sandwich, Kent, the largest church so far to come to the Fund.

The Fund is financed jointly by Church and State. Money comes from the Church Commissioners, the Department of the Environment and the sale of sites of demolished churches in the proportions 2:2:1. In the first Quinquennium a total of £500,000 was voted: in the second and current one up to £1,750,000 has been allocated. In addition the Fund has occasionally entered into useful partnerships with local authorities. For example, St Peter, Sandwich, received £12,000 from the former borough and £2,500 from Kent County Council. In its annual reports the Fund has continually stressed "its conviction, repeated year by year, that the Fund can accept all churches of architectural or historic interest no longer needed for worship and for which no suitable alternative use can be found" (1974). The decision to vest a church in the Fund is taken by the Church Commissioners, following a recommendation of the Advisory Board for Redundant Churches. As the Fund is financed jointly by Church and State it was obviously desirable from the start that the decision as to which churches were vested was taken on the best independent, expert advice and the Board's members are selected with this in mind.

So far the Commissioners have, in a vast majority of cases, followed the advice of the Advisory Board, but in a situation where the number of redundant churches increases year by year, where the cost of repairs and maintenance increases, and where there is an increasingly vocal lobby opposed to the Redundant Churches Fund, there is bound to be anxiety lest the Commissioners should grow more reluctant to vest churches in the Fund—and that this may lead to the demolition of notable churches including medieval churches and some that are listed as Grade A. In this setting we welcome the news that when once state aid begins the Secretary of State will be able to order a non-statutory public enquiry in any case where the Commissioners are disposed to demolish a church against the advice of the Advisory Board, or indeed in any case where he thinks such an enquiry desirable.

There are a number of further likely or desirable developments in the Fund's work in the next few years. Firstly, it should play a much more positive role in the field of tourism. While many of its churches were being repaired access was inevitably difficult, but far too many of the Fund's churches have subsequently remained locked, often without any indication of where the key is to be found. Since public money is involved this is unacceptable, as well as being contrary to the spirit in which the Fund was set up. Clearly there is an opportunity here for liaison between the Fund and regional tourist boards with leaflets available at tourist information centres. Some of the Fund's churches have groups of Friends who look after them and attend when they are open: at Pitstone, Buckinghamshire, the Friends are there on Sunday afternoons throughout the summer, while at Parracombe, Devon, one of the Fund's most visited churches, a local volunteer acts as curator.

The Fund's churches remain consecrated buildings, and can with the permission of the bishop be used for occasional services: six a year is the probable maximum—to discourage parishes from declaring churches redundant simply to pass on the burden of upkeep. The Fund's churches, however, are freely available for baptisms and funerals (which do not count as worship) and also for marriages, though a special licence is needed. Some Fund churches are also used occasionally for special events and festivals; Lower Gravenhurst, St Mary, Bedfordshire, has had a highly successful series of summer concerts; at Portland, St George Reforne, Dorset, the fine 18th-century organ is being restored; some Fund churches are used for annual flower festivals; at Albury, Surrey, the local historical society has staged a pageant; at St Peter, Wallingford, Oxfordshire, an exhibition has been held.

There is also a case for giving the Fund powers to lease its churches, rather as the National Trust leases some of its country houses to other users on repairing leases. At present the Fund can only alienate to a new owner. The Fund, however, can offer grants towards the repair of important redundant churches which are to be converted to other uses, the reasoning being that if the alternative use did not go ahead the Fund might have to bear the full costs of repairing and maintaining the building. Grants of £10,000 have been offered in this way to St George, Great Yarmouth, Suffolk and Holy Trinity, Tunbridge Wells, Kent. In certain cases where there were potential alternative uses but the tenants could not afford the initial outlay on repairs the building could be repaired by the Fund and then leased. Similarly quite a number of voluntary groups might be willing to take on the cost of repairing redundant country churches if freehold was vested in the Fund. In both cases it would be essential to use these powers sparingly so that all potential purchasers did not seek to take advantage of them.

Local authorities are responsible for a considerable number of ruined churches but, as yet, relatively few that are preserved intact. One of the best examples is the delightful Puritan chapel at Bramhope, near Leeds. This was in a bad state of repair when it was given to the Wharfedale District Council in 1963 (it had been neglected since 1927 and a beech tree had recently crashed through the roof), but it has since been beautifully restored by the Council's consultant architect, with the help of a Historic Buildings Council grant. More recently Tewkesbury

Borough Council have secured a 99-year lease on the remarkable old Baptist chapel in the town and restoration began in February 1977. When complete the building will be open to the public, and used occasionally for events such as lectures.

The National Trust also looks after a very small number of churches: James Paine's remarkable chapel at Gibside, Durham, the church at Clumber, Nottinghamshire, and the untouched Baptist meeting house at Loughwood, Devon.

CHAPTER TWENTY-TWO

New Uses

If the majority of redundant churches and chapels are to survive it is essential to find new uses for them. Fortunately there is abundant evidence that these are forthcoming. In many cases the uses are worthy of encouragement in themselves and the availability of a redundant church has played a major part in launching them. Broadly they may be divided into five groups, cultural and educational, community and public, commercial and industrial, residential and religious—this latter use usually meaning a change to a different denomination or faith. Many churches are on prime sites in the centres of cities and towns, and the fact that they are protected by listed building controls can provide a positive social benefit by making buildings available on desirable sites for activities which would normally be prevented by cost from establishing themselves where they are most likely to flourish. In architectural terms the need is, first, to identify a use that is in character with the building —which has been done very successfully in a great many cases—and, secondly, to ensure that any alterations and additions are sensitively and sympathetically designed, a far more difficult problem.

Though some redundant churches may cost considerable sums to repair or convert, raising the money is not necessarily the major problem. Very often it is simply the refusal of those in authority to accept that a converted old building can prove as satisfactory and rewarding to use as a new one. What so often happens is illustrated by the case of the potentially redundant medieval church of St Lawrence, Evesham, Hereford and Worcester (listed Grade A). In September 1976 an outline proposal was put forward to convert the church into a library but was rejected by the local authority on the grounds that a building of such an age was "quite unsuited to the concept of a modern public library". It is the purpose of this chapter to show that, contrary to this belief, a great many converted churches and chapels are proving wholly capable of meeting present day needs and standards.

Educational and Cultural

Churches converted into public libraries include the Roman Catholic church at Arnside, Cumbria, the former chapel of St Thomas Wymondham, Norfolk, the Friends' Meeting Houses at Coggeshall, Essex and Shipston-on-Stour, Warwickshire, and a chapel in Dunraven Street, Tonypandy, Mid-Glamorgan. In Oxford two churches have been converted with outstanding success into college libraries—St Peter-in-the-East for St Edmund Hall and All Saints for Lincoln College. Also comparable are a number of conversions into religious bookshops—including three for the Society for the Promotion of Christian Knowledge—Holy Trinity, St Marylebone, London; St Olave, Chichester, Sussex (Grade I) and St Nicholas, Rochester, Kent—while in Edinburgh, Wester Coates church has recently been converted for the National Bible Society of Scotland.

Quite a number of churches have been ingeniously converted into record repositories. The most ambitious example is St George Charlotte Square, Edinburgh (1814) which is now West Register House, and provides a much needed extension to the existing Old Register House, which contains the Scottish Records Office. The cost of essential repairs was £70,000 and of the conversion work £280,000 (which involved gutting the interior but provided a high standard of finish and 50,000 linear feet of shelving, equivalent to £61.14 per square metre of the total internal floor area). The total cost of £350,000 was higher than the estimate of £300,000 for a new building on the periphery of Edinburgh, but was more than compensated by the fact that the church was less than a mile from the existing archives—and no new building could have been provided on a central location at this price. In Winchester the large and imposing cruciform Victorian gothic church of St Thomas has become the Hampshire County Record Office. The first stage providing 3,306 linear metres of shelving was completed in 1972 at a cost of £86,000, and a second stage which will introduce multi-tiered stack areas and mobile shelving in the nave is soon to commence. In both these cases there has been no external alteration to the appearance of the building. Other comparable conversions are St Helen and All Saints, Worcester (county archives) and St Mary Mission Hall, North End Road, Hammersmith, London (borough records).

Another highly appropriate new use is conversion into a museum. The church has long been a great patron and churches can often be marvellous places to display works of art, or on a secondary level to store them. St Nicholas Church Museum, Bristol, is an example of the way a (bomb-damaged) church can be remodelled to create a flexible open space such as a new building would offer: at Woodham in Northumberland, by contrast, there is a church museum set up by a local authority where minimal alterations have been made. Another church museum is in St Peter Hungate, Norwich. At Colchester, Suffolk, two churches have become local museums, Holy Trinity (agricultural implements) and All Saints (natural history). The installation at the Agricultural Museum is particularly successful. With the development of tourism and leisure, the scope of museums is constantly broadening and it is interesting that some of the most unusual new museums are to be found in churches—including the Green Howards Regimental Museum in Holy Trinity, Richmond, Yorkshire and the concertina museum in a former Baptist chapel in Belper, Derbyshire. Currently Capell Babell, Cwmfelinfach, Gwent, is being converted to provide a museum and memorial to the poet Islwyn by the Islwyn Memorial Society. With the growth of county museum services churches can also be very suitable for local museums—as at Christ Church, Hartlepool, Cleveland.

Some churches have been transformed into flourishing local theatres or concert halls: indeed the layout of many nonconformist chapels with galleries and raked seats and an uninterrupted view of the pulpit has much in common with theatre design—as some contemporaries were not slow to point out. At Leicester the Dover Street Baptist Church is a theatre; at Chesterfield, Derbyshire, the Holywell Cross Methodist Church is now the North East-Derbyshire Young Peoples Theatre (a highly successful and inventive group); at Bridport, Dorset, a former Methodist Chapel has become a theatre with a single raked tier seating 250 people. In London the octagonal nave of St George, Tufnell Park (1867 by George Truefitt, Grade C) has been brilliantly transformed into an Elizabethan theatre in the round—the first production was staged on April 23, 1976. The pews have been rearranged to form a 485-seat auditorium with standing room for 110. Among other uses connected with the theatre are the Baptist Church, Glossop Road, Sheffield (University Drama Studio); the Welsh Chapel, Cromlech Road, Llandudno, Gwynedd (*c.* 1860) (local theatre society); the Cow Close Methodist Church, Wortley, Leeds (rehearsal room, store and offices for the Red Ladder Travelling Theatre Company); the Wesleyan Chapel (*c.* 1880), Berkeley Road, Coventry (amateur dramatic club); Nailsea, Avon, Methodist church (theatre club). Holy Trinity Southwark, London, is now an orchestra rehearsal hall, as Newington St Leonard, Edinburgh and Trinity Congregational Church, Glasgow, may soon be, while the Forbury Chapel, Leominster, is a dance studio.

Another exciting development is the number of churches and chapels being used by regional Arts Associations, or turned into lively multipurpose arts centres. The West Cornwall Arts Association is in a former chapel in Penzance; another arts centre has been set up in the former North and Trinity church in King Street, Aberdeen (listed Category A). Among other facilities this contains a theatre seating 386. Two particularly dynamic and flourishing arts centres have been set up in churches in Liverpool and Salisbury. In Salisbury the St Edmund Arts Centre runs a programme of daily events, many for children, which include creative writers workshops, sculpture, painting, portraiture, macramé and pottery workshops, "inventors" workshops, a local history group and life drawing, tap dancing, yoga classes, film festivals, poems and prints evenings, visiting theatre groups, jazz sessions, drama, crafts, fashion, music and dancing.

In Liverpool the exceptionally fine classical church in Great George Street, now known affectionately as the Blackie, is converted for use for concerts, theatres, rehearsals, TV recording, exhibitions and a host of community activities. Another excellent arts centre is to be found in the 13th-century church of St Andrew, Ox Market, Chichester, Sussex. At Buckfastleigh, in Devon, the John Loosemore Centre is housed in a former United Reformed church and now contains an organ-building workshop, teaching studio and a recital hall under the same roof. In Jackson's Lane, Haringey, London, another church has been converted into a community arts centre providing a venue for regular events both professional and amateur, such as poetry readings, drama and concerts. At Gravesend, Kent, St Andrew's Waterside Mission has been purchased by the local authority and leased to Gravesham Arts Centre. This is essentially a single-room chapel seating 100–120 people, and will be used for small theatrical and musical performances and help meet "the desperate shortage of rehearsal space in Gravesend".

Churches have also been put to a wide range of educational uses, nonconformist chapels in particular, serving as very practical examinations halls. For some 13 years Southampton Methodist Central Hall has been part of Southampton Technical College; in Manchester the striking First Church of Christ Scientist (listed Grade II*) is an annexe to Elizabeth Gaskell College of Education; at Kingston-on-Thames, St John the Evangelist is an examination hall for the Polytechnic (though still in use for worship); in Birmingham St James Edgbaston is a theological college for the Bible Institute; in Liverpool the former Welsh Chapel is now the University Department of Telecommunications and in Preston, Lancashire, St Peter's is now part of the Polytechnic. Certain churches are used for adult education, the Baptist Church in Belvoir Street, Leicester, known as the "Pork Pie" chapel (Grade II, by J. Hanson) is an adult education centre; in Chester

St Olave is an Adult Reading Centre; at Linburn, Lothian, a church serves as a Blind Peoples' Training Centre. A number of local authorities are considering using churches as Urban Studies Centres. St Mary-on-the-Hill, Chester, is already used in this way; similar proposals have been put forward for All Saints, Bristol, Avon and St Augustine, Pendlebury, Greater Manchester. Other educational uses include a school of dancing in the former Presbyterian church in School Street, Barrow, and a school of art and drawing in a church in Walham Grove, Hammersmith, London. Country churches can also be highly suitable for educational uses, particularly for field studies—at Newton, St Faith, Northamptonshire, there is an excellent Natural History Field Centre while Bowlees Methodist chapel, Durham, is an interpretative centre.

Community

Redundant churches can also make excellent community centres, particularly for the young, the old and groups with special needs for communal facilities—such as immigrants. General purpose community centres are to be found in London in Trinity Presbyterian Church, East Avenue, E12; Trinity Methodist Church, Greenwich, SE18 (Youth and Community); a chapel at Redmire, Yorkshire (community hall); the Belgrave Methodist Church in Leicester; St Mark, Bath, and the Psalm of David Synagogue, Reginald Terrace, Potternewton, Leeds. Churches specifically adapted for the young are the Quaker Meeting House, Holyhead Road, Coventry (built 1896, now a youth club); Tisbury, Wiltshire, Old Independent Meeting House (now a day nursery); Brunswick House Methodist Church, Marske, Cleveland (nursery school); St Francis Roman Catholic Church, Papworth Everard, Cambridgeshire (day nursery/play group); a chapel at Luckwell Bridge, Somerset (youth centre); a chapel in Mayrick Close, Salisbury (Youth Hall); Seion Chapel, Hill Street, Menai Bridge, Gwynedd (youth centre); St Paul, Shireshead, Forton, Lancashire (Boy Scout meeting hall); Tibshelf, St Thomas Mission Church (Scout and Guide Group HQ); Congregational Chapel, Leyburn, Yorkshire (club for stable lads); Comrie Parish Church (1806 by John Stewart) was converted into Comrie Youth Centre with Historic Buildings Council assistance in 1966–67.

In addition the churches themselves have established a number of youth centres in former churches. Asheldham, Essex, and Marrick Priory, Yorkshire, are both highly successful outdoor youth centres, giving a new lease of life to country churches. At Marrick Priory extensive hostel accommodation has been added. St Nicholas Chellington, Bedfordshire (Grade B), is now run by the St Albans Diocesan Board of Finance as a youth centre where groups of young people can spend several days together. Basic facilities (sanitation, cooking and heating) have been provided at a cost of £11,797, allowing each group to use the building as it wishes.

A number of city centre churches have been very successfully transformed into day centres for the old. The best known is St Sampson in York, opened in 1974 and now serving up to 1,000 cups of tea, coffee and soup every day. The work has been carried out with the help of grants of £67,000 from the Hayward Foundation and £7,000 from the York Round Table. Another day centre for old age pensioners is in a chapel at Williamstown, Rhondda, Mid-Glamorgan, and one is planned in the Methodist chapel at Sawston, Cambridgeshire.

Among churches used by particular groups are St Matthew, Southampton, which since 1974 has been a West Indian Social and Community Centre and St Matthew, Brixton, London, now known as Matthew's Meeting Place and used by a wide range of immigrant groups. Here the work has been aided by a grant of £150,000 from the Home Office, but has involved the total loss of an unusually complete late-Georgian interior. Comparable social work is carried out in the Plaistow Methodist Church, London, E13, by the Newham Community Renewal Programme. Some churches have been converted by their congregations into parish centres. St Andrew, Pershore, Worcestershire, which had not been regularly used for worship since 1943 has been transformed in 1971 for the modest price of £15,700, into a parish centre with a 150-seat hall and stage and a large recreation room for young people above. A similar scheme has been carried out at St James, Suffolk Square, Cheltenham, Gloucestershire. Other churches have become clubs including a social club in the Independent Methodist chapel at Brick Street, Warrington, Lancashire; a working men's club in the Friends Meeting House at Stebbing, Essex, and a night club in the Methodist Chapel at Stow Hill, Newport, Gwent.

The number of planning permissions given for conversion to community use has grown steadily over the last few years, though in some cases the work has been delayed due to the economic recession. In September 1976 for example the Brent Active Pensioners and Disabled Peoples Society was given permission to convert a church for their use in Fortunegate Road, London, NW10, while at Writhlington, near Radstock, Somerset, a church may be used for the mentally handicapped.

Churches and chapels also have considerable potential for conversion as indoor sports halls. The Sports Council, which gives grant to the provision of sports facilities, has produced an excellent booklet *Sport for All in Converted Buildings* "to show what can be achieved by initiative and imagination and relatively small capital investment in the provision of good facilities by converting existing buildings". Churches, and, particularly chapels, which rarely have aisles, often have the high ceilings and uninterrupted spans (roughly those of a badminton court) today required for indoor sports and can be adapted with fairly minimal additions. These facilities are in greatest need, according to the Sports Council, in city centres and remote country areas, precisely the places where most redundancies occur. The extent of the need is reflected in the target of 815 indoor sports centres by 1981: in the Eastern Region (where there are many redundant churches) the target is for 96 by 1981, of which 51 were in existence in 1976. Standard sizes for small sports halls are 32m by 17m, 29·5m by 16·5m and 26m by 16m (in each case with a ceiling height of 6·7m to 7·6m). This will provide space for badminton, basket ball, indoor cricket, fencing, five-a-side football, gymnastics, table tennis and volleyball. Other sports for which churches could provide suitable spaces are boxing, judo, karate, martial arts, keep-fit training, trampoline and wrestling, though some religious objections might be raised to potentially violent sports. The most interesting conversion on these lines so far is St Mark, Deptford, London. Here a church which had for some years been used largely as a warehouse was converted into a multi-purpose hall complete with stage on the upper level and a youth activity area below. Following the success of this project the adjoining church hall was converted into a sports hall with a viewing gallery and changing rooms. The windows are protected by metal guards and the walls have been boxed out flush to cater for local style football. The two phases of work were financed as follows:

	Phase I £	*Phase II* £
Cost	74,500	35,150
Grants		
London Borough of Lewisham	30,500	28,000
Parish Funds	11,000	3,150
Inner London Educational Authority	11,000	—
Department of Education and Science	22,000	—
Lady Florence Institute	—	4,000

The cost per square metre of the conversion of £70 for Phase I and £78 for Phase II, compares with an estimate in both cases of £180 per square metre in an equivalent new building.

Some churches are also of just the right proportions for conversion into one or more squash courts. Old Ranfurly Parish Church, on the outskirts of Glasgow (built *c.* 1900) has been converted in this way after lying empty for several years, by a local sports club. The total cost of £26,000 was aided by a grant of £12,000 from the Sports Council, with the landlord, a local leather company, providing a bank guarantee. Today the club has 250 members and the secretary, who has been involved in amateur sport for 15 years, considers that "this type of development could be repeated in many parts of the country". Other squash courts are to be found in former chapels at Northallerton, Yorkshire, and Crewkerne, Somerset; planning permission for squash courts was given for St Cuthbert's, Middlesbrough, subject to listed building consent. In Swindon the local subaqua club bought a former chapel in September 1975 to provide a workshop and storage for equipment and boats. Even where churches cannot provide indoor halls of standard size they can still offer useful community sports facilities. Local sports halls are not aimed at providing for top competitions but at meeting the needs of everyone who wishes to participate, and for this reason the Sports Council is encouraging small halls as much as prestige centres of international standards.

The large interior spaces of chapels and churches have in some cases made them very adaptable to medical use. In Glasgow a Physiotherapy and Rehabilitation Clinic has operated since 1930 in the former United Free Church in Bath Street (1874 by D. Sturrock). Today the clinic gives over 45,000 treatments a year, mostly to chronic and long-term patients with 250 people coming every day by appointment. Internally little alteration has been necessary apart from the installation of light-weight cubicles. The superintendent can emerge from his office behind the organ loft on to the gallery and—like the captain of a ship—take in everything that is happening and make immediate contact with any member of the staff. In the former Sunday School rooms beneath the church a gymnasium has been installed with bicycles, wall bars, rowing machines, mats and mirrors. In Coventry the church of St Mark in Stoney Staunton Road (1869 and Grade II) was recently acquired as an outpatients clinic for the nearby hospital. All Saints Church, West Pallant, Chichester, Sussex, is now a Red Cross Centre, used for therapeutic clubs, training in first aid and home nursing and monthly parties for house-bound and long-stay hospital patients.

Other forms of broadly public use are a conference centre in the Birchcliffe Baptist Chapel at Hebden Bridge, Yorkshire (sponsored by the Rowntree Trust); the chapel at Kelham Hall, Nottinghamshire (now Newark Council offices), which is to be used for banquets, buffets, receptions, conferences, exhibitions, concerts and indoor sports, and the Unity Church, Derby Street, South Shields, Durham, which is a Union Meeting Hall.

Commercial and Industrial

A great many urban churches and chapels, particularly in industrial towns and cities, have been converted to commercial and industrial uses. In most cases this preserves at least the townscape value of the building though, on occasions, the façade has been barbarously mutilated by the insertion of showroom windows. In broader economic terms however the use of these buildings has considerable relevance to the increasing concern for the survival of small businesses and industries and to the encouragement of traditional crafts and skills. The evidence we have received from planning authorities, particularly on light industrial uses, makes it very clear that nonconformist chapels in particular provide well-lit and well-ventilated flexible spaces that offer good working conditions and are suitable for many kinds of manufacturing machinery. There are, for example, printing works in the Methodist Chapel at Marsden Street, Chesterfield, Derbyshire, the Nant Paris chapel, Gwynedd and the Methodist Church at Old Brindsley, Nottinghamshire. Garment or clothing factories are established at a chapel in Clarendon Street, Leamington Spa, Warwickshire and Rock Ferry Presbyterian Church Birkenhead, Merseyside, while in the Methodist Church, Liverpool Road, Wigan, Greater Manchester, is a sewing factory. There are manufacturing joiners in the Methodist churches at Sutton Road, St Helens, Lancashire and Copsterhill Road, Oldham, Lancashire; that at Ilkeston, Nottinghamshire, is now used by Fairline Upholstery.

Very many former nonconformist chapels are used for various forms of light engineering and assembly, for example the Congregational Chapel, Regent Street, Oldham, Lancashire (light engineering goods); Capel Nazareth, Pont Rug, near Caernarvon (racing motor cycle components factory); the Methodist Church at Sandy, Bedfordshire (light engineering); the Methodist Churches in High Street, Clowne, Derbyshire (fork lift truck production), New Houghton (precision engineering), Pinxton (electronic assembly) and Pleasley (hydraulic equipment) all in Derbyshire. The old chapel in Chewton Street, Eastwood, Nottinghamshire, is used for the repair of gardening equipment, and the Methodist Chapel in Latchley, Cornwall, is a cardboard box factory. In country areas such activities can be eligible for help from the Council for Small Industries in Rural Areas (small industries are those not normally employing more than 20 skilled people and rural areas include country towns of up to 10,000 people). Loans of up to 80% of the cost of the project may be given, up to a maximum of £30,000, and repayment varies over 2 and 20 years. Examples are the Ebenezer Art Gallery, Polperro, Cornwall, the headquarters of the East Cornwall Society of Artists now housed in the former Ebenezer Chapel, built in 1877; and the Wessex Crafts centre in a former chapel at Tisbury, Wiltshire.

Chapels and churches are increasingly being re-used as workshops and studios: there are potteries in Millport West Church, Strathclyde and Priestweston, Salop. In the Friends Meeting House, Prebend Street, Leicester, there is a workshop for the blind. The Methodist church at Aughton, Rotherham, S. Yorkshire, is to become a stone masons' workshop and studio; St Peter, Little Oakley, Northamptonshire is a restoration workshop; St Jude, Shieldfield, Northumberland, is used by a picture framer; a chapel at Alvediston, Wiltshire, is a painting and photography studio. One of the best conversions of this type is the delightful early concrete church (in barn-like Tuscan style) in Dilston Grove, Rotherhithe, London, built in 1911 by Simpson and Ayrton as a mission from Clare College, Cambridge. This was rescued from abandonment and dereliction by a group of young people who now use it as a studio and workshop. Another communal use of this type is the Ballyhannan Church, Tarbet, now a crafts centre and tea room. Various churches are now used for photography: the Platt Chapel, Fallowfield, Manchester (listed Grade II) is now the headquarters of a photographic society and used for exhibitions; a synagogue near the University in Liverpool is now a commercial photographers studio. At Wareham, Dorset, Holy Trinity has become an art gallery; in Rotherham, South Yorkshire, Temperance Hall, in Wellgate, is now an antique gallery.

Many nonconformist chapels have become offices. Such conversions have been carried out at the Methodist Church in North Shields, Tyne and Wear, which forms an important group with the town hall; at a chapel in Brighton, Sussex (for Olivetti); at the Montgomery Wesley and Methodist Church in Sheffield; at St Nicholas Chapel at Nantmawr, Salop, and at chapels in Vann Road and Fernhurst, Chichester. To these can be added a number of supermarkets—at Barrow, Cumbria, a chapel in Main Street, Kimberley and the Methodist chapel in North Street, Barrow upon Soar, Leicestershire.

Churches and chapels have also been found very suitable for storage, notably for manufactured goods of different kinds, for antiques and for agricultural equipment. The United Methodist Church, Mansfield Road, Creswell, Nottinghamshire, is used for the storage of lubricating oil; the Congregational Church at Uxbridge Road, Hammersmith, for antique furniture; St Peter, Blossom Street, Manchester, as the University Theatre Group store; a chapel in Holly Walk, Leamington Spa, Warwickshire, for building materials and a Methodist Chapel in Trewidland, Cornwall, for an agricultural store. Such uses usually ensure the exterior of a building is kept intact, and on a temporary basis can mean that a redundant church with an interior of some quality is looked after and kept secure even though it will probably be inaccessible.

Residential Use

Strong feelings can be aroused by the conversion of churches to residential use. Local people may find it offensive that the parish church should become the exclusive property of an individual, to which they no longer have right of access. Others find it an assault upon the sanctity of the church and the churchyard where burials have recently taken place. Correspondence in *The Times* during the summer of 1976 showed especially strong feelings against the retention of religious fittings in churches converted into houses: "That a font where the sacred mystery of Christian baptism has been practised for generations should grace someone's 'chic' living room will admittedly be regarded with indifference by many, but most Christians will regard it as offensive. That the Royal Arms hang over the dining table, there are bells in the attic, brasses in the hall floor, stained glass in the kitchen window, and the dead of two World Wars recorded in the bathroom, surely cannot be right."

The Norfolk Churches Trust and the Friends of Friendless Churches are hardly less active in campaigning against conversion to residential use than they are against demolition. However, the Advisory Board for Redundant Churches and many Diocesan Redundant Churches Uses Committees consider that conversion into houses is in principle quite acceptable. The Diocese of Hereford Redundant Churches Uses Committee told us "it is the firm belief of this Committee that most country churches can best be preserved as residences". The Diocese of Carlisle's Redundant Churches Uses Committee while preferring public rather than private uses "favour houses rather than barns".

As yet there are relatively few conversions which are commendable in architectural terms, though Latchingdon and Langdon Hills, in Essex, and Mansel Gamage, in Herefordshire, are exceptions, where the essential character of the church has been respected both outside and in. At its worst the problem is illustrated by proposals for St John, Horsely Green, Manningtree, Essex, published in the *Architects Journal* (January 17, 1973). The problem appears to be that people who buy churches or chapels do so because they are cheaper than other houses, and such people will understandably be able to spend only the barest minimum on conversion work. Usually they will be hoping for improvement grants, and these are usually only given to schemes which meet stringent cost limitations. Any architectural alterations are therefore likely to be both plain and bald. One conversion in Scotland, for example, only attracted the grant-aid that made it possible by making two dwelling units (attracting two grants) which necessitated more windows and doors. From an architectural point of view a further objection arises over the inevitable problems of the churchyard. Usually an owner will want some land, but if a churchyard is still in use, an additional fence will have to be erected dividing one part of the churchyard from another: this is a disturbing intrusion in what should be a continuous and homogeneous open space. And where an owner wants to grow flowers or vegetables in front of a church this can look strangely out of place, and to some people profane.

A further problem over conversion to residential use stems with the attitude taken by certain local authorities, and also landowners. Some planning authorities refuse to give permission for conversion to residential use for any church outside the village envelope: this can be, however, in conflict with their role as the authority with responsibility for listed buildings. Considerable difficulties often arise over what appears to be unnecessary inflexibility about provisions for drainage: in one case an owner, forbidden to place a drainage tank in the obvious place, had to buy a patch of land from a neighbour—at the astronomical rate of £400,000 per acre.

One case of a redundant church converted into a house in Wiltshire suggests that churches may be particularly appropriate as dwellings for invalids. Here a paraplegic architect, who wanted a large single space in which to live and work where he could move round in a wheelchair without passing through doors or changing from level to level, has found a redundant church perfectly suited to his needs. Cases such as this confound all those who despair of finding new uses for churches.

In the last two years there have also been some ingenious schemes for converting urban churches into flats. At St James, Farnham, Surrey, the local authority architects' office has produced proposals for transforming the church into flats for young single people.

The conversion of redundant nonconformist chapels into houses can be numbered not just in dozens, but in hundreds, particularly in rural counties which were strongholds of Methodism. Eden District Council, in Cumbria, has given the following permissions for change of use to dwellings:

Methodist Chapel, Holt, Appleby (1972)
Methodist Chapel, Goglin (1973)
St Mary, North Stainmore (1974)
Methodist Chapel, Newbiggin (1976)
Methodist Chapel, Moreland (1976)

In the Cotswold District the following conversions have taken place:

Chapel, Aston Bank, Bourton on the Water (2 dwellings)
Old Chapel, Aston Magna, Blockley
Bethel Chapel, Brockhampton
Methodist Chapel, Chipping Campden (2)
Congregational Chapel, Loughborough (2)
Congregational Chapel, Northleach
Old Wesleyan Chapel, Tarlton, Cirencester

The best residential conversions in Scotland so far are the important late Georgian churches of Newburn, Fife (house) and Craig Tayside, Angus (house and studio).

Use by Other Denominations

The survival of numerous nonconformist churches is due to changes from one denomination to another. The Presbyterian chapel at Fulwood near Sheffield, which became Unitarian by the end of the 18th century, is a good example. Closed in 1876 it was leased to Wesleyans between 1878–80 and then closed again; then restored and re-used by the Unitarians between 1885–98, from 1899 to 1934 it was leased by the Congregationalists, when it reverted to the Unitarians only to return to the Congregationalists. It is only really since the Pastoral Measure of 1968 that Anglican churches have been taken over by other Christian denominations in any large numbers. The following is a list of redundant churches subject to such schemes since then.

1970	Oundle, Northamptonshire, Jesus Church	Roman Catholic
1971	Horsmonden, Kent, All Saints	Roman Catholic
1971	Swanscombe, Kent, All Saints	Roman Catholic
1973	Worsborough, Yorkshire, St James	Roman Catholic
1975	Dorchester, Dorset, Holy Trinity	Roman Catholic
1975	Huddersfield, St Andrew, W. Yorkshire	Roman Catholic
1976	Witham, Essex, All Saints	Roman Catholic
1976	Northampton, St Lawrence	Polish Roman Catholic
1975	Bedford, Holy Trinity	Polish Roman Catholic
1971	Bolton, Great Manchester, All Saints	Ukranian Catholic
1974	Wardleworth, Lancashire, St James	Ukranian Catholic
1972	South Kensington, London, St Peter	Armenian Orthodox
1970	Tolleshunt Knights, Essex, All Saints	Greek Orthodox
1972	Battersea, London, St Bartholomew	Greek Orthodox
1973	East Wickham, London	Greek Orthodox

1975	Camden Town, London, All Saints	Greek Orthodox
1975	Shepherds Bush, St Thomas, London	Greek Orthodox
1976	Bedford, St Cuthbert	Serbian Orthodox
1972	Leicester, St George	Greek & Serbian Orthodox
1976	Knightsbridge, London, All Saints, Ennismore Gardens	Russian Orthodox
1971	Leyton, Essex, St Edward	Elim Pentecostal Church
1971	Hastings, Sussex, St Mary-in-the-Castle	Assembly of God
1972	Derby, Holy Trinity	Assemblies of the 1st Born
1974	Everton, Liverpool, St Polycarp	Protestant Reformers Memorial Church
1974	Wicker, Yorkshire, Holy Trinity	New Testament Church of God
1976	Heigham, Norfolk, St Bartholomew	Mount Zion Pentecostal
1976	Walworth, London, All Saints	Church of the Lord
1976	Willey, Herefordshire, St John	Private Chapel

Of the 28 churches on the list, Roman Catholics have taken 6, Polish Catholics 2, Ukranian Catholics 2 and the Orthodox churches 9. The traditionalist Society of Pius X, supporters, like Archbishop Lefevre, of the Tridentine mass have, however, not been able yet to obtain a redundant Anglican church as the Church Commissioners only negotiate with the established hierarchy.

A different problem arises with non-Christian religions and sects. Islam is now numerically the second strongest religion in the United Kingdom, but there is considerable resistance in both the Church of England and the Church of Scotland to handing churches to Muslim communities. At the Church of England Synod strong feelings were expressed on both sides about the proposed sale of St Mary, Dewsbury, Yorkshire, for use as a mosque. The streets around were all solidly Muslim but local people fiercely objected, and the debate went against sale after an impassioned speech by an ex-Hindu convert, who argued that to hand churches to the very communities to whom missionary work was directed, could only sow doubts in both the minds of the converted and the unconverted. The Rev Jack Webb, however, put the point of view that "it is religious imperialism to use one's heritage and wealth to make life more difficult for other religions and this conflicts with the basic principle of freedom of worship which the church accepts".

Until now the growing demand for places of worship from immigrant Muslim and Hindu communities has been met largely by the sale of nonconformist chapels. In Leicester the Planning Officer stated there "is a major need for old churches to serve religions newly arrived in the City", and so far the following churches have been transferred:

Carey Hall Baptist Chapel, Roman Catholic Church, Harrison Road (both Muslim Temples); St George, Church of England (Orthodox); St Paul, Roman Catholic, Melbourne Road (Polish Catholic); and the Methodist Church, Hinckley Road (Ukranian Catholic). The Slough Planning Officer similarly confirmed "a continuing demand for churches by minority groups". Other examples of churches taken over by immigrant communities are the Baptist Church, Fern Street, Oldham (temple for local Indian Community); Great Synagogue, Fournier Street, Spitalfields, London (now a mosque) and the Baptist Church, Harnall Road, Coventry (now a Sikh temple).

A similar pattern of use by other denominations can be seen on a smaller scale in Scotland. In Glasgow the former Belhaven Church (James Sellars 1877) is now St Luke's Greek Orthodox Cathedral, Pollokshields West Church (W. G. Rowan 1875–76) is now the Christian Brethren Meeting House and Woodlands Parish Church (John Burnet 1874–76) is now Free Presbyterian. The last is a case where the fine Morris and Company and Stephen Adam stained glass had to be removed because of the beliefs of the congregation. In Edinburgh St Thomas's Church in Leith (John Henderson 1840) has become a Sikh temple.

Future Potential

From this survey it emerges that redundant churches are being re-used for a whole range of enterprising purposes and urgent community needs. All the evidence suggests that this demand is likely to grow. The potential of church buildings is stressed in the Inner City Studies commissioned by the Department of the Environment. That on Lambeth stresses that the need is not just to provide more open space . . . "but also to find ways of using buildings (for instance unused churches or church halls) so that they can, in an area where open land is at a premium act as indoor substitutes". Any covered space in a town is a potential asset and redundant churches could provide winter play space for children and act as crèches for mothers who need to be free of their children for a few hours. And where children are likely to be active it will not be necessary to go to the expense of heating the whole church.

In Norwich the church of St Martin-at-Oak has been adapted as a night shelter; could not many other disused city churches be used to make similar provision for the homeless? While these are often of no great architectural merit they are usually strongly built and could be adapted to serve in this way at little cost. Organizations such as Help the Aged, equally, often have difficulty in finding premises in towns and cities: redundant churches could sometimes provide the answer.

There is, in fact, a general case to be made that redundant churches are an excellent means of providing accommodation for the social needs the churches seek to meet.

The success of those churches like Asheldham and Chellington which have been adapted as youth centres by Diocesan authorities suggests that their example could well be followed elsewhere. There is also interesting potential for using redundant churches for exhibits relating to the church's work and patronage. At Colchester there is a proposal to transform a church into a museum of church life. Some could be used to collect treasures from other redundant churches. This could be done on a diocesan basis like the treasuries of church plate to be found in several cathedrals, or by subject on the model of the Stained Glass Museum in the triforium of Ely Cathedral which is opening (on selected days) for the first time this year. Given the current rate of redundancies there is clearly potential to establish relatively quickly good collections of church woodwork, metalwork, organs, and vestments. Though it is unlikely the Church of England or the other denominations would wish to take such an initiative on its own, such museums if they were in the development areas could qualify for substantial grants from the three national tourist boards, as well as forming a worthwhile contribution on the part of the churches to the tourist drive that is so vital to the economic well-being of this country.

Two churches have been converted into heritage centres with exhibitions and displays presenting local history through architecture to visitors. The first, in St Michael's, Chester, opened in June 1975 and cost £25,980 (aided by a Department of the Environment Grant). The second, in St Mary, Castlegate, York, which opened later that year was aided by grants of £40,000 from the Arts Council and £6,000 from York Civic Trust. The acclaim received by these two projects appears likely to stimulate similar ventures elsewhere.

Another interesting proposal, in the context of current concern for small businesses, is the proposal put forward by Bolton Metropolitan Borough Council and Bolton Civic Trust for using the Bridge Street Methodist Church as a small industries centre, providing facilities for conferences, exhibitions and receptions for firms which do not have these in their own works. This is an idea which could well apply elsewhere and win support from local chambers of commerce.

Here, as with many new uses, there is an opportunity for co-operation between local government and local businesses in raising finance to put churches to uses which would be beneficial to both. Partnership is in fact the key to the financing of many new uses. There are many central and local government spending programmes (quite apart from grants towards repairs to historic buildings) which can provide substantial sums if churches are put to social, educational, cultural or industrial uses. No public funded authority should embark on a new building if there is an existing one—worth retaining—which can be converted at a competitive price. This applies not only to local authorities but statutory undertakings like the Regional Health Boards, the Gas and Electricity Boards and the Post Office. In Edinburgh the delightful former Episcopal church of Holy Trinity, Dean Bridge (1838 by John Henderson) has been converted into an electricity substation with no alteration in its external appearance: at Wakefield, Yorkshire the Post Office use a former chapel as a sorting office. Both these examples could be followed elsewhere.

There also appears to be an increasing demand for disused churches as restaurants—another use closely connected with tourism. The Diocese of Guildford Redundant Churches Uses Committee has regular enquiries for churches to be used as "Elizabethan banqueting halls and the like". Just such a conversion is taking place at Bournemouth, Dorset, Holy Trinity. Some denominations—the Church of Scotland and some of the Free Churches—place covenants to prevent a church from being used for drinking (as they do for gambling), though such restrictions can be difficult to enforce if the building is resold. The covenants referred to restricting drinking can bring about the loss of the church as has been the case in 1977 at Macdonald Road, Edinburgh, where a good small Edwardian church and hall group by J. N. Scott and Lorne Campbell has disappeared because the clause deprived the building of its intending user.

One of the best examples of this type of conversion is a seamen's mission hall in Charleston, South Carolina, which has recently become a flourishing restaurant. This is a building to which no architectural guidebook would give more than a line as a church but which is memorable, almost noble, as a restaurant. Among the many people who eat there, a number would never normally go into a church: when, having admired the building they are told what it was, the thought has been sown that other churches might also be worth visiting. Thus, even transformed out of recognition, churches can still distantly fulfil some part of their purpose.

CHAPTER TWENTY-THREE

Church and State

Although the great majority of churches are the exclusive property of the Churches themselves, it needs to be remembered that quite a number could never have been built without generous state or municipal aid. Under an Act of 1670 the cost of rebuilding St Paul's Cathedral and the City churches after the Great Fire was met by a tax on coal entering the City of London. The same source of funds was made available under the Act of 1711 enabling the building of 50 new churches (though only a dozen new churches were in fact built), within London and its suburbs. Similar Acts, passed in 1818 and 1824, provided £1½ million for the construction of new churches which were seen as a means of combating the threat of mob-rule and the rise of nonconformity.

Towns and boroughs over the centuries have also made substantial contributions to parish churches, particularly to the building of towers which often contained the town clock and bells. The parish church at Newcastle-upon-Tyne is one example of quite a number given and still maintained by the town. In Aberdeen six of the principal churches were originally provided, or at some stage rebuilt, at the expense of the town council and until 1925 were wholly maintained by the council. That year ownership was transferred under Act of Parliament to the Church of Scotland, though the Corporation retained right of first refusal over churches being sold. In 1954 the City Corporation exercised its rights of pre-emption on the redundant North Kirk, which has now been converted into an arts centre; since then the General Trustees have sought, unsuccessfully, to end the local authorities rights. Similar situations have arisen in Edinburgh and Glasgow.

Ecclesiastic Exemption

The relation between the churches and the state over historic buildings has been dominated by the Church of England which has by far the largest number of historic churches: today it has some 11,000 listed buildings compared with the Church of Scotland's 1,000 and the Methodists 350. It was the determined intervention of Archbishop Davidson in 1913 that won the so-called ecclesiastical exemption from the provisions of the Ancient Monuments Act, which has been incorporated in all subsequent legislation extended to historic buildings. The reasons why this exemption was sought were forcefully expressed by Sir Lewis Didbin in his evidence to the select committee: "Anything like control by the Office of Works . . . I should regard as absolutely mischievous and under existing circumstances wholly impossible . . . it would cut clean across the whole ecclesiastical administration . . . it would so absolutely subvert the present administration of ecclesiastical affairs that I should regard it as anarchic . . . I think it would have this practical effect: that you would find that there would be a great many more interesting ruins in the country and fewer restored churches." Against this Lord Curzon argued: "I myself would like nothing better than to see our cathedrals—which, after all, are the most glorious national monuments we possess, excelling our palaces and our castles, put into the list of scheduled monuments, so that it would be impossible to touch them without the consent of the state as advised by the Ancient Monuments Board."

Following the submission of evidence the Select Committee recommended that cathedrals should be placed under the protection of the bill by a majority of one, but a motion to include parish churches was lost by a tie. Criticism levelled at the Church of England in the discussion, however, had the effect of making the Church authorities improve safeguards over repairs and alterations. As a result the Church of England has been fairly able to claim that its system for administering and protecting historic buildings has remained in advance of that of the state. This is argued to be a continuing justification for the ecclesiastical exemption. However as state measures to protect our heritage become more effective the real question that needs to be asked is whether the Church is continuing to maintain its lead. This is vital, as churches always were, and still are, the most important group of historic buildings in the country.

Grant Aid

The three Historic Buildings Councils for England, Scotland and Wales were set up in 1953 by the Historic Buildings and Ancient Monuments Act to advise on "the making of grants and loans towards the repair and maintenance of buildings of outstanding historic or architectural interest or their contents or adjoining land". Though the act was worded so that churches were included within its scope, grants have never in fact been made to churches because of the continuing exemption from the controls which apply to secular listed buildings. In 1960, however, the report of the Historic Buildings Council for England stated that "in future chapels forming part of, or within the precincts of, an outstanding house, and not in use as a parish church, could be included within our recommendations". In 1971–72 the English HBC affirmed its willingness to consider giving grants to redundant churches sold for conversion to alternative use.

On January 30, 1975, it was announced that the Government had accepted in principle the case for state aid for historic churches of all denominations still used for worship, other than cathedrals. Up to £1 million at 1973 prices was promised for England with proportionate amounts for Scotland and Wales. On November 11, 1976, Lady Birk announced in the House of Lords that broad agreement had been reached on conditions but that no date could be given for the commencement of grants and here, in June 1977, the matter still rests. As with secular buildings all churches recommended by the HBC as outstanding would be eligible for grants, and churches in outstanding conservation areas would be eligible for conservation grants. All churches would be subject to a means test which would in practice extend the exclusion of cathedrals to major analogous churches of other denominations. With the Church of England any repairs classed as urgent or immediate in the Quinquennial Inspection report would always be eligible while those essential within the Quinquennium would be considered on their merits. Applications would only be entertained within 12 months of the inspection. For other denominations similar rules would apply. In Scotland, unlike England, Cathedrals would be eligible for Grant-aid.

This scheme would run for an initial period of at least five years, during which no legislation would be introduced on the subject of the ecclesiastical exemption from listed building control. The Church Commissioners would, however, agree to consult the Secretary of State for the Environment before ordering the demolition of a listed church (or an unlisted church in a conservation area) and would allow him to hold a (non-statutory) local public inquiry. This would be done whenever the proposed demolition was taking place against the advice of the Advisory Board for Redundant Churches or representations and objections had been received. The findings of the inquiry, and the Secretary of State's conclusions and the Church Commissioners' reasons for accepting or rejecting these would all be published. For its part the General Synod of the Church of England would undertake to review the faculty jurisdiction if possible within five years. Finally, the Government would also make some provision for redundant churches, chapels and meeting houses of the other denominations to help balance the state's contribution to the Church of England's Redundant Churches Fund. One subject not mentioned is that of access to churches which have received HBC grants. As public access is a condition of grants to secular buildings the same provisions will presumably apply to churches. In view of the increasing problem of locked churches, however, the conditions on access need to be clarified not only in general principle but in specific undertakings in each case.

Listing

The listing of churches and chapels is to be operative in the administration of state aid and a review of the listing of ecclesiastical buildings is now under way. From the start Anglican churches both in England and Wales have been listed differently from secular buildings: A, B and C rather than I, II*, II, and III. (The supplementary list, containing only the now obsolete Grade III, was purely advisory and gave no legal protection; as the statutory lists are revised Grade III buildings are considered for upgrading.) Behind the curious system of dual grading was the fear that if the same standards were applied to both secular and ecclesiastical buildings churches would have outnumbered any other type of building in the top Grade, largely on grounds of age. As a result Grade A was even more exclusive than Grade I, and restricted to "first class churches that are more or less complete". As a result there were, on December 31, 1976, 5,095 Grade I listed buildings and 2,248 Grade A listed churches. Grade B by contrast is equivalent neither to Grade II* nor to Grade II, but rather embraces the lesser Grade I, all of II* and the better II in the following manner:

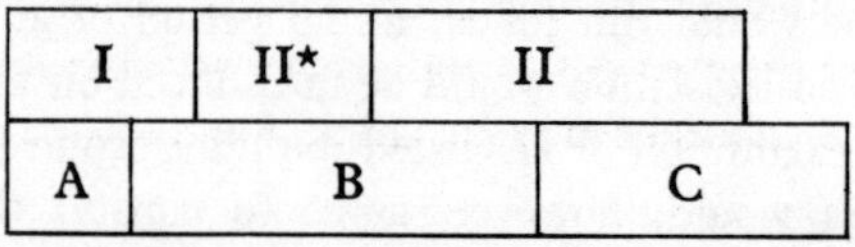

<table>
<tr><td colspan="2">I</td><td>II*</td><td colspan="2">II</td><td></td></tr>
<tr><td>A</td><td colspan="3">B</td><td colspan="2">C</td></tr>
</table>

This system is so confusing that there is a clear case for ending it and applying the same criteria for both secular and ecclesiastical building so that in future A = I, B* = II*, B = II and C like III is phased out.

In Scotland by contrast all buildings, both ecclesiastical and secular, have been classified identically as category (not grade) A, B and C from the start though C, like III south of the border, is being absorbed upwards or downwards. The terms of reference in Scotland for listing have also been drawn up with greater skill and foresight than in England and Victorian buildings included from a much earlier date. The criteria are:

17th, 18th and early 19th century parish churches

The meeting houses of the Secession Churches between 1817–40 and the very early Roman Catholic churches

After 1840 the works of the better known architects such as Thomson, Bryce, Wilson, Peddie and Kinnear, Pilkington, Rowand Anderson, J. J. Burnet, G. W. Browne, Robert Lorimer, John Kinross and Charles Rennie Mackintosh and the better buildings of the more gifted lesser known figures.

During the first round of listing in England and Wales not only were almost all the Victorian buildings omitted, but equally almost all the chapels and meeting houses of the dissenting denominations, and now that the lists are being revised it is vital that they should be included. As we have argued throughout this book, though they may not be of high architectural merit in a national sense they are often very important historically and architecturally distinctive in their neighbourhood. In view of this it is disturbing to hear that local authorities are still finding it difficult to get Victorian chapels listed, perhaps as a result of the statement by Lady Birk in 1976 that "too many marginal buildings, particularly of the later 19th century are being listed". The Director of the Amber Valley District Council for example told us "one way (of protection) is to get all good examples listed but this is not easy now". Recently Greater Manchester Council applied without success to have the Brunswick Methodist Church, Broad Street, Pendleton, Salford, listed, but the application was rejected by the Department of the Environment, and the building is now likely to be demolished. As local authorities are unlikely to make applications for spotlisting without good cause it seems unduly discouraging to local conservation teams and officers to reject their proposals and doubly so where the buildings are of a category which has been systematically underlisted in the past.

Control over Demolition

With state aid for churches now at last in prospect we believe that there should be a general move towards establishing standard procedures of control for all denominations both in the interests of preservation and of equity. As far as provisions for inspection and maintenance are concerned, and control over alterations and disposal of fittings, other denominations could usefully establish procedures modelled on those of the Church of England. However, we also take the view that Section 2 of the Redundant Churches Act (1969) should be repealed and that the Church of England should have to seek listed building consent to demolish both listed churches and churches in conservation areas in the same way as other denominations. So far no less than 27 listed Church of England churches have been demolished under Pastoral Measure Procedure and the Church Commissioners have refused to give an undertaking that no Grade A church will be demolished. We believe that in the Church of England's own interests it should submit to listed building procedures over demolition.

Though it is true that churches get no direct aid for repairs, they do, like all charities, receive considerable subsidies from the taxpayer through exemptions from many kinds of taxations. It seems reasonable to suggest that those who have paid the taxes should at least require that no church property be destroyed until the public has an opportunity to propose a means of saving it. In concrete terms every local authority should have the power to delay demolition of a building which has been subsidized by local or national taxes. Many redundant churches, even those of little architectural merit, are capable of being put to community use, and quite a number are strongly built and in sound condition, with a long life ahead of them. As the whole principle of exemption of churches from taxation is based on the fact that they do work of special value for the community we believe that buildings they no longer need should first be offered to the community, rather than the site sold for commercial purposes and the money used elsewhere, with no return to the place and people who have subsidized the building over the years.

Control over Alterations

While alterations to Anglican churches in England and Wales are subject to faculty jurisdiction the position over listed buildings of the other Churches which are in use for worship has been unclear. According to *Listed Church Buildings* a booklet issued by the Methodist Division of Property the law "would seem to allow several things without permission, for example: (1) partial or complete reconstruction of the interior, and (2) where a listed building is immediately flanked by other premises and the façade only is visible the accommodation behind the façade may be demolished and remodelled". However, the authors of this document say in their foreword that owners or trustees of listed churches "may not alter or demolish without listed building permission", and it appears to be the case that many denominations do in fact apply for listed building consent for alterations, presumably because of the uncertainty of the law. In Edinburgh three recent applications have been made for consent to demolish spires (a form of partial demolition)—two by the Episcopalian Church and one by the Church of Scotland. In many cases, however, alterations to listed buildings in ecclesiastical use have taken place without consent being sought: in Bath a disused chapel was sold recently to another religious group who removed all the stained glass from the windows as the iconography conflicted with their own doctrines. It is to be hoped that in view of the uncertainty over the law local authorities will insist that listed building consent is obtained for alterations and that the law is similarly clarified and strengthened at the earliest opportunity.

The lack of state control over both internal fittings and movable furnishings and treasure contrasts strongly with practice on the continent. In Sweden, for example, the Central Office of National Antiquities supervises "the whole body of internal church fittings of cultural interest, fixtures as well as moveables. Disposal of such an object is only allowed by permission of the state. The Central Office gives permission in every individual case to restore or repair items of this kind." In Finland the restoration or alteration of fixed furniture and the sale of church objects is controlled by the State archaeological commission. In France all churches classified as *monuments historiques* (of which there were 3,758 in 1972) are subject to the authority of the Ministry of Cultural Affairs, and controls extends to the maintenance or restoration of all classified movables (windows, murals, organs, altars, etc.).

Local Authorities

The survival of redundant churches, particularly in urban areas, will depend increasingly on the willingness of local authorities to take responsibility for them. Fortunately there is a very real awareness of the problem among many, though certainly not all, local authorities and quite a number have taken disused churches into their ownership and established new uses in them. In Chester for example the City Council own St Michael (Heritage Centre), St Olave (Adult Reading Centre) and Trinity Church (Guildhall) while St Mary-on-the-Hill, which is becoming an Urban Studies Centre, is owned by the County Council. The Heritage Centre in York also belongs to the City Council, acquired for 5p from the Church Commissioners before conversion. The City of Manchester owns four listed former churches: the First Church of Christ Scientist (Grade II*, now part of the college of education); the Welsh Baptist Chapel, Upper Brook Street; St Peter, Blossom Street and the Congregational Chapel, 154 Wilmslow Road. Leicester City Council has bought two former churches by agreement —the Belgrave Methodist Church, Belgrave Road, now a community centre and St John the Divine, South Albion Street, where the new use is currently being determined. In Honiton, Devon, the former Methodist Church in New Street is occupied jointly by the Day Centre and Town Council. The London Borough of Brent has also acquired two churches by agreement; the Brondesbury Park Congregational Church, Wrentham Avenue—now a youth club; and the Brondesbury Park

United Synagogue, Chevening Road, NW6—now converted to educational purposes. In Halifax the Calderdale Metropolitan Borough has acquired the remains of the burnt out Square Congregational Chapel and is to preserve the majestic spire though the fate of the much vandalized Georgian chapel beside it is uncertain. The former United Free Church of Scotland at Bora, owned by the Highlands Regional Council, now serves very successfully as the Divisional Roads and Transport engineers offices. Other local authority owned churches are All Saints Dorchester, Dorset (West Dorset District Council), and Carville Methodist Church, Wallsend (North Tyneside District Council). Overall, however, there is a growing body of evidence to show that both county and district councils are responding both energetically and imaginatively to the problem of redundant churches.

Mention might be made of the old Aberdeen County Council's restoration of Glenbuchat, the old Glasgow Corporation's rescue of St Vincent Street Church and Edinburgh's belated rescue of the Tron Kirk. Much less satisfactory is Glasgow's ownership of the magnificent baroque John Street Church (J. T. Rochead 1859) adjoining their City Chambers where, although used as a store and a shelter, the splendid ceiling with conch lunettes is falling in. Even worse is the state of James Adam's Tron Kirk (1794) which lies in a courtyard behind the 1595 Tron Steeple. Used by their works department the ceiling which was its best feature is collapsing. Lost completely while in their care was Greyfriars-Alexandra Parade Church (John Baird 1821) with its magnificent Doric portico. It was used as a salvage store by the Fire Department.

Whereas in the past local authorities tended to use compulsory purchase powers in connection with demolition, recently such powers have on occasion been used to rescue churches from abandonment or dereliction. Highland District Council acquired the former Rosskeen Church, near Invergordon, Ross and Cromarty, from the Church of Scotland as a result of a Purchase Notice, and though the building is still disused it is boarded up to ensure that it is wind and weatherproof. Cow Close Methodist Chapel, Wortley, is now in the process of acquisition by the City Council as a result of a purchase notice on the grounds of the lack of beneficial use after a potentially acceptable tenant failed to take the premises. Local authorities can also help with emergency protective measures. Tameside Metropolitan Borough for example recently gave a grant towards the vandal proofing of the large stained-glass windows in Christ Church, Ashton, Lancashire (local authorities, however, can only take such action when a church is closed). While local authorities have powers to serve repairs notices on owners of secular listed buildings, specifying the remedial work that needs to be done, and can if necessary carry out the work themselves, these powers do not apply to buildings in ecclesiastical use. The Church of England has its own system of quinquennial fabric inspection but the other Churches do not; and this is a very real cause of concern to many authorities, notably to Glasgow District Council.

Though local authorities cannot serve repairs notices on churches they can serve dangerous structures notices on churches, and a great number have been demolished as a result. Technically a dangerous structures notice can specify repairs that must be carried out to remove the cause of danger, but usually demolition is the solution. The fact that even the Church of England's inspection system sometimes fails to ensure churches are kept in proper repair is evident from a number of dangerous structures notices served on Anglican churches in London. Christ Church, Woburn Square, Camden, has been demolished as a result of one. Christ Church, Lancaster Gate, Paddington, could soon follow. A dangerous structures notice may also soon be served on Butterfield's masterpiece All Saints, Margaret Street, London. There is therefore a strong argument for empowering local authorities to serve repairs notices on Anglican churches before they actually become dangerous: in many cases this would be in the long term interest of the church and congregation as it would ensure that repairs were carried out at an earlier, and therefore less expensive, stage. As far as the churches of other denominations are concerned it is vital that local authorities should give powers to serve repairs notices as soon as possible.

Conclusion

Though we have argued for more state aid, and for more state control, we do not propose that the state should take over full responsibility for maintaining cathedrals or churches still in use. Looking at those countries where cathedrals or churches are vested in central or local government we do not find that the overall standard of care is higher: rather the reverse. Some certainly are supremely maintained, but many more are not properly cared for and local people are either apathetic, or indeed powerless to take action. Even in the most religious of countries governments tend, wisely or unwisely, to give the upkeep of monuments a low priority. If our churches are to be as well, and preferably better, cared for and protected than in the past, it is vital that responsibility and initiative remain at a local level, guided by the best advice available, and heartened by the knowledge that should their own best efforts to raise money fail they do not stand alone.

APPENDIX 1
Society of Friends

Meeting Houses *17th Century*

Broad Campden, Gloucestershire	1663
Portishead, Avon	1669
Hertford	1670
Almeley Wootton, Hereford & Worcester	1672
Alton, Hampshire	1672
Cirencester, Gloucestershire	1673
Earls Colne, Essex	1674
Brigflatts, Yorkshire	1675
Ifield, Sussex	1676
St Helens, Merseyside	1678
Settle, Yorkshire	1678
Stourbridge, Wiltshire	1680
Ettington, Warwickshire	1684
Colthouse, Cumbria	1688
Jordans, Buckinghamshire	1688
Marazion, Cornwall	1688
Swarthmoor, Yorkshire	1688
Fairfield, W. Yorkshire	1689
Lincoln	1689
Nailsworth, Gloucestershire	1689
Thakeham, Blue Idol, W. Sussex	1691
Yealand, Lancashire	1692
Skipton, Yorkshire	1693
Yarmouth, Norfolk	1694
Warwick	1695
Rawdon, W. Yorkshire	1697
Penrith, Cumbria	1699

18th Century

Airton, N. Yorkshire	1700
Brant Broughton, Lincolnshire	1701
High Flatts, S. Yorkshire	*c.* 1701
Aylesbury, Buckinghamshire	1704
Armscote, Warwickshire	1705
Gainsborough, Lincolnshire	1705
Macclesfield, Cheshire	1705
Warmsworth, S. Yorkshire	1705
Bewdley, Hereford & Worcester	1706
Painswick, Gloucestershire	1706
Bridport, Dorset	1707
Lancaster	1708
Burford, Oxfordshire	1709
Come-to-Good, Cornwall	1709
Countersett, N. Yorkshire	1710
Crawshawbooth, Lancashire	1715–36
Low Leighton, Derbyshire	1717
Long Sutton, Somerset	1717
Oakham, Leicestershire	1719
Hemel Hempstead, Hertfordshire	1720
Bridgwater, Somerset	1722
Capel, Surrey	1724
Wallingford, Oxfordshire	1724
Allonby, Cumbria	1725
Rookhow, Cumbria	1725
Pardshaw, Cumbria	1729
Stafford	1730
Herstmonceux, Sussex	1737
Hartshill, Warwickshire	1740
Broughton, Cumbria	1742
Beccles, Suffolk	1745
Pales, Powys	1745
Shaftesbury, Dorset	1746
Godalming, Surrey	*c.* 1748
Diss, Norfolk	1749
Bury St Edmunds, Suffolk	1750
North Walsham, Norfolk	pre 1800
Banbury, Oxfordshire	1751
Gildersome, W. Yorkshire	1756
Coanwood, Northumberland	1760
Marsden, Lancashire	1763
Low Bentham, N. Yorkshire	1768
Kettering, Northants	1769
Chesterfield, Derbyshire	1770
Uttoxeter, Staffordshire	1770
Kingston, Surrey	1772
Sawley, Lancashire	1777
Wandsworth, London	1778
Amersham, Buckinghamshire	1780
Evesham, Hereford & Worcester	1780
Wells, Norfolk	1783
Wooldale, W. Yorkshire	1783
Lewes, Sussex	1784
Brentford, London	1785
Horsham, Sussex	1786
Leighton Buzzard, Bedfordshire	1788

Kirkbymoorside, N. Yorkshire 1789
Winchmore Hill, Enfield, Greater London 1790
Pickering, N. Yorkshire 1793
Leek, Staffordshire 1794
Chesham, Buckinghamshire 1796
Cotherstone, Durham 1797
Esher, Surrey 1797
Folkestone, Kent 1798
Neath, W. Glamorgan 1799
Thirsk, N. Yorkshire 1799
Woodhouse, S. Yorkshire c. 1800

1800–50
Bardfield, Essex 1804
Ross on Wye, Hereford & Worcester 1804
Sudbury, Suffolk 1804
Brighton, Sussex 1805
Guildford, Surrey 1805
Spalding, Lincolnshire 1805
Derby 1808
Frenchay, Avon 1809
Guernsey, Channel Islands 1811
Maidstone, Kent 1811
Milford Haven, Pembrokeshire 1811
Huddersfield, W. Yorkshire 1812
Rochester, Kent 1814
Spiceland, Devon 1815
Whitby, N. Yorkshire c. 1815
Kendal, Cumbria 1816
Taunton, Somerset 1816
Berkhamsted, Hertfordshire 1818
Wellingborough, Northamptonshire 1819
Maldon, Essex 1820
Hereford 1822
Malton, N. Yorkshire 1823
Westhoughton, Greater Manchester 1823
Worcester 1823
Blackburn, Lancashire 1824
Truro, Cornwall 1825
Norwich, Norfolk 1826
Layer Breton, Essex 1827
Hoddesdon, Hertfordshire 1829
St Austell, Cornwall 1829
Calder Bridge, Cumbria 1830
Northampton 1830
Wigton, Cumbria 1830
Manchester, Mount St. 1830
Warrington, Cheshire 1830
Wilmslow, Cheshire 1831
Wincanton, Somerset 1832
Gloucester 1835
Reading, Berkshire 1835
Bainbridge, N. Yorkshire 1836
Great Ayton, N. Yorkshire c. 1843
Wellington, Somerset 1845
Darlington, Durham 1846
Dorking, Surrey 1846
Ackworth, W. Yorkshire 1848
Epping, Essex 1850
Street, Somerset 1850

APPENDIX 2
Methodist Churches built between 1800 and 1840

Note: this list is based on 1970 returns published in The Methodist Church *Statistical Returns* (see Bibliography) and does not take account of churches closed since that date.

LONDON NORTH-EAST DISTRICT

London (Waltham Abbey and Hertford)
Ware (New Road) 1839

Cambridge
Histon (Matthews Memorial, High Street) 1821

Hunts Mission
Earith (Chapel Road) 1828

Sawtry 1833

Colchester

Balls Green (Great Bromley) 1836
Elmstead Market 1817

Manningtree and Harwich

Manningtree (South Street) 1807
Ardleigh (Colchester Road) 1811
Great Oakley (Main Road) 1817

Clacton on Sea

Great Clacton (Valley Road) 1824

LONDON NORTH-WEST DISTRICT

St Albans

Shenley (London Road) 1839
Sleapshyde (Smallford) 1840

Hitchin and Letchworth

Steeple Morden 1835

Bedford (South)

Cardington 1823

Biggleswade

Shortmead (Trinity) 1834

Leighton Buzzard

Eaton Bray 1829
Totternhoe (Castle Hill Road) 1840
Stewkley (Central) 1839
Soulbury 1831

Milton Keynes

Newport Pagnell 1815
Aspley Guise (Mount Pleasant) 1813
Water Eaton (Mill Road) 1830
Bradwell 1839

High Wycombe

Downley (Moor Lane) 1824

Amersham

Lee Common 1839

Aylesbury

Weedon 1833

Thame and Watlington

Haddenham (High Street) 1822
Watlington (Shirburn Street) 1812

LONDON SOUTH-WEST DISTRICT

Hillingdon

Denham (Cheapside Lane) 1820

Dorking and Horsham

Effingham (The Street) 1834

LONDON SOUTH-EAST DISTRICT

Shooters Hill

Woolwich (William Street) 1815

Gravesend and Dartford

Shorne (Ridgeway) 1839

Tonbridge

East Peckham 1820

Hastings, Bexhill & Rye

Battle (Lower Lane) 1826
Beckley 1840

The Medway Towns

Hartlip 1820

Maidstone

Maidstone (Union Street) 1825

Sittingbourne & Sheerness

Sheerness (Ebenezer) 1821

Canterbury & Faversham

Canterbury (St Peter's) 1811
Dargate 1840

Margate

Birchington (Canterbury Road) 1830
St Nicholas-at-Wade (Down Barton Road) 1822

Dover and Deal

West Hougham 1840

Folkestone

Barham 1836
Elham 1839

Ashford (Kent)

Ruckinge 1839
Appledore (The Street) 1836

Wadhurst

Brede (Broad Oak) 1832
Northiam 1814

BIRMINGHAM DISTRICT

West Bromwich (Wesley)

Wesley (High Street) 1836

Lichfield

Alrewas (Post Office Lane) 1805

Nuneaton and Atherstone

Atherstone (Coleshill Road) 1836
Hartshill (Grange Road) 1836

Leamington

Harbury 1804

Kineton

Northend 1831
Oxhill 1814
Knightcote 1837
Fenny Compton 1837

Worcester

Leigh (Smith End Green) 1839

Evesham

Wyre Piddle (Chapel Lane) 1840
Pedworth (Chapel Street) 1840
Chipping Campden 1840

Oldbury

Tividale (Dudley Road West) 1840

Hereford

Eaton Bishop 1836
Birch 1834

Ledbury

Pendock 1824

Cwm and Kingstone
Newton 1830
Walterstone Common 1830

BOLTON AND ROCHDALE DISTRICT

Bolton
Delph Hill 1832
Rochdale (North)
Bagslate Moor (Edenfield Road) 1837
Bury and Heywood
Central (Union Street) 1817
Radcliffe
Close (Bury Street) 1839
Worsley
Worsley (Barton Road) 1832
Littleborough
Wardle 1809
Rawtenstall
Rakefoot (Crawshawbooth) 1810

BRISTOL DISTRICT

Bristol (North)
Olveston 1820
Oldbury on Severn 1835
Bristol (Bedminster)
Bedminster (Ebenezer, British Road) 1836
West Town (Backwell) 1800
Bristol (East)
Redfield (Gilbert Road) 1815
Bristol (Kingswood)
Wesley (Tower Road, Warmley) 1833
Longwell Green (Shellards Road) 1823
Bristol (South Gloucestershire)
Wesley (Inglestone Common) 1836
Cheltenham
Cheltenham (Wesley, St George's Street) 1839
Stroud and Cirencester
Chalford Hill 1823
Brimscombe 1804
Randwick 1807
Dursley and Stonehouse
Cam 1825
Leonard Stanley 1809
Halmore 1829
Bath
Walcot (Nelson Place East) 1815
Paulton
Paulton (Central, Park Road) 1826
Camerton (Red Hill) 1820
Marksbury 1838
Clutton (Upper Bristol Road) 1810
Timsbury (South Road) 1805
Cheddar Valley
Wells (Southover) 1838
Wedmore (Grants Lane) 1817
Easton (Wells Road) 1831
Weston super Mare
Worle (Lawrence Road) 1813
Brent Knoll 1840
Somerset Mission
Castle Cary (High Street) 1839
Frome and Shepton Mallet
Frome (Wesley, Christchurch Street West) 1812
Frome (Sun Street, Whittox Lane) 1806
Buckland Dinham (High Street) 1811
Leigh on Mendip (Ebenezer, Leigh Street) 1811
Nunney 1812
Oakhill 1825
Rode 1809
Rudge 1839
Waterlip (Doulting) 1816
Trowbridge and Bradford
Freshford (Sharpstone) 1827
Staverton 1827
Bradford-on-Avon (Coppice Hill) 1839
Mid-Wiltshire
Marston 1835
Bromham (Church Hill) 1802
Rowde (Marsh Lane) 1838
Tinhead (Edington) 1828
Seagry (Great Somerford) 1825
Spirithill 1825
Chippenham
Biddestone (Cuttle Lane) 1834
Brinkworth
Wootton Bassett 1838
Marlborough
Wilton 1811

CARDIFF AND SWANSEA DISTRICT

Newport
Caerleon 1814
Gwehelog 1822
Monmouth and Ross
Welsh Newton Common 1838
Trellech 1826
Llancloudy 1840
Monmouth (St James Street) 1837
Chepstow and Caldicot
St Briavels (Brockweir Common) 1819
Pwllmeyric 1833
Pontypool
Garndiffaith (Earl Street) 1840

Cwmbran New Town
Upper Cwmbran (The Square) 1820
Beaufort (Ebenezer, Primitive Place) 1836
Abertillery
Brynmawr (Orchard Street) 1840
Nantyglo (Wesley) 1825
Abergavenny
Abergavenny (Castle Street) 1828
Clydach Vale 1829
Mid Wales Mission
Brecon (Coke Memorial, Lion Street) 1835
Glasbury (Cwm Bach) 1818
Hay-on-Wye (Trinity, Oxford Road) 1828
Pembroke
Redberth 1822
Haverfordwest and Milford Haven
Haverfordwest (Wesley, Perrotts Road) 1825
Hakin Point (Chapel Lane) 1808
Waterston 1825
St David's (Bethel, Goat Street) 1818

CARLISLE DISTRICT

Carlisle
Scaleby Hill 1828
Dumfries (Buccleuch Street) 1818
Alston
Nentesbury 1825
Workington
Distington (Main Street) 1854
Keswick and Cockermouth
Greysouthen 1833
Lorton 1840
Kirkby Stephen, Appleby and Tebay
Hilton and Murton (Murton Village) 1837
Long Marton 1818
Kirkby Thore 1828
Blencarn 1840
Kirkby Stephen (Centenary, High Street) 1839
Orton 1833
Ravenstonedale 1839
Sedbergh
Dent 1834
Garsdale (Old Smithy) 1830
Penrith
Cliburn 1832
Morland 1819
Kirkoswald
Salkeld Dykes 1832
Culgaith 1830
Wigton
Welton 1834
Caldbeck 1832
Hesket-New-Market 1840
Kendal
Kirkby Lonsdale 1834

CHANNEL ISLANDS DISTRICT

Guernsey and Alderney
Vauvert (Salem) 1837
Alderney (Butes) 1820
Jersey
Aquila Road 1839
Bethlehem 1828
Eden 1833
Galaad 1832
Philadelphie 1833

CHESTER AND STOKE-ON-TRENT DISTRICT

Chester
Wesley (St John Street) 1810
Churton 1832
Frodsham
Crowton 1840
Dunham Hill (Village Road) 1834
Northwich
Acton (Chapel Lane, Acton Bridge) 1823
Pickmere (Pickmere Lane) 1826
Tarporley
Willington 1823
Eaton 1840
Congleton
Lower Withington 1808
Davenport 1834
Buglawton 1823
Cloud 1815
Nantwich
Nantwich (Central, Hospital Street) 1808
Poole 1834
Whitchurch
Whitchurch (St John's) 1810
Bronington 1828
Market Drayton
Hinstock 1831
Soudley 1837
Knighton (London Road) 1834
Stoke-on-Trent (Tunstall)
Bank 1839
Stoke-on-Trent (Burslem)
Burslem (Hill Top, Westport Street) 1837
Stoke on Trent (Burslem Mission)
Burslem (Swan Bank) 1801

Stoke-on-Trent (Hanley, Bethesda)
Bethesda (Albion Street) 1813
Stoke-on-Trent (Stoke)
Wesley (Epworth Street) 1816
Stoke-on-Trent (Longton and Fenton)
Lightwood (Mount Zion, Lightwood Road) 1816
Wolstanton and Audley
Englesea Brook (Balterley) 1828
Etruria (Wesley, Etruria Road) 1820
Audley (Central, Old Road, Bignall End) 1838
Newcastle (Staffs)
Higherland 1823
Leek
Leek (Mount Pleasant) 1811
Upperhulme 1838
Flash 1821
Thorncliffe 1839
Hartington 1809
Gratton (Chapel Lane) 1822
Bradnop (School Lane) 1840
Danebridge 1834
Cheadle
Alton (New Road) 1826
Boundary 1822
Wrexham
Bersham 1840
Rhosymedre (Chapel Street) 1840
Buckley and Mold
Penymyndd 1824

CORNWALL DISTRICT

Redruth
Redruth (Wesley) 1826
Busveal (Gwennap Pit) 1836
Carharrack (Wesley) 1815
Lanner (Wesley) 1828
Blackwater 1822
Camborne
Camborne (Wesley) 1828
Roseworthy 1810
Falmouth
Mawnan Smith (Maenporth Road) 1815
Mylor (Lemon Hill) 1836
Flushing (Kersey Road) 1815
Truro
Truro (St Mary's, Union Place) 1830
Chacewater (Station Road) 1832
Chacewater (East End) 1830
Hugus 1830
Kerley Downs (Billy Bray's Chapel) 1830
Truro (St Clement Street) 1835
Short Lane End 1840
Carnon Downs 1825
Hick's Mill 1821
Probus 1825
Ladock 1816
Tresillian 1831
St Columb and Padstow
Padstow (St John's, Church Lane) 1827
St Eval 1838
Talskiddy 1834
Perranporth and St Agnes
Mithian 1800
Mount Hawke 1820
Rose 1839
St Austell
Bethel 1836
Charlestown 1827
Tywardreath 1828
St Blazey Gate (Leek Seed) 1824
Gorran (High Lanes) 1817
Gorran Haven 1830
Roseland
St Mawes (Wesley) 1816
St Just 1817
Trewartha 1826
Bodmin
Bodmin (Fore Street) 1840
Warleggan (Mount) 1821
Roche (Chapel Road) 1835
Penzance
Newlyn (Trinity) 1832
Mousehole (St Clement's) 1833
St Just
St Just (Chapel Street) 1833
St Buryan 1833
Trewellard 1833
St Ives (Central)
St Ives (Wesley) 1834
Lelant 1834
Halsetown 1833
St Ives (Fore Street)
St Ives (Fore Street) 1831
Isles of Scilly
St Martin's (High Town) 1821
Helston
Ponsongath 1833
St Anthony 1829
Porthleven
Carleen 1833
Breage 1833
Hayle
Hayle (Chapel Lane) 1815
Gwithian 1810
Wall 1821
St Erth 1839
Praze (Central) 1828
Marazion
Crowlais 1834
Germoe (Balwest) 1829
North Hill
North Hill 1810

Liskeard
Liskeard (Greenbank) 1838
Duloe 1840
Quethiock 1839
Trewidland 1835

Camelford and Wadebridge
Camelford (Fore Street) 1837
Camelford (Chapel Street) 1810
Trewalder 1803
Trelill 1812
Helstone 1826
Michaelstow (Treveighan) 1828
Amble 1840
Tremail 1838
Boscastle (Fore Street) 1825

DARLINGTON DISTRICT

Darlington
Bondgate 1812
Hurworth 1827
Coniscliffe Road 1840
Barton (The Green) 1830
Gainford 1834
North Cowton (The Green) 1827
Haughton 1825
Stainton 1840

Stockton
Brunswick (Dovecot Street) 1823
Wolviston 1829

Stokesley
Carlton 1816
Newby 1826

Danby
Glaisdale Head 1821
Lealholm 1839

Loftus and Staithes
Runswick Bay 1829

Durham
Witton Gilbert (Sacriston Lane) 1832

Weardale
High House (Irehopeburn) 1825

Bishop Auckland
Etherley 1829

Teesdale
Eggleston 1828

Richmond (Yorks)
Hunton 1829

Reeth
Hurst 1815

Wensleydale
Bellerby 1839
Preston under Scaur 1805
Middleham (Market Place) 1836
Gayle 1833
Bainbridge 1836

Bedale
Thirn 1836

EAST ANGLIA DISTRICT

Ipswich
Holbrook (The Street) 1830
Stowmarket (Regent Street) 1836
Old Newton (Chapel Road) 1839

Newmarket
Burwell (The Causeway) 1835
Isleham (The Causeway) 1840
Mildenhall (High Street) 1829
Eriswell (The Street) 1834

Ely
Ely (Chapel Street) 1810

East Suffolk
Wenhaston (Stone, Chapel Lane) 1835
Peasenhall and Sibton 1809
Middleton 1828

Lowestoft
Hulver 1840
Sotterley (Waterloo Road) 1827

Loddon and Bungay
Burgh St Peter (Mill Road) 1835
Ilketshall St Andrew 1840
Woodton 1836
Rumburgh 1836

Martham
Catfield 1838

Acle
Wickhampton 1814

Cromer, Sheringham and Holt
Briston (The Lane) 1811

North Walsham and Aylsham
Edingthorpe 1829
Skeyton 1829
Reepham 1817

Swaffham
Swaffham (London Street) 1813
Beeston 1817
Great Massingham 1827

Wymondham, Attleborough and Watton
Deopham Green 1834
New Buckenham 1824

Diss
Banham (Mill Road) 1837
Long Stratton 1830

Thetford
Thetford 1830
Lakenheath 1835
Brandon (London Road) 1811

King's Lynn
Terrington St Clement 1840

Hunstanton and Docking
Sedgeford (High Street) 1830
Docking 1821

Wisbech
Parson Drove 1838
Terrington St John (Ely Row) 1813

Downham Market
Methwold 1831
Fenland
Benwick (High Street) 1833

ISLE OF MAN DISTRICT

Douglas
Abbeylands (Onchan) 1815
Quines Hill 1827
Lower Douglas (Victoria Street) 1820
Castletown
Castletown (Arbory Street) 1833
Ballamodha (Malew) 1834
Kerrowkeil 1814
Ramsey
Dhoor 1827
Lhen 1825
Kerrowmoar 1824
Peel
Peel (Atholl Street) 1838
Lhergydhoo 1837
Crosby (Station Road) 1832

LEEDS DISTRICT

Leeds (North East)
Woodhouse Street 1840
Leeds (Richmond Hill)
Halton (Chapel Street) 1840
Morley
Churwell (Back Green) 1821
Tingley (Westerton Road) 1838
Dewsbury
Centenary (Daisy Hill) 1839
Briestfield 1825
Knaresborough
Little Ribston 1818
Kirk Deighton 1819
Spofforth (Providence) 1810
Kearby 1809
Whixley 1808
Little Ouseburn 1815
Scotton 1825
Pateley Bridge
Darley (Wesley) 1829
Woodmanwray 1839
Hardisty Hill 1838
Otley
Stainburn 1836
Leathley 1826
Wakefield
Westgate End (Lanefield Lane) 1827
Lofthouse (Leeds Road) 1840
Pontefract
Badsworth 1830

LINCOLN DISTRICT

Epworth and Crowle
Sandtoft 1839
Owston Ferry (Centenary, High Street) 1837
West Butterwick (North Street) 1836
Lincoln (North)
Welton 1815
Ingham 1836
Stow (Sturton Road) 1824
Lincoln (Central)
Welbourn (High Street) 1839
Fulbeck (Washdyke Lane) 1825
Lincoln (South)
Bassingham (High Street) 1839
Gainsborough
Marton 1814
Willoughton 1807
Upton (High Street) 1822
Scunthorpe
Alkborough 1840
Messingham 1821
Barton-on-Humber
South Ferriby (Farishes Lane, Wesley) 1839
Sleaford
Helpringham (The Green) 1840
Dunston 1832
Market Rasen and Caistor
Tealby (Main Street) 1819
Legsby 1839
Normanby and Owmby 1814
Nettleton 1800
Louth
Louth (Centenary, Eastgate) 1835
Alvingham 1837
Grainthorpe 1818
Saltfleet 1815
Fulston 1836
South Willingham (Barkwith Road) 1840
Spalding
Holbeach Drove 1833
Holbeach
Moulton 1830
Whaplode Washway (Saracens Head) 1825
Horncastle and Bardney
Scamblesby 1835
Hameringham 1840
Horsington 1837
Minting 1838
Southrey 1838
Spilsby
Toynton St Peter 1811
Halton Holgate 1837
Partney 1835

Coningsby
Coningsby (Dogdyke Road) 1826
Moorside 1840
Boston
New Leake (Spilsby Road) 1838
Northlands (Sibsey) 1837
New Bolingbroke 1825
Skegness and Wainfleet
Chapel St Leonards (St Leonards Drive) 1836
Friskney 1839
Wainfleet Bank 1838
Friskney Fen 1836

LIVERPOOL DISTRICT

Warrington
Martinscroft (Manchester Road) 1827
Moore (Warrington Road) 1812
Whitley (Pillmoss Lane) 1802
Ormskirk
Moss Lane (Burscough) 1813
Altrincham
Dunham Massey (Woodhouses) 1813
Saddlesworth and Lees
Zion (County End, Lees) 1829
Stockport
Tiviot Dale (Lancashire Hill) 1827
Whaley Bridge
Whitehough 1840
White Knowle (Hayfield Road) 1809
Buxton
Longnor 1800
Hollinsclough 1807
Glossop
Hollingworth (Spring Street) 1830
Hollingworth (Water Lane) 1840
Hyde and Denton
Trinity (Talbot Road, Newton) 1815
Haughton Green (Two Trees Lane) 1810
Ashton under Lyne
Stamford Street 1832
Fairbottom (Lower Alt Hill) 1837
Macclesfield
Brunswick (Chapel Street) 1824
Presbury (Bollin Grove) 1816
Beech Lane 1830

NEWCASTLE UPON TYNE

Newcastle upon Tyne (Brunswick Central)
Brunswick (Brunswick Place) 1821
Newcastle upon Tyne (West)
Bell's Close (Front Street) 1838
Morpeth
Bedlington Colliery 1830
Hexham
Whittington 1835
Allendale
Limestone Brae 1825
Gateshead (East)
Sheriff Hill (Sodhouse Bank) 1836
Consett
Iveston (Iveston Lane) 1837
Accrington
Rhyddings (Chapel Street, Oswaldtwistle) 1836
Stanhill (Nab Lane, Oswaldtwistle) 1836
Colne
Trawden (Skipton Road) 1810
Barnoldswick
Mount Pleasant (Foulridge) 1822
Clitheroe
Harrop 1819
Paythorne 1830
Preston (Lune Street and Orchard)
Central (Lune Street) 1823
Garstang
Goosnargh (Whittingham Lane) 1832
Woodplumpton 1819
Bilsborrow 1811
Lancaster
Wesley (Sulyard Street, Lancaster) 1806
Caton (Brookhouse Road) 1837
Warton 1835

NOTTINGHAM AND DERBY DISTRICT

Nottingham (Central)
Oxton 1839
Nottingham (South)
Bradmore 1830
Nottingham (East)
Lowdham 1826
Epperstone (Chapel Lane) 1830
Derby (South)
Green Hill Central (St Peter's Churchyard) 1821
Findern (Lower Green) 1835
Barrow on Trent (Bethel, Chapel Lane) 1839
Ashbourne
Kniveton 1832
Milldale 1836
Rodsley 1823
Stanton 1824
Swinscoe 1835
Hanging Bridge (Mayfield) 1830
Hulland (Bourne) 1821
Ashby de la Zouch
Worthington 1820

Belper
Belper (Central, Chapel Street) 1825
Pottery (Kilbourne Road) 1816
Milford (Shaw Lane) 1823
Mercaston (Mercaston Lane) 1827

Bingham
Bingham (Union Street) 1818
Flintham (Spring Lane) 1805
Bottesford (The Green) 1820
Orston (Chapel Street) 1848
Scarrington 1818
Granby 1807
Colston Bassett 1838

Burton on Trent
Barton under Needwood (Crowberry Lane) 1828
Willington (Repton Road) 1838

Castle Donington
Wilson 1826

Dove Valley
Uttoxeter (High Street) 1812
Doveridge 1805
Sutton-on-the-Hill 1838
Church Broughton 1828

Grantham
Great Gonerby (Spring End) 1835
Barkston (West Street) 1838

Ilkeston
Wesley (Market Street, Heanor) 1839

Matlock
Tansley (Church Street) 1834
Wensley 1829
Winster 1823

Newark
Southwell (Prebend Yard, Westgate) 1839
Edingley 1838
Fiskerton (Upton Road) 1809
Brough (Lincoln Road) 1826

Ripley
Riddings (Spring Road) 1838

South Derbyshire
Swadlincote (West Street) 1837
Ticknall 1813

Wirksworth
Brassington 1834

OXFORD AND LEICESTER DISTRICT

Oxford
Tackley 1815

Witney and Faringdon
Newland (Witney) 1828
Charlbury 1823
Freeland (Wroslyn Road) 1805
Finstock 1840

Chipping Norton and Stow
Hook Norton 1807
Sibford 1827
Stourton 1809

Banbury
Shutford (West Street) 1837
Warmington (Chapel Street) 1811

Buckingham and Brackley
Arncott (Green Lane) 1834
Weston-on-the-Green (North Lane) 1838
Silverstone (High Street) 1811

Leicester (Central Mission)
Bishop Street 1815

Leicester (North)
Barkby 1823
Rothley (Howe Lane) 1823

Leicester (South)
Great Glan (Oaks Road) 1827

Leicester (East)
Halstead (Tilton-on-the-Hill) 1837

Loughborough
Costock (Chapel Lane) 1828

Hinckley
Sharnford (Chapel Lane) 1827

Melton Mowbray
Nether Broughton (Chapel Lane) 1839
Hoby (Chapel Lane) 1832
Uppingham (Orange Street) 1819
Barsby 1826

Northampton
Moulton (Cross Street) 1836
Great Billing (High Street) 1836
Brixworth 1811
Holcot 1815
Little Houghton (Lodge Road) 1815

St Neots
Toseland 1840
Tempsford (Station Road) 1804

Raunds
Catworth 1838
Old Weston 1839

Wellingborough
Wollaston (High Street) 1840

Daventry
Daventry (New Street) 1824
Norton 1817

Market Harborough
Naseby (Daventry Road) 1825

Peterborough
Yarwell 1840
Werrington 1835
Woodnewton 1840
Dowsdale 1840

PLYMOUTH AND EXETER DISTRICT

Plymouth and Devonport Mission
Plymouth Central Hall (Eastlake Street) 1816

Exeter
Silverton 1814

Saltash and St Germans
Botus Fleming 1840

Tavistock
Providence (Brentnor) 1809
Milton Abbot 1835

Brixham and Dartmouth
Brixham (Fore Street) 1816
Blackawton 1823

Buckfastleigh
Buckfastleigh (Chapel Street) 1835
Ashburton (West Street) 1835
Dunstone 1833

Kingsbridge and Salcombe
Kingsbridge (Fore Street) 1814
Modbury 1835

Holsworthy
Lana (Pancrasweek) 1838

Bude
Woolsery 1836
Thurdon 1840
Poundstock 1840
Woolley 1828

Tiverton
Tiverton (St Peter Street) 1814
Cullompton 1814
Sampford Peverell 1803
Halberton (High Street) 1816

Taunton
Taunton (Temple, Upper High Street) 1812
Taunton (Victoria, Victoria Street) 1839
North Curry 1833

Wellington (Somerset)
Hemyock (High Street) 1838

Bridgwater
Combwich 1838
Pedwell 1830

Devon and Dorset Mission
Lyme Regis (Church Street) 1840
Ottery St Mary (Mill Street) 1829
Colyford 1833
Churchill 1840
Smallridge 1812
Colyton (King Street) 1825

Bridport
Uploders 1827

Barnstaple
Braunton 1833
Fremington 1817
Ebberley Lodge 1839

Ilfracombe
Parracombe 1834

South Molton
West Buckland 1829

Bideford
Torrington (Windy Cross) 1832
Monkleigh 1833
Holwell (Horns Cross) 1834
Instow 1837

West Somerset
Timberscombe 1839
Bossington 1895
Exford 1835
Washford 1826

Shebbear
Shebbear (Lake) 1815
Thornhillhead 1824
Cockbury 1839

Chagford
Providence (Throwleigh) 1839

Ringsash
Burrington (Bethesda) 1829
Chulmleigh (Bethlehem) 1836
Stable Green 1840

Newton Abbot
Moretonhampstead (Cross Street) 1817
Hennock 1835

Okehampton
Sticklepath 1816
Broadley 1838

Northlew
Northlew 1815
Highampton 1836

SHEFFIELD DISTRICT

Sheffield (Carver Street)
Carver Street 1805

Sheffield (Norfolk)
Darhall (Wesley, Main Road) 1839

Sheffield (North)
Brightholm Lea (Wharncliff Side, Bradfield) 1807
Crane Moor 1839

Sheffield (South)
Ridgway (The Moor) 1806

Chesterfield
Wadshelf 1834
Cutthorpe 1837

Doncaster (Priory Place)
Priory Place (Printing Office Street) 1832
Auckley 1832
Finningley 1838

Doncaster (North East)
Thorne (Trinity, King Street) 1826

Doncaster (West)
Styrrup 1830
Scrooby 1830
Tickhill (Northgate) 1837

Barnsley (West)
Clayton West (High Street) 1835

Wath and Mexborough
Billingley 1818

Wombwell and Hoyland
Hoyland (Market Street) 1809

Rotherham
Laughton (Firbeck Road) 1813

Worksop
Oldcotes (Blyth Road) 1840

Retford
Laxton 1812
Laneham 1834
Hayton 1834
Clayworth 1834

The Peak
Ashford in the Water (Court Lane) 1830
Litton 1834
Bradwell (Wesley, Towngate) 1807
Edale (Barber Booth) 1811
Hope 1835
Great Hucklow 1800
Youlgreave (Wesley, Main Street) 1807

SOUTHAMPTON DISTRICT

Andover
Whitchurch (Wincester Street) 1813
Overton (Winchester Street) 1800
Nether Wallop 1819

Winchester
Alresford (Pound Hill) 1825
Houghton 1833

Romsey
Cadnam 1833

West Wight
Wootton (High Street) 1840
Newbridge 1837
Brightstone 1837
Rookley (Niton Road) 1832

East Wight
Godshill 1838

Newbury
Northbrook Street (Newbury) 1839
Boxford 1810
Thatcham (Chapel Street) 1832
Ashford Hill 1836

Hungerford
Hungerford (Bridge Street) 1807
Lambourn 1835
Ramsbury (Oxford Street) 1807

Poole
Lytchett Matravers (Wareham Road) 1824

Weymouth
Abbotsbury 1825

Salisbury
Church Street 1811
Woodgreen 1832
Fordingbridge 1836
Martin 1829
Handley 1835

Shaftesbury and Gillingham
Bourton 1833

Stour Valley
Sturminster Newton (Church Street) 1832

WEST YORKSHIRE DISTRICT

Halifax (North)
Denholm Clough (Halifax Road) 1834
Mount Sion (Ogden) 1815
Mount Tabor 1820

Huddersfield (West)
Slaithwaite (Centenary, Manchester Road) 1839

Huddersfield (North East)
Wiggan Lane (Sheepbridge) 1822
Cowcliffe 1836
Almondbury 1808

Holmfirth
Hinchcliffe Mill (Woodhead Road) 1839
Gate Head (Hepworth) 1836
Thurstonland 1836

Hebden Bridge
Mytholmroyd (Scout Road) 1825
Crimsworth 1834
Cragg Vale (Cragg Road) 1835

Denby Dale and Clayton West
Skelmanthorpe (Pilling Lane) 1836

Bradford (Great Horton)
Great Horton (Great Horton Road) 1815
Clayton Heights (Highgate Road) 1806
Shelf (Wade House, Wadehouse Road) 1821

Haworth and Oakworth
Marsh (Marsh Lane, Oxenhope) 1836

Bingley
Cullingworth (Lane Ends) 1824
Hillside (Green End Road, East Morton) 1827

Skipton
Embsay 1839

Grassington
Grassington (Chapel Street) 1811
Kettlewell 1835
Howgill 1836

Cleckheaton and Heckmondwyke
Roberttown (Roberttown Lane, Liversedge) 1839

Birstall and Birkenshaw
Hightown (St John's) 1828
Gomersal (Trinity) 1827

WOLVERHAMPTON AND SHREWSBURY DISTRICT

Wolverhampton (Trinity)
Coven (Lawn Lane) 1839

Cannock Chase
Brereton 1809
Cannock Wood (Chapel Lane) 1834

Stafford
Garshall Green 1835
Hixon 1840

Darlaston
Pinfold Street 1810

Willenhall
Trinity (Union Street) 1832
Ettingshall (George Street) 1806

Tipton
Bell Street 1823

Dudley
Pensnett (St James, High Street) 1837

Netherton
Providence (Northfield Road, Darby End) 1837

Stour Vale
Mount Pleasant (Quarry Bank) 1828

Kidderminster and Stourport
Trinity, Kidderminster (Central Premises, Mill Street) 1821
Stourport (Wesley, High Street) 1812
Frith Common 1811

Telford South
Little Dawley 1837
Stirchley 1840
Madeley Wood 1837
Jackfield (Coalford) 1825

Wellington (Shropshire)
Rodington 1834

Wem and Prees Green
Braden Heath 1832
Pool Head 1840
Ellerdine 1813

Oswestry, Ellesmere and Chirk
Maesbury 1832
Duddleston Heath (Chapel Lane) 1815
Pontfaen 1839
Moors (St Martin's) 1829

Llanymynech
Treflach Wood 1833
Morton (Bethel) 1838

Welshpool
Providence (Garthmyl) 1837

Minsterley
Asterley 1834

Bishop's Castle and Clun
Edgton 1834

Ludlow
Caynham 1836

Craven Arms and Church Stretton
Upper Hayton 1838

Leintwardine
Twitchen 1833

Knighton
Llanbister 1836

YORK AND HULL DISTRICT

York (Clifton and Monkgate)
Flaxton 1817

York (Centenary)
Gate Helmsley 1826
Stamford Bridge 1828

Hull (Trinity)
Little Weighton 1830

Hull (West)
Swanland (Main Street) 1828
Newport (Wallingfen) 1812

Snaith
Pollington 1835

Goole
Howden 1832
Blacktoft 1839
Swinefleet (Low Street) 1836

Driffield
Fridaythorpe 1840
North Dalton 1839

Bridlington
Barmston (Main Street) 1839

Withernsea
Roos (Main Street) 1808
Patrington 1811

Hornsea
Catwick 1839
Riston 1837
Leaton (Catfoss Lane) 1837

Filey
Muston (Hunmanby Road) 1830
Lebberston 1862

Market Weighton
Holme (Selby Road) 1826
Sancton 1840
Ellerton 1822

Whitby
Hawsker 1831
Newholm 1832

Tadcaster
Tadcaster (High Street) 1828
Wetherby (Bank Street) 1828
Wighill (Church Lane) 1828
Appleton Roebuck 1820

Pocklington
Pocklington (Chapmangate) 1815
Warter 1830
Bishop Wilton 1810
Bielby 1837
Melbourne (Wesley) 1809
Elvington 1809
Barmby Moor 1806

Malton
Malton (Saville Street) 1812
Rillington (Railway Street) 1803
Leavening 1824

Ryedale
Helmsley (Bridge Street) 1830
Appleton-le-Moors 1832
Lastingham 1804
Edstone 1823
Ampleforth East 1819

Scarborough
Bethel (Sandside) 1836

Sherburn
Sherburn (St Hilda Street) 1813
Wold Newton (Front Street) 1839
West Lutton 1817
Hutton Buscel 1822
Sawdon 1823

Pickering
Wrelton (Wesley) 1840

Easingwold
Easingwold (Chapel Street) 1815
Kilburn 1838
Thornton-le-Clay 1822

Thirsk
Skipton-on-Swale 1810
Sandhutton 1816
Carlton Miniott 1838
Kirby Wiske 1825

Boroughbridge
Topcliffe (Church Street) 1840

Ripon
Grantley 1815

Masham
Nosterfield 1813

Selby
South Milford (High Street) 1840
Micklefield 1837
Hemingbrough 1840

Northallerton
Appleton Wiske 1821
Newby Wiske 1814
Thornton-le-Moor 1836

FIRST NORTH WALES DISTRICT

Denbigh
Henllan 1816

Llangollen
Pontfadog (Seion) 1812
Pentredwr (Siloh) 1812

Holywell
Greenfield (Mynydd Gilead) 1830

Llanasa
Trelawynd (Capel-y-Gop) 1832

Mold
Mold (Pendref, Bailey Hill) 1828
Gwernymynydd (Carmel) 1827

Llanfair (Welshpool)
Gwaunynog (Saron) 1827

Newtown
Llandyssil 1827

SECOND NORTH WALES DISTRICT

Dyffryn Conwy
Llansantffraid (Ty'n Celyn) 1840

Abergele
Llanfairtalhaearn 1839

Mon
Trefor (Ebenezer) 1833
Bodedern (Zoar) 1822

Caernarvon
Llanddeiniolen (Seion) 1818

De Gwynedd
Talsarnau (Soar) 1840

Brynmawr
Hirwaun (Soar, Station Road) 1839

Llanidloes
Llangurig (Wesley Road) 1814

SCOTLAND DISTRICT

Edinburgh (Nicolson Square)
Nicolson Square 1815

Glasgow (St Thomas')
St Thomas' (Gallowgate) 1822

SHETLAND DISTRICT

Lerwick, North Roe and North Isles
Dunrossness 1830
Vidlin 1832
North Roe 1852

APPENDIX 3
Grade A Listed Churches in Welsh Dioceses

Diocese

St Asaph

Denbigh, St Marcella
Hope, St Cyngar
Llanrhos, St Mary
Mold, St Mary
Montgomery, St Nicholas
Ruthin, St Peter
Wrexham, St Giles
Caerwys, St Michael
Nerquis, St Mary
Northop, St Eurgain and St Peter
Whitford, St Beuno and St Mary
Overton, St Mary
Hanmer, St Chad
St Asaph, Cathedral
St Asaph, St Kentigern and St Asaph
Bangor Monachorum, St Dunawd
Worthenbury, St Deiniol
Dyserth, Saints Cwyfan and Ffraid
Cwm, Saints Mael and Sulien
Rhuddlan, St Mary
Tremeirchion, Corpus Christi
Holt, St Chad
Ruabon, St Mary
Marchwiel, St Marcella and St Deiniol
Llantysilio, St Tysilio
Gresford, All Saints

Bangor

Beddgelert, St Mary
Gyffin, St Benedict
Holyhead, St Cybi
Llanaber, St Bodfan
Towyn, St Cadfan
Llandegai, St Tegai
Capel Curig, St Curig
Dolwyddelan, St Gwyddelan
Llanbedr-y-Cenin, St Peter
Caerhun, St Mary
Trefriw, St Mary
Llanrhychwyn, St Rhychwyn
Llangadwaladr, St Cadwaladr
Llangeinwen, St Ceinwen
Llanidan, St Nidan (old church)
Newborough, St Peter
Penmynydd, St Gredifael
Trefdraeth, St Beuno
Llaniestyn, St Iestyn
Penmon, St Seiriol, Priory Church
Llangoed, St Cawdraf
Llangristiolus, St Cristiolus
Clynnog Fawr, St Beuno
Clynnog Fawr, nearby chapel of St Beuno
Llanberis, Old Church of St Peris
Llanfairisgaer, St Mary
Llanllyfni, St Rhedyw
Llanrug, St Michael
Llanfaglan, St Baglan
Bettws Garmon, St Garmon
Aberffraw, St Beuno
Llangwyfan, St Cwyfan
Llanbeulan, St Peulan
Talyllyn, St Mary
Llanfaethlu, St Maethlu
Trewalchmai, St Morhaiarn

Bodwrog, St Twrog
Bodedern, St Edeyrn
Llanaelhaiarn, St Aelhaiarn
Abererch, St Cawrdaf
Llannor, Holy Cross
Llanbedrog, St Pedrog
Aberdaron, St Hywyn
Llanengan, St Engan
Llangwnadl, St Gwynhoedl
Llandudwen, St Tudwen
Ceidio, St Cedo
Llaniestyn, St Iestyn
Pistyll, St Beuno
Llanarmon, St Garmon
Llangybi, St Cybi

St Davids

Haverfordwest, St Mary
Monkton, St Nicholas
Nevern, St Brynach
Newport, St Mary
Tenby, St Mary in Liberty
St Davids, Cathedral
Rudbaxton, St Michael
Kidwelly, St Mary, Priory Church
Pembrey, St Illtyd
Manorbier, St James
Pwllcrochan, St Mary
Warren, St Mary
Angle, St Mary
Angle, detached chapel
Rhoscrowther, St Decumanus
Castlemartin, St Michael
St Petrox, St Petrox
Stackpole Elidor, St Teilo
Lawrenny, St Caradoc
St Florence, St Florence
Bosherston, St Michael
Gumfreston, St Lawrence
Llawhaden, St Aidan
Loveston, St Leonard
Carew, St Mary
Tenby, St Nicholas, Penally

Llandaff

Cardiff, St John, Church Street
Llandaff, Cathedral
Margam, St Mary's Abbey Church
Llancarfan, St Cadoc
Llantwit Major, St Illtyd
Ewenny, St Michael

Monmouth

Bettws Newydd Church
Grosmont, St Nicholas
Llangwm Uchaf, St Hierom
Llantilio Crossenny, St Teilo
Mathern, St Tewdric
Llantilio Pertholey, St Teilo
Newport, St Woolos (Cathedral)
Usk, St Mary

Swansea & Brecon

Aberedw, St Cewydd
Brecon, Cathedral
Cregrina, St David
Glascwm, St David
Disserth, St Cewydd
Llanelieu, St Ellywe
Llanvillo, St Bilo
Llanfigan, St Meugan
Llanddew, St David
Llandefalle, St Matthew
Devynock, St Cynog
Patricio, St Ishow

APPENDIX 4—WALES

Grade	*Listed Churches and Chapels in Cardiff*
II	Methodist Church, Albany Road, Roath Park (1898: Gothic by Jones, Richards and Bugden—landmark value)
B	St Mary, Bute Street (1843: Romanesque by John Foster of Liverpool)
II*	Cathedral School Chapel, Cardiff Road, Llandaff (1850s: Ewan Christian)
II	Presbyterian Church of Wales, Cathedral Road (1903: Gothic and *art nouveau* by Edgar Down Melange)
II	United Reformed Church, Charles Street (1855 by R. G. Thomas)
26	St David's Roman Catholic Cathedral, Charles Street (1887 by Pugin & Pugin)
II	Former Wesleyan Methodist Central Hall, Charles Street, now used by Welsh National Opera Company (1850: Perpendicular Gothic by James Wilson, gutted in 1976)
B	St Augustine, Church Road, Rumney (medieval)
C	St Mary, Church Road, Whitchurch (1883: Gothic by J. Prichard)
A	St John the Baptist, Church Street (medieval)
II	Pembroke Terrace Presbyterian Chapel, Churchill Way (1877: Gothic by H. C. Harris)
II	Methodist Chapel, Conway Road (1869: Gothic)
II	Mortuary Chapels, Fairoak, Nonconformist and Church in Wales (1857–59: Gothic by R. G. Thomas and T. Warring)
A	Cathedral of St Peter and St Paul, Llandaff (medieval; restored in 19th century)
II	Masonic Temple, Guildford Crescent, formerly United Methodist Free Church (1863–64 by Hartland and Son of Cardiff)
II	Baptist Tabernacle Chapel, The Hayes (1842 and 1865 by J. Hartland & Son)
B	St Isan, Heol Hir, Llanishen (medieval)
II	Roman Catholic Church of St Mary of the Angels, King's Road, Canton (1907: Romanesque by F. A. Walters)
B	St Catherine, Kings Road, Canton (1883–84: Gothic by J. Prichard)
II	Presbyterian Church, Church of England, Marlborough Road, Roath Park (1897: Gothic by Habershon and Fawckner)
II	Casablanca Club, former Bethel Chapel (1858: classical)
C	St James the Great, Newport Road (1894: Gothic by Colonel Bruce Vaughan)
B	St Paul, Paul Street (1891–1902: Gothic by J. P. Seddon and J. Coates Carter)

B St John the Baptist, Radyr (medieval)

C Eglwys Dewi Sant, formerly Church of St Andrew, St Andrew's Crescent (1863 by John Prichard and J. P. Seddon)

B St John the Evangelist, St John's Crescent (1854–70: Gothic by J. Prichard and J. P. Seddon)

II Roman Catholic Church of St Peter, St Peter's Street (1861: Gothic by C. F. Hansom)

B St Saviour, Splott Road (1888: G. F. Bodley and T. Garner)

B Saint German of Auxerre, Star Street (1882–84: Gothic style by G. F. Bodley and T. Garner)

B St Margaret, Waterloo Road, Roath (1873: Gothic by John Prichard)

II English Presbyterian Church, Windsor Place (1866: Gothic by Frederick Pilkington)

C St Teilo, Woodville Road (1897: Perpendicular by G. E. Halliday)

II Pen-y-Groes Chapel, former Presbyterian chapel (*c.* 1800)

APPENDIX 5—SCOTLAND

The Listed Churches in Edinburgh

B Archepiscopal Chapel *Roman Catholic,* Morningside (1907: Byzantine by Robert Weir Schultz)

B Augustine-Bristo *Congregational* Church, George IV Bridge (1857–61: Romanesque and Renaissance by J., J. M. & W. H. Hay)

A Barclay Church *Church of Scotland,* Barclay Place (1862–64: Second pointed by F. T. Pilkington)

B Belford Church formerly *Church of Scotland,* Douglas Gardens (1888–89: Late Gothic by Sydney Mitchell)

B Braid Church *Church of Scotland,* Nile Grove (1886: Renaissance by Sir G. Washington Browne)

B Bristo *Baptist* Church, Queensferry Road (1932–35: Renaissance by William Paterson)

A Broughton Place Church *Church of Scotland* (1820–21: Classical by Archibald Elliot)

C Buccleuch Parish Church formerly *Church of Scotland,* Buccleuch Street (1753 & 1866)

B Buccleuch and Greyfriars Church *Free Church,* West Cross Causeway (1856–62: Second pointed by J., J. M. & W. H. Hay)

B Candlish Church *Church of Scotland*, Polwarth Terrace (1900: Late Gothic by Sydney Mitchell and Wilson)

A Canongate Parish Church *Church of Scotland* (1688–90: by James Smith)

A Former *Catholic Apostolic* Church now *Reformed Baptist*, Mansfield Place (1873–94: Neo-Norman by Sir R. Rowand Anderson)

B Christ Church *Episcopal*, Morningside Road (1878: French Gothic by H. J. Blanc)

B Colinton St Cuthbert *Church of Scotland* (1771: Byzantine interior by Sidney Mitchell 1907)

A Corstorphine Parish Church *Church of Scotland* (15th century, etc.)

B Craiglockhart Parish Church *Church of Scotland* (1889: Scots Gothic by George Henderson)

B Cramond Parish Church *Church of Scotland* (1656 onwards)

A Duddingston Parish Church *Church of Scotland* (12th and 17th century, etc.)

B Duncan Street *Baptist* Church (*c.* 1843: Neo-Greek)

B *First Church of Christ Scientist*, Inverleith Terrace (1910: Scots Romanesque by Ramsay Traquair)

B Glasite Chapel *Sandemanian* Church of Christ, Church of the Good Shepherd, 33 Barony Street (1836: Square domed meeting room)

B Gogar Parish Church formerly *Church of Scotland* (17th century onwards)

B Church of the Good Shepherd *Episcopal*, Murrayfield Avenue (1899: by Sir Robert Lorimer)

B Greenside Parish Church *Church of Scotland* (1836–38: Gothic by J. Gillespie Graham)

A Greyfriars Church *Church of Scotland*, Candlemaker Row (1601 onwards)

B Church of the Holy Cross *Episcopal*, Quality Street (1910–12: Round-arched by J. M. Dick Peddie)

A Abbey of Holyrood (ruin)

B Holy Trinity formerly *Episcopal* now transformer station, Queensferry Road (1838: Neo-perpendicular by John Henderson)

B Junction Road Church *Church of Scotland*, Leith (1824–25: Classical by William Bell)

B Former Lady Yester's Church *Church of Scotland* now University Works Department, 9 Infirmary Street (1803: Neo-Jacobean)

B Liberton Parish Church *Church of Scotland* (1815: Neo-perpendicular by J. Gillespie Graham)

B Lothian Road Church *Church of Scotland*
(1830: Classical by David Bryce)

A Magdalen Chapel *Church of Scotland*, 39 Cowgate (1614–15)

B Mayfield North Church *Church of Scotland*
(1876–79: French Gothic by H. J. Blanc)

C Morningside *Congregational* Church
(1929: Early Christian by James Maclachlan)

B Morningside Parish Church *Church of Scotland*
(1838: by John Henderson)

B Morningside South Church *Church of Scotland*, Cluny Drive
(1891–92: Late Gothic by Sir R. Rowand Anderson)

B Murrayfield Parish Church *Church of Scotland*
(1905: Curvilinear by A. Hunter Crawford)

B Church of the Nazarene formerly *Congregational* now offices, Broughton Street
(1816: Classical by David Skae)

C New Restalrig Church *Church of Scotland*, Willowbrae Road
(1891–92: Scots Gothic by Sydney Mitchell)

A Newington and St Leonard's Church formerly *Church of Scotland* now being converted to orchestral centre, South Clerk Street
(1823: Classical by Robert Brown)

A Nicolson Square *Methodist* Chapel (1814–15: Classical)

C Nicolson Street Church formerly *Church of Scotland* now saleroom
(1819: Tudor Gothic by J. Gillespie Graham)

A North Leith Parish Church *Church of Scotland*
(1813–16: Greek Revival by William Burn)

B Old St Paul's Church *Episcopal*, Jeffrey Street
(1881–83: by Hay and Henderson)

B Palmerston Place Church *Church of Scotland*
(1873–75: Italianate by Peddie and Kinnear)

B Pilrig-Dalmeny Street Church *Church of Scotland*, Leith Walk
(1860–62: Rogue Gothic by Peddie and Kinnear)

B Portobello Old and Regent Street Parish Church *Church of Scotland*
(1809: Classical by William Sibbald)

B Queen Street Church formerly *Church of Scotland* now commercial premises
(1852: Tudor Collegiate by John Henderson)

A Restalrig Parish Church *Church of Scotland*
(15th century onwards)

B Church of the Sacred Heart *Roman Catholic*, Lauriston Street
(1860: by Father Richard Vaughan)

A St Andrew's and St George's Church *Church of Scotland*, George Street
(1782–84: Classical by David Kay and Major Andrew Frazer)

B St Andrew's Place Church formerly *Church of Scotland*, Leith
(1826–27: Classical by Tait, Bell, Scott and Anderson)

B St Anne's Church *Church of Scotland*, Corstorphine
(1911–13: Romanesque by P. McGregor Chalmers)

A St Andrew's Chapel, Queens Drive (Ruin)

B St Bernard's Church *Church of Scotland*, Saxe-Coburg Street
(1823: Classical by James Milne)

B St Columba's Church *Church of Scotland*, Queensferry Road
(1899–1900: Romanesque by P. McGregor Chalmers)

B St Columba's Church *Free Church of Scotland*, Johnston Terrace
(1843–45: First pointed by Thomas Hamilton)

C St Columba's by the Castle *Episcopal*, Johnston Terrace
(1846–47: First pointed by John Henderson)

B St Cuthbert's Church *Church of Scotland*, Lothian Road
(1892–93: Renaissance by H. J. Blanc)

B St Cuthbert's Church *Episcopal*, Westgarth Avenue
(1888–97: Late Scots Gothic by Sir R. Rowand Anderson)

A St George's Church now West Register House, Charlotte Square
(1811–14: Classical by Robert Reid)

B St George's West Church *Church of Scotland*, Shandwick Place
(1867–69: Renaissance by David Bryce)

B St George's Chapel formerly *Episcopal* now showroom
(1794: Gothic by James Adam)

A St Giles (High) Church *Church of Scotland*, High Street
(1385 onwards)

B St James Church *Episcopal*, Constitution Street Leith
(1863: Early pointed by Sir George Gilbert Scott—Robert Rowand Anderson assistant responsible)

B St James the Less Church *Episcopal*, Inverleith Row, Goldenacre
(1888: Second pointed by Sir R. Rowand Anderson)

A St John's Church *Episcopal*, Princes Street
(1816–18: by William Burn)

B St John's Church *Roman Catholic*, Brighton Place, Portobello
(1904–6: Arts and Crafts Gothic by J. T. Walford)

B St Luke's Parish Church *Church of Scotland*, East Fettes Avenue
(1907–8: Neo-Romanesque by P. Macgregor Chalmers)

B St Margaret's Convent Chapel *Roman Catholic,* Whitehouse Loan
(1835: Saxon by J. Gillespie Graham)

B St Mark's Church *Episcopal,* High Street Portobello (1828)

B St Mark's Church *Unitarian,* Castle Terrace
(1834–35: Mannerist by David Bryce)

A St Mary's Cathedral *Episcopal,* Palmerston Place
(1874–79: Early pointed by Sir George Gilbert Scott, completed by John Oldrid Scott)

B St Mary's Cathedral *Roman Catholic,* St James Place
(1800: reconstructed 1828, 1858–61 and recently)

A St Mary's Church *Church of Scotland,* Bellevue Crescent
(1826: Classical by Thomas Brown)

B St Mary's Church *Church of Scotland,* Leith
(1848: Late second pointed by Thomas Hamilton)

B St Mary Star of the Sea *Roman Catholic,* Leith
(1853–54: Second pointed by Edward Welby Pugin and Joseph Aloysius Hansom)

B St Mary and St James Chapel, Newhaven (1508: ruins)

C St Matthew's *Church of Scotland,* Morningside
(1890: Early pointed by H. J. Blanc)

B St Michael's Church *Church of Scotland,* Slateford Road
(1883: Early pointed by John Honeyman)

A St Michael's and All Saints Church *Episcopal,* Brougham Street (1866–78: Early Gothic by Sir R. Rowand Anderson)

C St Oswald's Church formerly *Church of Scotland* now Boroughmuir School Annex, Montpelier Park (1899–1900 by H. F. Kerr)

B St Patrick's Church *Roman Catholic,* Cowgate
(1771–74: Classical)

B St Paul's Church formerly *Church of Scotland,* St Leonards Street (1836)

B St Peter's Church *Episcopal,* Newington
(1857–67: Early Geometrical by William Slater)

B St Peter's Church *Roman Catholic,* Falcon Avenue Gardens
(1906–8/1928/29: Free Early Christian by Sir Robert Lorimer)

B St Serf's Church *Church of Scotland,* Ferry Road, Goldenacre
(1899 and 1912: Late Gothic by G. Mackie Watson)

A St Stephen's Church *Church of Scotland,* St Stephen Street
(1827–28: Classical by W. H. Playfair)

B St Thomas's Church formerly *Church of England,* then Scottish Tourist Board, now disused, 2 Rutland Place
(1843 and 1882: Neo-Norman)

B St Triduana's Church *Roman Catholic,* Marionville Road, Restalrig
(1933: Scots Gothic by Sir Giles Gilbert Scott)

A Tolbooth St John's Church *Church of Scotland*, Castlehill (1841–44: English midpointed by J. Gillespie Graham and A. W. N. Pugin)

A Trinity College Church Apse formerly *Church of Scotland*, Chalmers Close (1460–1531: demolished 1848, choir re-erected 1872)

A Tron Church formerly *Church of Scotland*, High Street (1637–47: by John Mylne)

C Viewforth Church *Church of Scotland*, Gilmore Place (1871–72: Geometrical by Pilkington and Bell, interior gutted in fire of 1898; tower demolished)

B Apostolic Church, David Street (1812–13: Plain classic)

B Lady Glenorchy's Church *Church of Scotland*, Greenside Place (1844: Classical; 1846: John Henderson neo-perpendicular front)

B Lady Glenorchy's Church formerly *Church of Scotland* now University, Roxburgh Place (1909: Thomas Ross; 1913: Peter MacGregor Chalmers, late Scots Gothic)

B Quaker Meeting House, Pleasance disused (1791: plain box)

B Reid Memorial Church, *Church of Scotland*, West Savile Terrace (1929–33: Lorimer Gothic by Leslie Grahame Macdougall)

B St Bernard's Davidson Church *Church of Scotland*, Henderson Row (1854–56: Early decorated by John Milne)

B St Philip's Parish Church *Church of Scotland*, Abercorn Terrace (1875: Early decorated by John Honeyman)

C St Thomas's Parish Church formerly *Church of Scotland* now Sikh Temple, Sheriff Brae (1840: Neo-Norman by John Henderson)

B Slateford Church formerly *Church of Scotland* now workshop, Lanark Road (*c.* 1783 altered 1826: Plain classical)

B South College Street Church formerly *Church of Scotland* now University store, South College Street (1856: Renaissance by Patrick Wilson)

B Stockbridge Church formerly *Church of Scotland* Deanhaugh Street (1844: Neo-Norman by D. Cousin, re-erected here 1868)

C University Chaplaincy Centre, formerly New North *Church of Scotland*, George IV Bridge (1846–48: Early Decorated by Thomas Hamilton)

APPENDIX 6
The Episcopal Church in Scotland

A list of the most important churches with date and architect

Diocese of Aberdeen and Orkney

*** Aberdeen Cathedral of St Andrew, King Street (1817: Archibald Simpson, interior recast by Sir Ninian Comper 1936–43)

**** Aberdeen Chapel of St Margaret's Sisterhood, The Spital (by Sir Ninian Comper)

* Aberdeen St John the Evangelist, St John's Place (1851: by Mackenzie and Matthews)

* Aberdeen St Margaret of Scotland, Gallowgate (1869: by Matthews, good Comper additions)

* Aberdeen St Mary, Carden Place (1862: by Alexander Ellis)

** Aboyne, Aberdeenshire, St Thomas (1909: by Fryers and Penman)

* Ballater, Aberdeenshire, St Kentigern (1907: by A. Marshall Mackenzie)

* Banff, St Andrew, High Street (1833: by Archibald Simpson)

** Bieldside, Aberdeenshire, St Devenick (1903: by Arthur Clyne)

**** Braemar, Aberdeenshire, St Margaret (1899: by Sir J. Ninian Comper)

* Bucksburn, Aberdeenshire, St Machar (1880: by A. Marshall Mackenzie with Douglas Strachan murals)

**** Ellon, Aberdeenshire, St Mary-on-the-Rock (1871: by G. E. Street)

* Folla-Rule, Aberdeenshire, St George (1796: but present appearance Arthur Clyne *c.* 1900)

**** Fraserburgh, Aberdeenshire, St Peter (1892: by John Kinross)

* Inverurie, Aberdeenshire, St Mary (1842: by James Ross)

** Longside, Aberdeenshire, St John the Evangelist (1854: by William Hay)

*** New Pitsligo, Aberdeenshire, St John the Evangelist (1871: by G. E. Street)

* Old Deer, Aberdeenshire, St Drostan (1851: by Mackenzie and Matthews, chancel lengthened and glass by J. N. Comper)

* Peterhead, Aberdeenshire, St Peter (1814 by Robert Mitchell)

** Whiterashes, Aberdeenshire, All Saints (1850: fine Comper glass)

* Woodhead, Aberdeenshire, All Saints (1849: by John Henderson, good spire probably by James Matthews)

Diocese of Argyll and the Isles

*	Fort William, Inverness-shire, St Andrew (1880: by Alexander Ross)
*	Inveraray, Argyll, All Saints (1886: by Wardrop and Anderson, unfinished campanile detached from church)
*****	Millport, Bute, Cathedral of the Isles (1876: by William Butterfield)
****	Eorpaidh, Butt of Lewis, St Moluag (12th century: re-roofed and restored 1912)

Diocese of Brechin

****	Dundee Cathedral of St Paul (1853–65: by Sir Gilbert Scott, very good spire)
**	Arbroath, Angus, St Mary (1854: by John Henderson)
**	Brechin, Angus, St Andrew (1888: by Alexander Ross)
*	Broughty Ferry, Angus, St Mary (1858: by Sir Gilbert Scott, enlarged by Lorimer 1911)
***	Drumtochty, Kincardineshire, St Palladius (1885: by Pirie and Clyne)
**	Dundee St Luke, Baldovan Road (1903: by Gilbert Ogilvy)
*	Dundee St Mary Magdalene, Constitution Road (1867: originally Catholic Apostolic by Edward and Robertson, exterior badly scraped)
*****	Dundee St Salvador, Church Street (1868: by G. F. Bodley)
**	Invergowrie, Perthshire, All Souls (1891: by Hippolyte Blanc)
*	Lochlee, Angus, St Drostane (1879: by Matthews and Mackenzie)
*	Montrose, Angus, St Mary and St Peter (1858: by John Henderson; restored 1927 by H. O. Tarbolton)
**	Stonehaven, Kincardineshire, St James the Great (1877: by Rowand Anderson, chancel by Arthur Clyne)
*	Torry, Aberdeen, St Peter (1898: by Kinross and Tarbolton)

Diocese of Edinburgh

*****	Edinburgh St Mary's Cathedral (1879: by Sir Gilbert Scott)
*	Dalkeith, Midlothian, St Mary (1845: by William Burn)
***	Dunbar, East Lothian, St Anne (1882: by H. M. Wardrop and Rowand Anderson)
*	Edinburgh Christchurch, Morningside Road (1876: by Hippolyte Blanc)
**	Edinburgh Church of the Good Shepherd, Murrayfield Avenue (1899: by Sir Robert Lorimer)
*	Edinburgh Holy Cross, Quality Street (1913: by Dick Peddie)
*	Edinburgh St Columba, Johnston Terrace (1846: John Henderson)

** Edinburgh St Cuthbert, Colinton (1899: by Rowand Anderson)

**** Edinburgh St James the Less, Inverleith Row (1888: by Rowand Anderson, murals by William Hole, furnishings by J. J. Burnet)

*** Edinburgh St James the Less, Constitution Street, Leith (1863: by Sir Gilbert Scott)

***** Edinburgh St John the Evangelist, Princes Street (1818: by William Burn)

** Edinburgh St Mark, Portobello High Street (1826)

**** Edinburgh St Michael and All Saints, Brougham Street (1867: by Rowand Anderson)

*** Edinburgh Old St Paul's, Jeffrey Street (1883: by Hay and Henderson)

***** Edinburgh St Paul and St George, York Place (1818: by Archibald Elliot)

*** Edinburgh St Peter, Lutton Place (1860: by Slater and Captenter)

* Galashiels, Selkirkshire, St Peter (1854: by Hay and Henderson)

** Hawick, Roxburghshire, St Cuthbert (1858: by Sir Gilbert Scott)

** Kelso, Roxburghshire, St Andrew (1869: by Rowand Anderson)

* North Berwick, East Lothian, St Baldred (1862: by John Henderson)

* Penicuik, Midlothian, St James the Less (1882: by R. T. N. Spier; executed by Seymour and Kinross)

***** Roslin, Midlothian, St Matthew (1450–86)

**** South Queensferry, West Lothian, St Mary of Mount Carmel (15th century: repaired by Seymour and Kinross)

** Stirling Holy Trinity, Dumbarton Road (1878: by Rowand Anderson)

Diocese of Glasgow and Galloway

*** Glasgow St Mary's Cathedral (1871: by Sir Gilbert Scott)

*** Ayr Holy Trinity, Fullarton Street (1888: by J. L. Pearson)

*** Castle Douglas, Kirkcudbrightshire, St Ninian (1861: by E. B. Lamb)

** Dumbarton St Augustine (1873: by Rowand Anderson)

** Dumfries St John the Evangelist (1868: by Slater and Carpenter)

* Glasgow All Saints, Woodend Drive (1904: by James Chalmers)

***** Glasgow St Andrew-by-the-Green (1750; closed and becoming derelict)

** Glasgow St Bride, Hyndland Road (1904: by G. F. Bodley, additions by H. O. Tarbolton, incomplete)

*** Glasgow St Margaret, Kilmarnock Road (1912: by Dr McGregor Chalmers)

*** Greenock, Renfrewshire, St John the Evangelist, Union Street (1878: Paley and Austin)

*** Helensburgh, Dunbartonshire, St Michael and All Angels (1888: by Rowand Anderson)

Diocese of Moray, Ross and Caithness

*** Inverness Cathedral (1869: by Alexander Ross)

*** Aberlour, Banffshire, St Margaret (1875: by Alexander Ross)

* Fochabers, Morayshire, Gordon Chapel (1834: by Simpson)

**** Forres, Morayshire, St John the Evangelist (*c.* 1850: by Thomas Mackenzie)

** Gordonstoun, Morayshire, Michael Kirk (1705: Gothic)

* Inverness St Michael and All Angels (1904: by R. C. Bannantyne and Ninian Comper)

* Keith, Banffshire, Holy Trinity (1883: by J. & W. Wittet)

* Rothiemurchus St John the Baptist (1929–30: by Sir J. Ninian Comper)

Diocese of St Andrews, Dunkeld and Dunblane

*** Perth Cathedral (1850: by William Butterfield, much recast by the Pearsons)

** Alloa, Clackmannanshire, St John the Evangelist (1869: by Sir Rowand Anderson)

* Burntisland, Fife, St Serf (1905: by Pearson)

*** Doune, Perthshire, St Modoc (1878: by James Brooks)

* Dunblane, Perthshire, St Mary (1845: by John Henderson)

** Dunkeld and Birnam St Mary (1858: by Carpenter)

** Forfar, Angus, St John the Evangelist (1881: by Rowand Anderson)

*** Glenalmond, Perthshire, Trinity College, Private Chapel (John Henderson)

**** Kirriemuir, Angus, St Mary (1905: by Sir Ninian Comper)

** Rosyth, Fife, SS Andrew and George (1925–26: by Sir Ninian Comper)

*** St Andrews All Saints, North Castle Street (1923: by Paul Waterhouse—Chancel 1907 by John Douglas of Chester)

** St Andrews St Andrew, Queen's Gardens (1869: by Sir Rowand Anderson—spire dem)

APPENDIX 7
Demolished Churches

AVON

Bath: St Andrew
(1870–73: by Scott: dem 1950s)

Bath: St James
(1768–69: by J. Palmer: dem 1950s)

Bath: Holy Trinity
(1820–22: by John Lowder: dem 1957)

Bristol: Emmanuel Church, *C of E*, Guthrie Road, Clifton
(1865–69: by John Norton: dem 1977)

Bristol: St Andrew, *C of E*, Clifton Hill
(1819–22: Gothic, by James Foster: bombed, tower remained a landmark; dem *c.* 1956)

Bristol: St Augustine the Less, *C of E*, College Green
(15c, rebuilt 1840: dem 1962)

L Bristol: St Gabriel, *C of E*, St Gabriel's Road, Upper Easton
(1870: by J. C. Neale: dem 1975)

Bristol: St George, *C of E*, Summerhill Road
(1879: by P. E. Masey: dem 1976)

Bristol: St Mary, *C of E*, Woodland Road, Tyndalls Park
(1870–81: by J. P. St Aubyn: dem 1976)

Bristol: St John, Bedminster
(1855: by John Norton: dem 1967)

Bristol: Moravian Chapel, Maudlin Street
(1896: by Edward Gabriel: dem *c.* 1970)

Bristol: Old King Street *Baptist* Church
(1815: Classical: dem *c.* 1957 for redevelopment)

Bristol: All Saints, Clifton
(Street 1864ff.: burnt 1940; dem 1964)

Bristol: St Andrew, Montpelier
(S. J. Hicks 1845: dem *c.* 1955)

Bristol: St Andrew the Less, Hotwells
(J. C. Neale 1872: dem *c.* 1960)

Bristol: St Clement, Newfoundland Road
(Gabriel & Hirst 1854: dem *c.* 1955)

Bristol: St James the Less, Clifton
(Pope & Bindon 1862: dem 1974)

Bristol: St Luke, Bedminster
(John Norton 1861: dem *c.* 1962)

Bristol: St Matthias-on-the-Weir
(John Norton 1851: dem *c.* 1962)

Bristol: St Raphael, Cumberland Road
(Woodyer 1859: dem *c.* 1955)

Bristol: Christ Church *Congregational*, Sneyd Park
(Stuart Colman 1877ff.: dem 1961–62)

Bristol: Counterslip *Baptist* Church
(1810: burnt 1940; dem *c.* 1965 —stones said to have been numbered for re-erection)

Bristol: Ebenezer *Methodist*, Old King Street
(1795: dem 1954)

Bristol: Gospel Temple, Milk Street
(*c.* 1865–70: dem 1954)

Bristol: Grenville *Wesleyan* Chapel, Hotwells
(Foster & Wood 1875–9: dem *c.* 1965)

Bristol: *Countess of Huntingdon* Chapel, Lodge Street
(1830: dem 1967)

Bristol: Whitefield Tabernacle, Penn Street
(1753: dem 1958)

BEDFORDSHIRE

Bedford: St Paul, *Methodist* Chapel, Harpur Street
(1831: Italianate: dem *c.* 1970)

Bedford: *Methodist* Chapel, Hasselt Street
(dem 1960s)

Bedford: *Baptist* Church, Mill Street
(Italianate: dem 1960s)

III Biggleswade: St John, *C of E*
(1883: by Sir Arthur Blomfield: dem 1975)

Biggleswade: *Baptist* Church, Foundry Lane
(1785, enlarged 1818: good interior: dem early 1970s)

Billington: Primitive *Methodist* Chapel, Little Hill
(dem 1976)

Cranfield: *Quaker* Meeting House, Crossards Green
(dem *c.* 1966)

Houghton Regis: *Baptist* Chapel
(1846: neo-Gothic: dem early 1970s)

Kempston: St John, *C of E*
(1867–68: by Robert Palgrave: dem 1950s)

Leighton Buzzard: St Andrew, *C of E*, Church Street
(1885–87: by J. C. Neale: dem *c.* 1970)

Leighton Buzzard: *Wesleyan* Chapel, Hockliffe Street
(1864: Italianate: dem *c.* 1970)

II* Lidlington: All Saints Old Church, *C of E*
(1809 and 1886: dem early 1960s)

Lower Dean: *Methodist* Chapel
(dem 1970s)

Luton: *Baptist* Church, Park Street
(1850s: dem 1975 for redevelopment)

Luton: *Methodist* Church, Brache Street
(compulsory purchase order for redevelopment)

Luton: Wesleyan *Methodist* Chapel, Midland Road
(dem early 1950s)

Luton: *Congregational* Church, Stuart Street
(1864–65: Neo-Gothic, by J. Tarring: dem early 1970s)

Luton: *Methodist* Chapel, Walker Street
(dem early 1960s)

Milton Ernest: *Methodist* Chapel
(stuccoed neo-Classical chapel, due to be regraded II: dem 1976)

Stotfold: *Methodist* Chapel, Brook Street
(1869: dem 1976)

BERKSHIRE

Bradfield: SS Simon and Jude, Chapel of Ease
(1845: by G. G. Scott: dem 1954)

Kintbury: Christ Church, *C of E*
(1865–67: by T. T. Bury: dem 1954)

Langley New Town: St John, *C of E*
(1889: dem 1958)

Maidenhead: SS Mary Magdalene and Andrew
(1824–25: by C. H. Bury: dem *c.* 1964)

Maidenhead: St Paul, High Town Road
(1887–89: by E. J. Shrewsbury: recently dem)

Newbury: St Mary, *C of E*, Speenhamland
(1829–31 and 1876–1911: by G. Eard and A. E. Street: dem 1975)

Reading: *Unitarian* Church, 66 London Road
(dem 1975)

Reading: St Stephen, *C of E*, Rupert Street
(1864–66, enlarged 1886: by William White: dem 1976)

Reading: St John Evangelist, *C of E*, Watlington Street
(1872–73: by W. A. Dixon: dem scheme 1973)

Reading: *Salvation Army* Citadel, St Mary's Butts
(compulsorily purchased and dem for redevelopment late 1960s)

Reading: Chapel, Hosier Street
(compulsorily purchased and dem for redevelopment late 1960s)

Windsor: *Congregational* Church, William Street
(1832: Classical, by Jesse Hollis: listed building consent to dem granted 1971 but still standing)

BUCKINGHAMSHIRE

High Wycombe: Christ Church, *C of E*, Crendon Street
(1888-89: by A. Vernon: dem 1968)

High Wycombe: St James, *C of E*, Downley
(1938–39: by Cecil Brown: partly completed church dem and replaced with new church)

High Wycombe: St Andrew, *C of E*
(1897–98: by A. Mardon Mowbray: dem *c.* 1960 and replaced elsewhere)

High Wycombe: Free *Methodist* Church, Oxford Road
(dem 1968)

High Wycombe: Zion *Baptist* Chapel, Bridle Street
(dem 1970)

Prestwood: *Methodist* Church
(permission to rebuild 1974)

CAMBRIDGESHIRE

Cambridge: *Wesleyan* Chapel, Hills Road
(1870: by Hill & Swan: dem)

NL Chatteris: Salem *Baptist* Chapel, Huntingdon Road
(redeveloped as housing)

Denton: *C of E*
(17c: partly dem *c.* 1960)

Huntingdon: *Congregational* Chapel
(mid 19c: dem *c.* 1960)

NL Isleham: *Methodist* Chapel
(1840: dem 1976)

NL March: St Mary Magdalene, Whittlesey Road
(1874: by W. L. Spiers: dem *c.* 1971)

NL Peterborough: *Methodist* Church, Wentworth Street
(1874–75: by Johnson: permission granted for office block on site)

Wendy: All Saints, *C of E*
(1867: by R. W. Rowe: dem 1950 and replaced)

Wisbech *Baptist* Chapel, Ely Place
(1827–30: by William Swansborough: dem 1960s)

Woolley: *C of E*
(medieval: dem *c.* 1960)

CHESHIRE

Chester *Congregational* Chapel, Queen Street
(dem)

Crewe: *Methodist* Church, Heathfield
(one of the earliest chapels in Crewe: dem 1974)

II Nantwich: *Congregational* Chapel, Monk's Lane
(dem 1950s)

Nantwich: *Unitarian* Chapel
(dem)

Nantwich: *Methodist* Free Church
(dem)

NL Northwich: *Methodist* Church, London Road
(1888–89: Italianate: dem)

Runcorn: *Methodist* Church, Halton Road
(1871: Italianate: dem for housing)

Runcorn: Clifton *Methodist* Church, Cholmondeley Road, Clifton
(dem for housing)

Warrington: Golborne Street *Baptist* Church
(rebuilt elsewhere)

Warrington: Central Hall *Methodist* Mission
(dem following dangerous structures notice)

Warrington: *St Clement's Mission*, Bank Street
(dem for redevelopment)

Warrington: Bewsey Street *Methodist* Church
(1874: by C. O. Ellison: dem)

Warrington: Bold Street *Methodist* Church
(1850: late Classical with magnificent interior, by James Simpson of Leeds: replaced by offices and a new church)

Warrington: Martinscroft *Methodist* Church
(affected by road proposals awaiting dem)

Winsford *Methodist* Church, High Street
(to be dem for road improvements)

Wybunbury: St Chad, *C of E*
(1892–93: by James Brooks: dem scheme except tower 1976)

CLEVELAND

Hartlepool: *Methodist* Chapel, York Road
(1894: by Dunnipace: dem)

Hartlepool: Spion Kop Chapel, The Headland
(dem)

Hartlepool: *Jewish* Synagogue
(dem approved November 1973)

Haverton Hill: St John, *C of E*
(by Austin & Johnson: dem scheme 1976)

Middlesbrough: Providence Street *Baptist* Chapel, Grange Road
(purchased for dem for Northern Route Stage II)

Middlesbrough: *Congregational* Church, Canon Street
(purchased for housing development)

Middlesbrough: *Elim Free* Church, Brentnall Street
(dem as part of Central Area Redevelopment)

Middlesbrough: *Unitarian* Church, Corporation Road
(compulsorily purchased for slum clearance)

Redcar: St Andrew's, *C of E,* Chapel, Warrenby
(dem for slum clearance)

Thornaby: *Methodist* Church, Mandale Road
(to be dem for road scheme)

Thornaby: *Unitarian* Church, Mandale Road
(1873: by Clephan: to be dem for the A66 Stockton-Thornaby by-pass)

CORNWALL

L Redruth: the "Flowerpot" *Methodist* Chapel
(dem for redevelopment)

St Columb Major: Chapel
(dem)

CUMBRIA

Maryport: *Baptist* Church, Curzon Street
(1891: by C. Eaglesfield: replaced by new church)

Maryport: *Methodist* Church, Kirkby Street
(replaced by new church)

Pica: Chapel, near Whitehaven
(dem after dangerous structures notice *c.* 1972)

Uldale: St John the Evangelist, *C of E*
(1868–69: by G. Grayson: dem by 1967)

Whitehaven: *Congregational* Church, Scotch Street
(1874: by T. L. Banks: to be replaced by new county court and offices)

DERBYSHIRE

Bolsover: Town End *Methodist* Church, Welbeck Road
(dem 1972)

L Chesterfield: *Friends* Meeting House, Saltergate
(dem *c.* 1970 for multi-storey car park and road works)

NL Chesterfield: Trinity *Methodist* Church, Chesterfield Road
(dem 1974 for redevelopment)

NL Chesterfield: Ebenezer *Methodist* Chapel, Worksop Road
(dem 1974 because of damage by subsidence)

NL Chesterfield: *Congregational* Church, Avenue Road
(dem 1970)

NL Chesterfield: Mount Tabor *Methodist New Connexion* Chapel, Church Street North
(dem 1973 for redevelopment)

NL Chesterfield: Cross London Street *Methodist* Church
(dem 1972)

Creswell: Centenary *Methodist* Church, Elmton Road
(dem 1970)

Derby: St Alkmund, *C of E*
(1846: by Henry I. Stevens: dem for road improvements)

Derby: St Andrew, *C of E,* London Road
(1881: by Sir George Gilbert Scott, fine spire: dem)

Derby: *Baptist* Chapel, Osmaston Road
(1860: by Hine & Evans: dem 1968 and replaced)

Derby: *Baptist* Chapel, Watson Street
(dem as part of clearance proposals)

Derby: *Congregational* Church, London Road
(1843: by H. J. Stevens: dem post-war)

Derby: *Congregational* Church, Victoria Street
(1860: dem and replaced)

Derby: *Congregational* Church, Derwent Street
(1869–70: by Tait: dem)

Derby: *New Jerusalem* Church, London Street
(1819: dem)

Derby: *Primitive Methodist* Chapel, Kedlestone Street
(1871: by Giles & Brookhouse: dem)

Derby: *Primitive Methodist* Chapel, Traffic Street
(1865: by Giles & Brookhouse: dem)

Derby: William and Mary *Unitarian* Chapel, Friar Gate
(late 17c: dem 1974)

Derby: *Wesleyan* Chapel, King Street
(1841: by James Simpson: dem in last 15 years)

Derby: *Wesleyan* Chapel, Ashbourne Road
(1884: by John Wills: derelict in 1976)

Derwent Woodlands:
("eglise engloutie" submerged under Ladybower Reservoir)

Staintree: *Methodist* Church, Clowne Road
(dem 1971)

DEVON

Barnstaple: Emmanuel Church, *C of E,* Summerland Street (dem)

Dawlish: St Mark, *C of E,* Brunswick Place
(1849–50: by Hayward of Exeter: dem 1975)

Exeter: St Mary Major, *C of E*
(1865–68: by E. Ashworth: dem)

Exeter: St Edmund, *C of E*
(1834 with medieval crypt: dem scheme retaining crypt)

Exeter: St Sidwell, *C of E*
(15c and 1812: blitzed, later dem and replaced)

L Exeter: The Mint *Methodist* Chapel, Fore Street (1813, façade 1868: by the Rev William Jenkins: dem 1968)

Exeter: *Bible Christian* Chapel
(1839: heavy classical: dem 1950s)

Newton and Noss Parish: *Unconsecrated* chapel at Graton Hall
(proposal to demolish)

Plymouth: St Catherine, *C of E,* Lockyer Street
(1823: Classical, by John Foulston of Plymouth: dem after 1945)

Plymouth: Christ Church, *C of E,* Eton Place
(dem *c.* 1970)

Plymouth: St Matthew, *C of E,* Clarence Place
(1867: by J. Snell: dem *c.* 1970)

III Torquay: Belgrave *Methodist* Church, Union Street
(dem *c.* 1973)

NL Torquay: Belgrave *Congregational* Church, Tor Church Road
(dem 1973)

Torquay: *Methodist* Church, Market Street
(dem 1972)

Plymouth: *Zion Chapel* for Calvinists, Ker Street, Devonport
(by Foulston: dem)

Plymouth: *Plymouth Brethren* Chapel, Raleigh Street
(1831: by John Foulston: dem for new city centre)

DORSET

Bournemouth: *Quaker* Meeting House
(1912: dem 1964)

Chickerell: *Baptist* Mission
(permission for demolition and residential redevelopment)

East Burton: *C of E*
(1836–40: by J. T. Parkinson of Jersey: dem authorized)

East Stoke: Ruins of Old Church
(almost disappeared in recent years)

Hanworthy: St Michael, *C of E*
(*c.* 1820: dem *c.* 1960, replaced)

Holwell: *Methodist* Church
(permission to demolish)

Poole: St Paul, *C of E*
(1833: Greek Doric: dem 1963)

Poxwell: St John Evangelist, *C of E*
(1868: G. Evans: dem 1960s)

West Milton: St Mary Magdalene, *C of E*
(1869–74: by A. B. Hansford & G. R. Crickmay: dem since 1974)

Weymouth: Christ Church, *C of E*, King Street
(by E. Christian: dem *c.* 1950)

Weymouth: *Congregational* Church, Gloucester Street
(1864: Neo Norman, by R. C. Bennett: planning permission for demolition and redevelopment as old peoples flats)

DURHAM

Durham: Old Elvet *Methodist* Chapel
(1808: dem)

EAST SUSSEX

Brighton: Salem Chapel *Baptist* Church, Bond Street
(1861: dem *c.* 1973 for shops and offices)

Brighton: St Margaret, *C of E*
(1824: by Clarke: dem 1959)

Brighton: *Countess of Huntingdon* Church, North Street
(1870: by John Wimble, the "cathedral" of the Connexion: dem *c.* 1974 for offices, show rooms and maisonettes)

Brighton: St Mary Magdalene, Bread Street
(1864: by Bodley: dem 1960s)

Brighton: *Baptist* Church, Preston Park
(dem for four-storey flats)

Brighton: St Matthew, Sutherland Road
(1881–83: by John Norton: dem post 1965)

Eastbourne: St Clement, *C of E,* Priory Road
(dem after Compulsory Purchase Order)

Eastbourne: *Congregational* Church, Pevensey Road
(1862: by Searle, Son & Yelf: outline planning permission for redevelopment)

Eastbourne: *Elim* Church, Hartfield Road
(planning permission for new church and office building May 1973)

Eastbourne: St Peter, *C of E,* Meads Road
(1894–96: by H. Currey: dem 1972 for redevelopment)

Eastbourne: St George, *C of E*
(dem 1976 for redevelopment)

Eastbourne: *Baptist* Church, Victoria Drive
(dem 1973, site redeveloped, church rebuilt elsewhere)

Hastings: *Congregational* Church, Grove Road
(dem since 1968)

Hastings: Central *Methodist* Church, Cambridge Road
(dem after Compulsory Purchase Order)

Hastings: *Congregational* Church, Githa Road/Edwin Road
(dem since 1968)

Hastings: St Andrew, *C of E,* Queens Road
(1869: by Habershon & Brock: dem since 1968)

Hastings: St Clement, *C of E,* Priory Road
(1838: by Thomas Catley: dem since 1968)

Hastings: St Paul, Church Road, St Leonards
(1868: by John Norton: dem late 1960s)

Hastings: *Congregational* Church, Mount Pleasant Road
(dem since 1968)

Lewes: *Methodist* Church, Station Street
(1866–67: by Pocock, Corfe & Parker: permission to replace with shops, offices and flats October 1974)

Newhaven: Church, Baker Street
(permission to replace with three houses and garages 1974)

Willingdon: *Baptist* Church, Wannock Lane
(permission to replace with chalet bungalow and garage April 1976)

ESSEX

Colchester: St Nicholas, *C of E,* High Street
(1875–76, partly Medieval: by Sir G. G. Scott: dem 1955)

Creeksea: All Saints, *C of E*
(1878: by F. Chancellor: dem *c.* 1960)

Feering: Mortuary Chapel
(Victorian: dem 1974)

Frating: *C of E*
(Medieval and later: by C. F. Hayward: redundant 1976, tower declared dangerous and dem)

Great Warley: Old Church, *C of E*
(dem *c.* 1960)

Henham: *United Reformed* Church
(1864: by Jasper Cowell: permission to dem granted in 1976)

Kelvedon Hatch: St Nicholas, *C of E*
(1753: application to dem church in grounds of Hall)

Manningtree: St Michael and All Angels, *C of E*
(1616 and 1839: dem *c.* 1968–70)

Mistley Heath: St Mary the Virgin, *C of E*
(ruins levelled *c.* 1968–70)

Shopland: St Mary, *C of E*
(Norman: dem)

GLOUCESTERSHIRE

Cheltenham: St John, *C of E,* Albion Street
(1827–29, 1857 and 1870: by J. B. Papworth: dem *c.* 1970)

Cheltenham: St Matthew, *C of E,* Clarence Street
(1878–79: by E. Christian: spire dem 1952, church remains)

Cirencester: *Congregational* Church, Dyer Street
(by W. Gilbee Scott: dem 1970 for supermarket)

Gloucester: *Baptist* Chapel, Brunswick Road
(1872–73: by Charles G. Searle & Son: dem 1973)

Gloucester: *Wesleyan* Chapel, Northgate Street
(1877: by Charles Bell: dem *c.* 1972/73)

Gloucester: *Unitarian* Chapel, Eastgate Street
(1699: dem *c.* 1968)

Lassington: St Oswald, *C of E*
(Norman tower preserved, nave (1874/5: Medland & Son); dem after local opposition to house conversion)

Stonehouse: *Baptist* Chapel, Nympsfield
(dem)

Stonehouse: *Baptist* Mission, Woodcock Lane
(to be dem)

Stroud: *Congregational* Chapel, Chapel Lane, Ebley
(19c neo-Norman front: dem)

Stroud: *Congregational* Chapel: High Street
(dem 1970)

Stroud: Chapel at corner of Nympsfield and Northfields Road, Nailsworth
(dem)

Stroud: Monastery at Convent Lane, Woodchester
(dem)

Stroud: *Primitive Methodist* Chapel, Selsley Hill
(dem)

Walton Cardiff: St James, *C of E*
(rebuilt 1869: by John Middleton: dem *c.* 1976)

GREATER LONDON

Barking: *Methodist* Church, Rainham Road South
(dem 1958)

Barnet: St Peter, *C of E,* Cricklewood Lane
(1891: by T. H. Watson: to be dem for church school)

Barnet: St Margaret *Presbyterian* Church, Ballards Lane
(1874: by G. F. Stalker: to be dem for shops and offices)

NL Brent: St John, Cambridge Gardens
(dem 1974)

Brent: St Lawrence, *C of E,* Chevening Road
(dem site cleared)

NL Bromley: St Paul, Hamlet Road, Penge
(1865: by E. Bassett Keeling: dem after 1973)

Camden: St John Evangelist, *C of E,* Red Lion Square, Holborn
(by J. L. Pearson: dem unnecessarily after the war)

Camden: St Peter, Regent Square, St Pancras
(1822–24: by the Inwoods: damaged in the war, dem 1960s unnecessarily)

Camden: Christ Church, Somers Town, St Pancras (1868: by Newman & Billing: damaged, dem 1954)

Camden: St Andrew, *C of E,* Haverstock Hill, St Pancras (1866: by C. J. Heywocd: dem 1953)

Camden: Sinner Saved, *C of E,* St Pancras (1836: dem 1959)

Camden: St Stephen, *C of E,* Avenue Road, Hampstead (1849: by S. W. Daukes: dem 1960)

Camden: Christchurch, Woburn Square (dem 1975)

Camden: *Catholic Apostolic* Church, Caledonian/Hilmarton Road (dem)

Camden: St Matthew, Oakley Square (dem 1977)

City: Christ Church, Newgate Street (by Wren: gutted, shell partially dem for a new road 1976)

City: *Congregational* Memorial Hall, Faringdon Street (1872–75: by J. Farring & Son: dem pre 1970)

Croydon: St Matthew, *C of E,* George Street (1866: by A. Blomfield: dem)

Croydon: St Christopher, *C of E* (dem)

Croydon: London City Mission, Cairo Road (dem)

Croydon: St George's Mission, Whitehorse Road (dem)

Croydon: London City Mission, Gillett Road (dem)

Ealing: *United Reformed* Church, Spencer Road, Acton (1870: by J. Tarring: to be dem for old peoples home)

Greenwich: St Germain, Blackheath (1822: bombed, recently dem)

Greenwich: St Peter (1866: by S. S. Teulon: dem 1955)

Greenwich: Holy Trinity, Blackheath Hill (1838–40: by J. W. Wild: bombed, dem 1954)

Greenwich: Holy Trinity, Woolwich Road (dem 1975)

Greenwich: St Mark, *C of E,* Plumstead, Woolwich (dem scheme 1972)

Greenwich: St John, Woolwich (1883–84: by C. H. Cooke: dem 1959)

Greenwich: Holy Trinity, Beresford Square (1834: by Hopkins: dem 1962)

Hackney: St Peter, *C of E,* Hoxton, Shoreditch (1874–75: by R. W. Drew: dem *c.* 1953)

Hackney: St Paul, Broke Road, Haggerston, Shoreditch (1859–60: by A. W. Blomfield: dem late 1960s)

Hackney: St Saviour, Hoxton, Shoreditch (1866: by James Brooks: unnecessarily dem after the war)

Hackney: *Quaker* Meeting House, Yoakley Road, Stoke Newington (1828: by William Alderson: dem 1957)

Hackney: All Saints, *C of E,* Clapton Park (dem scheme 1976)

Hackney: Christchurch, Grove Road, Clapton (1870–71: by W. Wigginton. dem 1954)

Hackney: All Saints, Blurton Road, Clapton (dem 1973)

Hackney: St Matthew, Upper Clapton (gutted 1976, dem 1977)

Hammersmith: St Clement, Fulham Palace Road, Fulham (1885: by Sir Arthur Blomfield: dem for housing and new church-cum-hall)

Hammersmith: St Oswald, Anselm Road, Fulham (to be dem for housing)

Hammersmith: St Luke, Uxbridge Road (dem post 1973 for housing and new church-cum-hall)

Haringey: *Quaker* Meeting House, 594 High Road, Tottenham
(1831: dem 1961)

Haringey: St Paul, *C of E*, Tottenham
(1859: by W. Mumford: dem 1972)

Haringey: St Peter, *C of E*, Page Green, Tottenham
(1899: by J. S. Alder: dem scheme 1973)

Haringey: St Andrew, St Andrew's Road, Higham Hill, Tottenham
(dem 1973)

Haringey: St Mary, *C of E*
(1888: by J. Brooks: dem and replaced)

Harrow: *Methodist* Church, Benbrough Road
(dem)

Harrow: Trinity *United Reformed* Church, Station Road
(dem)

Hillingdon: *Methodist* Church, Yiewsley
(dem for redevelopment but replaced)

Hillingdon: Moor Hall Chapel, Harefield
(13c, secularized: dem *c.* 1960)

Hillingdon: *Methodist* Church at Northwood, now a *synagogue*
(to be dem for redevelopment)

Hillingdon: *Methodist* Church, Uxbridge
(to be dem)

Hillingdon: *Methodist* Church, Hayes
(dem for redevelopment but replaced)

Islington: St Matthew, *C of E*
(1850–51: by A. D. Gough: dem *c.* 1953)

Islington: St Barnabas, Holloway
(1865: by T. K. Green: closed 1945, since dem)

Islington: All Saints, Caledonian Road
(1838: by W. Tress: dem 1976)

Islington: St Paul, Upper Holloway
(1869–70: by H. Jarvis: bombed, dem 1950)

Islington: St John, *C of E*
(dem scheme 1972)

Islington: St Philip
(1855–56: by A. D. Gough: dem 1955)

Islington: St Luke, Old Street, Finsbury
(1732–33: Classical, by Hawksmoor & John James: unroofed and gutted by church authorities 1961)

Islington: Smithfield Martyrs Church of St Peter, Clerkenwell
(1869–71: by E. L. Blackburn: dem post war)

Kensington and Chelsea: St Matthias, *C of E*, Earls Court
(1868–71: by J. H. Hakewill: dem 1958)

Kensington and Chelsea: SS Andrew and Philip
(1868–69: by Bassett Keeling: dem *c.* 1951)

Kensington and Chelsea: St Mark, *C of E*, Notting Hill
(1864: by Bassett Keeling: dem scheme 1972)

Kensington and Chelsea: Essex *Unitarian* Chapel (1887: dem 1973)

Kingston upon Thames: Bunyan *Baptist* Chapel, 44–46 Cromwell Road
(1893: by T. Timberley: dem, replaced)

Kingston upon Thames: Surbiton Park *Congregational* Church, Grove Road
(dem)

Kingston upon Thames: Eden Street *Methodist* Church
(dem)

Kingston upon Thames: Richmond Road *Methodist* Church
(dem)

NL Lambeth: Auckland Hill *Evangelical* Church
(*c.* 1870: dem 1960)

NL Lambeth: Brixton *Baptist* Church, Stockwell Road
(1884: dem 1976 for road improvement scheme, replaced elsewhere)

NL Lambeth: Carlisle Chapel, Kennington Lane
(*c.* 1810: dem 1968)

NL Lambeth: Emmanuel Church, Clive Road
(1876: by E. C. Robins: dem 1966 for new church and housing)

NL Lambeth: Emmanuel Church, Distin Street
(1868: by H. E. Coe: dem *c.* 1955)

NL Lambeth: Knights Hill, Primitive *Methodist* Church
(dem *c.* 1960)

NL Lambeth: Loughborough Park *Congregational* Chapel, Coldharbour Lane
(dem *c.* 1970 for industrial development)

NL Lambeth: St Mary the Less, Black Prince Road
(1872: Gothic, by Francis Bedford: dem 1966 for GLC housing scheme)

NL Lambeth: St Philip, Kennington Road
(1863: by H. E. Coe: dem 1976 for housing development)

NL Lambeth: Railton Road *Methodist* Church
(1874: by R. Cable: dem 1968 for new church and community centre)

NL Lambeth: Roupell Park *Methodist* Church
(1879: by Charles Bell: dem 1968–69 for new supermarket and church by Poulson and Partners)

NL Lambeth: St Stephen, St Stephen's Terrace
(1861: by John Barnett: dem 1967 for new church and housing)

NL Lambeth: St Stephen, Weir Road
(1867: by James T. Knowles Junior: dem for new church)

NL Lambeth: Streatham *Methodist* Church, Streatham High Road
(1882: by Charles Bell: dem for supermarket)

NL Lambeth: Trinity *Presbyterian* Church, Clapham Road
(1862: by Habbershon & Pile: dem)

NL Lambeth: Upper Norwood *Methodist* Church, Westow Hill
(1874: by Charles Bell: dem 1964 for church, supermarket and flats)

Lambeth: All Saints
(1876–78: by A. Bedborough: bombed, dem 1952)

Lambeth: St Matthew, Denmark Hill
(1848: by Gough & Rounleu: bombed, dem 1962)

Lambeth: St George, *C of E*, Nine Elms
(1828: by Edward Blore: dem)

Lewisham: Holy Trinity
(1862–63: by W. S. Barber: dem 1960)

Lewisham: St Mary, Deptford
(1904–5: by P. Morley Horder: dem 1965)

Newham: St Saviour, Forest Gate
(1883–84: by E. Clare: dem 1975)

Newham: St Barnabas, North Woolwich
(1857: by Sir G. G. Scott: dem 1973)

Newham: St Barnabas, *C of E*, Silvertown
(dem scheme 1975)

Newham: St Peter, *C of E*, Upton Cross
(1892–93: by A. W. Blomfield: dem 1972)

Newham: St James, Forest Gate
(dem after 1966)

Newham: Christ Church, Stratford
(1850: by J. Johnson: dem after 1974)

NL Newham: Christ Church, *C of E*, Union Street
(dem, site now vacant)

Newham: St Peter, *Roman Catholic,* Upton Lane
(dem for school)

Newham: Upton Park *Methodist* Church, Green Street
(dem, now a filling station)

Newham: North Woolwich *Congregational* Church
(1891: by F. W. Troop: site to be cleared by Council)

Southwark: St Mark, Peckham, Camberwell
(1883–84: by C. L. Luck: dem 1959)

Southwark: St Chrysostom, Peckham, Camberwell
(1813: by David Riddell Roper: dem 1960s)

Southwark: St Michael, Camberwell
(1883–84: by J. W. Hunt: dem 1962)

Southwark: St Saviour, *C of E*, Ruskin Park, Herne Hill, Camberwell
(dem scheme 1973)

Southwark: St Paul, Kipling Street, Bermondsey
(1844–45: by S. S. Teulon: dem 1963)

Southwark: *Baptist* Chapel, Walworth Road
(1863–64: by Searle, Son & Yelf: dem 1960s)

Southwark: St Stephen Walworth
(1870–71: by Henry Jarvis & Son: dem 1958)

Southwark: St Mark Walworth
(1873: by Henry Jarvis & Son: dem 1955)

Southwark: St Andrew, New Kent Road
(1875–78: by Newman and Billing: dem 1959)

L Southwark: St Michael with All Saints, Grosvenor Park
(dem 1973)

Southwark: St Paul, Westminster Bridge Road
(1857: by W. Rogers: bombed, dem 1957)

Southwark: *Congregational* Church, Queens Road
(dem 1973)

Southwark: St Paul, Rotherhithe, Bermondsey
(1849–50: by William Beatson: dem 1958)

Southwark: St Barnabas, Rotherhithe, Bermondsey
(1870–72: by W. Butterfield: recently dem)

Tower Hamlets: St Gabriel, Poplar
(1868: by R. J. Withers: closed after the war, dem)

Tower Hamlets: St John, Isle of Dogs, Poplar
(1872: by A. W. Blomfield: dem 1953)

Tower Hamlets: St Stephen, North Bow, Poplar
(1857: by John Nicholls: bombed, dem 1961)

Tower Hamlets: St Peter, *C of E*, Limehouse
(dem scheme 1975)

Waltham Forest: All Saints, Selwyn Avenue, *C of E*, Highams Park
(by Hoare & Wheeler: dem scheme 1976)

Waltham Forest: All Saints, *C of E*, Capworth Street, Leyton
(1865: by W. Wigginton: dem 1971)

Waltham Forest: Shernhall *Methodist* Church, Shernhall Street, Walthamstow
(dem *c.* 1974)

Waltham Forest: Holy Trinity, *C of E*, Harrow Green, Leytonstone
(by J. T. Brassey: dem 1972)

Waltham Forest: St Andrew, *C of E*, Walthamstow
(1910: by Hoare & Wheeler: dem 1972)

Waltham Forest: St James, *C of E*, Walthamstow
(dem *c.* 1960)

Wandsworth: St Steven Mission Church, Fawe Park Road, Putney
(dem)

Wandsworth: St Faith, *C of E*, Fullerton Road
(partial dem 1974)

Wandsworth: St-Mary-le-Park, Albert Bridge Road, Battersea
(1883: by William White: dem *c.* 1966 and replaced by new church)

Wandsworth: All Saints, *C of E*, Prince of Wales Drive/ Queenstown Road, Battersea
(1883: by F. W. Hunt: dem)

Wandsworth: St George, *C of E*, Battersea Park Road, Battersea
(dem)

Wandsworth: St Andrew, *C of E*, Thessaly Road, Battersea
(1884: by Henry Store: dem)

Wandsworth: Providence Church, Speke Road, Battersea
(dem)

Wandsworth: St Peter, *C of E*, Plough Road, Battersea
(1875–76: by William White: destroyed by fire 1970)

Wandsworth: *Wesleyan* Church, Plough Road, Battersea (dem)

Wandsworth: St John, Battersea (dem)

Wandsworth: Christ Church, *C of E,* Battersea Park Road, Battersea (dem)

Westminster: St Peter, Elgin Avenue, Paddington (1869–70: by Newman and Billing: dem recently)

Westminster: St Saviour, Warwick Avenue, Paddington (1855–56: by John Little: dem early 1970s)

Westminster: St Michael, Star Street, Paddington (1861: by Major Rhode Hawkins: dem 1970)

Westminster: All Saints, Norfolk Square, Paddington (1847: by Henry Clutton: became deaf and dumb church, dem 1961)

Westminster: All Saints, Grosvenor Road (1871: restored post-war by T. Cundy III: dem 1976)

Westminster: St Paul, Portman Square (dem 1972)

Westminster: St Thomas, *C of E,* Tenison Court, Kingly Street (1702–1872: by Butterfield: dem 1973)

Westminster: Holy Trinity, Bishop's Bridge Road (dem 1972)

GREATER MANCHESTER

Bolton: St Saviour, *C of E,* Deane Road (1882: Paley & Austin: dem scheme 1974)

Bolton: *Quaker* Meeting House, Tipping Street (1820: dem 1965 for road scheme)

Brindle Heath: St Anne, *C of E,* Sharp Street (1914: by F. P. Oakley: faculty to dem 1971)

Cheadle: *Methodist* Church, Eden Place, High Street (dem)

Cheadle: *Congregational* Church, Massie Street (1860–61: by Poulton & Woodman: dem)

Dukinfield *Methodist* Church, Hill Street (to be dem for worship centre)

Hindley: *Unitarian* Chapel (1788: dem 1966)

Hyde: Central *Methodist* Church, George Street (dem for M67)

Hyde: *National Spiritualist* Church (dem for M67, resited)

Hyde: *Salvation Army* Mission (dem for M67)

Hyde: St Stephen, *C of E,* Bennett Street, Flowery Field (1889–91: by J. Eaton: dem proposed for housing)

Manchester: Chorlton on Medlock *Congregational* Church, Cavendish Street (1847–48: by E. Walters: dem *c.* 1973)

Manchester: Haslingden *Primitive Methodist* Church, Grange Road, Rossendale (recently dem, latterly used as warehouse)

Manchester: St Philip, *C of E,* Chester Street, Hulme (1859–60: by Shellard & Brown: dem scheme 1973)

Manchester: St Anne, *C of E,* Oldham Road, Newton Heath (1881–83: by A. Wellington Smith: dem 1974)

Manchester: St Barnabas, *C of E,* Pendleton (1887: by W. H. Booth: dem 1976)

Manchester: *Union Baptist* Chapel, Oxford Road (1868: by Medland & Taylor: dem 1931)

Manchester: St Clement, *C of E,* Chorlton (1782: dem 1949)

Manchester: St Stephen, *C of E,* Salford (1794: closed April 1955)

Manchester: St Matthew, *C of E* (1825: by Sir Charles Barry: dem 1951)

Manchester: St Andrew, *C of E* (1831: by Atkinson: dem)

Manchester: Christ Church, *C of E,* Salford (1831: by Thomas Wright: dem)

Manchester: St Saviour, *C of E,* Chorlton-on-Medlock (1836: dem)

Manchester: St Barnabas, *C of E,* Openshaw (1839: by T. W. Atkinson: dem)

Manchester: St Bartholomew, *C of E,* Salford (1842: by Starkey and Cuffley: dem)

Manchester: St Matthias, *C of E,* Salford (1842: dem)

Manchester: St John, *C of E,* Pendlebury (1842: dem)

Manchester: SS Simon and Jude, *C of E* (1842: by E. Walters: dem)

Manchester: St Silas, *C of E,* Aldwich (1842: by Starkey & Cuffley: dem)

Manchester: Holy Trinity, *C of E,* Hulme (1843: by Scott & Moffat: dem 1953)

Manchester: St Barnabas, *C of E,* Oldham Road (1844: by R. Tattershall: dem)

Manchester: St Simon, *C of E,* Salford (1849: by Richard Lane: dem)

Manchester: St Philip, *C of E,* Brandford Road (1850: by E. H. Shellard: dem)

Manchester: St Mark, *C of E,* Hulme (1852: by E. H. Shellard: dem 1950)

Manchester: St Stephen, *C of E,* Chorlton-on-Medlock (1853: by E. H. Shellard: dem)

Manchester: St John Evangelist, *C of E,* Oldham Road, Miles Platting (1855: by J. Edgar Gregan: dem 1973–74)

Manchester: St Paul, *C of E,* Paddington (1856: by E. H. Shellard: dem)

Manchester: St Catherine, *C of E,* Collyhurst (1859: by Speakman & Charlesworth: dem)

Manchester: St Philip, *C of E,* Hulme (1860: by Shellard & Brown: dem)

Manchester: Christ Church, *C of E,* Bradford (1862: by W. Hayley: dem)

Manchester: St Paul, *C of E,* Chorlton-on-Medlock (1862: by Clegg & Knowles: dem)

Manchester: St Michael, *Church of Scotland* (1864: by J. M. Taylor: dem)

Manchester: St Mark, *C of E,* Gorton (1865: by J. Holden: dem)

Manchester: St Matthew, *C of E,* Ardwick (1868: by J. M. Taylor: dem)

Manchester: St Gabriel, *C of E,* Hulme (1869: by J. M. Taylor: dem)

Manchester: St Stephen, *C of E,* Hulme (1869: by Horton & Bridgeford: dem)

Manchester: St James the Less, *C of E* (1870: by T. Ristey: dem)

Manchester: St Martin, *C of E* (1873: by Price & Linklater: dem)

Manchester: St James, *C of E,* Collyhurst (1874: by J. Lowe: dem)

Manchester: St Luke, *C of E,* Miles Platting (1875: by J. M. & H. Taylor: dem)

Manchester: St Mary, *C of E,* Beswick (1878: by Paley & Austin: dem)

Manchester: St Clement, *C of E,* Greenhays (1881: by H. R. Price: dem)

Manchester: St Ambrose, *C of E,* Chorlton-on-Medlock (1884: by H. C. Charlwood of Newcastle: dem *c.* 1969)

Manchester: St Anne, *C of E,* Brindle Heath (1914: by F. P. Oakley: dem)

Manchester: Brunswick *Methodist* Chapel, Broad Street, Pendleton, Salford
(to be dem 1977, Greater Manchester Council unsuccessfully attempted to spotlist)

Manchester: St Barnabas, *C of E,* Frederick Road, Pendleton, Salford
(1887: by W. H. Booth: dem 1976)

Middleton: *Unitarian* Chapel, Old Road
(1892–93: by Edgar Wood: dem 1965)

Oldham: St Peter, *C of E*
(by Wild, Collins & Wild: dem *c.* 1975 as part of town centre shopping scheme)

Oldham: *Independent Methodist* Church, Smith Street
(to be dem under compulsory purchase order, new church elsewhere)

Oldham: Bethel Church, Churchill Street
(to be dem under Compulsory Purchase Order, new church elsewhere)

Oldham: Waterloo Street *Methodist* Church
(to be dem under Compulsory Purchase Order, new site allocated)

Oldham: Waterhead *Methodist* Church
(dem under Compulsory Purchase Order, new church constructed)

Oldham: Brunswick Street *Methodist* Church
(dem under Compulsory Purchase Order)

Oldham: *Salvation Army* Citadel, Union Street
(1886–87: dem pre-1971)

Preston: St Paul, Rigway
(dem approved 1976)

Rochdale: St Alban, *C of E,* Manchester Road
(1855–56: by Joseph Clarke: dem scheme 1971)

Stalybridge: Booth Street *Methodist* Chapel
(dem for housing estate)

Stalybridge: *Baptist* Church, High Street
(1848: dem)

Stalybridge: Wakefield Road *Baptist* Church, Cocker Hill
(dem)

Stalybridge: Millbrook *Methodist* Church, Fitzroy Street
($\frac{3}{4}$ dem)

Stockport: St Paul, *C of E,* Great Portwood Street
(dem *c.* 1972)

Stockport: St Andrew, *C of E,* New Bridge Lane
(dem)

Stockport: *Methodist* Church, Cavendish Road, Heaton Mersey
(dem)

Stockport: Tiviot Dale *Methodist* Church, Lancashire Hill
(1826: by Richard Lane: dem)

Stockport: Trinity *Methodist* Church, Wellington Road South
(1884–86: by William Waddington & Sons: dem)

Stockport: *Methodist* Church, Woodsmoor Lane
(dem)

Stockport: Hanover *Congregational* Church, Lancashire Hill
(dem)

Stockport: *Welsh Presbyterian* Church, Wellington Street
(dem)

Stockport: Mount Tabor *Methodist* New Connexion Church, Wellington Road South
(1865–70: by William Hill: dem pre-1971)

Wigan: St Thomas, *C of E,* Caroline Street
(1849–51: by Messrs Hay: dem scheme 1973)

HAMPSHIRE

Bishopstoke: Old Church
(1825: church dem early 20c, tower dem 1965)

Blendworth: Old Church, *C of E*
(18c: dem *c.* 1960)

Laverstoke: Old Church
(Saxon, altered at various dates: dem *c.* 1950 by Lord Portal whose private chapel it had become)

Nutley: *C of E*
(dem)

Otterbourne: Old Church, *C of E*
(13c: nave dem 19c, Chancel dem 1971)

Popham: St Katherine, *C of E*
(1875–78: by J. K. Colling: dem *c.* 1960)

Portsmouth: St Bartholomew, *C of E,* Southsea
(1861: by Godwin & Butcher: dem *c.* 1961)

Portsmouth: *Evangelical* Chapel, Surrey Street, Landport
(1864: Rundbogenstil: dem *c.* 1961)

Portsmouth: St Mark, *C of E,* London Road, North End
(1874: by Sir Arthur Blomfield: dem *c.* 1971)

Portsmouth: St Mary, *Chapel of Ease,* Fratton Road
(1881: dem *c.* 1960)

Portsmouth: St Michael and All Angels, *C of E*
(1872 and 1886–92: by William Butterfield: dem 1960)

Portsmouth: St Paul, *C of E,* Southsea
(1820–22: by Francis Godwin: gutted in the War, impressive ruins dem in 1958 for new road)

Portsmouth: St Agatha, former *C of E,* Landport
(1893–95: by J. H. Ball: dem approved for road improvements)

Portsmouth: Circus Church, *C of E*
(1864: by B. Tabberer of London: dem)

Southampton: Carlton *Baptist* Church, London Road
(*c.* 1860: dem *c.* 1960)

Waterlooville: St George, *C of E*
(1830: by T. E. Owen: dem *c.* 1968 and replaced)

Waterlooville: *Baptist* Church
(1884–85: by G. Rake: dem and replaced)

Widley: St Mary Magdalene, *C of E*
(1849: Norman style, by John Colson: dem *c.* 1960)

Winchester: St Martin, *C of E,* Winnall
(rebuilt 1858: by William Coles: dem scheme 1971)

Winchester: St Maurice, *C of E,* High Street
(1841–42: by William Gover: dem 1957, medieval tower preserved)

HEREFORD AND WORCESTER

Bromsgrove: *Baptist* Church, New Road
(1866–67: Gothic: recently dem for new church)

Evesham: *Methodist* Meeting Hall, Mill Street
(1788: dem approved following inspection on structural safety)

Finstall: St Godwald
(1773: dem 1971)

NL Hereford: *St Barnabas Mission* Church, Barrs Court Road
(dem)

Kington: *Catholic* Chapel at the back of No 9 High Street
(1684: threatened)

Kidderminster: *Methodist* Church, Mill Street
(1803 and 1821: compulsorily purchased by the County Council and dem 1976 for Stage IV of the Kidderminster Ring Road programmed to be built in 1981)

II Redditch: *United Reformed* (formerly *Congregational*) Church, Evesham Street
(1st half 19c: Classical: dem as part of Town Centre Redevelopment Programme)

Redditch: *Gospel Hall,* Evesham Street
(dem as part of Development Corporation Town Centre Redevelopment Programme)

NL Worcester: St Peter the Great
(1836–38: by John Mills: dem August 1976)

Worcester: St Andrew, *C of E*
(15c: dem *c.* 1948)

Worcester: Holy Trinity, *C of E*
(1863–65: by Hopkins: dem *c.* 1965)

HERTFORDSHIRE

Hitchin: *Quaker* Meeting House, West Alley
(1693: sold 1840, dem 1960)

Hoddesdon: *Quaker* Meeting House, Essex Road
(1697: surrendered *c.* 1829, dem 1956)

HUMBERSIDE

Bridlington: Primitive *Methodist* Chapel, Chapel Street
(dem pre-1974 for department store)

Cleethorpes: Lovett Street Chapel
(dem proposed, permission given)

Cleethorpes: St Peter's Avenue Chapel
(dem, redeveloped as library and car park)

Cleethorpes: Chapel, Cheapside, Waltham
(dem proposed for highway improvements)

Driffield: St John's Parish Church
(1899: by Hicks & Charlewood: dem pre-1974 for bungalow)

Flamborough: *Primitive Methodist* Chapel
(dem, replaced with new chapel)

Full Sutton: *Methodist* Chapel
(to be dem)

Goole: St Paul, *C of E*
(1900: by Brodrick, Lowden & Walker: dem scheme 1975)

Grimsby: St Stephen, Roberts Street
(1911–14: by Sir Walter Tapper: dem scheme 1974)

Grimsby: St Luke, Heneage Road
(1912: by Sir Charles Nicholson: dem 1974)

Hessle: *Methodist* Church, South Lane
(dem proposed)

Hull: *German Lutheran* Church, Nile Street
(compulsorily purchased and dem, rebuilt Cottingham Road)

Hull: All Saints, Margaret Street
(1866–69: by G. E. Street: dem *c.* 1973)

Hull: St Mary and St Peter, *C of E,* Hessle Road
(1902: by W. S. Walker: compulsorily purchased and dem)

L Hull: St Augustine of Hippo, *C of E,* Queen's Road
(1890: by G. G. Scott Jnr, Temple Moore: dem 1976)

Hull: St Paul, *C of E,* St Paul's Street
(1847: by W. H. Dykes: dem 1976)

Hull: St James
(by Hansom & Welch: dem 1957)

Hull: St Jude, *C of E,* Spring Bank
(1873–74: by Edward Simpson: dem 1973)

Hull: St Barnabas, *C of E,* Hessle Road
(1873: by H. S. Constable: dem)

Hull: *Methodist* Church, 234 Beverley Road
(dem 1969)

Hull: *Methodist* Church, 297 Beverley Road
(dem)

Hull: *Elim* Church, Mason Street
(dem 1976)

Hull Bethesda *Methodist* Church, Holland Street
(dem)

Hull: All Saints, *C of E,* Margaret Street, Sculcoates
(1866–69: by Street & Samuel Musgrave: dem)

Hull: *Presbyterian* Church, 60–62 Holderness Road
(dem)

Hull: *Gospel Hall,* 148 Spring Bank
(dem)

Hull: *Methodist* Church, Brighton Street
(dem)

Hull: Transfiguration, *Roman Catholic,* Albert Avenue
(1904 and 1915: by A. R. Lowther: dem)

Hull: *Methodist* Church, Fountain Road
(dem)

Hull: King's Hall *Methodist* Church, Fountain Road
(dem)

Hull: *Methodist* Church, Carlton Street
(compulsorily purchased and dem)

Pocklington: Primitive *Methodist* Chapel, Union Street
(listed building consent (conservation area) for dem, not yet carried out)

Roos: *Methodist* Chapel
(dem proposed)

South Ferriby: *Methodist* Chapel, School Lane
(dem proposed, permission granted 1973)

ISLE OF WIGHT

II Ryde: *Congregational* Church, George Street
(1870–72: by R. J. Jones: dem 1974)

II Ryde: St Thomas, *C of E*, St Thomas's Street
(1827–28: Domestic Tudor: permission to demolish granted 1969, still there)

NL Ventnor: *Methodist* Church, High Street
(permission to demolish and redevelop 1976)

Ventnor: *Congregational* Church, High Street
(1836 (Church Hall), 1853–54 (new church): by Raffles Brown of Liverpool: permission to demolish and redevelop 1973)

KENT

Canterbury: Union Chapel, Watling Street
(1863: by W. F. Poulton: replaced)

Canterbury: St Andrew, *C of E*, Station Road East
(Victorian Gothic: dem)

Charlton-by-Dover: St Bartholomew, *C of E*, Templar Street
(1866: by Joseph Clarke: dem scheme 1974)

Chatham: St Paul, *C of E*
(1853–55: by A. D. Gough: dem scheme 1974)

Chatham: Zoar Chapel
(dem)

Chatham: Zion Chapel, Clover Street
(dem proposed)

Chatham: St Mary, Dock Road
(by A. W. Blomfield: dem proposed)

Dartford: St Anselm, *Roman Catholic*, Spital Street
(1900: by F. A. Watters: dem)

Faversham: *Congregational* Church, Newton Road
(1878–79: by Joseph Gardner: dem)

Folkestone: *Congregational* Church, Condon Street
(1865–66: by Joseph Gardner: dem)

Folkestone: *Methodist* Chapel, Grace Hill
(1865–66: by Joseph Gardner: dem)

Folkestone: St Michael, *C of E*
(by Bodley: dem *c.* 1950)

Gravesend: St Mark, *C of E*, Rosherville
(1851–53: Gothic, by H. & E. Rose: dem scheme 1974)

Gravesend: St Andrew *Presbyterian* Church
(1869: by A. Besborough: dem after 1948, resited)

Gravesend: Princes Street *Congregational* Chapel
(dem *c.* 1962 for Marks and Spencer building)

Gravesend: *Salvation Army*, West Street
(dem)

Gravesend: St Luke
(1889: by W. B. Smith: dem *c.* 1967)

Gravesend: Christ Church, *C of E*
(dem 1923, re-erected)

Gravesend: Holy Trinity
(dem after fire *c.* 1962)

Gravesend: St James, *C of E*
(1851: by S. W. Daukes: dem 1967)

Gravesend: St Faith, *C of E*, Central Avenue
(dem 1976)

Greenhithe: Chapel, High Street
(dem)

Herne Bay: St John, *C of E*, Brunswick Street
(1898–1902: by R. Philip Day: dem scheme 1974)

Maidstone: St Paul, *C of E*, Randall Street
(1859–60: by Peck & Stephens: gutted by fire 1963, dem 1971)

Maidstone: *Congregational* Church, King Street
(1860–62: by Peck & Stephens: dem)

Rochester: St Peter, Gravel Walk
(dem)

Rochester: St Peter, *C of E,* King Street
(1859–60: by Ewan Christian: dem 1970s)

Tonbridge: *Baptist* Chapel
(dem *c.* 1975)

Tunbridge Wells: Emanuel Church, Mount Ephraim
(1867: by Wimble & Taylor for Countess of Huntingdon's Connexion: dem 1974)

Upper Upnor: *Methodist* Chapel
(dem)

LANCASHIRE

Barnoldswick: *Baptist* Church, North Street
(dem 1975)

Barnoldswick: *Baptist* Church, Manchester Road
(dem 1976 for Old Age Pensioners flats)

Barrowford: *United Reformed* Church
(dem 1976)

Blackpool: Central *Methodist* Chapel
(1880–81: by John Gibson and Son: dem *c.* 1970 for shopping precinct, new chapel provided)

Blackpool: Trinity *Methodist* Chapel, Adelaide Street
(compulsorily purchased and demolished 1976 for central area redevelopment)

Blackpool: *United Reformed* Church, Alexandra Road
(dem for block of flats 1975)

Blackpool: *Methodist* Church, Rawcliffe Street
(1888–89: by J. H. Burton: dem for block of flats)

Blackpool: Marton *Methodist* Chapel, Chapel Road
(dem for block of flats 1976)

Bolton: St James, *C of E,* Waterloo Road
(1867–71: by J. Medland Taylor of Manchester: dem)

Burnley: *Christian Scientist* Church, Hammerton
(to be dem for Civic Office complex)

Fleetwood: Wesley *Methodist* Church, North Church Street
(1898: by J. J. Green: dem *c.* 1974)

NL Nelson: *United Reformed* Church, Manchester Road
(1884–85 by George Fell: dem 1973)

Nelson: *Baptist* Church, Carr Road
(1886: by George Baines: dem under special Environmental Assistance Scheme, site now landscaped and used as car park)

Roughlee: *Methodist* Chapel
(dem 1976)

LEICESTERSHIRE

Barrow: Chapel, *C of E*
(dem scheme 1972)

Barrow upon Soar: *Methodist* Church, North Street
(dem)

Barwell: Chapel Street
(to be dem for residential development)

Groby: *United Reformed* Church
(dem)

Hinckley: St Peter, *Roman Catholic* church
(1824: by J. Ireland: dem 1976)

Hinckley: Holy Trinity, *C of E*
(dem 1972)

III Leicester: *Salem Chapel,* Freeschool Lane
(1827: Huntingdonian, latterly a warehouse: dem 1974)

III Leicester: *Congregational* Chapel, East Bond Street
(1805 or 1821: dem 1965)

NL Leicester: Christ Church, *C of E*
(by William Parsons: dem 1957 for housing redevelopment)

NL Leicester: St Luke, *C of E,* Humberstone Road
(by Bellamy & Hardy of Lincoln: dem 1949)

NL Leicester: *Congregational* Chapel, London Road
(1886: James Tait of Leicester: dem 1966)

NL Leicester: *Baptist* Chapel, Archdeacon Lane
(1827: dem in 1950s)

Leicester: *Zion Baptist* Chapel, Erskine Street
(1872: by R. J. Goodacre: dem 1976 during area clearance)

NL Loughborough: Woodgate *Baptist* Church (by J. W. Chapman: dem 1976)

Mountsorrel: *Methodist* Church, Loughborough Road (1897: by John Mills: dem a "few years ago")

Shackerstone: Old Chapel (dem)

Syston: *Methodist* Church, Melton Road (dem *c.* 1972)

Thornton: *Methodist* Church (1902: by Tait & Herbert: dem 1976)

LINCOLNSHIRE

Boston: St James, *C of E,* George Street (1861–64: by George Hackford: dem 1972)

Gainsborough: *Primitive Methodist,* Trinity Street (1877: by William Freeman: dem pre-1971)

Lincoln: St Mark, *C of E,* High Street (1871–72: by Watkins: dem 1971)

Lincoln: St Martin, *C of E,* West Parade (1873: designed by A. S. Beckett: dem)

Lincoln: *Quaker Meeting House* (*c.* 1785: dem *c.* 1965 for ring road)

Lincoln: *Wesleyan* Chapel, Clasketgate (1836–37: by W. A. Nicholson: dem 1963)

Lincoln: *Wesleyan* Hannah Memorial Chapel (1873: by Bellamy and Hardy: dem 1965)

Lincoln: St Paul, *C of E,* Westgate (1877–78: by Sir Arthur Blomfield: dem)

Lincoln: Thomas Cooper Memorial *Baptist* Chapel, St Benedick's Square (1885: by J. Wallis Chapman: dem pending)

Old Woodhall: St Margaret, *C of E* (dem 1972)

Salmonby: St Margaret, *C of E* (1871: dem scheme 1975)

Totill: St Mary, *C of E* (1778: dem scheme 1976)

MERSEYSIDE

Birkenhead: St John the Evangelist, *C of E,* Grange Road (1845: by C. Reed: dem scheme 1976)

Birkenhead: Holy Trinity, *C of E,* Price Street (1837–40: by Cunningham and Holme: dem)

Birkenhead: All Saints, *C of E* (dem 1972)

Birkenhead: St Luke, *C of E,* Lower Tranmere (by G. Grayson: dem 1971)

Birkenhead: St Matthew, *C of E* (1889: by A. C. Ogle: dem by faculty)

Birkenhead: St Mary, St Mary Gate (1819: by T. Rickman: to be dem, local authority wish to retain steeple)

Birkenhead: Brunswick *Methodist* Chapel, Price Street (1830, enlarged 1844: dem since 1960)

Birkenhead: *Wesleyan* Chapel, Church Road, Tranmere (1861–62: by Walter Scott: replaced 1966)

Egremont: St Columba, *C of E* Seabank Road (1902–23: by C. E. Deacon: dem 1971)

Hoylake: Holy Trinity, *C of E,* Trinity Road (1833: neo-Norman, by Sir James Picton: dem scheme 1976)

Liverpool: Aigburth Street *Methodist* Church (dem in Housing Compulsory Purchase Order)

Liverpool: Palmerston Street *Methodist* Church (dem in Housing Compulsory Purchase Order)

Liverpool: Chinese Church, Prince's Avenue (dem 1973 after fire)

Liverpool: Prince's Gate *Baptist* Church, Prince's Avenue (1879–81: by Henry Sumners: dem 1974)

Liverpool: All Saints, Bentley Road
(dem 1974)

Liverpool: St Mark, Edge Lane
(now derelict, change of use refused by local authority)

Liverpool: St Cuthbert, *C of E*, Robson Street, Everton
(1875–77: by T. D. Barry & Sons: dem by faculty 1970 after fire)

Liverpool: St Chad, Everton
(1885: by Potts, Sulman & Herrings: dem scheme 1973)

Liverpool: St Jude, *C of E*, Edge Hill
(1831: by Thomas Rickman: dem 1966)

Liverpool: St Margaret, *C of E*, Belmont Road, Anfield
(1873: High Victorian Gothic, by W. & J. Audsley: damaged by fire in 1961 and replaced)

Liverpool: St Michael, *C of E*, Pitt Street
(1816–26: by John Foster: dem)

Liverpool: St Paul, *C of E*, Prince's Park
(1847–48: by Arthur Hill Holme: dem 1976)

Liverpool: Holy Trinity, *C of E*, St Anne Street
(1790–92: Classical: redundant prior to Pastoral Measure, but vandalized and demolished 1968)

Liverpool: St Anne, *C of E*, St Anne Street
(1870–71: by E. R. Robson: redundant prior to Pastoral Measure, dem *c.* 1970)

Liverpool: *People's Church*, Village Street, Everton
(dem)

Liverpool: St Timothy, *C of E*, Everton Brow, Rokeby Street
(1861–62: by W. H. Gee: dem 1970)

Liverpool: St Ambrose, Prince Edwin Street
(dem)

Liverpool: Rydal Youth Centre, former *Methodist* Chapel, Great Homer Street
(1839–40: fire and dem 1974)

Liverpool: Former *Welsh Methodist* Chapel, Shaw Street
(1866: Classical, by J. Denison Jee: commercial use, fire and dem 1976)

Liverpool: St Mary, *C of E*, Archer Street, Kirkdale
(1835: by A. H. Holme: interior gutted)

Liverpool: St Chrysostom, *C of E*, Queens Road
(1854: by Raffles Brown: destroyed by fire 1972)

Liverpool: Emmanuel, *C of E*, West Derby Road
(1866–67: by G. E. Grayson: declared redundant, dem *c.* 1971)

Liverpool: St Benedict, Heyworth Street
(1886–87: by Aldridge & Deacon, "exceptionally good": dem 1976)

Liverpool: St John, *C of E*, Breck Road
(1890: by E. C. Clarke: redundant 1971, dem 1974)

Liverpool: St Chad, *C of E*, Walton Breck Road
(1884–85: by John Sulman: redundant 1971, dem 1972)

Liverpool: St Cuthbert, *C of E*, Robson Street, Everton
(1875–77: by T. D. Barry & Sons: redundant 1971, dem 1972)

Liverpool: St Philip, Shiel Road
(1885–90: by J. Bevan: dem, new small church built 1974)

Liverpool: St David, Hampstead Road
(1910: by George Bradbury & Son: to be dem for housing)

Liverpool: St Margaret, West Derby Road
(dem, new church built 1962)

Liverpool: St Domingo *Methodist* Church, Breckfield Road North, Everton
(1870–71: by Hill of Leeds: sold privately 1972, dem)

Liverpool: Norwood *Congregational* Church, West Derby Road
(1862–63: by Poulton & Woodman: commercial use, to be dem for housing)

Liverpool: The Rock, *Methodist*, Whitefield Road
(1865: by C. O. Ellison: dem 1969)

Liverpool: St Brigid, *Roman Catholic*, Bevington Hill
(1894: dem 1967 for Mersey Tunnel approach road)

Liverpool: All Souls, *Roman Catholic*, Collingwood Street, Everton
(1870–72: by Henry Sumners: dem for Mersey Tunnel)

Liverpool: St Chrysostom, Aubrey Street
(1852–53: by W. Raffles Brown: dem 1972)

Liverpool: Kirkdale Cemetery Chapel, Longmoor Lane
(1881: dem 1977)

Liverpool: *Wesleyan* Chapel, Upper Stanhope Street
(1827: dem 1966)

Liverpool: St James, *C of E*, Mill Lane, West Derby
(1845–46 and 1876–79: by Welch and W. & J. Hay: spire removed)

Liverpool: *Unitarian* Church, Hope Street
(1848–49: by T. D. Barry and W. Raffles Brown: dem)

Liverpool: St Philemon, Windsor Street
(1872–74: by Culshaw and Sumners: dem 1976)

Liverpool: Trinity *Presbyterian* Church, Prince's Road
(1879: by H. H. Vale and G. E. Carroll: dem 1974 for housing)

Liverpool: *Congregational* Church, Aigburth Road/ Ullet Road
(1870–72: by H. H. Vale: dem 1975 for garage extension)

Liverpool: Brook Road *Methodist* Church
(to be dem for private housing)

Liverpool: Parkin Memorial Church, Lorenzo Drive
(1930–31: by George Downie: dem for private housing)

Liverpool: Mission Church, New Road
(to be dem for housing)

Liverpool: *Methodist* Church, Hilberry Avenue
(to be dem for housing)

Liverpool: *Methodist* Church, Banks Road
(1882: dem)

Liverpool: *Unitarian* Church, Hamilton Road
(sold privately 1972, dem)

Liverpool: Cottenham Street, *Baptist*
(included in Housing Compulsory Purchase Order 1974)

Liverpool: Liverpool City Mission Breck Road
(included in Housing Compulsory Purchase Order, dem)

Liverpool: St Saviour, *C of E*, Upper Huskisson Street
(dem for now abandoned road scheme *c.* 1970)

Newton-le-Willows: *Congregational* Chapel, Crow Lane
(1878: by W. & J. Hay: being dem—Pevsner)

St Helens: *Congregational* Church, Sutton Road
(dem pre-1974)

St Helens: *Baptist* Church, Park Road
(dem pre-1974)

St Helens: Wesley *Methodist* Church, Corporation Street
(dem 1974)

St Helens: St Anne, *Roman Catholic*, Monastery Road
(dem pre-1974)

St Helens: *Methodist* Church, Hamer Street
(dem since 1974)

St Helens: *United Reformed* Church, Warrington Road, The Holt Rainhill
(1890: by T. W. Cubbon: dem since 1974)

St Helens: *United Reformed* Church, Ormskirk Street
(1883: by Picton, Chambers & Bradley: dem since 1974)

Southport: *Congregational* Chapel, Lord Street
(1861–62: by E. Walters: gutted in 1964)

NORFOLK

Great Yarmouth: *Primitive Methodist* Temple, Priory Plain
(1875: by Freeman: dem)

Norwich: *Methodist* Church, Calvert Street
(1810: dem 1966)

Norwich: St Peter's *Wesleyan* Chapel, Lady Lane
(1824: by J. T. Patience: dem post-war)

Norwich: *Congregational* Church, Chapel Field
(1858: by Joseph James: des 1971)

Norwich: *Wesleyan* Mission Chapel, Ber Street
(1868: by Boardman: dem post-1960)

Norwich: Trinity *Scottish Presbyterian* Church, Theatre Street
(1875: by E. Boardman: des 1942)

Norwich: *Congregational* Church, Magdalen Road
(1900: by E. Boardman & Son: dem 1971)

Norwich: *Baptist* Chapel, Unthank Road
(1875: by E. Boardman: bombed and subsequently demolished)

NORTHUMBERLAND

Belford: *Presbyterian* Church to Kennels, Cragmore House
(1951: dem 1973)

Brandon: *Presbyterian* Church
(derelict 1976)

Crookham: *Presbyterian* Church
(dem 1930, replaced)

Donaldson's Lodge: *Methodist* Chapel
(1893: by George Reavell Jnr: dem)

Lowick: *Free Church,* Cheviot View
(dem)

West Fenton: *Presbyterian* Mission
(dem 1967)

Warenford: *Presbyterian* Church
(dem 1976)

NORTH YORKSHIRE

Harrogate: *Gospel Hall,* Lengs Road
(dem 1974)

Harrogate: *Quaker* Meeting House, Oxford Street
(1845: dem 1965)

Ripon: Coltsgate Chapel
(dem)

Ryedale: Stillington *Methodist* Chapel
(dem)

Scarborough: Trinity *Congregational* Church, Newborough Bar
(1850: by Raffles Brown: dem post-1955)

Scarborough: All Saints, Falsgrave Road
(1867: by Bodley: dem)

Thirsk: St James *Methodist* Chapel
(1816: dem)

Thorpe: St John, *C of E*
(dem scheme 1972)

Whitby: St Michaels, Church Street
(1847–48: by J. B. & W. Atkinson: dem)

York: Salem *Congregational* Chapel, St Saviour's Place
(1839: by J. P. Pritchett, townscape value: dem 1964)

York: St Mary, Bishophill Senior
(Saxon and later: dem 1963)

York: Grape Lane Chapel (formerly *Congregational*)
(1781: dem Aug. 1973)

York: St Maurice, *C of E*
(dem *c.* 1965)

NOTTINGHAMSHIRE

Mansfield: Rosemary Street *Baptist* Church and Lecture Hall
(1911: by John Wills & Sons: dem for central area redevelopment, listed building consent for Hall (*c.* 1800) granted 1972)

Mansfield: *Friends* Meeting House, Quaker Lane
(Mansfield holds place of honour in the minds of Quakers, Fox was a shoemaker here and started preaching in 1646: dem for Distributor Road)

Misterton: *Methodist* Chapel, High Street
(dem Jan. 1976)

Nottingham: *Quaker* Meeting House, Friars Lane
(1847: dem 1961)

Nottingham: St Bartholomew, *C of E*
(1895–1902: by J. L. Pearson: dem *c.* 1970)

Radford: St Michael, *C of E*
(dem scheme 1975)

OXFORDSHIRE

Banbury *Unitarian* Chapel, Horsefair
(1850: by H. J. Underwood · dem)

Banbury: *Baptist* Chapel, Bridge Street
(1839: façade only retained in rebuilding)

Fewcott:
(1871: by H. Woodyer: dem 1963)

Hook Norton: *Quaker* Meeting House, Burthrop
(1704: dem 1950)

Oxford: Holy Trinity
(1845: by H. J. Underwood: dem 1957)

Oxford: Old *Wesley* Memorial Chapel
(1817: by W. Jenkins: dem 1970s)

SALOP

Coalbrookdale: *Quaker* Meeting House
(1745: dem *c.* 1945–50)

Dawley: Chapel, Finger Road
(dem)

Dawley: Chapel, High Street
(dem)

Market Drayton: Emmanuel, *C of E*
(dem *c.* 1962)

Oakengates: Priorlee Chapel
(medieval: site redeveloped by Telford Development Corporation)

Preston Gubbals:
(tower and nave dem)

Shrewsbury: Chapel at Butlane Head Ford
(dem by County Council Highways Department for road improvement)

Weston Rhyn: Chapel
(dem by County Council for highway improvements)

Wombridge: Priory
(site of Augustinian Monastery redeveloped by Telford Development Corporation)

SOMERSET

Crewkerne: Christ Church, *C of E*, South Street
(1852–54: Gothic Revival: dem 1976 to be replaced by flats)

SOUTH YORKSHIRE

Barnsley: Ebenezer *Methodist* Church, Sheffield Road
(dem 1976)

Barnsley: St Thomas Church, Wood Street
(dem 1975)

Barnsley: St John, *C of E*
(1858: by Philip Boyce: dem scheme 1973)

Barnsley: Regent Street *Congregational* Church
(1854–56: by Joseph James: dem *c.* 1972)

Barnsley: *Friends Meeting House*, Huddersfield Road
(1816: replaced 1969)

Denaby Main: All Saints, *C of E*
(1899: by Fowler & Smethurst: dem scheme 1974)

Harley Wood: All Saints, *C of E*
(dem scheme 1974)

Rotherham: St John the Evangelist, *C of E*, College Road
(1865: by William White: dem)

NL Sheffield: St Paul, East Bank Street, Arbourthorne, *C of E*
(1939: by Romilly Craze: dem scheme 1975)

C Sheffield: Holy Trinity, *C of E*, Darnall
(dem 1976)

Sheffield: All Saints, *C of E*, Brightside
(1868: by Hockton & Abbott: dem scheme confirmed)

NL Sheffield: Duncomb Street *Methodist* Church, Walkley
(1898: by Joseph Smith: dem 1976)

NL Sheffield: Nether *Congregational* Chapel, Norfolk Street
(1827: by Watson Pritchett & Watson of York: dem 1970 though Grade II listing proposed)

III Sheffield: Queen Street *Congregational* Church
(1784: dem 1970)

NL Sheffield: *Methodist* New Connexion Chapel, Glossop Road
(dem 1970)

II Sheffield: *Methodist* Church, Broomhill/Broomspring
(1865: consent to demolish granted)

II Sheffield: Andover Street *Methodist* Church, Burngreave
(consent to demolish granted)

STAFFORDSHIRE

Boothen: All Saints, *C of E*
(1887–88: by C. Lynam: dem scheme 1974)

Burslem: Holy Trinity
(1851–52: by G. J. Robinson: dem 1959)

Burton on Trent: St Margaret, *C of E*
(1881: by R. Churchill: dem 1968)

Castletown: St Thomas, *C of E*
(1866: by W. Culshaw: dem 1971)

Newcastle-under-Lyme: *Wesleyan* Chapel, Lower Street
(1799: dem early 1960s)

Newcastle-under-Lyme: Brunswick *Wesleyan* Chapel
(1860: by R. Fuller: dem)

Silverdale: *Methodist* New Connexion
(1856: dem 1972)

Stoke-on-Trent: St Barnabas, *C of E*, Penkhull
(by Charles Lynam: dem scheme 1974)

Stoke-on-Trent: St Michael and All Angels, Fenton
(1887: dem scheme 1972)

Stoke-on-Trent: Holy Trinity, Burslem
(1851–52: by G. T. Robinson: dem 1959)

Stoke-on-Trent: *Congregational* Church, High Street, Hanley
(1881: by William Sugden & Son: dem)

Stoke-on-Trent: St Paul, *C of E*, Burslem
(1828–31: by L. Vulliamy: dem 1970s)

Stoke-on-Trent: Bethel *Congregational* Chapel, Hanley
(dem)

Stoke-on-Trent: *Congregational* Chapel, Longton
(1884: by Sugden: dem *c.* 1974)

Stoke-on-Trent: Jubilee Chapel, Tunstall
(dem)

SUFFOLK

Lowestoft: St Peter, *C of E*
(1833: by J. Brown; 1903: by E. P. Warren: dem 1974)

Lowestoft: St John, *C of E*
(by J. L. Clemence: dem 1975)

SURREY

Camberley: St George, *C of E*
(1892 and 1906: by Arnold H. Hoole: dem 1972)

Caterham: *Wesleyan* Chapel
(1883: by Ranger: dem 1969)

NL Chertsey: All Saints, *C of E*
(1900: by J. Henry Christian: dem *c.* 1975)

NL Cranleigh: St Andrew, *C of E*
(late Victorian: dem)

NL Dorking: *Methodist* Church
(Victorian: dem)

NL Guildford: *Methodist* Church
(1893: Victorian, by F. Boreham: dem)

Guildford: *Baptist* Chapel
(dem)

Redhill: Chapel at St Anne's
(1885: by Crickmay and Sons: proposal to demolish)

NL Reigate: *Congregational* Church
(1869 Romanesque: dem)

Staines: *Friends Meeting* House
(1844: by Samuel Danvers: dem pre-1946)

II Weybridge: *United Reformed* Church
(1864: by J. Tarring: applic to dem)

NL Weybridge: St Charles Borromeo, *Roman Catholic* Church
(1881: by A. S. Purdie: proposed demolition)

NL Weybridge: St Michael, *C of E*
(1874: by Butterfield: dem *c.* 1972)

TYNE AND WEAR

Herrington: St Cuthbert, *C of E*
(dem scheme 1975)

Jarrow: St Peter, *C of E* (1880: by Lamb & Armstrong: dem *c.* 1971)

TV Jarrow: *Congregational* Church, Napier Street (dem 1976)

Newcastle upon Tyne: St Barnabas, *C of E* (dem 1974)

II Newcastle upon Tyne: *Baptist* Church, Osborne Road (1889: Norman Style, very uncommon for this date, by Cubitt: dem)

TV Newcastle upon Tyne: *Methodist* Church, Clayton Road, Jesmond (spire very important: dem threatened)

II Newcastle upon Tyne: Chapel, Westgate Cemetery (dem)

Newcastle upon Tyne: St Cuthbert, *C of E*, Melbourne Street (1871: by A. R. Gibson: dem recently)

Newcastle upon Tyne: St Mary, *C of E* (1858: by Benjamin Green: dem recently)

II North Shields: St Cuthbert, *Roman Catholic*, Bedford Street (1821: by Robert Giles: empty and threatened with demolition)

TV South Shields: *Methodist* Church, Frederick Street (dem in 1976)

South Shields: *Gospel Temperance Union*, Alice Street (dem imminent)

Sunderland: *Salvation Army* Church, Southwick (dem)

Sunderland: *Baptist* Church, Beverley Street (dem)

TV Sunderland: *Methodist* Chapel, Herriston Street (dem 1975)

Sunderland: St Hilda, *C of E* (Hicks and Charlewood: dem recently)

Sunderland: *Quaker* Meeting House, Mile Street (dem 1974)

II Sunderland: *Unitarian Free Church*, Bridge Street (1830: Greek Doric: dem)

TV Sunderland: St Barnabas, *C of E*, Suffolk Street (1868: dem 1970 for redevelopment)

NL Sunderland: *Methodist* Church, Suffolk Street (1900: by W. & T. R. Milburn: dem 1975 for redevelopment)

TV Sunderland: *Methodist* Church, Cleveland Road (dem 1974 for redevelopment)

TV Sunderland: *Methodist* Chapel, Blind Lane, Silksworth (dem 1976)

II Sunderland: Chapel, *Roman Catholic*, Corby Hall, Ashbrooke Road (dem 1976 with Hall for redevelopment)

III Sunderland: *Friends Meeting House*, Nile Street (1822: dem 1974 for redevelopment)

NL Sunderland: Union *Congregational* Church, The Royalty (1890: by W. L. Newcombe: dem 1973 for redevelopment)

II Sunderland: St Paul, *C of E* (1852: dem 1970 for redevelopment)

Sunderland: St John, *C of E* (1764–69: by John Thornhill: recently dem)

Sunderland: All Saints, *C of E* (John Dobson: recently dem)

WARWICKSHIRE

Leamington Spa: Christ Church, *C of E*, Beauchamp Square (1825, the first of the new town: by P. F. Robinson, Norman Revival: dem 1961)

Leamington Spa: *Methodist* Church, Dale Street (1869–70: by George Woodhouse, Italianate: replaced by a new church)

Leamington Spa: *Methodist* Church, Warwick Street (dem 1973)

Stratford-on-Avon: St James, Guild Street (1853–55: by James Murray: dem *c.* 1968)

Warwick: All Saints, *C of E,* Emscote
(1854–56: by James Murray and Bodley & Garner, much painting inside: dem 1966)

Warwick: *Methodist* Church, Avon Street
(dem *c.* 1971)

WEST MIDLANDS

Bentley: St John, *C of E*
(1837: dem 1972)

Bilston: St Luke, *C of E*
(1852: dem scheme 1973)

Birmingham: *Quaker* Meeting House, Cotteridge
(1901: dem 1962)

NL Birmingham: All Saints, *C of E,* Boulton
(1833: by T. Rickman: dem 1973)

NL Birmingham: St Chrysostom, *C of E,* Boulton
(1887–88: by John Cotton: dem 1973)

NL Birmingham: St Stephen, *C of E,* South Aston
(1910: by Bidlake: dem)

NL Birmingham: St Cuthbert, *C of E,* Rotton Park
(dem)

NL Birmingham: St Mary, *C of E,* Aston Brook
(1863: James Murray: dem)

NL Birmingham: St Clement, *C of E,* St Clements
(extensively modified)

NL Birmingham: Holy Trinity, *C of E,* St Andrew
(demolition likely)

NL Birmingham: Hagley Road *Baptist* Church of the Redeemer
(1882: by James Cubitt, expensively fitted: dem 1975)

NL Birmingham: St Barnabas, *C of E,* Sparkbrook
(extensively rebuilt after fire)

NL Birmingham: Church of the Ascension, *C of E,* Pershore Road
(destroyed by fire)

NL Birmingham: *Baptist* Church, Boulton, Spring Hill
(dem)

NL Birmingham: *Methodist* Church, Heath Road, Washwood
(1899: by Ingall & Son: dem)

NL Birmingham: St Jude, *C of E,* Hill Street
(1850–51: C. W. Orford: restored in 1910 and early 1960s: dem)

NL Birmingham: *Methodist* Church, Gravelly Hill
(dem)

NL Birmingham: *Congregational* Church, Dulwich Road, Kingstanding
(dem)

II Birmingham: *Swedenborgian* New Church, Wretham Road, Handsworth
(1876: by Thomas Naden: dem)

L Birmingham: St George, Great Hampton Row
(dem 1959)

L Birmingham: St Patrick, Frank Street
(dem 1966)

Birmingham: St David, *C of E,* Bissell Street, Highgate
(1865: by F. W. Martin: compulsorily purchased, dem 1956)

L Birmingham: St Patrick, *C of E,* Frank Street, Highgate
(by J. L. Pearson: dem 1957)

Birmingham: St Asaph, *C of E,* Great Colmore Street, Lee Bank
(1868: by Thomason: dem 1957)

Birmingham: St Margaret, *C of E,* Ledsam Street, Ladywood
(1874–75: by F. B. Osborn: dem 1957)

Birmingham: St Barnabas, *C of E,* Ryland Road, Ladywood
(1857–60: by Bourne of Dudley: dem 1957)

Birmingham: *Methodist* Church, Monument Road, Ladywood
(dem 1968)

Birmingham: *Methodist* Chapel, Morville Street, Ladywood
(dem 1952)

Birmingham: St Nicholas, *C of E,* Lower Tower Street, Newtown
(1867–68: by Martin & Chamberlain: dem 1951)

Birmingham: *Ebenezer,* New John Street, Newton
(dem 1964)

Birmingham: *Evangelical Mission*, Ormond Street, Newtown
(dem 1956)

Birmingham: St Lawrence, *C of E*, Nechells Green
(dem 1952)

Birmingham: *Baptist* Chapel, Heneage Street, Nechells Green
(dem 1956)

Birmingham: Wycliffe *Baptist* Church, Bristol Street, Highgate
(1859–61: by James Cranston: rebuilt elsewhere 1968)

Birmingham: St Catherine of Sienna, *Roman Catholic*, Lee Bank
(1874–75: by W. Wainwright: rebuilt elsewhere 1964)

Birmingham: *Welsh Presbyterian*, Suffolk Street, Lee Bank
(1898: by Ingall & Son: rebuilt elsewhere 1968)

Birmingham: *Assembly of God*, Cregse Street, Lee Bank
(rebuilt elsewhere 1968)

Birmingham: *Mount Zion* Chapel, Graham Street
(1823: dem)

Birmingham: St Peter, *Roman Catholic*, St Peter's Place
(1786: dem 1969)

Blackheath: *Methodist* Church
(dem)

NL Coventry: All Saints, *C of E*, Far Gosford Street
(1869: Early English, by Paul and Robinson: dem *c.* 1970–74)

II Coventry: St Thomas, *C of E*, Albany Road
(1848–49: by Sharpe & Paley of Lancaster: dem 1975)

Smethwick: St Stephen, *C of E*, Cambridge Road
(1901–2: by F. T. Beck: dem 1974)

Tettenhall: St Michael, *C of E*
(1068, 14c and 15c, enlarged 1825, restored 1883: burnt down 1950, rebuilt)

Tipton: Park Lane *Methodist* Church
(brick with stone spire one of largest Methodist Churches in West Midlands: dem)

Walsall: St George
(1873–74: by Robert Griffiths: dem 1964)

Walsall: St Mark
(by Robert Griffiths: dem *c.* 1974)

Walsall: St John the Pleck
(1858: by Griffin-Weller: dem 1976)

Darlaston: St George
(dem 1973)

Wolverhampton: Christ Church, *C of E*
(1867: by T. H. Fleeming: dem scheme 1975)

Wolverhampton: St Paul, *C of E*, Penn Road
(1834: by Robert Ebbels of Trysull: dem 1970)

Wolverhampton: St Mary, *C of E*, Stafford Street
(1842: by William Raitton, Early English: closed 1948, dem 1950)

Wolverhampton: St James, *C of E*, Horseley Fields
(1843: Perpendicular: dem 1958)

Wolverhampton: Waterloo *Baptist* Church
(1863: Romanesque, by G. Bidlake: dem 1971)

Wolverhampton: Queen Street *Congregational* Church
(1864: by G. Bidlake: dem 1971)

Wolverhampton: Chapel Ash *Presbyterian* Church
(1869: Gothic, by Cockerell and Bidlake: dem 1966)

Wolverhampton: St Andrew, *C of E*, Coleman Street
(1865–70: burnt, replaced 1966)

Wolverhampton: St Matthew, *C of E*, Horseley Fields
(1848: Early English, by E. Banks: closed 1963, replaced 1970)

Wolverhampton: *Presbyterian* Church
(1869: Gothic, by G. Bidlake: dem 1960)

Wolverhampton: *Baptist* Church, Waterloo Road
(1863: Romanesque, by G. Bidlake: dem 1971)

Wolverhampton: St Patrick, *Roman Catholic,* Littles Lane (1865: by Edward W. Pugin: dem 1972, replaced)

Wolverhampton: Snow Hill *Congregational* Church (1849: by Edward Banks: collapsed and dem 1941)

WEST SUSSEX

Bognor Regis: St John, *C of E,* London Road (1882: by A. W. Blomfield: dem *c.* 1973)

Fishbourne: *Methodist* Church (dem 1975)

Horsham: *Congregational* Church, Springfield Road (permission to dem and replace with new church and office block)

Treyford: St Peter (1849: by B. Ferrey: dem 1951)

Chichester: St Peter-the-Less, *C of E* (early medieval: dem *c.* 1960)

Chichester: *Roman Catholic* Church, South Street (by W. W. Wardell: dem 1950s)

WEST YORKSHIRE

Bingley: Holy Trinity (1866–68: by R. Norman Shaw: allegedly unsafe, blown up *c.* 1973)

Bradford: St John, *C of E,* Thorpe Edge (1873: by Messrs Healey: dem scheme 1974)

Bradford: St Andrew, Legram's Lane, Listerhills (1851–53: by Mallinson & Healey: dem *c.* 1967)

Bradford: St Luke (1862: by Bowling: dem *c.* 1950)

Bradford: Holy Trinity, *C of E,* Lawkholme, Leeds Road (1864–65: by E. G. Baley: dem 1971)

Bradford: St Bartholomew, Ripleyville, Bowling (1871: by Healey & Son: dem 1965)

Bradford: St Jude, Manningham (1843: by Walker Rawstorne: dem *c.* 1967)

Bradford: *Independent* Chapel, Little Horton Lane (1860–63: by Lockwood & Mawson: dem)

Bradford: St Chrysostom, Bolton Road, Undercliffe (1890: by T. H. and F. Healey: dem *c.* 1967)

Bradford: Chapel Lane *Unitarian* Chapel, Town Hall Square (1868: by Andrews & Son & Pepper: dem for law courts)

Bradford: St James, Manchester Road (1836: by Walker Rawstorne: dem *c.* 1966)

Bradford: St John Evangelist, Little Horton Lane (1871–73: by T. H. and F. Healey: dem 1967)

Brighouse: St James, *C of E,* Bradford Road (1870: by Mallinson & Barber, excellent windows: dem scheme 1973)

Cleckheaton: *Methodist* Church, Greenside (1875–79: by R. Castle: dem)

Clifton: St Saviour, *C of E* (dem scheme 1975)

Dewsbury: Springfield *Congregational* Church, Halifax Road (1856: by Mallinson & Healey: dem)

Earlsheaton: St Peter, *C of E* (1825–27: by Thomas Taylor: dem scheme 1971)

Halifax: Square *Congregational* Church, Square Road (1855–57: by Joseph James: derelict since fire 10 years ago, spire remains)

Halifax: St Augustine, *C of E* (1881: by R. Coad and C. F. L. Horsfatt, dem scheme 1971)

Heckmondwike: St Saviour (1896: by W. Swinden Barber: dem scheme 1974)

Knottingley: Christ Church, *C of E* (by Vickers & Hingall: dem scheme 1975)

Leeds: St Peter, *C of E,* Hunslet Moor (by Perkin & Backhouse: dem scheme 1970, dem 1976)

Leeds: St Clement, *C of E,* Sheepscar
(1868: Gothic, by George Corson: gutted soon after redundant, dem 1976)

Leeds: St Andrew, Cavendish Street
(1844: by Sir Gilbert Scott: dem post-1951)

II Leeds: Chapel Allerton *Methodist* Church
(1874: Gothic by C. O. Ellison: consent to dem for District Centre redevelopment)

Leeds: Greenside *Methodist* Chapel, Chapeltown, Pudsey
(dem for residential redevelopment approved)

Leeds: Roscoe Place *Methodist* Chapel, Sheepscar
(1861: Gothic, by J. P. Pritchett: dem 1975–76 for road improvements)

Leeds: Beth Hamidrash Hagadol *Synagogue,* Potternewton
(dem 1973)

Leeds: St Mary Bethany, *C of E,* Tong Road, Wortley
(1886: by Adams & Kelly: dem 1975 for housing redevelopment)

Leeds: Trinity *Methodist* Church, Upper Town Street, Bramley
(1823: Georgian: dem)

Leeds: *Independent* Chapel, East Parade
(1841: by Moffat & Hurst: dem)

Leeds: *Wesleyan* Church, Oxford Place
(1896–1903: by Darby & Thorp: to be gutted for offices)

Leeds: Christ Church, *C of E*
(by R. D. Chantrell: dem 1971)

Leeds: St James, *C of E,* New York Street
(1795–1801: dem 1950)

Leeds: Christ Church, *C of E,* Meadow Lane
(1826: by R. D. Chantrell: dem 1972)

Leeds: St Andrew, *C of E,* Burley
(1842–45: by G. G. Scott: dem 1960)

Leeds: St Matthew, *C of E,* Little London
(1851: by C. W. Burleigh: dem *c.* 1965)

Leeds: St Jude, *C of E,* Hunslet
(1852: by P. Boyce: dem *c.* 1955)

Leeds: St John, *C of E,* New Wortley
(1852–54: by P. Boyce: dem 1970)

Leeds: St Mary, *C of E,* Hunslet
(1864: by Perkin and Backhouse: dem except tower 1974)

Leeds: St Simon, *C of E*
(1864–65: by T. Shaw: dem 1956)

Leeds: St John, *C of E,* Newtown
(1867: dem late 1950s)

Leeds: St Silas, *C of E,* Hunslet
(1869: by G. Corson: dem 1950s)

Leeds: St Alban, *C of E,* York Road
(1875: by Walford & Pollard: dem 1940s)

Leeds: Holy Trinity, *C of E,* Armley
(1872: by Adams & Kelly: dem 1950s)

Leeds: Holy Name, *C of E,* Woodhouse
(1881: by Chorley & Connon: dem 1974)

Leeds: St Cuthbert, *C of E,* Hunslet
(1884: by Perkin & Bulmer: dem 1955)

Leeds: All Hallows, *C of E,* Woodhouse
(1885–86: by Kelly & Birchall: dem *c.* 1970)

Leeds: Woodhouse Moor *Methodist* Church
(1874–75: Gothic, by C. O. Ellison: dem 1972)

Leeds: *Catholic Apostolic* Church, Cromer Road
(1866: by Woodhouse: dem)

Leeds: Burmantofts *Wesleyan* Chapel
(1875: by Hill & Swain: dem)

Leeds: Bellevue Road *Methodist* Church
(*c.* 1860: Classical: dem 1975)

Lightcliffe: Old Church
(1874: by W. Swinden Barber: dem early 1970s)

Ossett: The Green *Congregational* Chapel (1882: by J. P. Pritchett: dem 1970s)

Pontefract: *Quaker* Meeting House, Southgate (1698: dem 1947)

Savile Town: St Mary, *C of E* (1900: by Charles James Ferguson of Carlisle: dem scheme 1972)

Stainland: *Wesleyan* Chapel (*c.* 1830: dem)

Stourton: St Andrew, *C of E* (1898: by C. Hodgson & Fowler: dem scheme 1973)

Wakefield: *Methodist* Chapel (1802–44: closed 1966 and dem)

Whitwood: St Philip, *C of E* (1865: by Joseph Clarke: dem scheme 1974)

WILTSHIRE

Amesbury: Cemetery Chapel, *C of E* (dem scheme 1971)

Rodbourne: St Augustine, *C of E* (dem as dangerous structure)

Swindon: *Baptist* Tabernacle, Regent Street (1886: Classical, by W. H. Read: consent for dem and redevelopment as church and offices

Swindon: St Mary, *C of E,* Commonwealth Road (permission to redevelop)

Swindon: *Methodist* Central Hall, Regent Circus (1907: redevelopment pending)

Swindon: St Paul, *C of E,* Edgeware Road (1881: by E. B. Ferrey: dem 1965 and replaced)

Trowbridge: *Methodist* Church, Members Street (dem 1973)

SCOTLAND

A Aberdeen: Triple Kirk (2 *Church of Scotland,* 1 *Congregational*), Aberdeenshire (Grampian) (1843–44: consent to dem greater part 1976)

B Auchindoir: Aberdeenshire (Grampian) (1811: gutted recently)

B Bellochantuy: *Church of Scotland*, Argyllshire (Strathclyde) (1825: permission to dem)

C Blair Atholl: *Free* Church, Bridge of Lilt, Perthshire (Tayside) (1856: dem recently)

B Bridge of Teith: Perthshire (Central) (1831: dem)

B Craigend: *Church of Scotland,* Perthshire (Tayside) (1780: dem for motorway)

B Donibristle: Chapel, Fifeshire (Fife) (1731: by Alex McGill: gutted)

C Dunfermline: St Margaret, East Port, Fife (1827: consent to dem for commercial development)

B Dunfermline: St Paul, Canmore Street, Fife (1881: by James Sellars: gutted by fire 1976)

B Dundee: St Enoch's Church, *Church of Scotland*, Nethergate, Angus (Tayside) (1874: by T. S. Robertson: dem)

Dundee: Former St John, *Church of Scotland*, Tay Street, Angus (Tayside) (1839: by G. Angus: dem)

B Dundee: Former St Mary Magdalene, *Episcopal,* Blinshall Street, Angus (Tayside) (1854: by H. E. Coe: consent to dem 1976)

B Dundee: St Mary's Sisterhood Chapel, *Episcopal,* King Street, Angus (Tayside) (1871: by G. E. Street: dem for roadworks)

C Dundee: West Parish Church, *Church of Scotland*, Broughty Ferry, Angus (Tayside) (1844 and 1956: dem for lock-ups)

B Edinburgh: Kirkgate Church, *Church of Scotland*, Henderson Street, Leith, Lothian (1885: Italian Romanesque, by Thornton Shiells: permission to dem 1975)

Edinburgh: Marshall Street, *Baptist* Church, Lothian (1877: Lombard Romanesque, by Thornton Shiells: dem *c.* 1966)

Edinburgh: Netherbow Church, *Church of Scotland,* High Street, Lothian
(1851: by John Lessels: dem 1973)

Edinburgh: St Giles (West), *Church of Scotland,* Melville Drive, Lothian
(1881–82: by Hardy & Wight: dem 1975)

Edinburgh: St Margaret, *Church of Scotland,* Arthur Street, Lothian (dem 1971)

Edinburgh: Windsor Place Church, *Church of Scotland,* Portobello, Lothian
(consent to dem: 1977)

C Elie: Former *Free* Church, Fife
(1890: by Sydney Mitchell: dem)

C Falkirk: "Tattie Kirk" formerly *Anti-Burgher,* Stirlingshire (Central)
(1806: now a workshop: consent to dem for roadworks 1976)

B Galashiels: Old Parish *Church of Scotland,* Selkirkshire (Borders)
(1813: dem)

C Glasgow: Former Anderston *Free* Church, Cadogan Street, Lanarkshire (Strathclyde)
(1848: by Clarke & Bell: dem)

C Glasgow: Anderston Old Church, *Church of Scotland,* Heddle Place, Lanarkshire (Strathclyde)
(1839–40: by John Baird: dem 1967)

C Glasgow: Former Argyle *Free* Church, 14 Oswald Street, Lanarkshire (Strathclyde)
(1846: by Charles Wilson: dem)

B Glasgow: Former Barony *Free* Church, 45–53 Castle Street, Lanarkshire (Strathclyde)
(1866–67: by J. Honeyman: dem)

B Glasgow: Blochairn Church, *Church of Scotland,* Royston Road, Lanarkshire (Strathclyde)
(1883: by Malcolm Stark: dem)

C Glasgow: Brisby Memorial Church, *Church of Scotland,* South Portland Street, Lanarkshire (Strathclyde)
(1842: by John Baird I: dem)

A Glasgow: Caledonia Road Church, *Church of Scotland,* Lanarkshire (Strathclyde)
(1856: by Alexander Thomson: gutted by vandals and partly dem, ruins consolidated by Glasgow Corporation)

B Glasgow: Cambridge Street Church, *Church of Scotland,* Royston Road, Lanarkshire (Strathclyde)
(1834: by John Baird I: dem)

B Glasgow: *Catholic Apostolic* Church, 340–362 McAslin Street, Lanarkshire (Strathclyde)
(1852: by A. W. N. Pugin and James Salmon Junior: dem)

C Glasgow: Chalmers Memorial Church, *Church of Scotland* 11 Claythorn Street, Lanarkshire (Strathclyde)
(1838: dem)

B Glasgow: Chalmers *Free* Church, 43–50 Ballater Street, Lanarkshire (Strathclyde)
(1859: by Alexander Thomson: dem)

Glasgow: Elder Park Church, *Church of Scotland,* Govan, Lanarkshire (Strathclyde)
(1826: by James Smith; re-erected on another site 1884 by John Honeyman: dem)

B Glasgow: Gorbals John Knox Parish Church, *Church of Scotland,* 34 Carlton Place, Lanarkshire (Strathclyde)
(1806–10: by David Hamilton: dem)

B Glasgow: Ewing Place Church (Hope Street *Free* Congregation) Waterloo Street, Lanarkshire (Strathclyde)
(1858: by Hugh Barclay: dem 1958)

B Glasgow: Greyfriars and Alexandra Parade Church, *Church of Scotland,* 186 Albion Street, Lanarkshire (Strathclyde)
(1821: by John Baird I: dem)

B Glasgow: Johnston Memorial Church, *Church of Scotland,* 524 Springburn Avenue, Lanarkshire (Strathclyde)
(1873–74: by Clarke & Bell: dem)

B Glasgow: Laurieston–Renwick Church, *Church of Scotland*, 35 Cumberland Street, Lanarkshire (Strathclyde) (1869: by J. Barbour: dem)

B Glasgow: Lloyd Morris Memorial Church, *Congregational*, 155–157 Rutherglen Road, Lanarkshire (Strathclyde) (1902: by James Salmon Junior and Gillespie: dem)

C Glasgow: Nelson Street *E.U.* Church, Lanarkshire (Strathclyde) (1862: dem)

B Glasgow: Neptune *Masonic* Lodge, formerly St Mark's *Episcopal* Church, 430 Scotland Street, Lanarkshire (Strathclyde) (1910: by Sir Robert Lorimer: dem for road works)

B Glasgow: Park Parish Church, *Church of Scotland*, Lanarkshire (Strathclyde) (1858: by J. T. Rochead: dem except for tower)

B Glasgow: Pollok Street Church, *Church of Scotland*, Lanarkshire (Strathclyde) (1856: by Peddie & Kinnear: dem 1977)

B Glasgow: Former Renfield *Free* Church, latterly City Temple, 291 Bath Street, Lanarkshire (Strathclyde) (1858: by Boucher & Cousland: dem 1966–67)

C Glasgow: Former Renfield Street Church, *Church of Scotland*, Lanarkshire (Strathclyde) (1849: by James Brown: dem 1963)

B Glasgow: St George, *Church of Scotland*, Elderslie Street, Lanarkshire (Strathclyde) (1864: by Boucher & Cousland: dem)

C Glasgow: St George's Road Church, *Church of Scotland*, Lanarkshire (Strathclyde) (1876: by Robert Baldie: dem)

B Glasgow: St John, *Church of Scotland*, Bell Street, Lanarkshire (Strathclyde) (1819: by David Hamilton: dem)

C Glasgow: St John, *Church of Scotland*, George Street, Lanarkshire (Strathclyde) (1845: by J. T. Rochead: dem)

C Glasgow: St John the Evangelist *Episcopal*, Houldsworth Street, Lanarkshire (Strathclyde) (1849: by John Henderson: dem)

C Glasgow: St Mark, *Church of Scotland*, Argyle Street, Anderston, Lanarkshire (Strathclyde) (1848: by James Salmon: dem)

B Glasgow: St Michael, *Church of Scotland*, 50 Edrom Street, Lanarkshire (Strathclyde) (1902: by H. E. Clifford: dem)

Glasgow: St Peter, *Church of Scotland*, Brown Street, Lanarkshire (Strathclyde) (1908: remodelling with fine interior by Salmon and Gillespie: dem)

C Glasgow: St Thomas *Methodist* Church, 598 Gallowgate, Lanarkshire (Strathclyde) (1822: dem order November 1976)

C Glasgow: Somerville Parish Church, *Church of Scotland*, 435 Keppochhill Road, Lanarkshire (Strathclyde) (1894: by W. G. Rowan: dem)

Glasgow: Well Park Church, *Church of Scotland*, Lanarkshire (Strathclyde) (1854: by the Hays of Liverpool: dem)

C Glasgow: Former West George Street *Independent* Chapel, Lanarkshire (Strathclyde) (1819: by James Gillespie Graham, latterly British Rail Offices: dem)

C Glendoick: Kinfauns Former *Free* Church, Perthshire (Tayside) (1843: dem recently)

B Greenock: St Andrew, *Church of Scotland*, Renfrewshire (Strathclyde) (1881: by H. & D. Barclay: dem)

A Inchinnan: Parish Church, *Church of Scotland*, Renfrewshire (Strathclyde) (1899–1904: by Sir Rowand Anderson: dem for airport)

A Lasswade: Parish Church, Lothian
(1793: Greek cross plan: dem 1955)

B Monzievaird: Parish Church, Central, (Perthshire)
(1803: dem)

B Newburgh: Parish Church, *Church of Scotland,* Fife
(1833: by William Burn: dem for housing)

C Perth: The Wilson Church, *Church of Scotland,* Scott Street, Perthshire (Tayside)
(1896: by J. B. Wilson: dem recently for shopping development)

Rathillet: Fife
(dem for road widening)

C Stirling: North Church, Murray Place, Stirlingshire (Central)
(1841: ambitious Romanesque, by John Henderson: dem for shopping development)

C Trochry: Free Church, Perthshire (Tayside)
(1844: dem recently)

WALES

NG Blaina: St Peter, *Church in Wales,* Monmouthshire (Gwent)
(late 19th century: Norman central tower and spire, by Mr Norton: dem 1969, replaced by a new church)

NL Caernarfon: Moriah Chapel, Caernavonshire (Gwynedd)
(gutted, dem 1976)

Cardiff: St Dyffrig, *Church of Wales,* Wood Street, Glamorgan (South Glamorgan)
(1893: by Sedding and Wilson: dem for road scheme, major loss)

Cardiff: St Mark, *Church of Wales,* Glamorgan (South Glamorgan)
(1876: by C. J. Waring: dem for road works)

Cardiff: *Congregational* Chapel, Hannah Street, Glamorgan (South Glamorgan)
(1867: by Habershon & Pike, exceptional grand classical chapel: dem 1960s)

Cardiff: Wood Street Chapel, Glamorgan (South Glamorgan)
(*c.* 1850: vast interior: dem)

Cardiff: Bethany Chapel, Glamorgan (South Glamorgan)
(dem 1960s)

III Peneader: Yr Hen Gapel, Carmarthenshire (Dyfed)
(application to dem)

Chepstow: *Roman Catholic* Church, Monmouthshire (Gwent)
(1820: recently dem)

Chepstow: Chapel, East side of Welsh Street, Monmouthshire (Gwent)
(dem)

Ebbw Vale: St John, *Church in Wales,* Monmouthshire (Gwent)
(1899: by E. M. Bruce Vaughan, plain Gothic: walls reduced to height of 0·5 metres *c.* 1974 and site grassed over)

Gerlan: Bethesda Ebenezer Chapel, Caernarvonshire (Gwynedd)
(dem)

Kerneys: Kerneys Inferior, Monmouthshire (Gwent)
(dem *c.* 1965 for new A449 link in Usk Valley)

Llandudno: Zion *Baptist* Chapel, Mostyn Street, Caernarvonshire (Gwynedd)
(1860s: interesting chapel dem late 1960s for new shopping parade)

III Llanelli: Jerusalem Wesleyan Chapel, Wind Street, Carmarthen (Dyfed)
(1793: dem 1973 for road improvement)

NL Llanfairpwll: Salem Chapel, Holyhead Road, Anglesey (Gwynedd)
(dem *c.* 1975)

Margam: Beulah Calvinistic Methodist Chapel, Glamorgan (West Glamorgan)
(1838: taken down because of motorway and rebuilt)

C Nant-y-glo: Holy Trinity, Church in Wales, Monmouthshire (Gwent)
(1854: early English, by Daniells of Crickhowell: dem for extensions to Dunlop Semtex factory)

Newport: *Wesleyan* Chapel Fairview, Blackwood, Monmouthshire (Gwent)
(dem 1972)

Newport: Tabernacle *Congregational* Church, Park Street, Cwmcarn, Monmouthshire (Gwent) (dem 1963)

Newport: *Presbyterian* Church, Panlycefn Road, Markham, Monmouthsire (Gwent) (dem 1975)

Newport: *Roman Catholic* Church, Abernaut Road, Markham, Monmouthshire (Gwent) (dem 1972)

Newport: St Philip and St James, *Church in Wales*, Cwrtybella, Argoed, Monmouthshire (Gwent) (dem 1969)

Newport: *Methodist* Church, Gladstone Street, Crosskeys, Monmouthshire (Gwent) (to be demolished)

Pontypridd: Chapel by Market Place, Glamorgan (Mid Glamorgan) (dem)

Rhyl: Assumption *Roman Catholic* Church, Flint (Clwyd) (only complete church by J. Hungerford Pollen: dem 1975)

Bibliography

The Church of England Yearbook
The Catholic Directory of England and Wales
The Baptist Union Directory
Book of Meetings, Religious Society of Friends
The Church of Scotland Yearbook
The Episcopal Church in Scotland Yearbook
The Free Church of Scotland Yearbook
The United Reformed Church in England and Wales Yearbook
The Unitarian and Free Christian Churches Directory
The Bangor Diocesan Yearbook
The Cardiff Archdiocesan Yearbook
The Llandaff Diocesan Handbook
The St Asaph Diocesan Yearbook
The St Davids Diocesan Yearbook
The Jewish Yearbook

Advisory Board for Redundant Churches *Annual Reports*
Ageing Church Buildings (Occasional Paper, No. 1), Methodist Church Division of Property, 1975
Disestablishment and Disendowment of the Church in England and Wales, 1912
English Heritage Monitor, English Tourist Board, 1977
Facts and Figures about the Church of England No 3
Historic Buildings Council for England *Reports*
Historic Buildings Council for Scotland *Reports*
Historic Buildings Council for Wales *Reports*
Historic Churches Preservation Trusts *Annual Reports*
List of Ancient Monuments of England, Department of the Environment, 1971 (and supplements)
List of Ancient Monuments in Wales, Department of the Environment, 1974
Listed Church Buildings (Occasional Paper, No. 2), Methodist Church Division of Property, 1976
Nonconformist Congregations in Great Britain, Dr Williams Trust, 1973
Redundant Churches in Essex, County Planner, Essex 1976
Redundant Churches Fund *Annual Reports*
Report of the Archbishops' Commission on Redundant Churches, SPCK, 1960
Report of the Commission on Bristol Historic Churches
Report on the Future of the Churches of Inner Leicester, Diocese of Leicester, 1970
Report of the Salisbury Churches Committee, 1972
Report of the Sepulchral Monuments Committee, Society of Antiquaries of London, 1872
Sport for All in Converted Buildings, The Sports Council, 1975
Statistical Returns, Part 1 1972 and Part 2 1973, The Methodist Church Department for Chapel Affairs
The Church in Bedford, Diocese of St Albans, 1971
The Official List, List of Certified Places of Worship, General Register Office, 1974
Tourism in Wales: A Plan for the Future, Wales Tourist Board, 1976
Underused Church Properties: A Variety of Solutions, The Cheswick Centre, Cambridge, USA, 1975

Addyman, Peter and Morris, Richard (ed.). *The Archaeological Study of Churches*, Council For British Archaeology Research Report no. 13, 1976

Anderson, Mary D. *History and Imagery of British Churches*, 1971

Anson, Peter F. *Fashions in Church Furnishings*, The Faith Press, 1960

Barker, G. M. A. *Wildlife Conservation in the care of Churches and Churchyards*, Church Information Office, 1972

Barton, David A. *Discovering Chapels and Meeting Houses,* Shire Publications, 1975

Binney, Marcus and Burman, Peter (ed.). *Change and Decay: The Future of Our Churches,* Studio Vista, 1977

Briggs, Martin S. *Goths and Vandals*, Constable, 1952

Briggs, Martin S. *Puritan Architecture and Its Future,* Lutterworth Press, 1946

Clarke, Basil F. L. *Parish Churches of London,* Batsford, 1966

Clifton Taylor, Alec. *English Parish Churches*, Batsford, 1974

Davies, J. G. *The Secular Use of Church Buildings,* SCM Press, 1968

Dolbey, George W. *The Architectural Expression of Methodism—the First Hundred Years,* Epworth, 1964

Drummond, Andrew L. and Bulloch, James. *The Church in Victorian Scotland,* The Saint Andrew Press, Edinburgh, 1975

Earl Jones, Ezra and Wilson, Robert L. *What's Ahead for Old First Church Street*, New York, 1974

Gay, John D. *The Geography of Religion in England*, 1971

Gomme, Andor and Walker, David. *Architectura of Glasgow,* Lund Humphries, 1968

Hay, George. *The Architecture of Scottish Post-Reformation Churches 1560–1843*, Oxford University Press, 1957

Hilling, John. *Cardiff and the Valleys,* Lund Humphries

Holmes, Ann. *Church, Property and People*, The British Council of Churches, 1973

Jones, Jeremy. *How to record graveyards,* Council for British Archaeology and Rescue, 1976

Jones, Ronald P. *Nonconformist Church Architecture,* The Lindsey Press, 1914

Lidbetter, Hubert. *The Friends Meeting House,* The Ebor Press, York, 1961

Lindley, Kenneth. *Chapels and Meeting Houses,* John Baker, 1969

Little, Bryan. *Catholic Churches Since 1623,* Robert Hale, 1966

Martin, Frederick. *Property and Revenue of the English Church Establishment,* 1877

Newey, John. *The English Ecclesiastical Courts,* Diocese of Canterbury, 1976

Norwich, Bishop of. *Report on Disused Churches,* 1949

Sellwood, The Rev Bessie L. *Dissenting Meeting Houses in England before 1740,* unpublished thesis for Department of Theology, University of Birmingham, 1975

Southall, Kenneth H. *Our Quaker Heritage*, n.d.

Stapleton, Henry and Burman, Peter. *The Churchyards' Handbook* (second edition), Church Information Office, 1976

Thorncroft, M. E. T. *The Economics of Conservation*. The Royal Institution of Chartered Surveyors, 1975

Thorold, Henry (ed). *Lincolnshire Churches: Their Past and Their Future,* Lincolnshire Old Churches Trust, 1976

Underwood, A. C. *A History of the English Baptists,* 1947

Whiffen, Marcus. *Stuart and Georgian Churches,* Batsford, 1947–48

White, H. Lesley. *Monuments and their Inscriptions,* Society of Genealogists, 1977

INDEX

INDEX